Routledge Revivals

The Inspector General

Sir Jeremiah Fitzpatrick (c.1740-1810) was the first inspector general of prisons and lunacy inspector in Ireland and the first and only inspector of health to HM land forces in Great Britain. He also inspected convict vessels bound for New South Wales and the East India Company's troop ships, inquired into the Irish Charter Schools and attempted to alleviate the miseries of soldiers' dependents. His further ambitions ranged from a poor law for Ireland to a reorganisation of Dublin's police, to the regulation of noxious trades, from slave trade inspectorates to hospital management. He was therefore in many ways a precursor of the titans of early and mid-Victorian government. Originally published in 1981, much of the interest of the book lies in its revelation of late eighteenth century anticipations of mid-nineteenth century government. It also explores the differences between the two forms of administration and the reasons for the divergences and discontinuities.

The Inspector General
Sir Jeremiah Fitzpatrick and Social Reform, 1783-1802

Oliver MacDonagh

First published in 1981 by Croom Helm Ltd.

This edition first published in 2024 by Routledge
4 Park Square, Milton Park, Abingdon, Oxon, OX14 4RN
and by Routledge
605 Third Avenue, New York, NY 10158.

Routledge is an imprint of the Taylor & Francis Group, an informa business

© 1981 Oliver MacDonagh

The right of Oliver MacDonagh to be identified as the author of this work has been asserted by him in accordance with sections 77 and 78 of the Copyright, Designs and Patents Act 1988.

All rights reserved. No part of this book may be reprinted or reproduced or utilised in any form or by any electronic, mechanical, or other means, now known or hereafter invented, including photocopying and recording, or in any information storage or retrieval system, without permission in writing from the publishers.

ISBN 13: 978-1-032-85347-5 (hbk)
ISBN 13: 978-1-003-51774-0 (ebk)
ISBN 13: 978-1-032-85349-9 (pbk)
Book DOI 10.4324/9781003517740

The Inspector General

Sir Jeremiah Fitzpatrick and the Politics of Social Reform, 1783-1802

Oliver MacDonagh

CROOM HELM LONDON

© 1981 Oliver MacDonagh
Croom Helm Ltd, 2-10 St John's Road, London SW11

British Library Cataloguing in Publication Data

MacDonagh, Oliver
 The Inspector General.
 1. Fitzpatrick, Sir Jeremiah
 2. Great Britain – Officials and employees
 I. Title
 361'.9'410924   HV28.F5/

ISBN 0-85664-421-8

Printed and bound in the United States of America

CONTENTS

Preface

1. In Search of Sir Jeremiah	19
2. Prison Reform in Ireland, 1763-1783	42
3. A Prologue and an Act, 1784-1786	62
4. Sir Jeremiah and the Charter Schools, 1785-1788	86
5. The Greasy Pole, 1786-1788	105
6. Progress and Penitentiaries, 1788-1793	126
7. The Translation, 1793-1794	149
8. The Layman with the Lamp, 1794-1795	171
9. Waterloo, 1795	191
10. The Aftermath, 1795	214
11. A Sort of Tableland, 1796-1802	232
12. Service and Servitude, 1796-1802	257
13. Meanings	294
Appendices	330
Select Bibliography	332
Index	340

FOR DOLORES AND NIALL MEAGHER

PREFACE

This book is a biography, though one with the rather grave biographical defects of being practically confined to twenty years of its subject's life and to a single form of his activity, the official. But the twenty years are rich in matter, and the tumultuous nature of the man and of the times were such that the account of his career is almost a species of clerk's *Gil Blas*.

It is also a study in central administration, though again with serious deficiencies. In part, these arise from lacks in private records; in part, from 'lacks' in the governmental and parliamentary structures of the day whereby even such matters as the text of unenacted Bills, House of Commons debates or annual inspectorial reports enjoined by statute, are missing now. Moreover, a nineteenth-century historian is chastened to discover how many elementary biographical and institutional facts, readily accessible in his own time, remain obdurately hidden for even the 1770s and 1780s. Yet there is compensating profusion and colour in the Georgian caches which have here and there survived, in joyous contrast to the reticences and emasculations in Victorian files and printed papers; and several of the very 'lacks' in the eighteenth-century political and administrative systems provide keys to understanding the nature of later governmental growth.

This last is important. For if the book has ended as a sort of historiographical centaur, half human and half institutional, that is because it proved impossible to relegate Fitzpatrick to a subordinate role. Yeats once complained of George Moore's 'terrible gift of intimacy'. If the gift is to be deplored, Fitzpatrick stands condemned. He buttonholes, he grasps attention, he can somehow speak directly across two hundred years. So at least I have found. If caught like me, the reader may be occasionally exasperated by the tireless iteration and unflagging passion — but never to the point where any of that 'terrible' immediacy would be foregone. To find such a man was, however, an uncovenanted delight. The subject was chosen originally, not because of him, but for what it might contribute to an understanding of the genesis of the modern state, and particularly if paradoxically, for what it might contribute to a better understanding of the nineteenth-century revolution in government.

Work of mine on this last subject has aroused interest, and been of use to some and disputed by others, for over twenty years. When I decided to take it up again, my first thought was to repeat in another, contemporaneous field, the type of work which I had done for one branch of central government, in *A Pattern of Government Growth: The Passenger Acts and Their Enforcement, 1800-60*. The second field I chose, coal mines regulation, did indeed prove fruitful. But I found as I progressed that it was yielding, by and large, a customary harvest. This had of course its own significance; but the probable result seemed all too likely to smack of the 'replication of an experiment' (a dubious historical procedure) and of the mere defending of a fixed position. Gradually I became persuaded that it would be best to select from the coal-mines work those portions which broke out in (to me, at any rate) new directions and opened up fresh considerations; but to look elsewhere for major work which might carry forward the original ideas in some broad and general way.

In the end, I decided that it would be more promising to attempt a comparison of the late eighteenth and the mid-nineteenth centuries under this head. Such a comparison might clarify what was distinctive in the mid-nineteenth-century patterns, and perhaps also throw new light upon the early formation and first reasons for centralised social regulation.

The actual subject chosen had other advantages. First, the range of Fitzpatrick's interests was extraordinarily wide. His own administrative work covered prisons, madhouses, charity schools, troopships, convict vessels and the relief of soldiers' dependants; and his further specific administrative aspirations included the poor law, police, the woollen industry, the slave trade, urban pollution, army hospitals and animal protection. At the same time, this heterogeneity was counteracted by the constancy of his leading concerns. The bulk of his work was in the field of preventive public medicine, and all of it was informed by the same concept of state management through inspectorates and by a concentration upon the plight of the most vulnerable bodies in society.

A second attraction was that the subject permitted the exploration of dualisms which are generally, if not invariably, neglected by students of modern government in Great Britain. On the one hand, Fitzpatrick's bureaucratic career was divided almost equally between Ireland and England. The interrelationship of the two countries during the century and a half, c.1770-c.1920, was critically important in the development and shaping of state power. Ireland was in many ways a forcing house in this regard – even 'a social laboratory', in the judgement of one penetrating critic, W.L. Burn; and there was a very heavy traffic of leading British politicians between Westminster and College Green before 1801, and of politicians and civil servants alike between Whitehall and Dublin Castle thereafter. On the other hand, Fitzpatrick worked equally in civil and military government, and again it is rare for historians to concern themselves with the coexistence, let alone the interaction, of these two forms of social administration. More generally, they represent relatively open and closed types of bureaucracy; and although this particular distinction is not often made, it is rewarding to explore, both in its own right and for throwing many features of 'ordinary' government into high relief.

Thirdly, by its very nature a study which is perforce biographical raises (and profitably so, I hope) the problem of determining the relative parts played by individuals and processes in particular stretches of governmental growth. Correspondingly, in this case the problem of ideology as motivation is also raised, and in an especially interesting fashion. For at one level Fitzpatrick was a simple subscriber to the grand commonplaces of the day, and they may not have been without effect in furnishing him with impetus. But he did not conceive of them as either a philosophy or method (it was integral to the Enlightenment, as popularised, to appear 'self-evident'); and there is little to suggest that they had any effect on his administrative practice, or counted for much, against the fierce drive of his personality.

Finally, the subject is (to some extent, by unfortunate lacunae) sufficiently circumscribed to render a minute inspection of the process of growth practicable. This is crucial to a study of the *Pattern of Government Growth* kind; for it is only under the microscope that the accumulation and interworking of small changes reveal – or at any rate reveal to any considerable extent – their institutional dynamics.

May I append a still more personal note? If the foregoing seems already to intrude too much of the author into an introduction to his book, or even to strike a braggardly or portentous note about his earlier writings, this is not by choice – far from it – but because explanations of why one is silent here or expansive there are, at least tacitly, demanded in these days.

Jeremiah (or 'Jerome') Fitzpatrick is an obscure figure, forgotten for a century after his death, mentioned only incidentally in half a dozen later books on army medicine, convict vessels or the like, but generally unknown. So far as I am aware, the only substantial piece which deals with him is Richard L. Blanco's paper, 'The Soldier's Friend – Sir Jeremiah Fitzpatrick, Inspector of Health for Land Forces'. I cannot claim to have dispelled the obscurity: chapter 1, the attempt to reconstruct his life and rise to office, makes this all too clear. None the less quite enough material has survived (perhaps one should say, been discovered: it would be quite in character for Sir Jeremiah to yield up some secrets too late!) for his character as a public man, and his fortunes as a public servant, to be delineated. And these are in their turn quite sufficient to uncover a whole layer of government in hitherto undug soil. For all this, Fitzpatrick's own correspondence is the leading source.

For once, letters makyth man. The book, or twelve-thirteenths of it at any rate, may be read as a biography; and those for whom the strenuous disentanglement of administrative dynamics holds little charm, may escape them — not entirely but pretty well unscathed — by laying down the volume when they have ended chapter 12.

Generally I have retained Fitzpatrick's original spelling and punctuation, and those of his contemporaries, except in the very rare cases of obvious misprint or mistranscription; and I have not drawn attention to these retentions in the text unless (again rarely) not to do so might have led to some confusion. I have tried to distinguish between the departments of state headed after 11 July 1794 by Henry Dundas and William Windham, respectively the Secretaries of State for War and of War, by calling the first the 'War Department' and the second the 'War Office'. The ancestor of both was (in modern terminology) the 'Home Office', and the 'Home Office' it remains after they had broken off, although with the further loss of 'the colonies' to the secretary for war in 1801. All the pre-1801 statutes referred to in the text or footnotes are Irish, unless otherwise stated.

As so often — but would it were more often still — I must express my deep gratitude to my colleagues, Dr F.B. Smith and Dr A.W. Martin, for gentle but profound criticism and the elimination of some at least of the stylistic blunders. I am also deeply grateful to Professor R.M. MacLeod, of London University, who read almost all the work in typescript, too late, alas, for me to profit fully from his acute suggestions and store of knowledge, but still in time for his advice to improve the book materially. I must thank Professor E.M. Johnston of Macquarie University very warmly for helping me to find my way about the Irish parliamentary politics of the late eighteenth century during the early stages of exploration; and Dr A.P.W. Malcolmson for the Fitzpatrick materials which he searched for and found for me in the Public Record Office, Northern Ireland. Professor Blanco also kindly provided me with further Fitzpatrick references. Dr W.J. Lowe and Mrs Pamela Crichton gave me the most unstinting assistance in research, and (I should perhaps add) Frank and John very vigorous aid in scraping tombstones in lichened churchyards! Many other people have helped me with information or encouragement; nor is patient listening to be excluded, by any means.

I end with the warm acknowledgement of two very special debts: one to Mrs Lois Simms, who has typed so much of Sir Jeremiah, and so many times, and who has cherished him maternally from the cradle to the grave of his paper life; and the other, as always, to my wife.

Canberra

1 IN SEARCH OF SIR JEREMIAH

In the Anglo-Saxon analogue of life, a bird flies from the night into a lighted hall, veers this way and that, and then vanishes into the darkness from which it came. It might almost serve as an analogue for this book as well. A single penny-candle worth of information breaks the darkness which surrounds Fitzpatrick before he was knighted in 1782. All we know for certain is that he married an Elizabeth Fitzgerald in November 1770.[1] His end is almost equally mysterious. A handful of letters from,[2] and one concerning him;[3] an attempted intervention at a public meeting;[4] a deed of assignment,[5] and his will,[6] are the only surviving traces of the last eight years of his life, after his unsought retirement from the public service. His administrative career also fits the image. Parts of it were brilliantly illuminated, and parts remain in shadow, as Fitzpatrick swung left and right in his headlong passage. But perhaps a better metaphor for his official life would be the Roman candle: a racing fuse, a blaze, petty explosions, showers of sparks and at the last a black and empty shell — or rather several of them, for Fitzpatrick burned briefly in many fields.

We know where he was born, Kilbeggan, co. Westmeath, in the Irish central plain; but not when. Circa 1740 is the best guess which I can make. His marriage took place in 1770; in 1798 he spoke sadly of his advanced years; his portrait of 1801[7] suggests a man of sixty. His family too is practically unknown. It is certain that his parents lie buried in the Old Relic graveyard (from the Gaelic *reilig*, a burial ground), abutting the road between Kilbeggan and Tullamore.[8] But although most of the tombstones can be read, theirs, with characteristic Fitzpatrickian perversity, must be among the number which have fallen down or become indecipherable with weathering. We can infer that the elder Fitzpatricks were Catholics. The churchyard lies in the shadow of the ruined Durrow Abbey, and such places were used by Catholics as burial grounds in the eighteenth and early nineteenth centuries to elude the funeral rites of the established church. We may also infer, though less confidently, that they were people of some substance, for it was generally these who were buried in monastic grounds. Beyond these fragments, we know nothing of Fitzpatrick's ancestry.

His schooling and medical training lie in equal darkness. He knew French and was a practised Latinist. Possibly he could read, if not speak,

19

Italian. But his quite extensive Italian reading might have been in translation rather than the original. Undoubtedly he possessed a good working knowledge of mathematics and of the contemporary natural sciences, both chemistry and physics. But there is no evidence of literary training in his work, beyond a gentleman's acquaintance with the Bible and a capacity to write both chaste and ornate prose, given the licence of eighteenth-century grammar, spelling and punctuation. What are we to make of all this in terms of illuminating his education? Unfortunately, it excludes nothing. The evidence is compatible with a hedge school, a grammar school or private tutors. It was possible, though of course more difficult, to receive as good a grounding in classics and mathematics in surreptitious classes in haybarns or ditches or from wandering 'professors' as any regular 'academy' might provide.[9] If Jeremiah's parents were Catholics, the illicit hedge school or itinerant teacher was the more likely source of his early education. But we cannot put it any stronger, for many Catholic children attended the grammar schools of the established church.

His medical training is equally obscure. There is no record of his attending any British, Irish or Dutch college of physicians or surgeons — the standard channels of qualification in the mid-eighteenth century.[10] Yet he practised as a physician, and described himself on all formal occasions, and was always described officially, as 'MD'. It is of course conceivable that he was, medically speaking, an impostor, or that his doctorate in medicine was furnished by one of the German universities, perhaps at that time engaged in the business of selling higher degrees without examination or close enquiry. But neither supposition is at all likely. To look no further, he made many bitter enemies in Dublin, where he was well known, and later in the army medical service in Great Britain; and none would have hesitated to charge him with quackery, or worthless qualification, had there been the slightest ground for such a challenge.

The most likely explanation is that Fitzpatrick read medicine on the continent. In Ireland, the third quarter of the eighteenth century was marked by the rise of a Catholic middle class. With landownership barred to almost all Catholics by the penal legislation of 1691-1709, and the law, church and army altogether closed,[11] they naturally turned to trade and the demi-professions such as medicine for economic and social advancement. Not that they had a free run of either commerce or medicine: important parts of each were fenced off for the benefit of Anglicans. None the less from 1750 onwards Catholics became numerous and prosperous in the 'open' sectors.[12] They may even have been predominant numerically by 1775. Thus given Fitzpatrick's Catholic parentage and probable 'comfortable' background, medicine was a natural choice for a career; and for an eighteenth-century Irish Catholic the study of medicine meant, almost invariably, study in France or Italy. Some came through the medical schools of Padua or Bologna, and a few doubtless attended Strasbourg or Montpellier; but most were Paris trained. The best guess is, therefore, that Fitzpatrick qualified in medicine in Paris. This receives some slight measure of corroboration from his familiarity with the administrative systems and other aspects of life in the French capital, although it is also true that almost everything which he wrote of Paris could have been gathered readily enough from books and journals. Possibly he studied in more than one European centre. Certainly, he claimed to have visited hospitals all over the continent in his early life.[13]

By the early 1780s Fitzpatrick was practising as a physician in Dublin:[14] his address, Jervis Street, may suggest a connection with the nearby hospitals, Simpson's and the Charitable Infirmary. But where did he practise in the preceding fifteen or twenty years? It may well have been Dublin from the start. There are however one or two faint indications that he had lived in Kilkenny earlier in his career. Certainly he knew that city better than any other in the province. His marriage throws no light upon this question. In the settlement[15] his wife's residence is set down as Dublin: unfortunately, his own does not appear. But all her property in prospect lay close to Kilbeggan, and all the trustees but one – the former prime serjeant, Anthony Malone[16] – lived within twenty miles of the little town. Several of the trustees were her own relations. Thus, although Elizabeth Fitzgerald was a Dubliner in 1770, nothing in the marriage was incompatible with Fitzpatrick living elsewhere, for their common origin in Westmeath is the *prima facie* explanation of their acquaintanceship. The settlement does, however, throw a little light on other things. It tends to confirm Fitzpatrick's Catholic background, for Malone was the lawyer chiefly used by well-to-do Leinster Catholics. It also tends to confirm his middle-class milieu, first, in that there was considerable property to be settled, and secondly in that Elizabeth was evidently an educated woman: her signature is fluent and elegantly formed.

So far we have been dealing in the obscurity in Fitzpatrick's life. But there are also mysteries, in particular his religion and the reason for his knighthood. Such evidence as we have up to 1782 certainly indicates a Catholic origin and upbringing. But no open Catholic or even known nonconformer to the established church would have been knighted in 1782. Moreover, various of his reports to the Irish Parliament in the 1780s imply his attendance at Anglican services.[17] Of course this in itself presents no difficulty. In the third quarter of the eighteenth century the stream of prudential conversions from Catholicism in Ireland quickened considerably. But there is no record of Fitzpatrick conforming; and contrariwise he was spoken of as a concealed papist – if anything – in 1789.[18] Moreover, he was remarkable among late-eighteenth-century advocates of the penitentiary system in giving a negligible role to religion in the reformatory process. Possibly this expressed a general scepticism, or scepticism about the capacity of prison chaplains to touch men's hearts or change their courses of behaviour. But it may also have expressed a covert opposition to the state religion, for only clergymen of the established church would have been appointed to penitentiaries in Ireland in the 1790s. This view receives some support from Fitzpatrick's tentative suggestions that Catholic priests might be employed as a species of supernumerary chaplains for their co-religionists.[19] His army career throws no light upon the problem except in two negative respects. First, although Fitzpatrick's appointment as inspector general of health for the land forces in 1794 was militarily unique, his effective rank was that of colonel;[20] and to commission a Roman Catholic at that level would then have been in breach of the anti-popery laws, in an area in which they were still firmly upheld. On the other hand, his voluminous writings upon the care of the army sick and soldiers' morale and comfort contain no reference whatever to religious instruction, solace or ministration.

When we reach his years of retirement, after 1802, a similar ambiguity, or ambivalence, persists. In 1808 he was present at and attempted to address a meeting of the Catholic Committee – a body of Catholic aristocrats, landed proprietors and professional men – in Dublin.[21] Although this is not conclusive evidence, it strongly suggests that he was by then sailing openly under Catholic colours. Tangentially, his will, drawn up a year later, reveals close – not to say, militant – Catholic connections. Among the beneficiaries was Hugh Fitzpatrick, the Catholic bookseller and a leading member of the 'radical' Catholic faction, who was to be imprisoned four years later for publishing an anti-government tract.[22] It seems clear from the context that Hugh was either the nephew or (much less likely) the grand-nephew of Sir Jeremiah. Another of the beneficiaries was Patrick Vincent Fitzpatrick, at this time a youth, but later to become O'Connell's political manager and a prime organiser of the Catholic Emancipation campaign of the later

1820s.[23] He too was a collateral descendant of Sir Jeremiah, almost certainly a grand-nephew. It is tempting, in retrospect, to inject positive Catholicism into Sir Jeremiah from these links with the Irish Catholic *avant garde*. But the main beneficiary of the will was Sir Jeremiah's grandson, Jeremiah Tisdall, the fruit of a union between his daughter, Elizabeth, and John Tisdall of Ardee, a member of a leading Ascendancy family. From this it seems probable that young Tisdall and his other grandchildren by the same marriage were born into the Anglican ranks.

What type of religious identikit should we construct for Fitzpatrick from this medley of indications and implications? This seems to be the best that can be done: that Fitzpatrick was born and educated well into manhood as a Catholic; that he then, tacitly at least, conformed to the established church, while perhaps developing into a deist or some equivalent in belief; that he none the less retained a vestigial identification, at least, with the depressed community from which he had sprung; and that as his life closed in and the sects in Ireland became repolarised he reverted to the church in which he had been reared. This reconstruction has the additional merit, slight though it may be, of keeping in step with the general march of religious ideology and commitment in Ireland. The young among the Catholic middle class and aspirants to social rank or professional advancement conformed to Anglicanism in considerable numbers in the 1760s and 1770s. The years 1775-95 were marked by the rapid spread of indifferentism among the literate in Ireland, and by the rise of the sentiment that true religion (or humanity) transcended the ecclesiastical poles. From 1795 onwards, from a variety of causes, sectarianism and passionate religiosity returned to Ireland with redoubled force; the 'middle ground' contracted; and conversions to Anglicanism among the educated, and religious admixtures in families, fell away. Men – even the technical atheists and apostles of progress – had to choose their sides; and not a few of the conformers of the 1770s and 1780s returned to Catholicism in the new century. Fitzpatrick would certainly have been no curiosity in the land had he followed this general pattern.

At any rate, inconclusive though it may be, speculation about his religion is worthwhile. It is still the first question to be asked about any Irishman. It is also one of the first questions to be asked about any social reformer of the late eighteenth century. But most important of all an Irish Catholic boyhood amid the fears and repressions of the 1740s may provide the key to Fitzpatrick's extraordinary reticences in all the torrent of explanation and expostulation in his public life. It may even help to explain his rare but sharp shafts against his English betters and their order, as something akin to the ambivalence which Kramnick detects in Burke:

> Torn by personal misgivings about his own place in society, some of his basic inclinations seem, in fact, to have been not far removed from those of the very radicals against whom he thundered.[24]

Fitzpatrick's knighthood in 1782 is much more simply and blankly a mystery than his religion. His 'elevation' early in August in that year belonged to what would now be termed a list of resignation honours.[25] The Duke of Portland, who conferred the knighthood, was on the point of leaving the Irish lord-lieutenancy. It is true that two other Dublin physicians received the same title at the time.[26] But unlike Fitzpatrick they had official standing. It is also true that Portland's chief secretary was another Fitzpatrick, Colonel Richard, the crony of Charles James Fox, and the younger brother of the Earl of Upper Ossory.[27] Immediately, it is tempting to guess that Jeremiah was an illegitimate connection of this family, being hurriedly pushed up a rung or two while the noble Fitzpatrick had still some power in Dublin Castle. But the parents buried in the Old Relic graveyard seem to close off this avenue of conjecture once for all. On the other hand, there might have been a Catholic branch of the Upper Ossory family to which Jeremiah belonged, and he might have been useful to his hypothetical relative, the chief secretary, during the four months of the Portland administration in Ireland. Doubtless this may seem a farfetched explanation, although many Ascendancy families did have Catholic tails. But any other explanation seems more farfetched still. That Jeremiah performed some dark but valuable political service for Dublin Castle in 1782 might appear to offer a more substantial quarry for speculation. But not only is there no grain of evidence that he did, but also it seems impossible even to conceive of any political service which he might have rendered at all commensurate with a knighthood. Similarly, his career as social reformer or administrative philanthropist had not yet begun in 1782. At most, the foundations for it were being laid, out of sight. So this road, too, is closed, and we are left with either the mystery absolute or an airy construction resting on a mere coincidence of name and common region of origin — though possibly we might add to these the general principle that, in a question of eighteenth-century politics, family connection is the first place to look in seeking to explain an advancement.

The two decades 1783-1802 are the years of light. We know that

Fitzpatrick was practising as a physician in Dublin up to 1786, though with increasing absences from the city when voluntarily he undertook inspections about the country. In 1786 prison and other inspections became his full-time occupation, in which he continued until the end of 1793. He then took up army medicine, at first as a succession of *ad hoc* tasks, and later, in November 1794, as a properly appointed officer. In the summer of 1794 and again in December 1794 and January 1795 he visited the British army in the course of its successive retreats in the Austrian Netherlands and Holland, but otherwise spent most of 1795 and of the first half of 1796 dealing with various calamities at Plymouth. Thereafter Portsmouth was his main base, although he also worked for considerable periods at and around Southampton with occasional forays to east coast ports and the Thames. From 1797 he appears to have spent more and more time in London where he had maintained an office almost from the start, and where in July 1802 he received the dire news that, like many officers in the wake of the Peace of Amiens, he would soon be out on half-pay.

Although there is much that is obscure about his whereabouts and activities during these two decades, the broad outline is clear enough and there are also many phases in which his doings, virtually day by day, can be recorded. Strangely enough, it would seem that he never returned to Ireland from the day that he sailed with sick troops from the Cove of Cork to Plymouth, merely to tend them during the voyage, to the day of his enforced retirement from the service. One cannot be categorical about this. Various periods during these nine and a half years are not sufficiently accounted for to preclude absolutely a visit to his homeland. But his increasingly agitated – and unheeded – requests over the years to be sent to Ireland for one piece of business or another tend to support the inference that once caught up in army matters, he was held fast in the services without a break. He might as well have been a pressgang's prey, although it is also true that he was a most willing, not to say eager, victim.

As I have said above, the evidence of Fitzpatrick's life in retirement is sparse. In almost every instance what survives relates to one or other of his hobby horses. Even in powerlessness, the 'reforming' habit proved ineradicable. It is not clear where he lived from 1802 onwards – or rather all that is clear is that he was residing alternately in London and in Dublin. The 'Lady Elizabeth', as he sometimes called his wife, died in Ireland sometime shortly before July 1809[28] predeceased, it would seem, by the two children of the marriage, Elizabeth and John. But when Sir Jeremiah's own death came in February of the following year, he was living at 'his apartments in Frith-street', London.[29] Evidently, he made a final translation once his wife had died.

When J.B. Yeats the elder was asked to identify the essential difference between the English and the Irish, he replied that every Englishman had rich relations and every Irishman poor ones. Sir Jeremiah's will[30] provides mild confirmation of this grand dictum. Among the bequests was one of £110 to his grand-niece, Ann Kelly, 'to purchase a life annuity to prevent her becoming miserable and wanting the necessaries of life'; and another of £100 to Ann's brother, John, to purchase him a similar annuity. A niece-in-law and her four daughters were to receive £10 each, 'but to her that is deformed in the chest in order to get her a trade', £5 more; while to the future organiser of victory, P.V. Fitzpatrick, £12 to buy Malone's edition of Shakespeare and 'a set of geographical maps of the best kind' was bequeathed. Other Fitzpatrick relations received more substantial sums, up to £200, but it is clear from their addresses, Thomas Street, Capel Street and Petticoat Lane in Dublin, that these were people in trade, at a comparatively modest level. One general impression of Sir Jeremiah which emerges from his will is that of the successful member of a long-tailed upwardly mobile and moderately respectable tribe. Another is that of a feeling heart and sensitive conscience. Apart from his bequests to grand-nieces and -nephews, he left £120 each to his former servants, remembered old debts (including one owed by his son, John, presumably dead for some time), and was concerned that a woman who had, at his request, made clothes for small boys in the Penitentiary or Bridewell of James's Street should not be out of pocket if the government had failed to settle her account. The will also makes it clear that Sir Jeremiah was tolerably well-to-do. The cash legacies amounted to approximately £1,000; a residue of unknown amount was, at any rate, notionally allotted; there were many carriage horses to be distributed among his nephews; and the income from rentals of lands owned in Westmeath and King's County, divided between the two principal heirs, Jeremiah Tisdall and Jeremiah Fitzpatrick, grandson and godson respectively, may well have exceeded £1,000 per annum. At a hazard, his annual income in his last years may be put at about £1,400, quite enough to make him a very substantial man in Ireland (particularly in Catholic Ireland), though still far from the category of 'rich'. It is to be noted that the bulk of his money, deriving from land, appears to have come to him through his wife. This might help to explain how he could afford the career of philanthropy from the mid-1780s onwards: possibly Elizabeth came into the inheritance foreshadowed in her marriage settlement about this time.

Fitzpatrick's career as a public servant may fairly be described as philanthropic, despite the fact that he was a salaried officer from its formal commencement. In his early years as inspector general of prisons in Ireland, the expenses of running his 'department', which he had to meet, exceeded his stipend;[31] and even later, if matters mended at all, he cleared at best £200 a year – meagre compensation for the abandonment of a profession. Certainly the inspectorship of army health was a more rewarding occupation. But again his pay, £730 per annum, must have been considerably higher than his net income from his employment. He was forced to meet some of the costs of his office – precisely how much is uncertain, as the matter was lengthily disputed and the outcome unrecorded.[32] He suffered greatly moreover from another of the misfortunes of the eighteenth-century public servant, delays and arrears in payment; and years of putting up in English inns and lodgings, for which he received no compensation, must have eaten heavily into his earnings. In short, his army career, while not run absolutely at a loss, cannot have been a profitable substitute for private practice.

In some respects, Fitzpatrick was far from the stereotype of the mid-Georgian public servant. He worked, not few and occasional hours, but day and night in crisis. In place of the fee'd parasite, he was the salaried official. So far from appropriating, he himself sometimes paid for government supplies. There can be little doubt that he was incorruptible, even if he were sufficiently a man of his time to look upon the malversation of other public servants resignedly. Only once was an observation made which might conceivably be construed as a charge that he manufactured jobs for his own advantage. In June 1791 he appeared in a mid-year squib in the *Freeman's Journal* under 'the Art of Humbugging by Sir J- F-p-k'.[33] But, as Shaw once remarked, one of Dublin's marks is a 'certain flippant futile derision and belittlement which confuses the noble and serious with the base and ludicrous'.[34] Many of Dublin's other leading men were made to stand in still less flattering lights in the lampoon; and in any event Fitzpatrick was a *bête noire* of the reactionary Irish Anglicans by that time. On the other hand, it cannot be denied that the system of patronage and personal influence was – and doubtless had to be – his natural air. Such posts and power as he attained could not have been won unless he had been adopted by great men; and to some extent his successes in office depended on the continuance of such a backing. Conversely, he himself may have patronised others in his lilliputian way. In particular he was accused, probably with good reason, of trying to push the fortunes of his indigent fellow-countrymen in England. Certainly, his governmental world was poles apart from one of 'merit', competition and examination; and certainly he was marked by the supposedly Irish characteristic of attachment to persons rather than 'principle'.

There remains a question, which opens into broader matters: was Fitzpatrick a government agent, in the political sense? As has been said, one cannot even think of any useful role which he might have played during the crises of 1780-2. But he did provide the Irish government with political intelligence in 1792-3. He later called upon the Earl of Westmorland, who had been lord lieutenant at the time, to confirm 'my capability of obtaining early and true information, since the time of the formation of the Catholic Convention [1792]'.[35] But the information provided appears to have been general and innocuous. It was his knowledge of Catholic opinion, and of the influence and status of various prominent Catholic 'Individuals of each County, City or District within the Kingdom', which Fitzpatrick put at the service of the Castle.

Such information might have had its political uses – for example, in briefing Hobart and Nepean as to the respective characteristics and sticking points of the members of the Irish Catholic delegation whom they met in London early in 1793. But we need not regard this as sinister. In the early 1790s, most educated Irish Catholics, especially of the older generation, still looked to Britain for deliverance. Many of them feared that by pressing for too much too soon the Catholic Convention might frighten London off, while at the same time creating appetites at home which could not possibly be satisfied, but would issue finally in revolutionary violence and bloody suppression. Moreover, we must note that it was the British element in the Irish government that Fitzpatrick was attempting to enlighten. The corollary of Catholic trust in the British Parliament in 1792-3 was distrust in the Irish, and in particular distrust of the Anglo-Irish office-holders in Dublin Castle. It might well have seemed important to Fitzpatrick to provide London with an alternative view of the Irish situation to that furnished by the Ascendancy faction. Whether he was asked to report or volunteered to supply information – there is no evidence either way, but the second course would certainly have been in character – he was probably doing no more than the cautious Catholic party (which at that stage included the entire episcopate and most priests) would have approved.

On 3 May 1797, after he had served in England for over three years, Fitzpatrick proposed collecting political information during a visit of inspection of the Irish ports. He observed that 'for some months back' this had been

> a wished for object of mine; indeed from the Moment I heard of the intended French Invasion in that Country; but more particularly, — when I found that a disappointed party was determined, at every risk to render the Catholic Body dissatisfied, to answer their own Views.[36]

The 'French Invasion' was Hoche's (and Tone's) expedition which after maddening delays had reached Bantry Bay on 21 December 1796, only to fail to land its army. The 'disappointed party' was the United Irishmen, already losing its northern Presbyterian base and turning to the Catholic peasantry for a substitute.[37] Fitzpatrick had good reason for his concern. The French were soon to attempt an invasion once again, and the 'disappointed party' was certainly maintaining its efforts to embroil the Catholic masses.

Fitzpatrick's primary aim, in proposing to visit Ireland, was, he said, to counsel the Catholics against the United Irishmen and to open Catholic eyes to the perils, for them, of violence and conspiracy. But he also hoped 'by the confidence reposed in him . . . [to] receive the best information and make proper use of it'. Clearly he envisaged some form of subterfuge, if not espionage, for he spoke of 'keep[ing] clear of suspicion'[38] and later, travelling 'inadvertently as it should have appeared'.[39] What he hoped to discover is not made plain. The only indications contained in his letters suggest the projected landing place and the Irish exiles most likely to participate in the next French invasion.

In the event Fitzpatrick's proposal came to nothing, although he pressed it more than once on Huskisson and Dundas. Perhaps they felt that the qualities which he himself had prescribed as indispensable for such a mission, 'judgement' and 'delicacy',[40] were not his forte. But he also asserted roundly that certain native members of the Irish administration had determined that 'unprejudiced, accurate and true accounts . . . [of] that distracted, disturbed Country'[41] should not reach London. This was not altogether implausible. Fitzpatrick might have been exaggerating the divergence between British policy and Ascendancy interests at this particular stage. But as yet the gap between the two had by no means closed. In fact mid-1797 marked the crisis here, for it was now that the revolutionists were beginning to make serious inroads amongst the Irish masses; it was now that the Orange Societies were swelling monthly in numbers, menace and official favour; and it was now that the militia were sowing the seeds of the next year's rebellion in Leinster by their gross brutality and exactions in the course of stripping the peasantry of arms.[42] Whether or not it actually played a part in frustrating Sir Jeremiah's scheme, there was unquestionably a faction in Dublin Castle eager to drive the British government and the Irish Catholics into conflict.

When the Wexford rising did take place in May 1798, Fitzpatrick became frantic in his endeavours to be sent to Ireland. Even as late as 12 June, when the rebellion had been practically crushed, he begged, vainly, 'in the Name of Charity, Humanity and Policy' to be despatched: 'much time has been lost — every day I get essential information from that unhappy country'.[43]

How is all this to be evaluated? On the face of it it might seem as if he were offering himself as an informer. But this would probably be a misreading of the business. Fitzpatrick was not being moved by fear or greed. He had no access to secret information. His Irish knowledge was either four or five years old, or distant gossip. In short, though he may have deceived himself, he could scarcely have deceived anybody else, in pleading information-gathering as a justification for government sending him on a tour of Ireland in 1797 or 1798.

The truth would seem to be that he found absence and inaction unendurable when his country and community were in their supreme crisis. Of course this feeling was augmented by his self-importance. But the prime notes in his importunity were the desperate need to turn the Irish Catholics — 'the poor deluded peasantry' — from their fatal course, and his horror of the impending blood bath. When the slaughter actually began, in May 1798, his voice rose to the pitch of agonised impotence. Irishmen far to the left of Fitzpatrick politically, and with far less natural sympathy with the common people, were reacting in essentially the same fashion. Tone, writes his principal biographer,

> was shocked to find such old friends as Griffith and Plunket taking an active part among the forces of the Crown. Perhaps he did not know that even Burrowes and Stokes had joined the yeomanry. So indeed had someone else of whom Tone had probably never heard, but of whom the world was to hear a great deal — no less a patriot than Daniel O'Connell. The fact is that the state of mind of large numbers of educated Irishmen of liberal views was by no means what Tone supposed it to be. It was entirely possible to hate the ascendancy system, to despise religious intolerance, to long to better the lot of the poverty-stricken masses, even to have sympathized at

one time with the French Revolution, and yet to shrink from civil war and to feel that the French had lost all title to be considered deliverers of mankind.[44]

A decade later Fitzpatrick flickered again upon the Irish political scene. 1808 was a fateful year in Irish Catholic politics, marking the beginning of the rise of O'Connell to the leadership of the emancipation agitation and the supersession of the aristocrats by the professional men as controllers of the movement. The most interesting development of all was a *volte face* by the Irish prelates. In secret negotiations with the Irish executive in 1799, their representatives had agreed to an unlimited government veto on appointments to vacant sees. By 1808, partly from middle-class lay pressure, partly because the emancipation tacitly promised them in 1799 had been denied, and partly because of the continuation of full Protestant ascendancy in Ireland after the Act of Union of 1801, almost the entire body of bishops had swung around to condemn every form of interference by the crown in appointments to the Irish Catholic church.[45]

The critical meeting held in Dublin on 19 January 1808 ended in defeat for the conservatives. But there had been a struggle during the meeting, and an unsuccessful attempt by Fitzpatrick to propose a moderating amendment.[46] As published two days later in the newspapers, his proposal amounted to a species of inverted veto. The diocesan chapters were to nominate the candidates for the bishoprics, the Irish executive to approve them (or otherwise) and the papacy merely to robe the *faits accomplis* in canonical form.[47]

Although Fitzpatrick's burked motion had no further public effect than to provoke some newspaper correspondence,[48] it may have been otherwise behind the scenes. An unsigned letter of 31 January from Dublin Castle, directed to Lord Liverpool, then Home Secretary, and possibly written by Sir Arthur Wellesley himself, as Irish Chief Secretary, contains this interesting passage:

> Sir Jerome Fitzpatricks publication produced an alarm among the Bishops . . . They had a meeting on Monday last (the 25th) & it is supposed they were to consider Sir Jerome's proposition. But it is not known what passed – one of them had previously called on Sir J. & represented the injury or inconvenience to the Clergy if he persisted in agitating this subject & in engaging the Lay Catholics to take it up . . .

It is considered by some that Sir J. is set on by Governmt.

If the Laity thought they could carry their points they would readily engage the Clergy & succeed in making them adopt some measure like Sir J.'s. The Pope would for the good of the Catholick cause agree to it even in his present circumstances.[49]

It seems clear that Fitzpatrick had not been 'set on by Governmt.': the communication was an intragovernmental one. It also seems clear that the writer did not really grasp the nature of the conflict within the Catholic agitation: his 'Laity' was the cisalpine, loyalist, aristocratic faction, which was on the point of losing control of the movement in Ireland to the gallican, nationalist, middle-class thrusters epitomised and marshalled by O'Connell. Fitzpatrick's resolutions expressed substantially the views of the waning aristocratic element. If he were acting as anybody's mouthpiece, it was theirs.

But there is no reason to suppose that he was speaking on behalf of others. His sentiments were typical of the Catholic lay conservatives even as late as 1808. But we should remember that these had been 'advanced' sentiments in an earlier generation. In fact, there is consistency in Fitzpatrick's various political interventions or attempted interventions over nearly a quarter of a century. From first to last he spoke the language of a liberal Catholic of c. 1775. That is, he looked to the British government for relief; he regarded the Anglo-Irish members of the executive as inherently inimical to Catholic claims; and he was increasingly alarmed and dismayed by the growth of Catholic radicalism in and after the 1780s.[50] Fitzpatrick's behaviour was also consistent from first to last. He was on all occasions (to use his own ironical self-description) 'Sir Jeremiah-the Busybody', pressing himself into others' business, often absurd in his pretensions and maddening in his prolixity and persistence. But this was merely the dark side of Sir Jeremiah the compassionate man. Given his reading of Irish Catholic politics, his periodic drives to involve himself in their working out were no less feeling than meddlesome. Predominantly, it seems to have been the prospect of suffering, of blood and death, which rendered him, so to say, a man possessed. Nor was this 'possession' solely tribal. In June 1798 he had pleaded passionately to be given a hand in the setting up of field hospitals and ambulance services in the wake of the crown forces during the Leinster campaign.[51]

Perhaps he did really see himself as a political agent at certain junctures. Perhaps he even had at some time or other a specific political

In Search of Sir Jeremiah

principal, though this seems unlikely. But his 'politics' were immediate and crude. We need probably say no more than that anything was liable to be taken on as his concern when the prospect of pain or popular degradation met his inconstant eye.

So much for Fitzpatrick's disposition and situations for the present; the rest can be left to show themselves in his administrative career. But what of his intellectual equipment and the body of his ideas and inclinations? His published writings draw on 27 other authors, the great majority of them men of science or medicine. Priestley,[52] Harrington,[53] Black,[54] Lavoisier[55] and MacBride[56] are his main sources for general chemical theory, Robert Boyle[57] and William Hooper[58] for air compression, Stephen Hales[59] for air putricity, and the physicians Ramazzini,[60] Mezery, Tissot[61] and William Buchan[62] for the practical relationship of all these to preventive medicine. He made much greater use, however, of the works of the great eighteenth-century military and naval doctors, his near contemporaries Sir John Pringle,[63] Donald Monro[64] and James Lind.[65] From them he derived the belief that the main generator of all 'fevers and fluxes' was the exhalations from human and animal excrement, with fetid air, marshy locations and damp the next most important causes. They agreed that camp, gaol, cottage and the rest of the fevers of the poor were essentially but different names for the same infectious disease — typhoid, as we should say; and they allowed that such factors as poor housing, overcrowded rooms, dirty clothing, scanty and ill-balanced diet and bad water must predispose or contribute towards the outbreaks. Fitzpatrick's approach to public health was based upon these writings. His theoretical carapace of humoural physiology and phlogistic chemistry does not appear to have had any bearing on his practice. At any rate, his struggle for sanitation, ventilation, space, cleanliness and better food, drink and clothes was not a wasted or irrelevant undertaking.

His other authorities were few. There are a handful of references to chronicles recording the circumstances of gaol fevers. Only two sources, Beccaria[66] and Eden,[67] are employed for general criminology, although he also draws on Eden extensively when writing upon the penitentiary system. On the slave trade, Wilberforce's concepts and plans,[68] doubtless as publicly reported, impressed him deeply. But Howard was by far the greatest influence upon him outside the field of medicine proper. *The State of the Prisons in England and Wales*[69] (1777) largely determined Fitzpatrick's view of prison reform. He added many details of his own, and differed from Howard on a few minor questions and on one matter of significance — the role of religion in the gaols. But by and large he was a faithful and open disciple. 'The second Howard' — an accolade he was frequently awarded — had itself a second meaning.

Thus Fitzpatrick dealt for the most part in other men's ideas, although he discriminated intelligently amongst them, and modified his own conclusions with experience. He was however an inventive person in a characteristically eighteenth-century way. When faced with a practical mechanical difficulty he would not have dreamt of delegating the search for a solution to an 'expert'. Instead, he devised and sketched endlessly — ventilation mechanisms, smokeless lanterns, folding beds. No less was he an administrative gadgeteer — planning diet schedules, designing hospital wards, arranging office hierarchy, composing draft legislation. At the same time, his instinct was to reduce the data from which all these were drawn to order and simplicity: he kept creating new forms of tabulation as he went along. His statistics were the only innovations in which he took much pride. The rest were put down to mere natural reaction to a stumbling-block and (very rightly in most cases) common sense. Nor was it very remarkable that he should have seen nothing extraordinary in this. It was the day of the Franklins and the Benthams, even if few of the second rank of devisers showed Fitzpatrick's fertility or range. Similarly with his habits of quantifying and search for the most economical and readily comprehensible forms of classification. For it was also the day of the first literary and philosophical associations, bent on gathering and arranging independent social and medical statistics, the data which might make 'improvement' practicable.

In general philosophy, however, he was a man of his time in a much more commonplace fashion. The enlightenment touched Dublin late and feebly; and Fitzpatrick was steeped in its clichés rather than conscious of its deeper implications. His cosmic optimism was facile. Again and again he looked back complacently on vanished barbarism. Curiously enough, current miseries, cruelty and exploitation — his constant professional concerns — never struck him as incompatible with the age of beneficence. On the contrary, he spoke of them repeatedly as strange, shameful survivals from 'the darkened centuries', all the more necessary to uproot because they contrasted so disgracefully with the general advance. Of course, the sunlit uplands of the present had been won by knowledge, magnanimity and the softening of manners. Of course, ignorance and superstition (whether from prudence or not, he never added priestcraft and aristocracy) were still forces of the fading night, and the most powerful restraints on further progress. It must be said, however, on Fitzpatrick's behalf that most of these expressions of simple faith belonged to the years 1782-93, one of those delusory phases of convergence and amelioration which have interrupted the turbid flow of Irish political history. Retrospective satisfaction and prospective hope would not perhaps have seemed quite so callow in Dublin then as they were to look only five or ten years later.

The blessed trinity which Sir Jeremiah invoked most often, in the prayers for action which composed much of his official writing, was Economy, Policy and Humanity. Sometimes Common Sense was added. In arguing that the various social reforms which he proposed were economical, he did so in no candle-end-saving sense. When he thought that an improvement should be made or a need supplied, he gave money little consideration. He did emphasise from time to time that this or that innovation would cheapen the governmental process, and he occasionally showed a species of housewifely pride in 'using up' unwanted scraps of labour or materials.[70] But essentially his economical arguments were on a grander level. For example, his unceasing opposition to sending ill, old or decrepit soldiers overseas was based on the financial waste implicit in their uselessness, their need for support and their proneness to infect the remainder with disease. Similarly, lack of investment in hospitals or clothing or food for the troops was presented as a most costly form of cheeseparing; it reduced the effectiveness of the army so drastically that the net loss ran into hundreds of thousands of pounds in the worst years.[71] Nor were Fitzpatrick's arguments on the social costs of 'economy' confined to the circumstance of an army at war. High among the evils flowing from overcrowded and insanitary prisons was the danger of spreading contagious diseases into the community at large — expensively in all senses. Of course there were other fields in which he could not so easily call up 'economy' to his support. For example, it was difficult in the 1790s — perhaps it still is — to convince anyone that neglecting soldiers' wives or the insane would cost society dearly. We may infer from his excursions into such fields as these — certainly it would be true — that economy was not the driving force in Sir Jeremiah's various campaigns. At the same time his hatred of waste was genuine, and his concept of waste at once more generous and more penetrating than that of the great majority of his Victorian and Edwardian successors.

The concept of 'Policy' Fitzpatrick never defined. But he probably meant by it the political equivalent of his Economy. Repression and illiberality were as injurious to the cause they were supposed to serve, public and social order, as blinkered parsimony in government was to true economy. In other words, Fitzpatrick was a moderate and gradualist reformer, arguing that greater equity and equality and judicious change were the best security of established society. He might have smiled at Foucault's aphorism, 'The first task of the doctor is therefore political: the struggle against disease must begin with a war against bad government',[72] as a Wildean extravagance: soberly, he would have thought it an inversion of the truth. He was certainly anti-radical. He would uproot nothing, although there was a great deal that he wished to modify. True perhaps to a Catholic upbringing in the 1740s and 1750s, he remained fearful of democratic action and agitation. Conversely his faith in the ultimate good will of government — of Westminster, that is, not Dublin Castle — was practically boundless. But there are two qualifications to be made. He feared mass activity as more terrible for the masses than for the classes. Irish experience had branded deeply in him the knowledge of the peasant suffering which followed every challenge to their masters. Secondly, every so often one is startled by some savage phrase in his writing, seeming to show, for the moment, a burning hatred of the powerful. It is almost as if the slack has shifted and an incandescent glow in the interior been suddenly revealed. But this comes and goes so swiftly that it may be an illusion, after all.

Economy, Policy, Humanity: for Sir Jeremiah the greatest of these was certainly Humanity. It was the argument most commonly and most confidently deployed. What was economical, or what politic, in particular cases might be disputable. What was humane was taken to be self-evident; and it needed no justification beyond itself, for was not humanity the very mark of his more enlightened time? Fitzpatrick's supporting self-image was that of a heart responding generously, and boundlessly, to human suffering. Sympathy for the miserable welled irrepressibly in the breast, and impelled one headlong into battle to alleviate and console the wretched.

Can there be a species of pathetic fallacy between a man and a book? Although it seems improbable that he ever read Henry Mackenzie's *The Man of Feeling* (1771) and although he may never have so much as heard of its existence, Fitzpatrick's administrative career is strangely reminiscent of the novel. The bureaucracy of sensibility may seem an absurd conflation. Yet it would not be inaccurate as a categorisation of Sir Jeremiah's view of his role, or even of the considerable majority of his undertakings, and like the Man of Feeling, he was repeatedly being diverted by new calls upon his commiseration. Of course, the parallel is not to be closely pressed. Fitzpatrick was not absorbed by the moral beauty of his own reactions. He was not essentially concerned with inducing an emotional condition in himself or in his readers. Without exception his cases for compassion were inherently pitiful, to any generation or to any class; and without exception they concerned the most helpless and abandoned in the community. None the less sensibility was important to his work, and in a subjective as well as an objective sense. It provided him with endorsement and validation for his tireless importunity; it maintained his impetus in the teeth of failure and rejection; it kept finding him new fields for struggle as soon as or even well before he had reached his limits in the old.

In a sense then Fitzpatrick was an ideologue of his time. Almost every commonplace of the day, from the reign of reason to the man of feeling, found its way repeatedly into his writings, informal as well as printed. But this is not to say that ideology shaped what he did or attempted. In the first place, he was no theoretician; he dealt in shibboleths and the surfaces of ideas. Secondly, the concepts which engaged him were not readily reducible to administrative rules of thumb. In itself, the general notion of enlightenment suggested nothing about the mechanics of government; that of sensibility would never of itself produce a principle of social regulation. Finally, his ideology was in certain respects anti-ideological in tendency. At any rate, it could masquerade as the absence of ideology. Feeling, common sense, the practical responses to the specific difficulty – in such terms did men like Fitzpatrick interpret their own courses of action, and look on them as 'natural' and independent of philosophy. On the other hand, serene faith in the *Aufklarung* and the certainty that one was fighting not merely the good but also the winning fight were an inexhaustible resource for the early social reformer. Sir Jeremiah's world-picture – a patchwork of contemporary thought and sentiment – did not teach him how to sail. But it somehow seemed to conjure up, in foul weather and fair, the wind which drove him onward.

Notes

1. See marriage settlement, no. 183346, Registry of Deeds, Dublin.
2. See particularly, Fitzpatrick to H. Dundas, 3 August 1804, Melville Papers, National Library of Scotland MS. 1041, f.22; Fitzpatrick to Earl of Hardwicke, June 1805, British Museum Additional MS. (hereafter cited B.M. Add. MS.) 35760, ff. 174-5.
3. Unsigned, undirected letter dated 31 January 1808, Liverpool Papers, B.M. Add. MS. 38242, ff. 190-1.
4. *Freeman's Journal*, 20 and 21 January 1808.

38   In Search of Sir Jeremiah

   5. This was between Sir Jeremiah and his wife 'Dame' Elizabeth and Richard FitzGerald, dated 9 February 1807. It 'Granted and Confirmed unto . . . Richard FitzGerald . . . one Annuity, yearly rent Charge or sum of Two hundred pounds sterling', no. 398441, Registry of Deeds, Dublin.
   6. Dated 23 July 1809. In Kirkpatrick bequest, Royal College of Physicians Library, Dublin.
   7. '.1 Mezz. 60.4 x 41.7 cm. WL to R, face frontal, hat and cane in L hand which is pointing towards group of soldiers and women at seashore; on table books on prison reform and abolishment of slave trade; below plan of County Prison dated 1785 . . . W. Barnard after a painting by S. Drummond, 1801', R. Burgess, *Catalogue of Portraits of Doctors and Scientists in the Wellcome Institute of the History of Medicine* (London, 1973), no. 982, p. 118. One copy is in the mess of R.A.M.C., London, W. Drew, *Commissioned Officers in the Medical Services of the British Army 1660-1960*, 2 vols. (London, 1968), vol. 1, p. 82, another in the National Gallery, Dublin. The portrait is titled 'Inspector General of Health to His Majesty's Land Forces' and has the following lines of verse inscribed on it:

Nature's warm advocate this print wou'd shew
The man who feels and softens human woe
Behold him watchful of that Godlike end
The prisoners refuge and the soldiers friend.

   8. See Fitzpatrick's will, R.C.P. Library, Dublin.
   9. D. Kennedy, 'Education and the People' in R.B. McDowell (ed.), *Social Life in Ireland 1800-45* (Dublin, 1957), pp. 60-4.
   10. Professor Blanco was also unable to locate any evidence of Fitzpatrick's medical degree. See R.L. Blanco, 'The Soldier's Friend — Sir Jeremiah Fitzpatrick, Inspector of Health for Land Forces', *Medical History*, vol. xx (1976), p. 402.
   11. See W.E.H. Lecky, *A History of Ireland in the Eighteenth Century*, 5 vols. (London, 1902-6), vol. 1, pp. 137-70.
   12. As early as 1719, Archbishop King of Dublin noted 'that the Papists . . . have turned themselves to trade, and already engrossed almost all the trade of the kingdom', quoted in E.M. Johnston, *Ireland in the Eighteenth Century* (Dublin, 1974), p. 42. See also L.M. Cullen, *Life in Ireland* (London, 1968), pp. 93-7; and generally M. Wall, *The Penal Laws, 1691-1760* (Dublin Historical Association pamphlet, 1961).
   13. Cf. Fitzpatrick's testimony that he 'visited Prisons and Hospitals in various parts of Europe' in Fitzpatrick to Pelham, 25 August 1801, B.M. Add. MS. 33107, ff. 341-5.
   14. *Wilson's Dublin Directory for the Year 1783*, p. 90.
   15. No. 183346, Registry of Deeds, Dublin.
   16. *DNB*, vol. xii, pp. 876-7. See also Johnston, *Ireland in the Eighteenth Century*, pp. 119, 121-2; D. O'Donovan, 'The Money Bill Dispute' in T. Bartlett and D.W. Hayton (eds.), *Penal Era and Golden Age: Essays in Irish History, 1690-1800* (Belfast, 1979), pp. 60-2.
   17. E.g. his comments on Ray Charter School, *Report of the Committee on the State of the Protestant Charter Schools*, 14 April 1788, *Journals of the House of Commons* (Ire.), vol. xii, p. dcccxxv.
   18. R. Woodward to T. Conolly, 6 January 1789, Conolly Papers/957, Trinity College, Dublin.
   19. J. Fitzpatrick, *An Essay on Gaol Abuses, and on the Means of Redressing Them: Together with the General Method of Treating Disorders to which Prisoners are Most Incident* (Dublin, 1784), p. 106.

20. H.O. 51/147, p. 349, n.d.
21. *Freeman's Journal*, 20 January 1808.
22. B. Inglis, *The Freedom of the Press in Ireland* (London, 1954), p. 231.
23. D. Gwynn, *Daniel O'Connell* (Oxford, 1947), pp. 14, 174, 191-2.
24. I. Kramnick, *The Rage of Edmund Burke: Portrait of an Ambivalent Conservative* (New York, 1977), p. 3.
25. *Freeman's Journal*, 3-6 August 1782.
26. One of the doctors who was knighted on 28 July 1782 was Robert Scott, *Dublin Gazette*, 27-30 July 1782. See also notes attached to will, R.C.P. Library, Dublin.
27. Col. Richard Fitzpatrick and the Duke of Portland were part of 'a Protestant reform group anxious to break ... [the] power concentrated in the hands of members of the Established Church'. T.H.D. Mahoney, *Edmund Burke and Ireland* (Cambridge, Mass., 1960), p. 129.
28. His wife died between 9 February 1807, the date of the deed of assignment to Richard FitzGerald, and 23 July 1809, when Sir Jeremiah drew up his will.
29. Obituary, *Gentleman's Magazine*, vol. 80 (February 1810), p. 187.
30. Will, R.C.P. Library, Dublin.
31. Foster Papers D562/8967B, P.R.O., N.I., f. 494.
32. Fitzpatrick to Dundas, 26 June 1797; Fitzpatrick to W. Huskisson, 13 July 1797; Fitzpatrick to Huskisson, 19 August 1797; Fitzpatrick to Huskisson, 4 September 1797; Fitzpatrick to W. Windham, 4 July 1798, W.O. 1/897, ff. 537-40, 541-4, 545-8, 555-60, 681-5.
33. *Freeman's Journal*, 23-25 June 1791.
34. A.M. Gibbs, *Shaw* (Edinburgh, 1969), p. 7.
35. Fitzpatrick to J. King, 4 May 1797, W.O. 1/897, f.533. Cf. Johnston, *Ireland in the Eighteenth Century*, pp. 166-8.
36. Fitzpatrick to King, 4 May 1797, W.O. 1/897, f.533.
37. F. MacDermot, *Theobald Wolfe Tone and his Times* (London, 1939), pp. 207-33. The Griffith referred to here was Richard Griffith, the prisons reformer, and a close supporter of Fitzpatrick.
38. Fitzpatrick to King, 4 May 1797, W.O. 1/897, ff.534-5.
39. Fitzpatrick to Huskisson, June 1797, W.O. 1/897, f.508.
40. Fitzpatrick to King, 4 May 1797, W.O. 1/897, ff.534-5.
41. Fitzpatrick to Huskisson, June 1797, W.O. 1/897, f.506.
42. Lecky, *History of Ireland*, vol. 3, pp. 421-92.
43. Fitzpatrick to Huskisson, 12 June 1798, W.O. 1/897, ff.607-8.
44. MacDermot, *Wolfe Tone*, pp. 282-3.
45. B. Ward, *The Eve of Catholic Emancipation* (London, 1911), pp. 53-4, 76-7; O. MacDonagh, 'The Politicization of the Irish Catholic Bishops, 1800-50', *Historical Journal*, vol. xviii (1975), pp. 38-9.
46. *Freeman's Journal*, 20 January 1808.
47. Ibid., 21 January 1808.
48. Ibid., 30 January 1808.
49. Liverpool Papers, B.M. Add. MS. 38242, ff.190-1.
50. A typical example of the attitudes of a Catholic 'liberal' born in the second quarter of the eighteenth century is furnished in this comment of 1800: 'For me I have always disapproved of what I conceived to be an unwise and intemperate conduct in that body for some years back, whether they assumed the character of the Catholic Convention or the aggregate or select meeting of the Catholics of Dublin ... They seem to me totally to have lost sight of what in my humble opinion should be the main object for their consideration and that was, whether it was to the benignant interposition of the executive [British]

40 In Search of Sir Jeremiah

Government or to the generous and sponteneous liberality of their countrymen who composed the two houses of parliament that they were really beholden for the favours they had received and to which it was, upon sober and rational reflection, they were to look up for a farther extension of them . . . is it not peculiarly unfortunate that the Catholics of the metropolis would not attend to that consideration, and not deprive themselves and their brethren of the only support and shelter they had — the countenance and kindness of the executive Government [?] ', Maurice O'Connell to Daniel O'Connell, 30 January 1800, O'Connell Papers, National Library of Ireland MS. 15473. For the speech of Daniel O'Connell to which this was a response, see *Dublin Evening Post*, 14 January 1800.

51. Fitzpatrick to Huskisson, 12 June 1798, W.O. 1/897, f.608.

52. J. Priestley, *Directions for Impregnating Water with Fixed Air, in order to Communicate to it the . . . Spirit and Virtues of Pyrmont Water* (London, 1772); *Observations on Respiration, and the Use of the Blood* (London, 1776); *Experiments and Observations on Different Kinds of Air*, 3 vols. (London, 1774-7).

53. R. Harrington, 'Philosophical and Experimental Enquiry into the First and General Principles of Life', *Monthly Review*, vol. lxvi, p. 98.

54. J. Black, *Dissertatio medica inauguralis; de humore acido a cibis orto, et magnesia alba* (Edinburgh, 1754); *Experiments upon Magnesia Alba, Quick Lime and other Alcaline Substances* (Edinburgh, 1777).

55. A.L. Lavoisier, *Opuscules physiques et chymiques, tom. i* (Paris, 1774); *Sur l'existence de l'air dans l'acide nitreux, et sur les moyens de décomposer et de recomposer cet acide Receuil des mémoires* (Paris, 1776); *Essays on the Effects Produced by Various Processes on Atmospheric Air; with a Particular View to an Investigation of the Constitution of the Acids.* Translated from French by Thomas Henry (n.p., 1783).

56. D. MacBride, *Experimental Essays on Medical and Philosophical Subjects* (2nd edn, London, 1767); *An Historical Account of a New Method of Treating the Scurvy at Sea: containing Ten Cases* (London, 1767); *A Methodological Introduction to the Theory and Practice of Physic* (London, 1772); *A Methodological Introduction to the Theory and Practice of the Art of Medicine*, vol. 2 (2nd edn, Dublin, 1777); 'Metodo di conciare la pelli, publicato nella transazioni filosofiche, e quindi dello Societa di Dublino' in Amoretti and Loave, *Opera coli scetti sulle scienze e sulle arti*, tom. ix (n.p., 1778).

57. R. Boyle, *The Works of the Honourable Robert Boyle*, 5 vols. (London, 1744).

58. W. Hooper, *Rational Recreations, in which the Principles of Numbers and Natural Philosophy are . . . elucidated by a series of . . . Experiments*, 4 vols. (London, 1744).

59. S. Hales, *Philosophical Experiments, containing . . . Instructions for such as undertake Long Voyages at Sea . . .* (London, 1739); *A Description of Ventilators: whereby . . . Fresh Air may . . . be conveyed into Mines . . . Hospitals* (London, 1743); *A Treatise on Ventilators* (London, 1758).

60. B. Ramazzini, *A Treatise of the Diseases of Tradesmen, shewing the Various Influence of Particular Trades upon the State of Health* (London, 1705); *De contagiosa epidemia, quae in Patavino agro, et tota fere Veneta ditione in boves irrespsit* (Patavii, 1712); *B. Ramazzini . . . Opera omnia, medica et physica* (London, 1717); *Health Preserved, in Two Treatises: I. on the Diseases of Artificers . . . II. On those Distempers which arise from Particular Climates and Methods of Life* (London, 1750).

61. S. Tissot, *Practical Observations on the Smallpox, the Apoplexy, Dropsy and Nervous Cholic . . . in a Series of Letters to Albert Haller* (Dublin, 1733);

An Essay on Bilious Fevers; or the History of a Bilious Epidemic Fever at Lausanne, in the Year 1755 (London, 1760); *Advice to the People in General with Regard to their Health* (London, 1765); *A Letter to . . . Dr Zummerman on the Morbus Niger* (London, 1776).

62. W. Buchan, *Dissertatio medica inauguralis de infantum vita conservanda* (Edinburgh, 1761); *Domestic Medicine or the Family Physician* (Edinburgh, 1769).

63. J. Pringle, *Observations on the Diseases of the Army in Camp and Garrison* (London, 1752); *Observations on the Nature and Cure of Hospital and Jaylfevers. In a Letter to Dr Mead* (London, 1750); *A Discourse on the Different Kinds of Air* (London, 1774); *A Discourse upon some Late Improvements of the Means for Preserving the Health of Mariners* (London, 1776).

64. D. Monro, *Dissertatio de hydrope* (Edinburgh, 1753); *An Account of the Diseases which were Most Frequent in the British Military Hospitals in Germany from January 1761 to March 1763. To which is added an Essay on the Means of Preserving the Health of Soldiers, and Conducting Military Hospitals* (London, 1764); *A Treatise on Mineral Waters*, 2 vols. (London, 1770); *Praelectiones medicae ex Cronii Instituto annis 1774 et 1775; et oratio anniversaria ex Harveii Instituto, die Octobres 18 . . . 1775* (London, 1776).

65. J. Lind, *A Treatise of the Scurvy* (Edinburgh, 1753); *An Essay on Diseases incidental to Europeans in Hot Climates* (London, 1768); *An Essay on the Most Effectual Means of Preserving the Health of Seamen in the Royal Navy . . . And an Appendix of Observations, on the Treatment of Diseases in Hot Climates* (London, 1757); *Two Papers on Fevers and Infection* (n.p., n.d.).

66. Marquis of Beccaria, *An Essay on Crimes and Punishments* (London, 1767).

67. W. Eden (Lord Auckland), *Thoughts on Penal Law* (London, 1771).

68. W. Wilberforce, *Correct Copies of the Twelve Propositions submitted . . . by Mr Wilberforce, to the Consideration of the Committee to whom the Report of the Privy Council, Various Petitions for the Abolition of the Slave Trade, and other Papers Relative Thereto had been Referred. The Speeches of Mr Wilberforce, Lord Penrhyn* (n.p., 1789).

69. J. Howard, *The State of the Prisons in England and Wales with Preliminary Observations and an Account of Some Foreign Prisons and Hospitals* (Warrington, 1777).

70. E.g. Fitzpatrick to Huskisson, 26 April 1795, W.O. 1/897, ff.325-6.

71. E.g. Fitzpatrick to Lord G. Lennox, n.d. no. 1, W.O. 1/896, ff.27-9; Fitzpatrick to Transport Commissioners, 26 August 1795, Adm. 108/36, 29 August 1795; Fitzpatrick to Huskisson, 2 February 1796, W.O. 1/897, ff.484-5.

72. M. Foucault, *The Birth of the Clinic* (New York, 1975), p. 33.

2 PRISON REFORM IN IRELAND, 1763-1783

I

Fitzpatrick entered the field of prison reform some time in the 1770s, probably towards the decade's close. Apparently his interest in it was first engaged by his work as a prison physician; and if he needed any encouragement to move on from mere practice to reform, it was supplied by Hussey Burgh, a leading 'liberal' politician who was later to become Chief Baron of the Exchequer. Fitzpatrick wrote in 1790 that it was Burgh who had originally recommended as 'objects' for him, 'To propose the means of rectifying gaol abuses, and the reform of manners in our prisons'.[1] But Fitzpatrick was no pioneer. There had been a remarkable, if short-lived, burst of prison reforming legislation in Ireland long before he involved himself in the question, and he may well have been throwing himself upon another, well-launched wave of 'rectification' when at last he did so. Thus, as he freely admitted, he was — to start with, at least — following in others' footsteps; and it is necessary to trace them at some length before Sir Jeremiah's part in the long process of change can be properly estimated.

Prison reform in Ireland in the eighteenth century dates effectively from 1763, with two Bills introduced in the Irish House of Commons in the autumn of that year. The first was narrow and specific, dealing with what seemed *prima facie* a particularly irrational and cruel anomaly. At that time acquitted prisoners were kept in prison if they were unable to pay the gaoler's fees accumulated while they were awaiting trial; and the new Act was meant to exempt them from further detention.[2] It was, however, well-meaning rather than effective. The prescribed legal processes were involved, and enforcement was left to the discretion of the local justices, who rarely took advantage of it, doubtless because the grand juries of the counties had to compensate the gaolers for lost fees. It was also widely believed that almost all of those found 'not guilty' were in fact habitual criminals for whose incarceration, on whatever pretext, society should be grateful. Needless to say, this sentiment also worked against the Act's enforcement. Nevertheless, it was an interesting measure, not least because it dealt with the precise issue which launched John Howard upon his career as prison reformer. In fact, the first statute which Howard caused to be passed in the British Parliament, in 1774,[3] was substantially a copy of the Irish Acquitted Prisoners Act of 1763.

The second Irish measure of 1763[4] was however, both wide-reaching and revolutionary. Two of its clauses, one dealing with the authorisation and display of the scale of gaolers' fees and the other with the sale of drink and food by gaolers in the prisons, may have had partial English precedents. But most of the other provisions of the Act appear to have been as original as they were, in contemporary conditions, radical. First, the gaoler was to be made, in part, a salaried official instead of someone who derived his income solely from fees and from trafficking with the prisoners: this last was absolutely prohibited. Secondly, the health of prisoners was brought into consideration for the first time: 'whereas', clause VII ran, 'many infectious disorders are daily produced by the confinement of numbers in close prisons', exercise grounds were to be enclosed and set out for inmates. Thirdly, the segregation of prisoners was to begin. The separation of the insane from the remainder was to take place immediately, and men and women prisoners to be separated as soon as new gaols, suitably arranged, could be erected. Fourthly, and most interesting of all, a rudimentary form of inspectorate was proposed — or, to be precise, a still more rudimentary form of inspectorate, which dated from 1665,[5] was to be developed. By the 1763 Act, the parish clergy of the established Church of Ireland were enjoined to visit the gaols and prisoners in their districts regularly, and if they considered that any prisoner needed food or medicine or medical attendance, they were to order it to be furnished at the public expense. A final innovation provided a primitive species of 'legal aid'. Whereas a common informer secured or shared a fine only if his action succeeded, under the Prisons Act of 1763 a judge could order that any 'prosecutor' bringing a charge under its provisions be compensated from public funds for his expenses and loss of wages.

What was the provenance of these extraordinary pieces of legislation — extraordinary because they anticipated the late eighteenth-century British prison reform movement by more than a decade, and still more extraordinary in anticipating nineteenth-century developments in several particulars? They certainly belonged to a long-established paternalistic Irish tradition. The clauses of the Irish 3 Geo. III, c.28 which dealt with the provision of medicine and food to poor prisoners at the expense of the county, and with the administration of this 'charity' by the parochial Anglican clergy, were, as we have said, refinements of similar clauses in earlier legislation. Specifically, they extended provisions of an Irish Prisons Act of 1729,[6] which had in its turn built upon a more rough and ready Caroline statute, half a century old.⁷ The 1763 Acts were also characteristic of Irish penal legislation throughout the eighteenth century in their intense concern with enforcement. In contrast to the British, almost every Irish prison statute of the eighteenth century attempted, painfully, to envisage and to circumvent the difficulties of its being carried into effect. Enforcement was an *idée fixe* in Ireland — perhaps so because legislation was peculiarly difficult to realise there. As Howard was to observe some twenty years later, although the Irish Prison Acts contained 'many articles highly laudable and worthy of imitation . . . the police of this country [Ireland] in these matters is as defective in point of execution, as it is commendable in theory'.⁸

More generally, although the evidence on the point is indirect, it seems plausible to derive the 1763 legislation, in part, from two of the most common motives for trying to regulate prisons in the eighteenth century — fear of disease, and the feeling that debtors needed and deserved different treatment from the other inhabitants of gaols. Gaol fever was one of the intermittent terrors of the day. Even from within the walls of the prison it might break out into the exterior world, either carried by visitors or those who worked there or airily transported in some other, incomprehensible fashion. But the necessity of taking prisoners out into the open streets for exercise or the performance of 'natural functions', and their appearances in court for trial or as witnesses, were much more immediate threats. If, as was often the case, fever were abroad or brewing in the prisons these excursions seemed to thrust the infected directly against the world at large. Thus, the eradication of disease within the gaol was not just the prisoner's but everyman's precaution.

Correspondingly, more than half the prison population comprised, not people convicted or accused of any crime, but defaulting debtors. Now imprisonment for debt was a not wildly improbable fate for a middle- or even an upper-class man in the eighteenth century. A legislator could, in a real sense, see it as something which might befall himself. At any rate, he should have done so: as Howard reminded them:

> Those gentlemen who, when they are told of the misery which our prisoners suffer, content themselves with saying, *Let them take care to keep out* . . . forget the vicissitudes of human affairs; the unexpected changes to which all men are liable; and that those whose circumstances are affluent, may in time be reduced to indigence, and become debtors and prisoners.⁹

With several of the clauses aimed at preventing fever or reducing the charges for incarceration, we may plausibly suppose that these two commonplace forms of self-interest also acted as general promoters of the statutes of 1763.

But all this — even in the unlikely event that usage, fears and repulsive empathy provided between them a comprehensive explanation of the 1763 Acts — still leaves two questions open: who were the moving forces, and why did they move at that particular time? Here the first clue is, of course, the Bills' sponsors. The various proposers and seconders were Henry Flood, Sir Hercules Langrishe, Sir John Parnell (the elder)[10] and Henry Sheares,[11] the father of the Sheares brothers who were to be executed as United Irishmen in 1798. Flood, whose father was a judge and who had himself practised at the English bar a short time before, may have had a special knowledge of and interest in the plight of acquitted prisoners detained for poverty: at any rate, his introduction of the first Bill was virtually the maiden action of his parliamentary career. Neither Langrishe nor Parnell (moderately distinguished members) seems to provide even so tenuous a connection as this with the cause which they were espousing in 1763. Sheares, however, can be firmly linked with prison reform. In 1774 he established a charity in Cork to relieve small debtors, and this soon developed into a general prison reform association of some significance. Moreover, he co-operated in 1767 with Dr Charles Lucas in introducing a Bill to strengthen the position of the accused in treason trials. Lucas himself may well have played a more telling part, behind the scenes, in the preparations of the 1763 Bills than any of the leading actors. He was the promoter of a Bill in 1761 to secure the release of debtors; and he had come within an ace of possessing the best of all qualifications for a mid-eighteenth-century prison reformer: he had been committed to prison himself in 1749, although he had foregone the critical experience at the eleventh hour by fleeing to the Isle of Man.[12] Moreover, he had shown a professional interest in his *An Essay on Waters* (published in 1756) in one of the matters dealt with specifically in 3 Geo. III, c.28. 'It would likewise', he had written,

> be not onely an act of great and true charity, but the best policy, to establish proper baths in all bridewells, gaols and other places of confinement; where, by obliging the wretched, who from filth and nastiness, contract the most malignant and pestilential diseases frequently to wash and cleanse themselves, much of the calamity, and the dreadful infection may be obviated, which they so commonly

suffer and so often impart to the rest of society, in general gaol deliveries.[13]

We might also note that Lucas was a frequent contributor to the new opposition paper, the *Freeman's Journal*, from the start, and that the *Freeman's*, which began publication on 12 September 1763, acted as a mouthpiece for the prison reformers. Lucas may well have written some or even all of the several pieces favouring prison reform which the newspaper published in October and November 1763. If only for want of a better hypothesis, then, we may propose Sheares and Lucas as the most likely authors of the 1763 Acts and in particular of the second, which evidenced a first-hand knowledge of, and perhaps also some systematic inquiry into, the proceedings of contemporary prisons.

A second clue to the immediate provenance of the Bills may lie in the general Irish movement towards colonial nationalism, and of opposition to the established 'undertaker' mode of rule, which had got under way in the 1750s.[14] The members of the House of Commons involved in moving the 1763 prisons Bills belonged to the 'Patriot' group or faction, as these early colonial nationalists were named. So too did the *Freeman's*; and its campaign of support for them is worth some notice. On the day on which the first Bill was proposed, 27 October 1763, it denounced the illegal purchase of offices, including gaolerships, from sheriffs. Part of the proceeds of gaolers' extortions, its editorial ran, went to paying sheriffs for their appointments: 'what cruel exactions have not these foul practices produced'. A second editorial, a fortnight later, which almost coincided with the introduction of the second Bill, and which attacked the entire process of imprisonment for debt, included these comments on prison life:

> We are credibly informed that it is usual with such keepers to amass considerable fortunes from the wrecks of the wretched, to squeeze them by exorbitant charges and illicit demands, to huddle them together in naked walls and windowless rooms . . . even a sufficiency of water is refused to their necessities.
>
> That public and private benefactions are dispersed of at the pleasure of the keepers, regardless of the intentions or orders of the donors. And that the apartments appointed to these miserable men are generally damp or shattered in the flooring and exposed by breach or want of windows to the inclemency of the weather and all the rigours of the seasons.[15]

On 22 October the newspaper had carried an appeal from the debtors in the City Marshalsea for 'alleviation of numberless most deplorable and piercing miseries . . . being totally destitute of food, raiment, fire and candle light', and this was repeated in the issues of the next few weeks; and on 19 November the sale of alcohol in prisons was condemned. This ended for the time being the *Freeman's* interest in prison reform. The fact that it was expressed so freely but so briefly, and that it coincided so neatly with the introduction of the two reforming measures in the House of Commons, certainly suggests the existence of a concerted campaign, as well as a close association of the new 'liberalism' and this particular assault upon a branch of Irish government.

To summarise, the flurry of activity in 1763 was in part the product of one of those periodic Irish realisations that what had been statutorily enjoined was not in fact being done; it may well have been forwarded by outbreaks or apprehensions of an outbreak of gaol fever; it almost certainly reflected concern − whatever the immediate occasion − with the plight of debtors; and last but far from least, it seems also to have been an early expression of the colonial nationalist opposition to the entrenched administrative order, which was expressed in the Irish House of Commons at this time. In almost all these respects it was the forerunner of the next significant wave of change, in 1778-88, in the midst or on the crest of which Fitzpatrick was to ride.

II

Meanwhile, from 1764 to 1778 prison reform in Ireland proceeded on a different tack, or different tacks. In the later 1760s it was determined to rebuild two of Dublin's largest prisons, the City Marshalsea and Newgate, after committees of the House of Commons had reported them to be 'inconvenient', 'unwholesome', 'ruinous' and cramped;[16] and as late as 1777 further committees were appointed to settle the final building accounts.[17] Contemporaneously, various measures for the relief of debtors were passed, with Lucas as one of the leading sponsors;[18] and again as late as 1777 and 1778 committees were enquiring into the effects of the recent Insolvency Act upon such relief.[19] Finally, in 1778, the Irish Parliament followed the English example of 1776[20] in sanctioning the use of hulks, to be moored in the Liffey, to accommodate prisoners awaiting transportation, now that the American colonies no longer provided receptacles for those sentenced to expatriation. The Irish Hard Labour Act of 1778 required felons from all over

Ireland to be sent to the Dublin hulks, from which 'base' they were to be despatched to toil on public works ashore, at any rate until their transportation overseas could be arranged.[21] All three developments, the rebuilt prisons, the freeing of debtors and the transference of felons to hulks, were concerned either with providing new or alternative accommodation for prisoners or with reducing the number incarcerated. The consequential measures might of course also improve the quality of the life of prisoners within the four walls of the gaol. But if so it was a secondary and incidental consideration.

Yet the distinction between the two should not be too sharply drawn. For example, the 1777 committee which granted a final £1,000 for the rebuilding of Dublin's New Prison considered also 'the pestilential disorders' raging in the gaols of the capital — the 'ruinous state' of prison buildings forming the connecting link.[22] More particularly, the Irish Hard Labour Act of 1778 led on to a revival of the concerns of 1763-4. Before its passage each Irish county was responsible for its own transportees until they were embarked. But now 100 to 120 country convicts would be added to Dublin's prison population every year. As things turned out they were to be additions to the existing gaols in the capital, and not to its waterborne inhabitants. No hulks were ready in 1778, nor in fact was any ever to be moored upon the Liffey. Even before the Hard Labour Act was passed fears were being expressed in Dublin that the increase in the number of the imprisoned would lead to new and worse outbreaks of gaol fever; and early in the year it was reported that the disease was again spreading rapidly in the City Marshalsea.[23] As always, the fear of gaol fever acted as a spur to 'reform' in terms of what went on within the gaol. An act 'for preserving the health of prisoners in gaol and preventing the gaol distemper' was hurried through in the spring of 1778.[24] Although the new statute bore a close resemblance to English legislation of 1776, it was a more comprehensive measure. It also looked back to the second Irish statute of 1763, and was marked by characteristic Irish emphases upon the means of financing the prescribed operations, and on machinery for the steady review by some superior body of what was actually happening in the gaols.

According to this Prisoners' Health Act of 1778, all prison rooms were to be scraped and whitewashed at least once a year, and kept clean and well ventilated. Separate sick rooms were to be provided for men and women; prisoners were required to be washed in warm baths and cleanly clothed before they left the prison; and courts of justice were to be properly aired. These and similar provisions were clearly related to the purpose set out in the preamble, the eradication of the current outbreak of gaol fever which had already occasioned deaths in Dublin and elsewhere. The discretions and obligations which were heaped upon the grand juries and magistrates in the final clause of the Act evidenced the degree of alarm which was being felt. But perhaps the most interesting feature of the Act, in terms of this particular book, was the provision requiring each set of magistrates at quarter sessions 'to appoint an experienced surgeon or apothecary at a stated salary' to attend each gaol, and to report quarterly to the justices on the health of the prisoners in his charge.[25] This brought closer to adumbration the idea of a regular prison inspectorate. It may also have been the actual gate through which the future inspector general of prisons, Fitzpatrick, first entered the field. He was described in 1781 as having already worked 'for *many* [my italics] years as a physician in the Dublin prisons'. But he might well have moved from voluntary and casual to regular and salaried prison work in 1779.

The revival of interest in prison reform in the late 1770s did not die away after the fashion of the early 1760s. Instead it issued in a reform 'movement', broad, deep and persistent. By the beginning of the 1780s, a pressure group had formed in Parliament which kept the issue before the Irish House of Commons, and won general support there. This group concentrated much more single-mindedly and doggedly than ever was the case before upon the enforcement of the existing legislation. It did not neglect altogether prison construction and renovation, or the amendment of various clauses and requirements of the earlier Acts. But its main concern was life within the prison, and its main endeavour to carry into effect what was already upon the statute books.

The derivation of the new reform movement was multiple and complex. One root went back, of course, to the Prisoners' Health Act of 1778. In so far as the statute established in the gaols a network of surgeons and apothecaries, who had to report to each quarter sessions, it ensured that the subject did not drop out of notice — especially so as the medical attendants were now paid officials whose stipends had to be sanctioned regularly by the local gentry.[26] The recurrent outbreaks of 'malignant fever' obviously worked in the same direction, of keeping the 'gaol question' in the public view.

A second root was English example, and in particular the work of the two great contemporary publicists of prison reform in England, John Howard and William Eden (who served as chief secretary in Ireland between November 1780 and April 1782). Howard's work may even have done something towards igniting the second Irish blaze. But though the first edition of his *State of the Prisons* did have some reference to Ireland, which he had visited briefly in 1775, two years before the publication, these were scanty; and there is nothing to indicate that Howard himself or his book had any influence upon the initial revival of concern with prison reform in Ireland in 1777-8. His visit in 1779 may have brought him closer to Irish reformers; and perhaps even introduced him to Fitzpatrick. At any rate, his 'inspections' in Dublin in that year appear to have been more extensive, minute and active than those of 1775. Certainly, by the time of his third visit, in 1782, he was both well known to, and respectfully received by, the Irish reformers. He was the key witness before the House of Commons committee on prisons in 1782, and at the instigation of the provost, John Hely-Hutchinson, was honoured, shortly after his testimony, by the degree of LL.D at Dublin University.[27] From then onwards, Howard was of first importance to the movement, although mainly as a sanctified exemplar and authoritative source.

William Eden may well have been more influential than Howard in the very early days. Eden had been a leading – perhaps one might say, the leading – British prison reformer for a decade, when he took up the Irish Chief Secretaryship at the end of 1780. His *Principles of Penal Law*, avowedly in the Beccarian tradition, had been published in 1771; and he was the author of the English Hard Labour Act of 1779, a major and revolutionary measure, which had involved him in efforts to establish a national penitentiary system. With such interests and such a recent experience, and with the immense powers of a chief secretary to initiate and sustain behind him, Eden was perfectly placed to direct and sustain an Irish prisons movement. At this stage, however, he would certainly have been out of sympathy with Howard.

Whether or not Eden took the lead in assembling it, the pressure group for prison reform did take shape in the Irish House of Commons during his period of office. Its leading member was Peter Holmes, owner of and member for the borough of Banagher (the second seat of which he sold) and comptroller of stamps.[28] The most notable of the other members of the group was Sir John Parnell, the younger, who had succeeded to the baronetcy in 1782: he was then a Commissioner of Revenue, and soon to become chairman of the Ways and Means Committee and later Chancellor of the Exchequer.[29] Of the rest, the two most active reformers were Sir John Blaquiere, who had served as Chief Secretary between 1772 and 1775, and who now held the sinecure position of Alnager, worth £3,000 per annum,[30] and Richard Griffith, who was described in 1784, in a confidential government memorandum, as a 'well meaning Young Man . . . who made his fortune in the East Indies — is hot and impetuous, yet certainly is not of mischievous intention, though much tainted with popular prejudices. He is warm for reform of Parliament and protecting duties'.[31] Clearly, the pressure group was not politically homogenous. Blaquiere was one of the most conservative and Griffith one of the most radical members of the House of Commons while Holmes and Parnell were both borough owners, placemen, moderate government supporters and eager for further advancement.

Thus the reformers of the 1780s were not as a whole 'progressives', even in the very limited sense in which their counterparts of the 1760s might be so described. On the other hand, there are some interesting similarities in the gestation periods of the two groups. An Irish House of Commons struggling to assert its independence and its ability to rule, and to compensate for the want of ultimate power by exploiting to the full the petty powers which it did possess, is a marked feature of each little phase. Possibly this indicates as well a critical difference between pre-Union and post-Union Ireland. In 1750-90, it might be argued, the nationalist impulses (or colonial nationalist impulses, to be more precise) among the Ascendancy were being sublimated into attempts at the humane reform of various contemporary institutions. Direct political reform would have soon raised very awkward questions for even the most advanced members of the Protestant nation. How to ensure that the drive towards independence of British control stopped short of separation? How to ensure that the drive towards parity for Catholics stopped short of the loss of Anglican ascendancy? How to ensure that parliamentary reform stopped short of popular determination of the actions of the legislature or executive? In these circumstances, perhaps it was tempting to turn to less dangerous fields such as lunacy, disease, prisons or sanitation.[32]

Half a century later the entire situation was reversed. By the 1830s a new species of nationalism, grounded in an increasingly self-conscious and aggressive Irish Catholic culture, was filling the field in public life. This meant that in so far as subjects like public health or penal institutions were disputed in Ireland, the struggle was essentially political — a contest as to who controlled patronage in dispensary or prisons appointments, or which sections of the community met the majority of the bills. In the second quarter of the nineteenth century, in sharp contrast to the rising outcry in England, there was general silence in Ireland on the substance of civic government and the amelioration of daily living. In so far as they involved spoils or served as symbols of superiority or inferiority of station, sanitation, arterial drainage, housing, roads, lighting and similar affairs in Ireland might engage attention. But practical changes, if any there were to be, were treated as the business of the public servants.[33]

At any rate, whatever the truth may be about the general relationship of colonial nationalism, nationalism and social reform, the prison 'rectification' movement of the last quarter of the eighteenth century in Ireland coincided in point of origin with the upsurge of Irish Protestant independence in Volunteerism. It began with a House of Commons committee which sat from 9 May to 28 August 1780.[34] The committee was primarily concerned with the relief of debtors, and as such part of a now familiar pattern by means of which, in almost every parliamentary session, a number of specified insolvents secured their release. But on this occasion the inquiry was enlarged to embrace the sufferings and injustices of the imprisoned bankrupts of Dublin. Parliament was prorogued almost immediately after the 1780 committee reported, but as soon as it next met, in October 1781, another committee was appointed, this time specifically 'to inspect the state of all Debtors places of confinement in Dublin', and this second committee included at least one member of the administration. Ten days later, the second committee was enlarged both in membership (the lord mayor of Dublin was among the additions) and in scope.[35] All the capital's prisons were now to come under review. In turn, the enlarged committee was superseded by a third in March 1782, which was commissioned 'to inquire into the state of the gaols and prisons of this Kingdom' (and not of the metropolis alone); and again the scope of inquiry was extended later, finally to include all bridewells and houses of correction, as well as gaols, throughout the entire country.[36]

It was Fitzpatrick's friend, Peter Holmes, who was responsible for turning the inquiries towards both prison health and the provincial gaols. Shortly before the recess at the close of 1781 he had moved that the House consider

> the state of our gaols and prisons, which he feared would be found more defective than in any other country in Europe, particularly with regard to the danger of infection, as experience had manifested; for we had instances of the jurors, the lawyers, the witnesses and almost every person attending in our courts, being swept away by the violence and malignancy of the jail infection.[37]

When the session resumed, he also raised 'in a most affecting speech'

Prison Reform in Ireland

the question of the country prisons, giving 'from authentic documents, a clear account of the insufficient accommodation in the county gaols'.[38] Almost certainly the 'authentic documents' and, very probably, the inspiration for Holmes came from Sir Jeremiah. It is most likely, too, that Holmes himself was chairman of the March 1782 committee: he had proposed the motions which led to its setting up.[39]

The March committee reported on 15 June 1782, but this was not the end of its labours. It was instructed to remain in session even after Parliament rose at the end of July. Meanwhile two 'interim' pieces of legislation had been spawned,[40] as well as yet another prisons committee (this time specified as under the chairmanship of Peter Holmes) to prepare the more important of the two.[41] The first statute ordering the release of all acquitted prisoners then in gaol in Ireland from inability to pay sheriff's or gaoler's fees, removed *pro tem.* one small portion of the problem. The second measure, that in Holmes's charge, sought merely the enforcement of existing legislation, although, as we shall see, it adopted heroic, not to say draconian, remedies to try to bring to life the virtually extinguished and forgotten Prison Acts of 1763 and 1778. Both Bills of the 1782 session were debated and revised extensively during their passage through the House of Commons.

The first striking aspect of the prison agitation of 1780-2 is of course that it absorbed a considerable proportion of parliamentary time during two of the most intense and crowded sessions in the history of the Irish House of Commons: these were the years of the struggle which culminated in the repeal of Poynings' law and of the declaratory Act, the notorious 6 Geo. I. Secondly, the prison campaign involved a considerable proportion of the membership of the Lower House in the inquiries. Sixteen MPs were named as members, but each of the four committees (or derivations of the original committee of 1780, if one wishes) which have been noticed had additional members whose names were not recorded in either the Commons journals or the *Parliamentary Register*. When we add to these the membership of three further prisons committees of 1780-2, which dealt with the now-separated issues of debtor relief and prison building, it becomes clear that the level of knowledge of the subject generally in the House of Commons must have been rising fast.

Thirdly, in its final version, the 1782 inquiry included 'field-work'. In June 1782, the committee visited Dublin prisons, and these were not cursory inspections but prolonged as well as painful traversings of the gaols. The practice of direct investigation and interrogation was to become a regular element in the prison inquiries of 1783-93 and from first to last it was of crucial importance in giving an altogether sharper and deeper apprehension of the evils to those who had seen and heard and touched and smelt them for themselves. Finally, in the course of these developments both Howard and Holmes decidedly entered the scene, while the reports on the country prisons make it clear that Fitzpatrick was already working in the wings. Possibly Eden, too, may have intervened, in the sense of pushing the old issues of debtors' relief and prison construction into the area of gaol regulation and management generally in 1781. But certainly Howard was the dominating witness before the committee set up in March 1782, and Holmes was its dominating member. It was he, possibly in collusion with Fitzpatrick, who advertised for witnesses and evidence even before the committee had come formally into being.[42]

Howard really set the direction of prison reform in 1782 by his evidence before the March committee. He had found Newgate 'in every respect the very Reverse of every Idea he can form to himself of a perfect and well-regulated Gaol'. Sick and dying lay on stone floors in the cells, unattended; the chapel was never used; morals were 'totally neglected', with several men living on the 'female Side' and some women on the men's; no work was available or prescribed for anyone, even for those condemned to hard labour; spirits were sold openly, and neither scale of fees nor regulations were anywhere displayed; and the entire prison was 'dirty beyond Description', and ripe for an outbreak of gaol fever at any hour.[43] The committee concluded, upon inspecting Newgate for themselves on 11 June, that 'no Part of Mr Howard's evidence . . . was exaggerated'. On the contrary it had omitted or understated some of the horrible particulars, such as the promotion of debauchery, the corruption of children from nine to sixteen years 'mixed indiscriminately with the most hardened Felons and Malefactors', and the 'narrow, dark, close, noisome and filthy' dungeons in which it was 'cruel and inhuman to confine any Persons'. To their astonishment, the committee also discovered that Newgate was practically without supervision. The high sheriffs repudiated all responsibility; the head gaoler was an absentee; the undergaoler knew nothing of the legislation governing prisons; some of the turnkeys were prisoners themselves; the chaplain had long ceased to visit the gaol; and no surgeon attended regularly. The prison officers were 'paid' by what they could extort from the prisoners for 'fees', food and drink, or in the case of the head gaoler, by running a 'Warehouse' to sell 'Wines, Spirits, etc.' to the inmates. The total salary bill for Newgate was £20 p.a.[44]

The committee's report was essentially an expression of horror at what had been disclosed. Its only specific recommendation was the curiously panopticon-like proposal that the neglected chapel should be used to enlarge accommodation, 'by which Alteration the Gaoler would have the opportunity of inspecting, from a single Spot, the State of the Male and Female Wards at any Time, which he cannot do from any Part of his present Habitation'.[45] But when the report was presented on 15 June 1782 a most unusual step was taken. It was ordered that it be printed immediately and that a copy be delivered at once to every member of the House of Commons.[46] Clearly, this was the beginning rather than the end of a campaign.

It is true that the committee's report practically coincided with the passage of the second (or Holmes's) Prison Act of 1782, which indeed it had helped to procure. But it cannot have expected that this statute would achieve much, at any rate in the short run. Essentially, it evidenced the virtual rediscovery of the existence of the Gaol Regulation Acts of 1763 and 1778, which were not only dead-letters but also practically forgotten. Both had relied ultimately upon the grand juries to ensure their execution, and the grand juries had failed altogether in their duty. Holmes's 1782 Act[47] attempted to remedy this by empowering a still more weighty authority to coerce the grand juries in their turn. The judges of assize were enjoined to look to the enforcement of the 1763 and 1778 Acts, and where grand juries failed or refused to do what was required of them, to fine the counties up to a limit of £500. The judges were also enjoined 'to make such orders, and impose such fines, in cases of neglect or misconduct of gaolers, as shall seem to them just, according to the circumstances'.[48] This statute is of the highest interest in throwing light upon late eighteenth-century attitudes towards central government. Characteristically, the existing legal and administrative system has the new functions heaped upon it; characteristically, the established superior authorities are given a virtual *carte blanche* in terms of coercive power once the failure of lesser penalties to achieve the desired results is apparent. None the less, the second 1782 Act was really following in the tracks of the earlier legislation, simply nominating another institution as the final arbiter and increasing the scale of punishment for neglect. All earlier experience suggested — as was in fact to prove to be the case — that mere intensification of the old practices would not suffice to produce significant change. Besides, the new regime of the assize judges was not to come into force until mid-1783.

In these circumstances, the 1782 committee was not likely to rest on its oars after it had reported in June of that year. The report had come too late in the session to form the subject of fresh legislation. Moreover, as the paucity of its recommendations and its post-prorogation sittings indicate, the committee's inquiries were far from complete when it was issued. But the day after Parliament next assembled, on 15 October 1783, either the old committee was confirmed or a near replica was endorsed[49] — it is impossible to tell which without knowing the full membership of either — with Holmes now undoubtedly in charge.

III

It was at this point that Fitzpatrick first entered the public stage. He was the witness examined at much the greatest length by the 1783 committee, as well as the only witness who was not a gaoler or a turnkey or a magistrate. Instead, he had been chosen as 'a Gentleman, who from his Profession and long Attendance on Jails, they [the committee] considered capable of giving them useful and interesting Information'[50] — in short, the counterpart of Howard in 1782. For not only had Fitzpatrick been 'long attending' Dublin gaols, but he had also been 'inspecting' prisons across the country on his own account for several years. Those which he described at his examination were gaols which he had visited in the course of a journey to Kilkenny towards the end of November 1783, and three others in Dublin which he had visited immediately after his return to the capital. But he spoke of these as altogether typical of Irish prisons in general, both from place to place and over the last few years.

The 1783 prisons committee's concerns at this stage may be summarised as a characteristic late-eighteenth-century amalgam of eclectic altruism and self-interest. The members did manifest some pity for the misery of prisoners — most often, although by no means altogether, for the misery special to incarcerated debtors. But they also spoke of the medical deficiencies as 'a Grievance productive of the worst Consequences, by endangering the lives of those respectable Characters whose Duty it is to attend the Courts of Justice, as has been fatally evinced in recent Instances'.[51] Fitzpatrick steered a way between response to the committee's lead and enlargement of the reforming view.[52] He made the widespread use of dungeons, or subterranean cells, and irons the pivot of his prison critique. These, he argued, predisposed prisoners to disease because of the damp, dirt, want of ventilation, cold, accumulations of filth and lack of exercise inherent in such modes of confinement. Not that the suffering involved was merely physical: 'the melancholy State of Mind in which Prisoners generally are' opened them wider to disease. But even the fact that this mental depression was 'irremediable' was turned to account, for Fitzpatrick observed that it rendered a still greater 'Degree of Precaution' necessary.

His essential points were, however, that the dungeons-and-irons regime was a direct consequence of prison insecurity, and that the cause of insecurity was, in turn, the faulty construction and fittings of almost every Irish gaol. This line of reasoning enabled Fitzpatrick to enter into an entire scheme of prison reform. Its centrepiece was the construction or reconstruction of the gaols, so as to eliminate the need for dungeons or irons, while providing room for exercise and sufficient sanitation, warmth and 'airiness' within the buildings themselves. His strictures on even the most modern of Irish prisons, the new Carlow gaol completed only five months before, revealed, obliquely, his reforming plan. Although Carlow was provided with a paved exercise yard, it was

> fifteen Steps below the Surface or first [i.e. ground] Floor, ... the Prisons are flagged with a Sort of Stone, which on the Changes of the weather becomes damp. There are no Passages for the free Circulation of the Air, nor are there Necessaries on any of the different Floors, which are three in Number, nor is there a Communication from the Cells, to the only Necessary, which is in the lower Court Yard. There is no Hospital.

Later in his evidence Fitzpatrick pointed to three other general deficiencies: bad food, insufficient and dirty bedding (even where it was merely straw) and the lack of medicines and medical attendance. As with the location, construction and design of prisons, he had no difficulty in relating these to what appears to have been the committee's leading concern, infectious diseases. But he himself spoke as if the sources of gaol fever and 'the general Hardship that the Prisoners Labour under' were practically identical. A good example of this conflation is his handling of the insecurity of prisons, which he presented as the key to explaining the miseries and the diseases alike.

> The Jail of Naas, is a strong Proof of this Assertion, for as the upper Parts of it are so insecure, the Criminals are confined in the most loathsome dark Dungeons, the Passage to those is from the Street, through a dark Entry, guarded by three different strong Doors, and

so dark are those Dungeons, that there is no seeing without Candles, and . . . [so] damp and filled with stinking Vapors, that Candles with Difficulty burn; the only Passage for either Light or Air, is a small Window to each of those Cells, scarce fourteen Inches square, and even that small Space is, in a great Measure, occupied with Iron Bars; in the smaller of those Dungeons, the 29th of last Month, there were lying on the cold damp Ground, scarce defended with Straw, six double-bolted Criminals, two of them without any Sort of Covering, save a little Straw and Mats made of the same, which they substituted for Blankets.

Fitzpatrick went on to describe one of the pathetic implications of the want of 'necessaries', yard and proper food at Naas: the gaoler, in his 'humanity', allowed the chained prisoners to beg in the street all day outside the prison door.

Similarly, he skilfully connected the antiquated and ruinous condition of the Dublin Bridewell with other prison evils, and allowed the mere account of these to stand in the place of overt condemnation. The range of those incarcerated in the bridewell ran from lunatics to those 'confined to Hard Labour'. Lack of space and the ill-repair of many of the rooms crowded them indiscriminately together. Thus, for example, two young boys occupied the same chamber as three lunatics, one of whom was constantly chained down; and hard-labour prisoners being forbidden fire and candlelight, all their involuntary companions shared their deprivation. Correspondingly, despite the large number of the insane in the bridewell, no medical attendance whatever was provided; and Fitzpatrick believed that several of the 'insane' women had been improperly committed. Even the delirious might end up there. He reported the case of a young man, who had been brought in a few days before, 'raving' from an inflamed wound. There was no physician to tend either the injury or the delirium. Again Fitzpatrick's was a rounded account. The 'insane' poor ended in the bridewell, cheek by jowl with the criminal sane, because there was no other place to lodge them; the 'insane' included many who were not mad because there was no medical practitioner to determine which was which; and in turn the absence of medical attendance aggravated all the sufferings which the overcrowding and indiscrimination had originally inflicted.

Two characteristics of Sir Jeremiah as a reformer stand out at once in this, his first recorded essay in social criticism. First, he was a synthesiser. He looked for cardinal causes and fundamental remedies; as a matter of course he sought to rearrange everything that he perceived

Prison Reform in Ireland

into trunk and branches. At the same time, he did not draw attention to his mental proceeding, but depended heavily upon his audience drawing inferences from his sequences and descriptions. It was an unusual but effective conjunction of techniques. Habits of self-justification and glorification, and some successes, made inroads upon them as his administrative career progressed — or perhaps one should say, jerked forward. But he never lost altogether his native tact, inassertiveness and obliquity. Even less did his eye for the central or his instinct for systematisation weaken with time. Meanwhile he was to receive some return for both qualities in the provisions of the Irish Prisons Act of 1784.

The 1784 Prisons Act[53] derived from the testimony before Holmes's committee, which reported on 17 December 1783.[54] The Bill, probably drawn up by Holmes and Griffith, was broadly divisible into three parts. Sir Jeremiah's evidence received its reward in the clauses enjoining new prison building or prison reconstruction to ensure both security and adequate sanitation, and also in the particular provisions which rendered dry and airy cells, and sufficient water supplies and privies obligatory. He may also deserve the credit for a clause empowering magistrates to commit minor offenders to houses of correction rather than to gaol, for this was clearly inspired by two purposes which he had closely adopted — the reduction in numbers in the gaols and the separation of the merely 'giddy' from the deep-grained criminals. On the other hand, the Act assailed the system of paying gaolers by fees and by the profits which they made from trafficking with the prisoners. It rendered gaolers liable to heavy fines for selling drink, and made the grand juries responsible for paying them adequate annual salaries. These reforms derived not from Fitzpatrick's evidence but from the disclosures about the conduct of Newgate and other Dublin prisons first made by Howard. Nor does Fitzpatrick appear to have had any hand in the shaping of the third general feature of the 1784 Act, the enforcement clauses. These relied heavily, in the traditional way, upon the activity of the grand juries. It was to the grand juries that the investigation of the physical state of particular prisons, and their renovation or replacement, was left. It was they who received discretionary power to spend up to £50 in an emergency. It was they who were to appoint from among their own members the justices of the peace who, by quarterly visits and reports, were to ensure the observance of the Act. Fitzpatrick was no believer in gentry government; but for the present he had to be content with the paper advances of the earlier clauses of the Act.

Notes

1. J. Fitzpatrick, *Thoughts on Penitentiaries* (Dublin, 1790), p. vi.
2. 3 Geo. III, c.5.
3. 14 Geo. III, c.20.
4. 3 Geo. III, c.28.
5. 17 & 18 Chas II, c.8.
6. 3 Geo. II, c.5. This is 'An Act for continuing several Temporary Statutes made in This Kingdom, and now near expiring, and for the Amendment of other Statutes therein mentioned'. Section vi deals with the procedure for giving relief to poor prisoners.
7. 17 & 18 Chas II, c.8.
8. J. Howard, *The State of the Prisons in England and Wales* (4th edn, London, 1792), p. 202.
9. Ibid. (2nd edn, London, 1780), p. 15.
10. See *DNB* for all three: vol. vii, pp. 331-5; vol. xi, pp. 556-7; vol. xv, pp. 347-9.
11. *DNB*, vol. xvii, pp. 1393-4, under his son John Sheares.
12. Ibid., p. 1394.
13. *Freeman's Journal*, 13-15 February 1781, quoting from Charles Lucas, *The Theory and Uses of Baths* (Dublin, 1772). The passage is in turn an extract from *An Essay on Waters* (London, 1756).
14. See O'Donovan, 'The Money Bill Dispute' and T. Bartlett, 'The Townshend Viceroyalty, 1767-72' in Bartlett and Hayton (eds.), *Penal Era and Golden Age*, pp. 55-112.
15. *Freeman's Journal*, 11 November 1763.
16. *Journals of the House of Commons* (Ire.), vol. viii, pp. 48, 52, clxx.
17. Ibid., vol. ix, p. 345.
18. 7 Geo. III, c.25; 11 & 12 Geo. III, c.32; 13 & 14 Geo. III, c.44; 17 & 18 Geo. III, c.14.
19. E.g. *Journals of H of C* (Ire.), vol. ix, pp. 408, 412, 447.
20. 16 Geo. III, c.43 (G.B.).
21. 17 & 18 Geo. III, c.9.
22. *Journals of H of C* (Ire.), vol. ix, pp. 336, 363.
23. *Freeman's Journal*, 4-7 April 1778.
24. 17 & 18 Geo. III, c.28.
25. Ibid., s.i.
26. By the twice yearly presentments at quarter sessions.
27. Dublin University *Register*, 31 May 1782.
28. E.M. Johnston, 'Members of the Irish Parliament, 1784-7', *Proceedings of the Royal Irish Academy*, vol. 71, section C, no. 5, p. 185.
29. Ibid., pp. 196-7. E.M. Johnston, 'The State of the Irish House of Commons in 1791', *Proceedings of the Royal Irish Academy*, vol. 59, section C, no. 1, p. 39.
30. Johnston, 'Members of the Irish Parliament', p. 171.
31. Ibid., p. 183.
32. Of course, many modern historians would regard such fields as 'dangerous' in the sense of being central to social order and control, cf. M. Foucault, *Discipline and Punish: the Birth of the Prison* (London, 1977) and *The Birth of the Clinic*. The point here is that they both were non-partisan issues and issues which did not threaten the interests of the Anglican Ascendancy *vis-à-vis* other Irish groups and sections.
33. Cf. O. MacDonagh, *Ireland: The Union and its Aftermath* (London, 1977), ch. 2.
34. *Journals of H of C* (Ire.), vol. x, pp. 124, 192, 196.

35. Ibid., pp. 217, 241.
36. Ibid., pp. 319, 369.
37. *Parliamentary Register* (Ire.), vol. i, p. 196.
38. Ibid., p. 265.
39. Ibid.
40. 21 & 22 Geo. III, cc. 41 & 42.
41. *Journals of H of C* (Ire.), vol. x, p. 308.
42. *Freeman's Journal*, 24-27 December 1781.
43. *Report of the Committee Appointed to Enquire into the State of the Gaols and Prisons in this Kingdom*, 15 June 1782, *Journals of H of C* (Ire.), vol. x, p. dxxxiii.
44. Ibid.
45. Ibid., p. dxxxiv.
46. *Journals of H of C* (Ire.), vol. x, p. 370.
47. 21 & 22 Geo. III, c.42.
48. Ibid., s.i.
49. *Journals of H of C* (Ire.), vol. xi, p. 17.
50. *Report from the Committee Appointed to Enquire into the Present State, Situation, and Management of the Public Prisons, Jails, and Bridewells, of this Kingdom*, 17 December 1783, *Journals of H of C* (Ire.), vol. xi, p. cxxxi.
51. Ibid.
52. Ibid.
53. 23 & 24 Geo. III, c.41.
54. *Journals of H of C* (Ire.), vol. xi, p. 171.

3 A PROLOGUE AND AN ACT, 1784-1786

I

The 1784 Act proved ineffectual. Its basic weakness was to entrust the stock agencies of law and order, the judiciary, the magistrates, the established clergy, and above all the grand juries, with the task of galvanising the prison officers into activity, and frightening them into good conduct. As usual, these agencies remained embedded in their ordinary routines. But the forces which had thrown up the deadletter statute were not spent. Chief among them were the zealous people, and chief among the zealous members of parliament was Peter Holmes.[1] Already in 1784 it could be said, 'Ireland can [now] boast of her Howard in the person of Mr P. Holmes'. Holmes had, however, zealous support — from above, so to say, in Thomas Orde, the new Chief Secretary, from the side, so to say, in Richard Griffith; and from below, in Sir Jeremiah himself. All three were important in their ways — though Griffith's usefulness was lessened by his being regarded by most other members as a firebrand. But only Fitzpatrick's help was really crucial, for it was he *par excellence* who revealed the present ills and proposed the future remedies. At a secondary level, Holmes could also rely on the general approval of the most influential members of the Irish executive, the Chancellor of the Exchequer, Foster,[2] and the Attorney-General, Fitzgibbon,[3] as well as the former Chief Secretary, Blaquiere. Foster spoke of Holmes as the true friend of 'the cause of humanity',[4] and Blaquiere spoke of his endeavour as 'humane and benevolent',[5] and of course the majority of the House of Commons followed where such men led, especially in an extra-factional field.

Next, there was unfinished prison business hanging over from the 1784 parliamentary session. In particular, neither the Acquitted Prisoners Fees Act[6] nor the Insolvent Debtors Bill of that session had ended well. The first had been opposed in the Commons, partly on the ground that it would set criminals (even if they had escaped convictions on the actual charges brought against them) loose upon the community, and partly because crown clerks would lose that part of their income which derived from prisoners' fees![7] Although Holmes, Foster and Fitzgibbon were outraged by such arguments, the measure appears to have been emasculated in committee in response. Holmes's Insolvent Debtors Bill — designed to clear the gaols once more of at least some of these unfortunates — did pass the House of Commons. But it failed in the House of Lords, although supposedly because of its defects in form rather than opposition to its principle.[8] However that may have been, the miserable insolvents remained incarcerated; and even an interim form of relief proposed by Holmes on 19 April 1784 — that creditors be compelled to grant a small subsistence allowance to those whom they had forced into prison[9] — also came to nothing. Thus the 1784 Prisons Act had certainly not stilled concern nor diverted public attention from the gaols question. The plight of the insolvents alone was bound to bring it to the front again when the Irish Parliament next met at the beginning of 1785.

Meanwhile, Holmes's agitation had set off another train of events which was to lead indirectly to new legislation. The principal debtors prison in Dublin, the Four Courts Marshalsea, had come under scrutiny during the debate on the Insolvent Debtors Bill in the House of Lords on 21 April 1784. A week later the House went into committee to investigate the running of the Marshalsea;[10] and though the outcome is unknown, it is clear that the inquiry was quite protracted, that several witnesses were examined and that, once again, the matter did not end with the close of the parliamentary session in June, but was carried forward into the following year when the lord mayor himself conducted an inspection of the gaol.[11]

Moreover, the usual medley of 'public feeling', some of it disreputable, some moderately decent, helped to keep the prisons question alive in the last six months of 1784. Fears of gaol fever revived, particularly at assizes time, and early in 1785 another outbreak was reported in the capital.[12] On 17 July 1784 a mass escape from the New Prison (the rebuilt Newgate) in Dublin was reported,[13] and in the same month a recent increase in crime became the talk of the day.[14] People were agitated by the need for security, yet also by the inappropriateness of the death penalty for most capital offences. They were frightened by the horrific accounts of squalor in the gaols, yet also by the insufficiency of gaol accommodation for the incarceration of the dangerous. In a confused way all this perturbance of opinion funnelled itself, in the end, into a collective demand for more, safer, roomier and (above all) healthy prisons.

The pot was kept boiling — or perhaps brought to the boil — by Fitzpatrick's first pamphlet, *An Essay on Gaol Abuses and on the Means of Redressing Them*, published some time in 1784. It probably appeared late in the year. Internal evidence suggests that it was not even begun until after Holmes's committee had presented its report on 17

December 1783, and the dedication to the new Lord Lieutenant, the Duke of Rutland, who was not appointed until February 1784, praises his activities in Ireland. Thus the pamphlet would not have appeared in time to influence the Prisons Act of 1784, for that statute received the Royal Assent on 14 May, and the committee stage had been completed by 23 April.[15] However much Sir Jeremiah's evidence before the 1783 committee or his friendship with Holmes might have helped to shape certain of the clauses, his essay itself must have been much too late to do so. However, it was clear, as we have seen, almost from the start that the new statute was by no means a final measure. The pamphlet would soon have its chance of determining the course of Irish penal regulation. As the first 'native' plan of prison reform, as well as the first considerable piece of Fitzpatrick's administrative writing, it is worth close attention.

II

The *Essay on Gaol Abuses* was shot through with Sir Jeremiah's inimitable sketches in a phrase or two of this or that particular facet of Irish prison life; but its philosophy and programme alike were largely derivative. Howard's *State of the Prisons in England and Wales* was the source of both much of its reasoning and several of its recommendations. On prison construction and siting, the segregation of prisoners, their exercise, keepers, and ventilation, Howard was clearly Fitzpatrick's inspiration. This he fully — not to say, fulsomely — acknowledged by repeated obeisances to the *'all worthy Howard'* and the *'observing Howard'*, 'whose name cannot be made too frequent mention of'.[16] There were also specific attributions to the *State of the Prisons*. Quite commonly, however, Fitzpatrick carried forward Howard's proposals even in such Howardesque matters as the location of gaols with a view to air, sun and wind flow; and in practical ingenuity he particularly shone. For example, where Howard had simply proposed ventilating machines for cells,[17] Fitzpatrick went on to prescribe that part of the farmer's winnower or corn cleaner, with 'small wings annexed to a slender axis', which could be fixed in the window, with the prisoner turning the axis to draw in fresh and expel stale air:[18] the advantages being those which he always looked for in social management, simplicity, ease of operation and cheapness. Again, where Howard had recommended that irons be as little grievous as practicable,[19] Fitzpatrick added the idea of breeches especially tailored so that prisoners who were bolted could remove them.[20]

In more general terms there were significant differences in emphasis and points of concern between the two works. Howard was a strait and narrow evangelical, but the *Essay on Gaol Abuses* was if anything deist in tone, with the usual ritual bob or two towards 'Divine Providence'. Even in so far as Fitzpatrick followed Howard in asking for chaplains to 'exhort' the prisoners, he sketched, though cautiously, the notion of adding Catholic priests to those of the established church — and this at a date when the popish priesthood still worked furtively and often illegally in Ireland:

> although there may be no possibility of making provision compatible with the nature of the laws of this country for a roman catholic clergyman, yet I am convinced that many of them, from the sense they have of their duty, would be happy to have an opportunity of reforming the principles of lawless wretches; and do believe, that the greatest advantages would arise to the community, from the adoption of this method; by giving the clergymen an opportunity of exercising their influence ...[21]

Overall, however, secular virtue took the place of religion in the *Essay*. Its air is caught exactly when Fitzpatrick asks rhetorically whether Irishmen would 'in an age, when bigotry, superstition and persecution are fled . . . deny every comfort to the wretched, and security in respect to the lives of those, whose duty it is to superintend them — Avert it heaven!'[22] Nor was heaven's benevolence to be doubted. 'The iron age has fled, and the spirit of emulation having charity and *true* policy for its objects, pervade almost every breast'.[23] Even more breasts would be pervaded, he believed, if Orde, the new Chief Secretary, got his way with educational reform. A future plan of Orde's[24] was to include a diminution in the Church of Ireland's control of schools and an increase in 'rational' teaching and the inculcation of 'the principles of rectitude and beneficence into the hearts of the rising generation'.[25]

Similarly, medicine and the natural sciences loomed much larger in Fitzpatrick's work than in Howard's. More than half the *Essay* was taken up with the chemistry of air, the causation of infectious disease, diagnostic procedures, preventive measures and modes of treatment. Again there was no pretence at originality, unless modest accounts of one or two of his own cases implied such a claim. Instead, the argument relied heavily on contemporary authorities, most of all on Pringle and

Monro, the leading men on army medicine, and on Lind's *Essay on the Health of Seamen*.[26] For Fitzpatrick saw infectious diseases as in one sense a simple problem in public health. Whether it was soldiers in encampments, sailors between decks, the poor in crowded cabins, ocean passengers, debtors in spunging houses or prisoners in gaols was comparatively insignificant. Overcrowding, dirt, damp, foul air, bad or no sanitation, poor food, tainted water, ragged clothes and filthy bedding were the likely concomitants of each condition of confined living. Thus the lessons of one field could be transferred confidently to another, and — treatment of contracted disease being so uncertain and unhopeful — the critical thing was to identify the sources of infection, and concentrate upon eliminating them.

Again, the difference between Howard and Fitzpatrick was essentially one of degree. Howard too saw the physical circumstances of prison life as predisposing the inmates to infection, and he looked largely to physicians and surgeons as the executors of reform. But Fitzpatrick had a coherent theory and a universal view. This led him into much more radical health proposals than Howard's. Two of his recommendations in the *Essay on Gaol Abuses* may serve to illustrate the happy consequences of the more comprehensive, professional and root-and-branch approach. First, Sir Jeremiah argued that each prisoner should be subject to a medical examination on first entering the gaol.[27] This was important not only to check the importation of infectious diseases into the prison, but also to try to reduce the miseries of those who might otherwise be incorrectly classified as insane, and to identify those in need of treatment for some other malady or defect. The second example is Fitzpatrick's dictum — from which he never deviated through his career — that where infectious disease had broken out, there was nothing for it but to burn all the clothing and bedding of the infected to halt its further spread.[28]

As these instances may indicate, Sir Jeremiah's was, if not an original medical mind, at least a shrewd one. His account of the symptoms and cures of fevers began, 'The physician who wishes to discharge his duty, must be a close attendant on nature';[29] and it was surely a mark of virtue, or at least of sense, in an eighteenth-century doctor to be slow to prescribe anything for a patient. He set out the Harrington-Priestley controversy on phlogiston simply but fairly, inclined towards Harrington but ended by saying that what really mattered for public health was the common ground between the two, as the place on which the medical reformer — 'the servant of humanity' — could build.[30] At the same time, he moderated his book-medicine by the experience of 'many

A Prologue and an Act

years' of gaol attendance, which, he added, had led him to believe that 'in no one instance is the exertion of the physician more necessary' than prison reform.[31] For (to complete the circle) Fitzpatrick spoke of medicine as the 'healing art' in social as well as individual terms. He seemed to see the physician as the equivalent, if not the supersessor, of the parson, in contemporary society. Ideally, at any rate, medicine, like the church, was less a profession than a form of public service, 'one of the most laudable and beneficient occupations about which a friend to mankind can employ himself'[32]

The next arresting mark of the essay is its immediacy. In certain veins, Fitzpatrick had an almost Sterne-like capacity to grasp an audience, and plunge it into his allusive flow. He habitually personalised problems, and this far more effectively than Howard because, as a regular gaol worker over years instead of a lightning visitor from Olympus, he could describe an individual plight in complex terms, and over a considerable period. But perhaps the most interesting aspect of Fitzpatrick's immediacy in the *Essay* was his attempted use of empathy. Repeatedly, he tried to induce the reader to suppose himself in the role of the sufferer — or rather to recall his own discomforts and fear in situations in which he had immeasurable advantages over the poor prisoner. A characteristic passage runs:

> Those who will for a moment, turn their thoughts on the general effects of different states of the atmosphere, on the human body, will readily conceive what extraordinary changes may take place in our frames, by its immediate transition from heat to cold, from dry to moist, &c. but when we reflect on the sudden alteration which takes place in us, if affected by a disagreeable smell, the langour on our spirits, inclination to faint, defect of brisk circulation, &c. what are we not to suppose of their sufferings, who are shut out from the light of Heaven, deprived of the pure air, so bountifully bestowed by Providence; loaded with irons; bedewed with unwholesome vapours; perhaps that instant impregnated with the discharge of putrid lungs; their bodies not half covered; no place to rest their languid frame, but a naked damp floor, scarce coated with straw, the vital spark almost extinct (in so much as it depends on proper food), and the horrors of either a capital punishment, or long imprisonment hanging over them?[33]

Even the rich were reminded of their own itches and scratchings (doubtless many in 1784), and then asked to imagine themselves in the places of the lousy, threadbare wretches in the gaols, and to consider what it must be to endure their bodies. Whether innocent or contrived, this mode of exposition-argument was well pitched as propaganda. Of course, induced empathy as a literary method was not idiosyncratic to Fitzpatrick; and sensibility (in nerve physiology no less than literature) was a growing vogue. But they were also invariable and incessant in Sir Jeremiah. It is difficult to think of any contemporary who turned to them more naturally or more often.

Finally, and of most immediate significance, the *Essay on Gaol Abuses* concentrated attention upon the enforcement of prison reform. The need for stringent and continuous regulation, Fitzpatrick felt, scarcely needed to be argued. The evidence of even a single observer such as Pringle was 'sufficient to prove the necessity'. 'Divine Providence' having marked out the human race by its capacity to improve and to forestall evils, 'how eagerly ought we [not] to embrace every method which can be devised, towards the further preservation of the species?'[34] But remedial legislation was worthless unless implemented; and Fitzpatrick took as examples seven major provisions of the existing Irish prison legislation, and showed from his own experience that they were thoroughly and universally neglected.[35] Conversely, there was the example of France.

> Notwithstanding that there is no part of the world in which the laws are better executed than in France, yet it was found, that the best regulations were liable to abuse, and that prisoners were not sufficiently provided for, by the enaction of the best laws, except, the execution of them was attended to.[36]

From Howard, from Treforiers' *Ou dames de charité* and possibly from knowledge of his own of Paris, he had gleaned the French countermeasures. In particular, he was impressed by the weekly prison visitations of members of the attorney-general's department, by the grander visitations by members of the *Parlement*, and by the *Parlement*'s appointment of one counsellor as *commissaire* to each prison — and especially that this office was 'perpetual'.[37] Why, he asked, should not Ireland imitate France in more worthy matters than her fashions?

Fitzpatrick's recommendations for an inspectorial system at this stage were neither ambitious nor much further forward than Howard's. He merely asked that a physician or surgeon, appointed to each prison and visiting it twice weekly, should make it his business to ensure that the health and cleanliness regulations were enforced, while the chaplain

A Prologue and an Act

on his twice weekly visits should see to it that the gaolers observed the other provisions of the law. This was fully in the eighteenth-century mode of amateur enforcement of social legislation — as indeed *mutatis mutandis* was the Parisian practice. But Sir Jeremiah ended the 'reform' chapters of the pamphlet with this 'quere':

> Would not the having a general inspector who would visit the gaols once or twice a year, and see that the regulations prescribed by law were punctually executed, be one of the most effectual methods of carrying the intention of the legislature into effect?[38]

Possibly the *commissaire* was the remote inspiration of this pregnant proposal. But Fitzpatrick was thinking not of the casual philanthropy of 'a gentleman of fortune', a counsellor of the *Parlement*, but of a paid, permanent and powerful officer of the state.

To complete the 'prologue' to the Prisons Act of 1786, it may be useful to consider here also two other schemes of Fitzpatrick's, devised in 1785. These did not influence the Prisons Act of 1786 in any direct fashion. But they do throw more light upon Sir Jeremiah's concept of the role of central government in managing society, as well as extending our knowledge of his administrative thought, and of his *modus operandi* in expounding these ideas to key politicians. For it was to Foster, still Chancellor of the Exchequer but soon to become the Speaker of the House of Commons,[39] that the schemes of 1785 were submitted; and not only was Foster the most powerful of the native politicians at this juncture but he was also the one who reflected the attitudes of the Ascendancy *en bloc* most faithfully. In all senses, he spoke with the accents of the resident Irish gentry; he reacted instinctively as they did; he rationalised their prejudices. As to his main rivals, Fitzgibbon was English by desire, and Beresford[40] by family connection and ambition. But for Foster the link with Britain was but a marriage of convenience, or rather of mutual necessity; he neither brought love to nor expected love from such cold conjugality. In short, among the leaders of the Irish 'cabinet' in 1782-1800, he was much the closer in spirit and elemental feeling to the mass of his fellow members.

The precise direction and detail of Fitzpatrick's proposed reforms have not survived, but their general outlines are clear enough. The first concerned the Irish wool trade. In the 1770s English rams had been introduced to improve the Irish sheep stock. One consequence had been the coarsening of the wool generally, and a greater admixture of qualities. This may not have produced a net loss, as the quantities of wool grown were much greater than before. But it did create — or at least accentuate — the need for specialisation both in sorting the wool and in directing it to the appropriate branches of manufacture. It also placed woollen manufacture in Ireland, where neither form of specialisation was nearly so advanced as in England, at greater risk in terms of English competition. Or so, at any rate, Fitzpatrick saw the situation.

Were Irish entrepreneurship sufficiently developed, doubtless no great problem would arise.

> I confess that if the original Purchaser of the Place had such a Capital as would intitle him to become what is called a Sorter, and lived in a Town or Country where he could vend the different brands of Wooll to those who wanted them, that he would become a considerable Gainer...[41]

But as things were, there was little hope that the necessary specialisations would develop 'spontaneously' in Ireland. Consequently, 'Parliament must interfere'. Fitzpatrick did not elaborate, in his letter to Foster, the parliamentary interference which he thought appropriate to 'the infant State of the Woollen Manufacture in the Kingdom'. But he did make it clear that it should follow the already common Irish practice of employing legislative 'Penalty' or 'Reward', or 'Threat or Encouragement', to move matters in various desired directions. He also stressed that such interference was often temporary; and he expected that things would eventually so fall out 'in respect to Wooll Sorters, for as their Utility and Profits will be evident, numbers after some time will follow the Business'. None the less, state support and regulation were the indispensable preliminaries.

In the case of Fitzpatrick's second scheme — the provision of a metropolitan police force — we do not know even the outline of his proposal, the relevant part of the manuscript having been destroyed. But it is clear that it was inspired by the protracted political riots in Dublin in the preceding year, when the city's watchmen were overwhelmed and the troops had several times to disperse the mobs bloodily. Foster, as an anti-protectionist, was one of the particular objects of popular execration, so that Fitzpatrick might confidently have expected to find here a ready ear. It is also clear that to some degree Fitzpatrick used the current police system of Paris as a model, and that he intended that, apart from the initial expenditure for arms and uniforms for the 'City Guards', as the new force was to be termed, it should pay for itself, doubtless by some form of levy from the protected.[42]

Although these projects were both fragmentary and stillborn, they are in their way revealing. Perhaps their most interesting feature is their anticipation of the framework of the 'radical' administrative reform of half a century hence. Each of Fitzpatrick's cases of social engineering envisaged an initial intrusion by the state to supply a want or correct a deviation, but also to produce in time a self-regulating system. Whether stick or carrot should be used to achieve the desired end was merely tactics: the vital thing was to get the appropriate social mechanism so wound and set that it would, so far as practicable, run itself. None the less all was ultimately and always subject to central control, even if it were best that this should not be called into action: doubtless it was no coincidence that Fitzpatrick, like certain of his counterparts in the 1830s, should have turned to France for patterns. The distant hills of omnicompetent state and omnipresent intendant must have looked green indeed.

III

Early in the 1785 parliamentary session Holmes returned to the attack on behalf of the insolvent debtors. In June 1784, the lord chancellor had promised to direct the judges to draw up a new Bill free of legal defects, when the old one had been rejected by the House of Lords. But nothing had been done; bankrupts continued to starve; and on 3 March 1785 Holmes threatened to introduce another measure himself 'for those miserable helpless creatures' unless the judges bestirred themselves immediately.[43] In fact, the question was subsumed in the larger issue of prison reform generally when Holmes secured another committee of inquiry into gaols and bridewells on 13 April.[44] But this committee had been already anticipated. Doubtless in collusion with Holmes, Fitzpatrick had begun an inquisitorial tour (of almost four weeks' duration, and including the county gaols of Wicklow, Wexford, Waterford, Tipperary and Kilkenny, as well as a dozen prisons, bridewells and spunging houses in Dublin) on 30 March. Thus Sir Jeremiah had virtually completed his inquiry before the committee, whose principal witness he was to become, began to sit.

Fitzpatrick's evidence before the 1785 committee[45] was more extensive than that of all the other witnesses together. These others consisted of sheriffs and bailiffs — in effect defendants, and of imprisoned debtors — in effect the accusers: the review of gaol conditions as such rested on Sir Jeremiah's testimony. Although his evidence was considerably above two thousand words in length, it was far from prolix, but instead terse, almost telegrammatic. This for example was his account of the women's chambers in the New Prison:

> much crouded and dirty; the smoaking of them is scarce supportable. They [the women] are confined in the Apartments in Consequence of the Work going on in the Yard, which is neglected, as not a Stone was laid these fifteen Days past. This is a great Hardship on the poor Creatures. They have no Hall or Kitchen. The Time of getting Straw is to be next Saturday, but at present they have not a single wisp under three-fourths of them, nor a Blanket to cover them. On the Whole these Apartments, or rather Cells, are stinking, shocking Places, and in every Respect ill-contrived. The Necessaries on the different Corridores are yet open, and emit a most foetid Smell. There are two Women ill lying on the naked Flags, with scarce a Wisp of Straw under them, in the Cells, as there is no Hospital for Women; nor is there a Kitchen or Wash-house. Bars are wanting for the top Lobby, to prevent Persons falling over the Stairs. The stairs are one Foot ten Inches wide.

Fitzpatrick's general 'findings', all of them implicit, were, first, that the existing legislation was practically ignored (only in Kilkenny did he find that the existing regulations were obeyed), and that the prison officers of all kinds were practically unsuperintended and unchecked; secondly, that squalor and privation almost beyond description — except that he succeeded in describing it — was the lot of the incarcerated; thirdly, that health, cleanliness and the sick were especially neglected; next, that systematic extortion and failure to adhere to or even compose set scales of fees were commonplace; next, that gaols, even new gaols, were badly designed and built, and lacked many or most of the features prescribed by law; and finally that, were two evils to be chosen above all the rest, dungeons and drunkenness should be the choice.

Naturally, given the immediate provenance of the inquiry and Holmes's temporary obsession with the subject, debtors and spunging houses loomed extraordinarily large in Sir Jeremiah's evidence. But he did not neglect his own admirable *idées fixes*. Locking up the sane as mad, and virtual enslavement by extracting unpaid labour from those in one's power were two of these; and he killed both birds with one stone in this passage on women in the Dublin Bridewell.

There are sixteen Women under the Idea of being insane in the Womens Apartments below Stairs, and the Nurse of those. There were three Women, viz. Anne Hynes, Hannah Osborne and Mary Gorman, who appeared to Witness, at the Time he visited the Prison, to be rational, but by being kept in the Room with the other unfortunate Creatures who were in a State of Real Madness, and not one Moment passed without every Species of Turbulence and Confusion, they told Witness they were distracted, and begged to be released. Witness examined them separately, and found them consistent. This might have been their lucid Interval; but even so, they should be removed to other Apartments, and some Aids applied which might assist in restoring them to their Reason. Anne Narry has been confined nine Years, and seems rational. She is made Use of by the Keeper as a Servant for two Years past. Witness saw her nursing an Infant for the Mistress of the Prison. Wishes to be released. Mary Greene seems rational. Confined five Years. Has worked frequently some very fine Work for the Mistress of the Prison, which the Mistress acknowledges, but does not choose to report her as perfectly sensible.

A final noteworthy feature in Fitzpatrick's evidence was the tabulations which he submitted to the inquiry. These specified each room in the Dublin debtors' prisons; its rent; the number of people and beds it held (the second often less than the first); and its particular sanitary condition. These tables, though simple, provided both a quantitative and a comparative view of the problem, which even the least informed Member of Parliament (or for that matter newspaper reader, for the tables were set out, together with the rest of Fitzpatrick's evidence, in the Dublin press) could readily grasp. The prison 'charts' are doubly interesting — for the very early date of their devising, and for their being the first surviving venture of Sir Jeremiah into a form of reporting which he was to use constantly in his administrative life.

As we shall see, Fitzpatrick's tours of inspection and the *Essay on Gaol Abuses* largely determined the next Irish penal legislation. But the road to the actual statute was long and broken. Not that the work of the 1785 committee on gaols and prisons went slowly. On 4 May 1785, little over a fortnight after its appointment, Holmes read its report — essentially the setting out of the evidence which it had heard — from his place in the 'deeply affected' house.[46] Five days later 'in a short but most pathetic speech', he moved three resolutions calling for new prison building in Dublin as the principal remedy of the debtors' miseries and exploitation.[47] The resolutions were sympathetically received: not so, however, Holmes's suggestion that the House should not dwell upon the past, but look exclusively to the future. Blaquiere, and later another member, Ogle, pressed hard for the punishment of those whom the committee's report had exposed as 'guilty of such abominable cruelties'; and in fact seven sheriffs and bailiffs, accused of running a species of 'protection racket', were soon summoned before the bar of the House of Commons, four of them to be charged later in the criminal courts with extortion and assault.

But mere bricks and mortar and retribution were not a sufficient response to the report, and on 24 May Griffith was called on by the House to produce 'his plan, for amending the state of the jails'. Griffith, nothing loth, declaring that this reform 'was the wish nearest his heart and the main object for which he had solicited a seat in that House', moved a resolution for an inspectorate to ensure that prison legislation was 'properly and duly executed'.[48] Practically, Griffith proposed a form of inspectors general, two for the entire country, alternating the provinces in their charge every other year.

> This produced a conversation [debate] of three hours, in which, although every gentleman agreed in the idea, yet they differed as to the mode. Mr Daly thought four inspectors would be better than two and Mr Secretary of State [Hely-Hutchinson] wanted five, one for each circuit . . . Sundry other differences arose about grand juries — about whether the surgeons of the county infirmaries would not be the most proper persons for that office? — Whether the inspectors should reside in the towns, or be sent from other parts of the country? — And whether the appointment of these inspectors might not degenerate into court jobs? On either side of each opinion much was said, but nothing decided.[49]

None the less the House was in committee on the report on three further days of the week beginning 21 May — a degree of attention to a measure of social reform altogether unprecedented in the Irish Parliament — and at the sitting of 27 May Griffith produced a set of resolutions giving shape, he hoped, to the movement of opinion up to that time. The first three proposed that grand juries appoint prison inspectors for their counties at a salary of £20 per annum, unless the grand juries themselves (under pain of fines for neglect) undertook the duty of inspection. The fourth resolution — exactly in line with Sir Jeremiah's final recommendation in his *Essay* — proposed the appointment of an inspector general to visit, and report annually to Parliament upon, all the prisons in the Kingdom. Griffith also put forward a body of regulations for the inspectorates, local and national, to enforce upon gaolers or prisoners, as the case might be.[50]

When the final form of the proposals was determined next day, some wing-clipping of the inspectorates took place. The local inspector's salary was reduced to £10, and he was forbidden to act 'in any Manner interfering with the Authority of Sheriffs or Grand Juries'. In some respects the inspector general's role became more substantial in the course of the revision. All the local inspectors were to report regularly to him on the conditions in their prisons, he in turn making a digest of these reports for Parliament. He was, moreover, to advise on the physical reconstitution of the entire Irish prison system over the next two years — to recommend additions, alterations and improvements to existing gaols, with an eye especially to the prisoners' health; and not merely to advise on, but also to assist in deciding upon the locations, and plans for, gaols being or soon to be erected. Here again he was to act as the direct agent of Parliament. On the other hand, Dublin was half-removed from his sphere. The capital was to have its own inspector — at £150 per annum, altogether a superior personage to the county inspectors — who would report directly to King's Bench twice a year. But far worse, the inspector generalship was declared to be a temporary office, two years at most in duration, 'as it may be expected that a complete Arrangement in the Prisons of this Kingdom may be effected within that Time'. Clearly, the inspectorial proposals had met considerable opposition. Even the revised resolutions on the inspectorates, when they came up for final determination on 30 June, passed only after the House had divided on each[51] — again an almost unheard-of proceeding in the Irish Parliament on an issue of social reform. Obviously some, and possibly many, members were concerned at inroads into the powers and standing of the local authorities, or lest a permanent inspector generalship open the way to uncontrolled bureaucracy, or further jobbery. Obviously, too, the city members wished to maintain as much as possible of Dublin's administrative autonomy.

Griffith's fifth and last proposal of 27 May had survived almost intact when the resolutions were finally revised on the 28th. This set out the detailed regulations for gaols, twelve in number, which the inspectors and the inspector general were specifically directed to press home. The first group of regulations concerned the gaolers. They were to be resident, salaried and full-time officers; and neither bailiffs nor dealers in liquor. Rules 5-6 enjoined the segregation of sick from healthy, debtors from felons, men from women and 'atrocious' offenders from the rest. The use of wine or spirits was forbidden. But so too was the use of dungeons (except in such extremities as riots or mass escapes), and the levying of 'Penny-Pot or Garnish . . . on Prisoners on their Entrance into Prison, on any Account or Pretence whatsoever'. A table of fees, to be displayed in every prison, was to be drawn up by the local inspector and approved by the assizes judge. Health was to be secured, so far as might be, by exercise yards and exercise hours for prisoners; and by baths and necessaries; the daily scraping and sweeping of rooms; twice-yearly whitewashing (in good time for the assizes); and fresh straw weekly. The sanitary rules were to be the particular charge of the local inspector who was to visit each room thrice a week, and investigate all complaints against the gaolers. But the chaplain (if he were not the inspector too) was also to look to cleanliness. As the thrice-weekly distributor of bread (as well as homilies to prisoners 'willing to listen') he would visit the prison and see each prisoner regularly. The sick were to be attended by a surgeon (one was to be appointed to each gaol) who would supply medicine, treatment and sustenance while they were ill.

The resolutions passed, Holmes and Griffith were charged with drafting a Bill — entitled, significantly, 'for establishing inspectors of jails' — to embody them.[52] Another Bill to empower the grand juries to present for the repair or building of bridewells, and a third to amend the Acquitted Prisoners Act of 1784, were also set in train. But the session was too far advanced for any of the three to reach the statute book. It was 5 September before Griffith introduced the measure which he had prepared with Holmes, and Parliament was prorogued only two days later.[53] But there was no danger that the Bill would die with the session of 1785. Apart from the members' heavy investment of time and trouble in prison reform, public conern was sustained by an outbreak of fever in the City Marshalsea in July[54] and an outbreak of correspondence from *Verax, Humanitas* and the like to the Dublin press during September and October.[55] A few touches in these letters suggest that Fitzpatrick had some hand in this; even more so a report on the new English houses of correction in the *Freeman's Journal* of 30 August, which anticipated in several respects his later writings on the subject. Certainly, he played a part in maintaining the agitation at the end of 1785, when he set off on another tour of prisons, covering most of the southern counties. His reputation and effectiveness as an agitator by this stage may perhaps be gauged from his reception at Cork, which he reached on 4 January 1786. After his gaol visitations ('where, we are

A Prologue and an Act 77

sorry to hear, he discovered many deficiencies, and very great abuses'),[56] he was entertained by the mayor and sheriffs on two successive days, and then waited upon in the lodgings by the Cork Society for the Relief of Debtors who

> zealous to testify the respectful sentiments they entertain of the benign and truly patriotic exertions of Sir Jerome Fitzpatrick, cannot omit the present opportunity of inscribing to his virtues a page of this little book [their printed proceedings] as a small mark of their high approbation of his amiable attention to the wretched, in undertaking the dangerous and laborious task of visiting the prisons of Ireland, for the very laudable purpose of detecting abuses, and of pointing out what improvements they may admit of in their structure for the health and convenience of the miserable and unhappy prisoners.[57]

After a modest deprecation of his own influence, Fitzpatrick in reply observed that both the lord lieutenant and the legislature had given sufficient indications of humane concern to render hopeful the prospect of a new Prisons Act in the coming session. This was over-cautious. The revival of the 1785 Bill had already been assured.

IV

When the House of Commons reassembled on 23 January 1786 Holmes successfully moved the revival of the gaols committee. Much good, he said, had flown already from the inquiries of 1785; 'the attentions and the feelings of the public had been rouzed, and it only remained for parliament to give them a proper direction'.[58] Next day he and Griffith were again authorised to prepare a Prisons Inspection Bill,[59] and new Bridewells and Acquitted Prisoners Fees Amendment Bills soon followed.[60] The Bridewells Bill slipped easily and unopposed through all its stages;[61] and although the Fees Bill was initially resisted by some members as threatening to loose vagabonds upon the country, a fierce intervention by Hely-Hutchinson scorning the attribution of 'humanity' to himself, and proclaiming it to be the most rudimentary justice that 'no innocent person should ever suffer punishment', silenced the critics once and for all — at any rate, for that particular session.[62] The Prisons Inspection Bill however was considered at the most extraordinary length, and formed part of the business of almost every sitting between

7 February and 8 March.

Thirty-four amendments were debated, to say nothing of the amendments to amendments. Most of these concerned Dublin. At one point it was proposed to exclude the capital altogether from the measure. But in the end Dublin was subjected to a more minute and complex regulation than the country as a whole, with several *ad hoc* and *ad hominem* provisions to quieten immediate clamour or to satisfy established interests.[63] One at least of the city members remained disgruntled. On 7 March Alderman Warren attempted to get the entire Bill recommitted as essentially a new measure because of the number of fresh clauses proposing prison officials of various kinds in Dublin – 'so many useless and expensive offices'.[64] In general, the amendments had whittled away the more daring innovations in the first proposals. For example, a proposal that Catholic as well as Anglican prison chaplains be appointed was lost. But one of the amendments, almost certainly Sir Jeremiah's in inspiration, was strikingly original. This was, to provide the country with a continuous series of criminal statistics.

On 9 March the House of Commons at last released the much-cobbled Bill. From then on it was in smooth waters, slipping unchanged through the House of Lords and receiving the Royal Assent two months later.[65] Its centrepiece was of course the inspector generalship. This was justified in part by timeliness – many prisons were being rebuilt or repaired; in part because 'a general reformation is required' for health and cleanliness; and in part because the existing legislation was ignored. As in the original resolutions, the inspector general's first duty was to inspect every prison in the kingdom, more than once if he thought it necessary, and to report on his visitations on the first day of each parliamentary session. He was also to report then on the reports which he had received from the individual local inspectors, and to inform Parliament if any inspector had failed to send him a return. The Dublin inspector, however, was exempted from this requirement, and allowed to report to Parliament directly.

The inspector general's role *vis-à-vis* prison building remained the same. But in the course of the amendments he had, as we have seen, acquired another function, that of ultimate collector and collator of national criminal statistics. At each assizes the crown clerks were to furnish the local inspectors with a complete schedule of all prisoners tried, the crimes with which they were charged, the verdicts, the sentences if found guilty, the execution or otherwise of the sentences, and the nature of the remissions if there were any. The inspectors (post boxes in effect for the inspector general) were to forward this information to him when they reported in the ordinary way. As we have said, there can be little doubt that this was Fitzpatrick's brainchild, stepfathered though it may have been by Holmes or Griffith. Throughout his career, Fitzpatrick referred proudly to, and used as a model for other forms of data-gathering, 'my Criminal Chart'. As he saw it, the 'Chart' and its like had two purposes; to reveal at a glance the well- or ill-being of society (the medical imagery is interesting) in one or other of its aspects; and to provide a firm basis for determining future policy. The 'Succession and Comparative View of these Annual *Charts*', he told the Duke of Portland in 1798, enabled the statesman

> To know the partial or general disposition to oppose the Laws, or any other particular Law; to discover the locallity of such criminalty in the first instant, and further in a Moment to see whether a Country is getting more depraved . . . ; consequently the Maladies of the State are at once laid before its political Physicians.[66]

It was the second of these purposes which the 1786 Act stressed: 'the legislature', the relevant clause began, 'should receive every possible information relative to offences committed [so] that effectual laws may be framed from time to time'.[67]

At the base of the administrative pyramid stood the local inspector. He was to be appointed by the grand jury. But he need not be the parish clergyman who 'distributes or directs the distribution' of the prisoners' bread rations. True, the clergyman still had the preference. But if he were reluctant or ill suited to serve, some local medical man might be appointed. Moreover, the local inspectorship was to be a paid office, at the rate of £20 per annum (after repeated shuttling between £10 and £20 in the draft Bills, the larger sum was finally approved), and this in addition to whatever sum the inspector might receive as prison chaplain or surgeon. The inspector's duty was of course the enforcement of the twelve prison regulations agreed upon in the 1785 resolutions — together with a curious thirteenth, for another rule, prohibiting the employment of women as gaolers (one wonders what this derived from!) had been added in 1786. He had besides to see to the setting up and heating of a common hall in each county gaol (the minimum summer and winter hours when fires must burn there were prescribed), and to indent and account for money from his grand jury twice a year to pay for firing, blankets and other sources of warmth.

The word 'pyramid' was used advisedly above. For the chain of surveillance from inspector to inspector general and ultimately Parliament had been carefully forged. Not only had the inspector to report on the condition of the prisons, and to furnish the criminal statistics, of his district, but he was also required by the act to complete a sort of questionnaire asking how each of the thirteen regulations *seriatim* had been observed locally in the preceding year. Again, the minute tabulation suggests Sir Jeremiah's hand.

About half the Act's clauses were taken up with the special case of Dublin.[68] It was still to have a superior inspector of its own. But this inspector's annual stipend had been reduced from £150 to £100 during the vagaries of the debate; and much the largest prison in the city, the new Newgate, was removed from his charge and placed instead in the hands of the current Newgate physician, George Doyle. Moreover — strange qualifying clause — 'If a person of publick spirit, or liberal fortune, should undertake the office [of inspector] in Dublin, without any emolument, he may appoint a deputy [at a salary of £60 p.a.] to be approved of by the grand jury and King's Bench'. On the other hand, not only was the Dublin inspector to report directly to Parliament and not to the inspector general, but he was to take over all the inspector general's national functions once this office had been wound up.

The Dublin grand jury, 'correspondent with feelings of humanity, and requisite to the well being and safety of the community at large', was also to appoint 'a regularly bred physician' as prison medical officer. Because his work would be 'very laborious and painful', he too was to receive £100 per annum as his stipend. Again, the city's largest prison, Newgate, was excluded from his charge. Conversely, the chaplain of Newgate had the City Bridewell (but no other Dublin prison) added to his 'parish'; and as his was now regarded as a full-time task his stipend was increased from £20 to £60 per annum. In yet another category was the new office of prison apothecary for Dublin. He alone was appointed to all the gaols of the capital, and he alone was to receive no salary, the profits on the medicine which he supplied being regarded as a sufficient reward. Various other changes were made in the prison management of the capital. The city marshal was replaced as superintendent of the infamous City Marshalsea by a keeper 'elected' by Dublin corporation, which was also ordered to increase the salary of the Newgate gaoler from £20 to £100 per annum, as this was 'a place not only of trust but of considerable trouble'.

V

Thus the 1786 Act was an ill-knit amalgam of revolutionary and traditional governmental forms. Over most of the country an extraordinarily 'nineteenth-century' system had been far advanced. A network of paid — if still part-time — inspectors was established; they were given a large number of specific duties; and among these duties was the supply of information for appraising current success and for formulating future policy. An elaborate if oblique surveillance of their work was to be provided by a central office, the inspector generalship, in both its peripatetic and its collating roles.

Although, formally, the inspector general was the mere adviser of Parliament, he was bound in the nature of things (if the office worked at all) to determine largely the operation of current, and the formulation of new, legislation. His was a crown appointment, removed from the hands of Parliament and grand jury alike. His stipend, £200 per annum, was considerable both by Irish standards generally, and was ten times larger than that of his inferiors in the localities and twice as high as that of his nearest rival, in Dublin. He suffered, it is true, from the rather heavy drawback of having only two years to live. But after all this was to be a common pattern in new ventures in social regulation in the nineteenth century — to bring permanent arms of government into the world, in the belief or on the argument that one was making mere temporary excursions of inquiry. The expeditionary forces became armies of occupation, as a rule. Finally, the new 'bureaucracy' of 1786 was related to regular political authority in reasonably close approximation to the later forms. The inspector general reported and was directly responsible to Parliament. The grand juries, who appointed and paid the inspectors and met the prison bills, were directly responsible to the judiciary. The judiciary were responsible for explaining their duties under the Prisons Act to the members of the grand juries, and were empowered to fine them up to £200 if they failed to fulfil their obligations under the statute before the end of the relevant assizes. All in all it was a colourable imitation — or rather prefiguration — of early Victorian government in the social fields.

On the other hand, the Dublin provisions in the Act were disorderly responses to particular pressures and interests. Neither the inspector's nor the physician's nor the chaplain's writ ran over all the city's gaols. In some cases the appointments were annual, in some indefinite; in some cases, absolute, in others, subject to the approval of King's Bench. The metropolitan inspector was to report to King's Bench as well as

Parliament, but not (as we had seen) to the inspector general; and there was no consistency in the arrangement governing the relationships between him and his various 'subordinates'. Where responsibility lay if the inspectorship were honorary, and a deputy appointed, was not made clear; and the proposal that the Dublin inspector step into the inspector general's shoes in two years time was obviously *faute de mieux* and ill-conceived. All in all, the metropolitan clauses, in a sort of inverted *déjà vu*, strangely remind us of the London imbroglios of sixty to seventy years hence in such fields as burials and water sanitation, when the powerful contending interest groups in the capital effectively removed London from national planning and threw it into a state of administrative confusion and ineffectuality.[69]

There were other indications in the 1786 Act of resistance to the new 'rationality'. For example, the established church crept back, to some extent, to its traditional role as national social worker-cum-controller. Not only were Catholic priests (as indeed were Presbyterian or other nonconformist ministers) tacitly excluded as chaplains, but the parish clergy also retained the function of buying and distributing the prisoners' food despite the creation of the new office of inspector. Moreover, the parish clergyman was to be 'preferred' to the medical attendant for this office; and his pastoral utility, particularly in striving for repentance and regeneration, was much more strongly stressed in the 1786 Act than in any earlier piece of Irish prison legislation. If the secular-medical drive had not been altogether beaten back, neither had it carried the day. On the other side of things, there were some provisions of unexpected 'modernity'. Clause 43, to take one instance, empowered the MPs for the county (yet another existing 'authority' being cast in a strange executive role) to acquire land compulsorily for prison building — the price to be settled by jury because of the exorbitant demands which the owners were wont to make when their property was needed for public purposes. Such powers were not unknown in Ireland. The Dublin wide streets commission already enjoyed similar rights.[70] None the less compulsory purchase and an external valuation from which there was no appeal are arresting features in a Prisons Act of 1786.

Fitzpatrick's part in shaping the statute cannot be gauged exactly. Much of the detail of the day-to-day regulation proposed for the prisons derived from Howard, though with some i's dotted and some t's crossed by Sir Jeremiah and some twists and wrenchings in various directions derived from the play of prejudices and interests in the course of the debates. With the cat's cradle of metropolitan clauses,

A Prologue and an Act

Fitzpatrick can have had little to do, except — a vital exception, of course — to provide the evidence which effectively forced the House of Commons to tackle the various Dublin institutions and offices which it 'reformed' so variously. But it is a fair speculation that the enforcement system was basically his concept. Of course, Howard had adumbrated local surveillance, and inspector generalships were to be found already in other forms of Irish central government, military and economic; the barracks and linen boards and mines are three examples.[7] But the elaboration and interrelation of the local and central inspectorates, and the efficient connection of the two to the parliamentary process, were emblematic of Fitzpatrick's administrative approach, as well as sketched out in part in his earliest administrative writings. To him we may confidently attribute the conjunction of the functions of adviser on the execution and amendment of the law, and adviser on prison planning and reconstruction. To him too both the concept of, and the particular scheme for, the collection of criminal statistics can be confidently ascribed.

Finally, while we cannot measure precisely his importance in creating and maintaining the pressure which produced at last the 1786 Act, he was clearly indispensable to the reforming lobby in Parliament as the supplier of data and administrative ideas. He was also of course an independent propagandist. In fact, in the midst of the Bill's vicissitudes, Sir Jeremiah's star had been rising fast. On 5 April 1786 he was even placed upon a common pedestal with the saintly Howard in the Dublin press. 'Our worthy country-man', the *Freeman's Journal* continued, '. . . with infinite humanity distinguished himself in this Kingdom to effect a reformation in our gaols . . . the comfortless situations of whose unhappy tenants were sufficient to still a heart not totally callous to human feeling.' Of course, there were then (as now) some dangers in being proclaimed a Schweitzer in Dublin — at least, for a native son. None the less it could have caused no surprise in the capital when on 24 May 1786 the lord lieutenant's choice for the new office of inspector general of prisons was announced to be Sir Jeremiah Fitzpatrick, MD.

Notes

1. Fitzpatrick, *Essay on Gaol Abuses*, p. 30.
2. For a full account of Foster's career, see A.P.W. Malcolmson, *John Foster: the Politics of the Anglo-Irish Ascendancy* (Oxford, 1978).
3. John Fitzgibbon (1749-1802), became Attorney-General in 1783 and Lord Chancellor in 1789. See *DNB*, vol. vii, pp. 156-9.

4. *Parliamentary Register* (Ire.), vol. v, p. 183.
5. Ibid., p. 184.
6. 23 & 24 Geo. III, c.34.
7. *Parliamentary Register* (Ire.), vol. 4, pp. 415-16.
8. Ibid., vol. iii, pp. 112, 144, 170.
9. Ibid., vol. iii, pp. 170-1. General Luttrell had suggested that Holmes do this.
10. *Freeman's Journal*, 27-29 April 1784.
11. Ibid., 19-22 March 1785.
12. Ibid., 1-3 February 1785.
13. Ibid., 15-17 July 1784.
14. Ibid., 24-27 July 1784.
15. *Journals of the House of Commons* (Ire.), vol. xi, p. 259.
16. Fitzpatrick, *Gaol Abuses*, pp. 28, 29, 76.
17. Howard, *State of the Prisons in England and Wales* (2nd edn), p. 29.
18. Fitzpatrick, *Gaol Abuses*, p. 51.
19. Howard, *State of the Prisons* (2nd edn), pp. 18-19.
20. Fitzpatrick, *Gaol Abuses*, p. 96.
21. Ibid., p. 106.
22. Ibid., p. 84.
23. Ibid., p. 95.
24. *Parliamentary Register* (Ire.), vol. vii, pp. 486-96.
25. Fitzpatrick, *Gaol Abuses*, p. 94.
26. See chapter 1, p. 33.
27. Fitzpatrick, *Gaol Abuses*, p. 54.
28. Ibid., p. 57.
29. Ibid., p. 118.
30. Ibid., pp. 97-8.
31. Ibid., pp. 13-14.
32. Ibid., p. 13.
33. Ibid., pp. 71-2.
34. Ibid., p. 70.
35. Ibid., pp. 84-92.
36. Ibid., p. 82.
37. Ibid., p. 83.
38. Ibid., p. 114.
39. Johnston, 'Members of the Irish Parliament, 1784-7', p. 160.
40. John Beresford (1738-1805) became first Commissioner of Revenue in 1780; under Pitt he practically managed Irish affairs. See *DNB*, vol. ii, pp. 327-8.
41. Fitzpatrick to Foster, Foster Papers, D562/8673, P.R.O., N.I., ff. 433-4.
42. Ibid.
43. *Parliamentary Register* (Ire.), vol. v, p. 55.
44. *Journals of H of C* (Ire.), vol. xi, p. 413.
45. *Journals of H of C* (Ire.), vol. xi, pp. ccccxiv-vi.
46. Ibid., vol. xi, p. 430.
47. *Parliamentary Register* (Ire.), vol. v, pp. 182-3.
48. Ibid., vol. v, pp. 227-8.
49. *Freeman's Journal*, 24-26 May 1785.
50. Ibid., 26-28 May 1785.
51. *Parliamentary Register* (Ire.), vol. v, pp. 251-4.
52. Ibid., vol. v, p. 254.
53. Ibid., vol. v, pp. 482-3.
54. *Freeman's Journal*, 9-12 July 1785.
55. Ibid., 13-15 September 1785; 29 October-1 November 1785.
56. Ibid., 14-17 January 1786.

A Prologue and an Act

57. Ibid., 19-21 January 1786.
58. *Parliamentary Register* (Ire.), vol. vi, pp. 29-30.
59. Ibid., vol. vi, p. 39.
60. *Journals of H of C* (Ire.), vol. xii, pp. 22, 38.
61. *Freeman's Journal*, March-May 1786.
62. Ibid., 28 February-2 March 1786.
63. *Journals of H of C* (Ire.), vol. xii, pp. 66, 92.
64. *Freeman's Journal*, 4-7 March 1786.
65. *Journals of H of C* (Ire.), vol. xii, p. 100.
66. Fitzpatrick to Portland, 5 January 1798, B.M. Add. MS. 33105, ff. 325-6.
67. 26 Geo. III, c.27, clause 39.
68. Ibid., clauses 4-20, 24-9, 34-6, 47.
69. See O. MacDonagh, *Early Victorian Government 1830-1870* (London, 1977), pp. 147-8.
70. See R.B. McDowell, *The Irish Administration 1801-1914* (London, 1964), p. 190.
71. Ibid., pp. 15-16, 195-6; MacDonagh, *Early Victorian Government*, pp. 82-95.

4 SIR JEREMIAH AND THE CHARTER SCHOOLS, 1785-1788

Sir Jeremiah's first excursion in humanitarian serendipity — the discovery at least was happy, if not the discovered — was into the charter schools.[1] These schools, managed by the Incorporated Society for Promoting English Protestant Schools in Ireland, numbered fifty in 1785, rather more than half a century after the foundation of the Society.[2] An anonymous supporter described the Society in 1752 as

> a Charity that will make those who are at present a Nuisance and a Burden to their country, to become a Treasure and a Blessing to it; that will make honest and industrious Men of those who would have been bred up to Thieving and Rags . . . that will multiply obedient and peaceable Subjects to the King, and render the *Protestants* of *Ireland* safe in their Lives and Possessions.[3]

More simply, the purpose was, as Locker Lampson put it, 'to proselytise by separating catholic children totally from their families and rearing them as anglicans',[4] for there seemed to be no surer way of rendering the Protestants of Ireland safe. In certain respects, then, the charter schools anticipated the 'Protestant crusades' of the early and mid-nineteenth century in Ireland.[5] They represented an attempt to solve the Irish question by anglicising, in terms of language, manners, habits, disposition and religion, the rising generations of the Irish poor. Forty-eight of the fifty schools accepted only Catholic children, and at that only Catholic children who were between the ages of four and ten. The children were taken far from their native districts — as the secretary of the Society confessed, 'the Motive of transplanting them is to remove them from the Influence of Popish Parents, and Seduction by them or their Means'.[6] They might be — and often were — later moved from school to school across the country.

By contemporary standards, the Incorporated Society represented a very considerable semi-state undertaking. Parliamentary grants, both direct and indirect in the form of the revenue from a tax on pedlars and hawkers in the capital, and a regular royal bounty, provided between them some £10,000 per annum, or roughly two-thirds of the Society's annual income, in the 1780s.[7] But the management of the business was delegated to a board, which met monthly and had its central office in Dublin. The board operated through three committees, executive, legal and financial, and supervised local committees, which were composed of Protestant ladies and gentlemen in the respective districts. In turn, these local committees were meant to oversee the schools.[8]

But all this was the merest façade, for in effect the Society, in true eighteenth-century fashion, contracted out the evangelical work. The masters of the schools received, over and above their accommodation, board and small annual salaries of £12-14,[9] *per capita* allowances for each child[10] and the right to use the children's labour in agricultural work or textile manufacture.[11] They were also permitted to cultivate the school lands, for a very small or even nominal rental.[12] Presumably they profited considerably from both the business and the farms, to say nothing of what they might save in the feeding and clothing of the children, or gain from the invention of imaginary pupils. (It was discovered in 1785 that nearly 30 per cent more children were being charged for than existed.)[13] In the interstices of work, the children were meant to be taught and effectually converted to the Protestant religion. But, as might be expected, the time allotted to the schoolroom and the catechism was contracted, while that available for what was in effect slave-labour was enlarged. By the 1780s the children were spending about eight hours daily at their 'tasks' as against four in secular and religious education.[14] In all, it was not a system likely to be free from either cruelty or corruption.

Fitzpatrick's first visit was to the Kilkenny Charter School on 12 February 1785. He reported:

> The House is situated a Mile from the City. There were thirty-two Children, many of them very small and almost all looked miserable; and their wretched Appearance was enhanced by their being barefooted and ragged. Though Boys, they were employed in carding and spinning, and sat on Stools and Stone-seats in a cold Work-shop. On the Morning of the Day of my Visit it snowed heavily, yet the Room in which they were at work was without Fire, although it was ready for lighting. I asked why it was not lighted? A Person who superintended the Labour of the Children demanded of them (with an angry Tone of Voice) why they had not lighted it before? Two of them with a look of Terror arose and instantly obeyed. After having examined the Situation of the House, where I found the Beds abominably filthy, Education most culpably neglected, and many of the Children afflicted with Itch and Scald, I rode off; but suspecting

from what I had seen that the Children would not long enjoy the Benefit of the Fire, I returned on foot through the Fields, and found that they had already extinguished it by pouring Water on it.

The Barbarity of this Treatment to the wretched Objects of public Benevolence was one of my first and principal Inducements to persevere in the Inspection of Charter Schools.[15]

Charter Schools Visited by Fitzpatrick

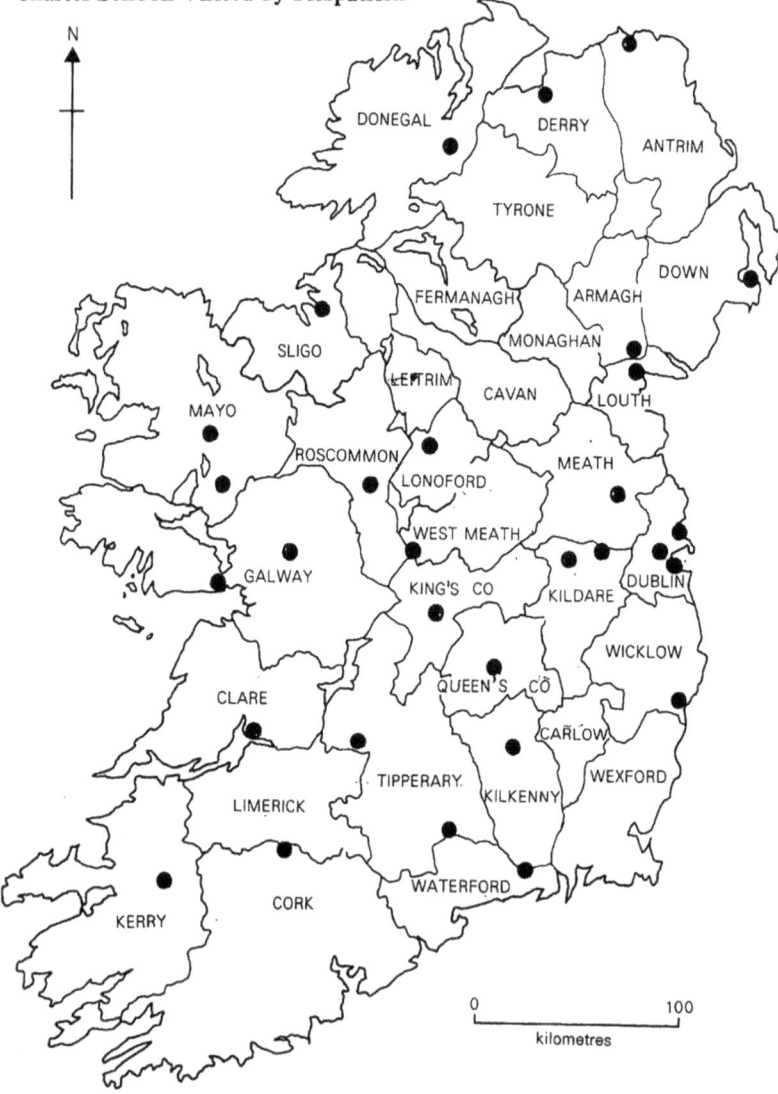

Fitzpatrick's last sentence gives a reason for his continuance in this work. Why had he entered it? Possibly because of the example of John Howard, who had taken in some charter schools on his tour of Irish prisons in the preceding years, and reported equally unfavourably upon them. Subsequently, it was said that Fitzpatrick 'was *sent* in order to *find fault*' with charter schools, and acted 'not as a visitor but a spy'.[16] This is unlikely. When Fitzpatrick reported confidentially on the schools in February 1787, to Orde, then Irish Chief Secretary and the most likely employer of 'spies' in such a business, his letter suggested no prior design.[17] It is far more probable, in the light of the pattern of Fitzpatrick's subsequent career, that some accidental encounter or reference (perhaps Howard's book or work or the gossip which it engendered in Dublin, in this particular instance) first drew his attention to schools, and that, having once caught the scent of another form of 'inhumanity' (to use his own favourite word), he was soon in full cry in pursuit.

Fitzpatrick had been in Kilkenny on other business in February 1785, and this may well have been prison investigation. Certainly prison inspection explains his presence in Arklow, co. Wicklow, two months later, when his next charter school visit was made. Thenceforward, his inspections became more systematic. Immediately after Christmas 1785 he visited three schools fairly close to his own home country in co. Westmeath within six days: this may have been a vacation period for him. He visited six other schools, four of them in Munster, during the autumn of 1786; and between 13 July and 11 August 1787, nine others in the west of Ireland. Then he turned his attention to the north and visited six of the Ulster schools between late September and mid-November 1787. In between his tours of 1786 and 1787, he appears to have inspected certain of the schools in Dublin regularly, and he certainly paid second or third visits to several of the country schools, which happened to be close to the district of his main, i.e. prison, investigation, while he was on tour. In all, Fitzpatrick examined thirty of the fifty Irish charter schools between 1785 and 1787, and a considerable number of them more than once. Although it is impossible to say certainly, it is probable that his earliest visits to charter schools in 1785 were adjuncts of his first systematic tours of prisons and bridewells throughout Ireland, made in anticipation − or any rate in anticipatory justification − of his appointment as inspector general of Irish prisons in the following year. Certainly for 1786 visitations were superogatory accompaniments of his prison tours. We might note, finally, that he had no official standing whatsoever during 1785, although he did hold an inquisitorial office in another field in 1786 as well as a quasi-commission from the Society itself during 1787.

There is evidence to suggest that even Fitzpatrick's earliest reports, those of 1785, reached, and had effect upon, the Incorporated Society. He later implied, for example, that it was his report on the Arklow Charter School, insinuating improper relations between the master and the female ushers and enumerating other abuses, which was responsible for the master's dismissal at the close of that year.[18] But certainly his summer and autumn tour of 1786 put him in direct communication with the Society. He would have regarded it as 'criminal',[19] as he himself expressed it, had he not reported his fearful findings to the Incorporated Society, immediately upon his return to Dublin in November 1786. The 'committee of fifteen' (so the executive committee of the board termed itself) was duly impressed by his reports. Sir Jeremiah was invited to proffer testimony in person; and at the meeting of 15 December 1786, at which he appeared, resolutions were passed unanimously expressing the Society's fervent thanks for his 'humane and charitable inspection', and approving of his enrolment as an honorary member.[20] When he was enrolled[21] (at the next meeting when membership might be considered, on 7 February 1787), he was asked by the committee to furnish further and more systematic proposals of reform. Meanwhile, his earlier reports had produced the dismissal of several other masters and an usher.

Even before he became an honorary member of the Society, however, Fitzpatrick was off upon another tack. On 5 February 1787 he attempted to enlist Orde's aid in a scheme for reorganising the entire system of the charter schools. The school buildings and the children's employment, lodging, clothing and education were, he wrote to Orde, the subjects most in need of the Chief Secretary's 'fostering hand'.[22] Characteristically, Fitzpatrick cast his appeal for assistance in terms of feeling and expediency alike – 'your humanity will rejoice – independent of its being highly political'. It was also characteristic of Fitzpatrick's *modus operandi* that he should have aimed at both wings of his target by, on the one hand, pandering to Orde's love of power and arrangement, and, on the other, stressing the educational opportunities which would be afforded – education being Orde's hobby horse. Evidently Orde was successfully enlisted. In his plan for the reorganisation of Irish education expounded in the House of Commons on 12 April 1787, Orde included four 'Christ's Hospitals' to be 'supported by a gradual change of the application of the funds now given to the Charter Schools';[23] and during the parliamentary session of 1787-8 the house was induced to set up a committee of inquiry into the conduct of these schools.[24] Perhaps it was in preparation for this inquiry that Fitzpatrick inspected and reported on the charter schools of Connaught and Ulster during his tour of the Irish country prisons in the summer and autumn of 1787. Possibly he also intended at the start to fulfil his engagement of February to the Incorporated Society, and submit to them elaborated proposals for reform. But if this were so he evidently changed his mind, for the Society was to complain later[25] that their first sight of Fitzpatrick's 1787 reports was in the printed parliamentary proceedings of the following year.

When the House of Commons committee met, Fitzpatrick's evidence, though it corresponded closely with Howard's, was widely divergent from the reports upon the schools from the local committees of management and local clergymen. On various points of fact there was a direct clash of testimony, as well as a great gap between what Fitzpatrick and his opponents considered reasonable or practicable in school arrangements. The parliamentary committee of inquiry, although in difficulties over these contradictions, came down on Fitzpatrick's side so far as possible; and the Incorporated Society was given neither forewarning of the hostile evidence, nor an opportunity to muster a contrary case to that of the outside reformers.

Fitzpatrick's condemnation of the secular features of the charter schools was forthright and comprehensive. In a schedule attached to the committee's report, his statement was summarised as follows:

> that he visited twenty-eight Charter Schools [during 1786-7], in most of which he found the Children rather delicate, many of them afflicted with Itch, Scald &c. and that the Athleticity, so strongly marked in the Children of the Poor in this Kingdom, however shabby their Clothing, is not to be found in Charter Schools, which he attributes in a great Measure to the Nature of their Employments, the bad Quality of their Food, to Confinement, and to the Effects of unwholesome Exhalations from filthy Bed-clothes and foetid Straw inclosed in odiously besmeared Tickens. He says the Nature of their Labour injures the Health of many who sit carding and spinning at the Linen Wheels; the Attitudes cripple their Limbs, whilst the constant discharge of Saliva to wet the Thread injures their Digestion; and employed at the large Wheels, their Limbs being yet in a gristly State, they contract the Habit of turning in their Knees and Toes, and otherwise become distorted, which follow from the Positions into which they are thrown, which even at the State of

Manhood speaks their early Employments; and by the Master's paying for the Childrens Labour he becomes more interested in the Profits arising from it than in their making the wished Progress either in a proper Knowledge of the Principles of Religion or Education. He also states that the Charter School Lands are in general in worse Condition than their neighbouring Grounds; this he attributes to Masters not being allowed for their Improvements, as also to the uncertainty of their Tenures.[26]

To this statement may be added the following passages from the summary of his earlier evidence before the committee:

The Children in general filthy and ill-clothed; he has seen them without Shifts or Shirts, and in such a Situation as was indecent to look at: He found the Diet in general insufficient for the Support of their delicate Frames; the Potatoes very often bad; very bad poor Milk, and in small Quantities; the Oatmeal good. He is convinced that the Instruction of the Children is in general very much neglected ... He has seen many of the Reports of the Local Committees entered in the School Books that did not correspond with the State in which he found the Schools; in general the Reports were more favourable than he found the Schools deserved, and believes there could not be a Difference in the Time of his visiting. Says he objected to the Masters to some of the Reports when he saw them, and received no satisfactory Answer. His Objections were in general to the Childrens Health and Information ... Says that the Schools he visited were in bad Repair, with an Exception of five or six ... He observes that by one of the Regulations of the Incorporated Society, the Girls are to be bound out at the Age of fourteen, but the Masters and Mistresses find it their Advantage to keep them ignorant, so as that no Person may be induced to take them Apprentice, by which Means they have the Advantage of their Labour, though their Diet and Clothing is paid for.[27]

By now the opposition, temporal and spiritual (and it is a nice problem to distinguish them), had been thoroughly aroused. From the start the high churchmen had spoken of the threat to the charter schools in the tones of early Victorian evangelicals, as the 'most fatal blow to the protestant religion in Ireland ... nothing would be more grateful to the society *de propaganda fide* in Rome'.[28] Now the Incorporated Society, having struggled vainly to present a defence against its accusers before the committee reported, protested in a memorial to the lord lieutenant against being 'criminate[d] . . . in a very high degree' and 'being held up to public suspicion without a possibility of being heard in their defence against many of the charges till the next meeting of Parliament'.[29] Howard's evidence was pooh-poohed as hastily compiled, as formulated in ignorance of Irish conditions, and (so far as his 1787 tour went at least) as never communicated to the Society. It had to be admitted that Sir Jeremiah had reported unfavourably to the board as recently as November 1786; but since then he had not thought it 'proper to communicate to your memorialists a copy of his remarks, tho' requested to do so, but stood forth their accuser before Parliament'. Despite these brave words, the Society was on the defensive, even in its memorial of protest. It ended by pleading the inadequacy of its resources in relation to the extent of its commission.

None the less, an attempt was made, later in 1788, to turn the tables upon the 'reformers'. In the autumn, at the opening of the parliamentary session of 1788-9, the Anglican bishop of Cloyne, Richard Woodward, moved for another committee of inquiry into the charter schools — but this time a House of Lords' committee,[30] which would presumably deal with the Incorporated Society more tenderly. On 6 January 1789, Woodward wrote privately to Thomas Conolly,[31] one of the leading members of the House of Commons, to secure his aid in repelling what he spoke of as the attack upon religion. For Woodward the assault upon the charter schools was part of a general liberal undermining of order in church and state. Portland's administration, he wrote, under the influence of men like Burke and Grattan, seemed bent on subverting the Protestant ascendancy in Ireland. The evidence before the Commons committee on the schools was untrustworthy. Howard 'did not make allowances, nor, in truth, was he disposed, being a bigotted Presbyterian', to do so; while Fitzpatrick, the administration's chief tool of destruction, sent to gather adverse testimony, deserved neither 'notice' nor 'confidence'. 'As far as his religion can be traced, he is a papist. He did not deny it when asked by Mr Ford of Dawson St. *A pretty visitor of Protestant Charter Schools!*' Woodward was, however, notorious as an extreme advocate of exclusive Anglican supremacy,[32] and despite his further lobbying for support, his effort to discredit the House of Commons committee of 1788 came to nothing in the end. The Society was reduced to getting what satisfaction it could from revenging itself upon Sir Jeremiah personally. The Prison Reform Bills of 1788 and 1789 were, as we shall see, to be rejected by the House of Lords; and one, and probably the essential, reason for the rejections was that each contained a clause doubling the stipend of the inspector general of prisons.[33]

There can be no doubt that Fitzpatrick was in the right in the contests with the defenders of the charter schools. A commission of inquiry held in 1809 admitted that the Incorporated Society had failed in its primary object, 'the conversion of the lower orders of the Inhabitants of Ireland'. The numbers in the schools still constituted a minute portion of the poor Catholic children, and a large proportion even of these 'returned to the Popish persuasion'.[34] As Howard has observed more than a quarter of a century before, the state of the children in the schools was 'so deplorable as to disgrace Protestantism and encourage Popery in Ireland'.[35] The 1809 commission tacitly admitted the abuses of earlier years when it spoke of recent improvements (which were to be later still dismissed as illusory, in their turn).[36] But the strongest support for Sir Jeremiah's findings lies in the nearly contemporaneous, though sporadic and unsystematic, comments of Howard and John Wesley. Howard had found the children 'sickly, naked and half-starved', the buildings often in ruinous disrepair and the masters and mistresses skimming profits from the miserable allowances for the children's food and clothing. Among the 'blackly humorous' items in Howard's testimony was his discovery that the inadequacy of the soap allowance was 'an inducement to preserve the urine for washing the children's linen, which is one cause of cutaneous disorders'.[37] In May 1785, Wesley visited the school at Ballinrobe, co. Mayo, and reported in his *Journal* in these terms:

> I went thither about five in the afternoon, but found no master or mistress. Seven or eight boys, and nine or ten girls (the rest being rambling abroad), dirty and ragged enough, were left to the care of a girl half the head taller than the rest. She led us through the house. I observed first the school-room, not much bigger than a small closet. Twenty children could not be taught there at once with any convenience. When we came into the bed-chamber, I inquired, 'How many children now lodge in the house?' and was answered, 'Fourteen or fifteen boys, and nineteen girls.' For these boys there were three beds, and five for the nineteen girls. For food, I was informed, the master was allowed a penny-farthing a day for each! Thus they are clothed, lodged, and fed. But what are they taught? As far as I could learn, just nothing! Of these things I informed the Commissioners for these schools in Dublin.[38]

The significance of Fitzpatrick's work in the field of charter schools certainly does not lie in a material improvement in the daily life of the children. He may have produced some changes in staff and supplies in 1785-8 (which is probably more than either of the distinguished men, Wesley or Howard, could have claimed). He may also have done more considerable good through his evidence before the 1788 committee, which was followed almost immediately by the Society's dismissing more masters, increasing the food and clothing allowances, preparing a new dietary scale, discontinuing the making of clothes in Dublin, and in other ways responding to Fitzpatrick's and Howard's condemnations and recommendations, as well as resolving 'that a committee be appointed to enquire into the state of such schools against which they find any complaints to have been made'.[39] But the effect of the intrusion was neither deep nor lasting – in plain words, it was negligible.

But in other terms Fitzpatrick's charter school inquiries have their interest. To begin with, this little episode in his career is an early revelation of his approach and methods of advance. First, he appears to have been led, tangentially, into a reforming work by what he encountered in the news and writings of the day and in the course of another reforming task. Secondly, he sought to work through men of power, appealing at once to their humanity and their political self-interest, and seeking to enlist them in his support. Thirdly, he secured, or sought to secure, a position or station in which he could influence policy and carry into effect the schemes of reform which his fertile administrative imagination rapidly suggested. In this case, he may well have considered that he could improve upon the foothold which he had gained as an honorary member of the Incorporated Society by organising a parliamentary inquiry, to be sprung upon the unsuspecting society. Fourthly, after initial success – at least he himself would have so regarded the sacking of the unworthy schoolmasters and the request of the Incorporated Society to compose an elaborate remedial programme – the enemies whom his zeal had called into being began to denounce, and sought to disable, his endeavours. It is remarkable how precisely this pattern was to be stamped on piece after piece of his attempted work in later years.

Fitzpatrick's remarkable qualities as a social investigator are clearly apparent in this early set of reports. They are brief, lucid and powerful. The report on the Kilkenny Charter School has been quoted in its entirety, and it is no longer than several of the remainder. But description clear as glass and simple detail are used most dextrously to stamp a general impression deeply upon the auditor or reader. For example,

Fitzpatrick wrote of his first visit to Charleville, co. Cork, in 1785 when snow lay twenty inches deep on the ground, 'This precaution [entering the school unannounced] afforded me the Opportunity of seeing two little Girls sitting on a Table in the School-room, which was damp and clay-floored, without any Fire; their little Legs were under each other's Petticoats to keep them warm . . .'[40] A second instance may be taken from his report on Frankfort Charter School, which he had visited during the same short Christmas tour. On Fitzpatrick's being told to his amazement that despite the snow frozen upon the ground, some of the boys were working on the farm, he

> determined to see the Fact myself, and immediately rode to the Field they were in at some Distance from the House, where I found five Boys nearly perished with cold, for they were miserably clothed; the two who were digging the Potatoes had old Brogues on, but the two who were picking them, and a small boy who was making a Fire of a few rotten Sticks at some Distance in a Ditch for the Purpose of warming them, had neither Shoe nor Stocking.[41]

The nineteenth-century official report is not often considered as literature: by 'literature' here I mean of course composition and selection effective both in conveying information and in creating a desired impression upon a general readership. Technicality, specialisation and fixed and complex administrative procedures have long since rendered this form of 'literature' obsolete. But in the dawn and early morning of the administrative revolution it was of first importance in gathering together, and infusing with horror and anger, powerful bodies of opinion. It was, in one sense, the obverse of the nineteenth-century 'social' novel. Just as the 'social' novelist used the data of communal evils as materials for literary entertainment, so contrariwise the administrative reformer used — or rather was most effective when he used — the graphic, selective and economical techniques of the novelist to press the facts of suffering upon the minds of his public. In a period without a special language of the social sciences, or a special language of bureaucracy, or fixed modes or conventions of evaluation, the vignettes of misery, the choice of case, the concreteness of the instance, were often the critical matter. In this, Fitzpatrick was a master stylist, the precursor of the Chadwicks of half a century hence.

A second striking characteristic of Fitzpatrick's reports is his practice of counting and measuring, virtually as a matter of course. The 1788 committee of inquiry noted that his reports detailed 'the Situation of each School, the Number and Dimensions of the Apartments, their Vicinity to Towns, Villages &c',[42] although because of their 'Prolixity' they were not printed among the evidence. We can however guess both their character and their impact from the enumeration and quantification threading his general summaries of the conditions in the various schools. 'This House, which contained forty-one girls, consisted of eleven rooms, three of which the Master occupied, besides a Hall and a Kitchen', was a characteristic opening to an account of a visitation. Almost always the number and the sex of the children are noted. Usually the number – as well as the state – of the beds, the sheets, the blankets and the mattresses; the elevation and the weatherliness of the buildings; the location – as well as the brackishness or filth, respectively – of the water supply and the privies; the state or absence of windows or ceilings; the numbers of pairs of stockings and shoes; the numbers of shifts or shirts; and much else that could be counted or calculated, are carefully recorded. Nor was this random enumeration and measurement. Primarily, the statistics which he gathered bore upon communal health, as he understood its sources and its enemies; although, of course, some of them related also to welfare and happiness in the most ordinary sense. Fitzpatrick's report of his visit of 23 September 1787 to Ray Charter School, co. Derry, includes a fine example of his method and procedure.

> This House, which contains twenty-one Boys and thirteen Girls, is situated in the interior mountainous Part of the Country, five Miles North of Raphoe, on the Declivity of a Glen, and twelve Miles North-west of Derry; the Road to the House is through a Valley, and the Yard which forms the Entrance to it is confined and dirty, and was a Receptacle for Pigs, Poultry, Cattle &c. The Ascent to the Hall, which is rather promptly steep, the perpendicular Height being ten Feet, and the sloping Passage but nineteen Feet and a Half, is the worst and most dangerous of the kind I ever saw; it would be difficult to ascend or descend the Curve of the Arch, on which is a Pavement smooth and slippery, were it not for the Battlements, which are three Feet high. The Under-part of the House was filthy beyond Description, one of the Apartments, which measured seventeen Feet by fourteen Feet, served as a School-room and Work-room for both Sexes; in it were twenty-two Wheels, two Reels, a Table and two Forms; and it was the only Place for Education and Labour, except that some of the strongest Children were daily engaged in digging and picking Potatoes, herding Cattle, and other Business in

the Farm. The Room in which the Boys slept, was eighteen Feet by fourteen Feet, and shamefully dirty; several of the Sheets but filthy Rags, most of the Tickens rotten, the Bedsteads old and broken, and the Beds in Want of Stuffing; many of the Bolster-cases were quite empty, and the Walls were shamefully filthy. The Room in which the Girls slept, of equal Size with that of the Boys, was in every Respect as disgusting, with the additional Circumstances of their Sheets being rent in Rags. The Children were wretchedly clothed; and this being Sunday, notwithstanding their tattered Garbs, nineteen of them were brought to Church by the Master, fifteen remaining at home, two through Indisposition, and thirteen for Want of Shoes or Stockings . . .[43]

On this occasion, the beds and linen were not counted, but almost everything else was; and Sir Jeremiah had excelled himself with the setting.

Thirdly, Fitzpatrick not only reported; he also acted and arranged himself. Even as early as 1785 he tried to intervene in the management of some of the schools which he visited. He recommended fires to be lit, periods for exercise to be set aside and rooms to be rearranged. In these initial interventions, he appears to have relied on his standing as a physician, advising 'medically'. In the following years, 1786-7, however, with some shadow of authority thrown before him by his inspector generalship of prisons, Fitzpatrick went much further. Many of his recommendations could still be broadly categorised as concerned with health. At Roscommon and indeed most other schools, he found it 'absolutely necessary to recommend Play and Exercise in the open Air'[44] — perhaps the most endearing feature of these reports is Fitzpatrick's constant stress on children's need of time for play and playgrounds. At Farra, co. Longford, he prescribed for eye and throat infections, and for diarrhoea.[45] At Ballinrobe, co. Mayo, he left instructions with 'a Mrs. Finn, who acted as Apothecary' for the treatment of the various diseases, ranging from measles and convulsions to idiocy, which he had found among the children.[46] In other schools, he left other advice; and in all he laid down 'a mode of Conduct' for bedwetting,[47] which was a universal problem. But a great deal of Fitzpatrick's intervention was extra-professional. For example, in Ballinrobe he also procured the alteration of the children's clothing, which fitted very badly;[48] in Athlone, the whitewashing of interior walls;[49] in Strangford, co. Down, the removal of the schoolroom from a chamber where, because of 'the unparalleled bad Structure of the Chimney,

Sir Jeremiah and the Charter Schools 99

Fire would not burn';[50] in Creggane, the rearrangement of damp rooms, their airing by fires in metal pots, and their reslating;[51] and in Dundalk, the establishment of the 'infirmary' in a dry room, with the maidservant to sleep there regularly to tend the children sick at night.[52] At Ballykelly, co. Antrim, he 'communicated', he said, an entire set of proposals for reformation.[53] Everywhere, he strove to replace the rotten tickens.[54]

It is also worth noting that Fitzpatrick often – perhaps as often as he could – persuaded persons of standing to accompany, or to join, him when he visited a school. Sometimes the person was a magistrate or a member of the local committee; once, an unparticularised 'gentleman from co. Limerick', shanghaied upon the public road. On both his visits to the Athlone Charter School, he was flanked by Major Ormsby, the commanding officer of the local garrison, and his subordinate, Captain Dennis. In part, Fitzpatrick adopted this practice to secure independent testimony. But in part – or at any rate on some occasions, such as the Ballykelly inspection – it was meant to add to the weight of his injunctions. Generally, with or without support, Sir Jeremiah got his way – at any rate until his back was turned. Only once did he report open defiance. In this case, interestingly enough, the master's wife believed that she could shelter behind counter-authority. Upon Fitzpatrick's complaining about the filth, vermin and disorder of the girls' school at Castlebar, 'Mrs. King very insolently told me, in Presence of a Magistrate of the County, that she disregarded me, as she had powerful Friends'.[55]

In one light, Fitzpatrick stands out as the forerunner of those masterful Victorian officers who, in the infancy of their corps, and from a combination perhaps of humane impatience and overbearing spirit, assumed powers and directed people hither and thither without any formal authority.[56] The first generation of emigration officers and of factories and mines inspectors threw up several men of this quality, who behaved like frontiersmen before the frontier was defined. In another light, however, what we observe is eighteenth-century man operating in an eighteenth-century milieu.

Authority was strangely diffused in a society where rank was clear cut, but office at once indefinite in scope, and large in menace. In such a society, rights against the state and resistance to official exorbitance were comparatively feeble concepts or forces among the mass of people, and station and influence comparatively strong. Except in extraordinary cases, men bent instinctively before the prevailing wind: 'superiors' were rarely challenged. Mrs King resisted Sir Jeremiah, not because he lacked official standing, but because she thought that he could be out-trumped in that species of governmental whist where magistrates were kings and magnates aces, and where the loudest voice, the most peremptory manner and the commanding air took the trick in the majority of rounds. It was second nature to Fitzpatrick to play such a game, even if, in the end, too many easy rubbers led him to overplay his cards.

Fourthly, Fitzpatrick was a restrained and conformist critic. In almost half the schools which he inspected he described some feature or other, or several, as satisfactory. In one or two instances his praise was general and unqualified; and in two or three others he noted improvements which had been made between his first and second visits. Moreover, in the case of charter schools, as in the case of all the other causes which he adopted, he did not assail the existing institutions as such, but merely proposed their modification and reformation. This was so even where he regarded the institution as intrinsically bad. In short, he was, deliberately, a meliorist, a gradualist, a Fabian. At the same time, his exposures of sloth, corruption and cruelty in the working of the system may have been all the more effective for being oblique, and his criticism all the more effective for being implicit. For example, Fitzpatrick never discussed directly the efficiency, or the probity, of the central government of the Incorporated Society. But it is manifest from the individual reports on schools that the Society's headquarters were to blame for the lack of clothing, books, linen and all sorts of other equipment, which were producing a vast sum of human misery across the country. Again and again, Fitzpatrick noted the masters' complaints of Dublin's failure to honour its promises to supply materials, or else of its furnishing the schools with the shoddy and inappropriate. Similarly, he established both the piteous condition of the children and the gross privilege of their superiors most effectively, albeit indirectly, by constant contrasts between their respective accommodation. The report on Clonmel Charter School, for example, begins with nineteen 'barefooted and ragged' boys having to sleep in one 'exceedingly filthy' room. It ends laconically, 'The Master's and Mistress's Apartments and the Committee Room were comfortable and well-furnished'.[57] 'By the Master's conveniencing himself with Lumber Closets, Potatoes- and Fowl-rooms below Stairs', Fitzpatrick wrote of Ballykelly, 'he has narrowed and darkened to Passages the several Parts of the House.'[58] After describing a dining hall at Ballycastle so crowded and narrow that the children had to eat standing up, and their small schoolroom which was none the less 'incumbered with a large Meal

Bin, a Bed for two Servant Boys, two Tables, eleven Wheels, three Reels, seven Forms, large and small, and a Shoemaker at work', he went on to note later in the report that six rooms which had recently been added to the building, and which were 'neatly Kept', were reserved for the mistress's children and the usher.[59] The most savage irony was reserved for Sligo. Fitzpatrick's horrific account of the two foul, cramped chambers in which twenty-five boys and seventeen girls slept in squalor of every kind was followed, after many other matters had been soberly considered, by this concluding sentence: 'Young Master and Miss Hart [the superintendent's children] occupy two Rooms on the middle Floor, which are well lighted and measure each Twenty-eight Feet by eighteen Feet'.[60]

How are we to evaluate this characteristic of Fitzpatrick's? There can be no doubt that this meliorism was a considered attitude to both society at large and administrative change. Nor can there be any doubt that his selective praise is sincere: he generally gives specific reasons for his satisfaction with particular aspects of the running of the schools. The fact remains, however, that his audience and his readership were members of the eighteenth-century Irish gentry; and in the sharply graded society of which they were the absolute masters circumspection in dealing with the powerful was the natural counterpart of assertion in dealing with inferiors. In short, it seems all too likely that Sir Jeremiah was no egalitarian in his condemnations, and that his tone was carefully modulated according to whom he addressed. If so, does this explain the obliqueness and reticences which we are now considering? Was this habit of Fitzpatrick's a calculated method of conveying revulsion and indignation without ultimately overstepping the limits of propriety or prudence? Is it possible that the Austenesque prose conceals an Austenesque ambiguity, that the apparently meek acceptance of the established order hides – to apply D.W. Harding's celebrated judgement upon Jane Austen herself – 'regulated hatred'?[61] When Fitzpatrick wrote, apparently apropos nothing in particular, that John Dempsey of Galway Charter School, whom he thought to be nineteen years of age instead of the fourteen and a half entered in the school books, 'has a Contraction in his Elbow, and might, had he been attended to in Time, have made a Clerk, Taylor &c. but the poor Wretch cannot even spell; he is five Feet six Inches in Height, and none of the Clothes sent down will fit him'[62] – when Fitzpatrick concluded his report of 7 August 1787 with this, was he excoriating the entire system of the charter schools, the cruel bumbledom of the Dublin management, or the neglect of the Galway master or the Galway usher — or merely sorrowing in all the sorrow of the world?

A fifth and final trait which seems to deserve notice is Fitzpatrick's implicit acceptance of the necessity for what the next age, or the next age but one, would call 'espionage' in inspecting. Immediately after his very first visit, to Kilkenny Charter School in 1785, he had returned on foot through the fields to catch the superintendent extinguishing the fire which he had caused to be lighted[63] earlier in the day; and this remained his *modus operandi*. He tried to come upon the schools unawares, riding, as he reports, swiftly across country to forestall the warning messengers sent to arouse the next victim in his tour. There is of course some simplicity, as well as comedy, in all this. Fitzpatrick attempted no apology whatever for his efforts to surprise the inspected. He appears to have considered it self-evident that only in this way could he discover how things really stood within the institutions. In Ireland loyalty to abstract justice was extraordinarily weak at all levels of society. At the same time, the informer was universally despised there. This renders Fitzpatrick's attitude unusually interesting. No less interesting is the fact that he went straight and clearly to, and through, the heart of one of the great problems of the early Victorian inspectorates. The first nineteenth-century inspectors were faced with an almost universal hostility to government 'espionage' before which many of them quailed. Perhaps Fitzpatrick lived in a simpler society and simpler times, in which quasi-war between authority and subject was taken as a matter of course, and no particular opprobrium attached to the appropriate battle tactics. At any rate, what was to be, half a century later, a delicate and complex issue taking decades to arrange was here almost casually brushed aside as a matter of the plainest common sense.

There are of course other and more important dimensions to Sir Jeremiah as a social investigator than those which have just been noted. But even the five considered here, his characteristic modes in exposition and enquiry, have their own significance. He was at once an artist and a counter and measurer; at once an actor in the field, an ironist (or so it seems to me) in his reporting, and a ruthless inquisitor in investigation. It is enough, for the present, to note these five qualities in the first full-length part he played upon the administrative boards.

Notes

1. 'The Charter for establishing Protestant Schools in Ireland, was granted by his late Majesty George the second, in the year 1733, on the Petition of the princi-

pal Nobility, Clergy and Gentry of Ireland, setting forth the gross ignorance, disaffection and want of civilization that prevailed among the Popish Inhabitants, who in the provinces of Leinster, Munster, and Connaught, were stated as far exceeding the Protestants in number; and praying the incorporation of a Society for establishing and maintaining a sufficient number of English Protestant Schools in proper situations, as one of the most effectual means of converting and civilizing the Irish natives; and in which the Children of the Poor might be instructed *gratis* in the English tongue, and the fundamental principles of true religion and loyalty', *Third Report of the Commissioners of the Board of Education in Ireland on the Protestant Charter Schools*, 1809, vii (142), 16.

2. See M.G. Jones, *The Charity School Movement: a Study of Eighteenth Century Puritanism in Action* (Cambridge, 1938), pp. 238-59, for a description of the charter schools. For the names of charter schools visited by Fitzpatrick, 1785-8, see Appendix I.

3. *An Address to Persons of Quality and Estate* (1752), quoted by C. Maxwell, *Dublin under the Georges 1714-1830* (London, 1946), p. 136.

4. G. Locker Lampson, *A Consideration of the State of Ireland in the Nineteenth Century* (London, 1907), p. 132.

5. R.B. McDowell, *Public Opinion and Government Policy in Ireland, 1801-1846* (London, 1952), pp. 23-33. See generally, D. Bowen, *The Protestant Crusade in Ireland, 1800-70* (Dublin, 1978).

6. *Report on the State of the Protestant Charter Schools*, 14 April 1788, *Journals of the House of Commons* (Ire.), vol. xii, p. dcccxix.

7. Ibid.; *Third Report on Protestant Charter Schools*, p. 17. See also various Acts entitled 'An act for licensing hawkers, and pedlars, and for encouragement of English protestant schools', e.g. 3 Geo. III, c.4.

8. *Third Report on Protestant Charter Schools*, p. 19.

9. This calculation was based on Howard's evidence, *Report on Protestant Charter Schools*, p. dcccxvi.

10. *Third Report on Protestant Charter Schools*, p. 20.

11. Ibid., p. 21.

12. Ibid., p. 17.

13. *Report on Protestant Charter Schools*, p. dcccxvi.

14. Schedule annexed to the same, pp. dcccxxiii, dcccxxv.

15. Ibid., pp. dcccxx-dcccxxi.

16. Woodward to Conolly, 6 January 1789, Conolly Papers/957, Trinity College, Dublin.

17. Fitzpatrick to Orde, 5 February 1787, Bolton Papers, MS. 15881, f.5, National Library of Ireland.

18. Schedule annexed to *Report on Protestant Charter Schools*, p. dcccxxi.

19. Fitzpatrick to Orde, 5 February 1787, Bolton Papers, MS. 15881, f.5.

20. Incorporated Society, Board book, 1775-90, 15 December 1786, Trinity College, Dublin, pp. 376-7.

21. Ibid., 7 February 1787, p. 384.

22. Fitzpatrick to Orde, 5 February 1787, Bolton Papers, MS. 15881, f.5.

23. *Parliamentary Register* (Ire.), vol. vii, p. 490.

24. *Journals of H of C* (Ire.), vol. xii, p. 282.

25. Board of Incorporated Society to Lord Lieutenant, I.S. Board book, 25 April 1788, IS/5226, pp. 421-2.

26. Schedule annexed to *Report on Protestant Charter Schools*, p. dcccxx.

27. Ibid., p. dcccxix.

28. Sir Francis Hutchison in *Parliamentary Register* (Ire.), vol. vii, p. 500.

29. Board of Incorporated Society to Lord Lieutenant, I.S. Board book, 25 April 1788, IS/5226, pp. 421-2

30. *Journals of the House of Lords* (Ire.), vol. vi, p. 15.
31. Woodward to Conolly, 6 January 1789, Conolly Papers/957.
32. It was the tithe agitation of the 1780s which drove Woodward altogether into the ranks of the reactionaries. He saw the Church of Ireland as the bulwark of law, property and the British connection: 'the establishment was to be a many-sided civilizing influence on *une gendarmerie noire*', R.B. McDowell, *Irish Public Opinion, 1750-1800* (London, 1944), p. 120.
33. *Journals of H of L* (Ire.), vol. vi, pp. 204, 303; *Parliamentary Register* (Ire.), vol. viii, pp. 425-6.
34. *Third Report on Protestant Charter Schools*, p. 25.
35. *Report on Protestant Charter Schools*, p. dcccxvi.
36. *Third Report on Protestant Charter Schools*, pp. 24-5.
37. *Report on Protestant Charter Schools*, pp. dcccxv-dcccxvi.
38. J. Wesley, *Journal*, 8 vols. (London, 1938), vol. 7, p. 80.
39. Incorporated Society, Board book, 1775-1790, 25 April 1788, IS/5226, p. 421.
40. Schedule annexed to *Report on Protestant Charter Schools*, p. dcccxxi.
41. Ibid.
42. Ibid., p. dcccxx.
43. Ibid., p. dcccxxv.
44. Ibid., p. dcccxxiii.
45. Ibid.
46. Ibid., p. dcccxxiv.
47. Ibid., p. dcccxxvi.
48. Ibid., p. dcccxxiv.
49. Ibid., p. dcccxxv.
50. Ibid., p. dcccxxvi.
51. Ibid.
52. Ibid., p. dcccxxvii.
53. Ibid., p. dcccxxvi.
54. Ibid., p. dcccxx.
55. Ibid., p. dcccxxiv.
56. Robert Low, the first emigration officer, provides an excellent example of the type, O. MacDonagh, *A Pattern of Government Growth 1800-60: the Passenger Acts and their Enforcement* (London, 1961), pp. 91-114.
57. Schedule annexed to *Report on Protestant Charter Schools*, p. dcccxxii.
58. Ibid., p. dcccxxvi.
59. Ibid.
60. Ibid., p. dcccxxiv.
61. D.W. Harding, 'Regulated Hatred: an Aspect of the Work of Jane Austen', *Scrutiny*, vol. vii (1940), pp. 346-62.
62. Schedule annexed to *Report on Protestant Charter Schools*, p. dcccxxiv.
63. Ibid., p. dcccxxi.

5 THE GREASY POLE, 1786-1788

I

The new broom swept vigorously if sometimes wildly. Fitzpatrick's first concern, once installed as inspector general of prisons, was to reduce the gaol population, especially in Dublin. Many awaited transportation, and it was an urgent though also a most difficult matter to remove at least some of these. Over 150 Dublin debtors were promised release under the Insolvent Prisoners Bill still before Parliament at the end of May 1786; and it was vital that this too should go through and the consequent liberation take place immediately. In most cases, the unfortunate families of the debtors shared their incarceration, so that as many as two or even three hundred additional persons may have been involved in this.[1] Lastly, Fitzpatrick found no fewer than 166 people in the gaols without any sort of legal committal whatever;[2] and he went to work to have them freed at once unless they were charged in due legal manner. His first concern in all this was the danger of gaol fever, particularly with the onset of hot weather. But he also expressed the more exalted motive of human rights, as well as the more bizarre argument that the lives of innocent wives and children and comparatively innocent insolvents were being equally imperilled with those of hardened criminals by the sheer pressures of contiguity. For that matter, he might have gone on to contend that even the hardened were being put at an unjustifiable risk by the number of those improperly confined with whom they were being forced to live!

On 26 June 1786, just one month after his appointment, Fitzpatrick made an oral report to the judges of King's Bench on the Dublin prisons. He had of course no standing in the capital, but since no metropolitan inspector had yet been appointed, he could step nimbly into the vacuum. His reception by the judges was not uniformly favourable. One of his 'humane' proposals, that criminals be executed without caps in order to deter vicious onlookers from attempting capital crimes, was very properly scouted. Lord Earlsfort, a former attorney-general, told him (and with the first of these observations at least the other members of the court agreed)

> that the distorted features of the expiring criminal, in the last convulsive agonies, would be a spectacle too shocking for public

105

exhibition; and in the case of women seeing such horrid objects, might produce the most deplorable consequences.³

But generally his report and 'plans' were welcomed. Only the testimony and recommendations concerning the Four Courts Marshalsea survive.⁴ But from these we can fairly guess the whole. Nineteen prisoners, he reported, occupied no less than thirty of the Marshalsea's rooms. These were of course the *crème de la crème* of insolvents, whose servants often shared their fate. A Mr Ledwell for example occupied three chambers, with his valet as his sole companion. But the remaining nineteen rooms held over two hundred people, in indescribable confusion and distress. To take one instance, room no. 41, eighteen feet long by seventeen feet wide, housed nine prisoners, three wives, three children and a stocking frame in full whir. Next door, a prisoner with fever was bedded under the stairway.

Briskly, Sir Jeremiah set out the leading wants and needs. First, the Marshalsea needed extension, with perhaps double the number of apartments. Equally, a hospital was required, as 'the Sick and Healthful are indiscriminately confined, and the former sometimes perish, to the no small Danger of the other Prisoners'. But the Marshalsea also lacked common-rooms, kitchens, washrooms and baths, and even 'proper Privies', while the absence of both corridors and 'Windows in contrary Directions' left the air still and fetid. Clearly, so many and such large changes were imperative that an entirely new prison − Holmes's demand of more than a year before − was pointed to. Meanwhile, Fitzpatrick attempted off his own bat to make some small alleviation of the current miseries. When, for example, he found that a corner of one of the rooms (containing eighteen people) had been enclosed to form a pawnbroker's office, he ordered this 'Closet' to be removed. He had no clear authority to do so, and it was re-erected soon after his back was turned. None the less this sort of impetuous, 'creative' destruction was an earnest of things to come.

Fitzpatrick's appearance before King's Bench was probably made more to help the Insolvent Debtors Bill on its way through the House of Lords than in the hope of immediate reformation of the Four Courts Marshalsea. The passage of the Bill practically cleared the prison (the aggregate debts of those released exceeded £22,000), although the overcrowding was almost as great again within six months of the massive clearance.⁵ Fitzpatrick could now turn to the country at large, and during the remainder of the summer he was on tour once more, visiting and inspecting the gaols of seventeen counties and five of the county boroughs. We do not know for certain where he went, but very likely it was to the midland, western and northern regions. He had covered the south-east in 1785, and much if not all of Munster during the preceding winter. Meanwhile, he established a species of central department in miniature, with an office and clerk in Dublin, and a groom and horses for travelling about the country. Of course, in eighteenth-century fashion, the expenses of these administrative adjuncts were met from his own pocket, and not in any direct sense by government.

Unfortunately Sir Jeremiah's report for 1786 (for some seven months of which he was in office) has not survived. Nor has that for any other year. Doubtless the reason why none was printed was their extent, for Irish parliamentary papers of the eighteenth century were very brief indeed. As the 1787 select committee on the state of gaols said of the inspector general's 1786 report:

> it contains a full Representation of the State and Situation of the different Gaols, the Abuses that he found existing, and the Steps that were taken to redress them. This Detail has rendered it so voluminous that your Committee have not judged it expedient to annex it to this Report: It contains many Particulars well worthy the Attendion of those who wish for fuller Information on this Subject.[6]

Luckily, however, this committee quoted extensively from and summarised many portions of the document so that it is possible both to recover the general findings and to learn a good deal about Fitzpatrick's *modus operandi*.

Thirty-three of the forty Irish counties and county boroughs had appointed local inspectors by the end of 1786; the seven delinquents were of course named — among them, ironically, Fitzpatrick's near native county, King's. Of the thirty-three inspectors, twenty-eight had reported in the prescribed fashion, and on this occasion Sir Jeremiah was indulgent towards the laggards, and placed no greater stigma upon them than that of 'not having been regular'. Many, though not all, of the twenty-eight 'good' counties were found to have made a worthy effort to present as they should for bedding, fuel and provisions, and to see that the regulations were observed 'in as much as the Structure of their Prisons will admit'. Overall, the inspector general was pleased with the initial response to the new legislation. There were grounds to hope that 'a few Years Perseverance will effectuate a complete Reform . . . a Reform as necessary to every Idea of well-regulated Police, as consonant to every Sentiment of Humanity'.[7]

By a happy chance, the 1787 committee reprinted Sir Jeremiah's first criminal chart, incomplete though it had to be. He had continued his practice of tabulation when reporting to King's Bench in June 1786. On that occasion, the Four Courts Marshalsea statistics were neatly arranged in ten columns, specifying the size and occupiers of the rooms, the numbers of women, children and servants sharing imprisonment, the number of beds, the trades pursued, and similar matters. The criminal chart was still more elaborate. Sixteen types of serious crime were distinguished, and the numbers tried and the numbers convicted in each category in each county (or county borough) at each assizes were set out. Cross-tabulation gave the national – or in the case of 1786, the near-national totals. Fitzpatrick was not satisfied with the assize clerks' classification in all cases, and sometimes, in his extensive 'Remarks' opposite each line of figures, he either elaborated or corrected the returns. For example he drew attention, where he himself had discovered them, to cases where the current agrarian 'criminals', the Rightboys, had been charged with or convicted of offences which would not indicate the true reason for their being tried; and he suggested revision of the statistics accordingly. When we envisage the chart extended into an annual series, Sir Jeremiah's boast that the casual eye would instantly apprehend the state's 'maladies', and the progress of the various 'complaints', seems warranted. Even in the single set of figures for half a year we can see at once, to take a simple instance, that with (in order) the three commonest serious offences, assaults and riots, Rightboyism and murder, the conviction rates were respectively 33, 24 and 7 per cent, while at the other end of the scale seven charges of rape or abduction produced no convictions, though five charges of coining produced four.[8] As Fitzpatrick would have been delighted to know, speculation on the causes of the variations, however futile, is irrepressible.

The only portion of his report of 1786 which was reproduced in detail covered the metropolitan prisons, still without an inspector of their own and therefore open to his encroachment. It need hardly be said that he again found them to be in a deplorable condition. Worst of all was the New Prison,

> crouded with an indiscriminate Assemblage of Offenders, many of them often lying without Straw to defend their almost naked Bodies from the Effects of the cold wet Flags, their Heads pillowed with Bricks or Stones, and their nightly covering ragged threadbare Garbs.[9]

Those awaiting hanging, those awaiting transportation, 'the untried Desperadoes' and 'the artful Felons' were cheek by jowl with mere 'impudent Drunkards' and children of nine. It was imperative that the petty offenders and the young should be removed from this forcing house of vice, as much to check the appalling death-rate as to prevent corruption, for overcrowding, and its children, filth and foul air, contributed heavily to 'the putrid and malignant Diseases, so prevalent there'. Fitzpatrick proposed as an immediate and short-term remedy the transformation of the Dublin Bridewell into a minor offenders and juvenile gaol. As ever he was practical, specific and pound-wise. But the reader will have supped full of the metropolitan horrors by now, and we need not follow Sir Jeremiah again, notebook in hand, on his Dublin round, like a rescuer picking his way about some earthquake-shattered site.

II

When the Irish House of Commons reassembled on 18 January 1787 one of its first acts was to institute a committee to inquire into the state of public gaols.[10] This was of course virtually a reconstitution of the committee which had sat through the 1786 session, just as that in turn had been a virtual reconstitution of the committee of 1785. In fact the succession of prisons committees since 1780 had been so little broken that they might reasonably be regarded as a single standing body, all the more so because of the core of 'permanent' members, Holmes, Blaquiere and, later, Griffith, with a few others like Sir Edward Crofton very commonly included. This had as we shall see important constitutional and governmental implications. It also meant that there was a specialised group within the house to which Fitzpatrick's report for 1786, presented at the bar on 29 January 1787, could be directed immediately. Having received this report, the 1787 committee set to to investigate the entire prisons question once again, making its recommendations some seven weeks later, having meanwhile examined several witnesses. It was however the inspector general's report which formed the substance of and set the agenda for the inquiry, and the witnesses were called primarily to substantiate his findings on Dublin.

The committee first found that Sir Jeremiah had 'discharged the Trust reposed in him with Zeal, Diligence and considerable Ability',[11] and then step by step endorsed his evaluations and proposals. It followed him in his general satisfaction with the progress in the country at large, accepting the few malingerers among the grand juries, and the initial errors and omissions of some of the local inspectors, as inevitable concomitants of the first six months of a new order; and like Fitzpatrick it looked to two or three years of guidance and control to set most things to rights. It followed him too in his wholesale condemnation of the metropolitan prisons. Dublin still had no inspector. The person nominated by the grand jury had been rejected as unfit by King's Bench[12] — jobbery seems to have been the reason — and once again Sir Jeremiah was able to insert himself into the problems of the capital. In this instance, however, the Commons committee checked his evidence against that of half a dozen of the city's leading prison officers, Gamble and Lynch, respectively the chaplains of Newgate and the Four Courts Marshalsea; Doyle and Scott, the physicians respectively to Newgate and the remainder of the Dublin prisons; Powell, the apothecary to the city gaols in general; and Osbrey, the late keeper of the City Marshalsea. All fully corroborated Fitzpatrick's horrific accounts of gaol life in Dublin. Scott, for example, testified

> that in the Marshalsea every Species of Debauchery and Immorality is practised; does not apprehend that sufficient Powers are vested in any Person at present to prevent Irregularity; and thinks that the greater Part of the Diseases occurring in those Prisons arise from the Excesses of the Prisoners, and their being subjected to the Action of cold and damp, and that were those Inconveniences obviated, Diseases would be much less frequent, and consequently the Expence of Medicines lessened: Says the City Marshalsea is in a very ruinous State, and that were it even repaired it would still be a very improper Place of Confinement. Witness further gave your Committee a melancholy Picture of the State of the Bridewell, in which above forty miserable Prostitutes are confined, the greater Part of whom are exceedingly ill with venereal Disorders, and lie on the Flags of a common Hall, with scarcely a Covering to defend them from the Inclemencies of the Weather, the Windows being all unglazed, and no Fire-place in the Room.[13]

It became clear from the evidence of the Dublin witnesses that there were other sorts of deficiencies in the 1786 Act. Scott himself could not be paid because the grand jury could only present for his salary if there were a Dublin inspector to certify the due performance of his duties. Doyle found that the New Prison alone absorbed more than the total sum allowed for medicine for all gaols, and Powell's apothecary's bill for even five months of the year was larger than the permitted maximum for annual presentment. The committee agreed that, in part because no inspector had been appointed, Dublin gaols generally had not benefited at all from the reform legislation, the Four Courts Marshalsea in particular being 'a Scene of Disorder, Irregularity and Intoxication'; and it was scandalised by the failure of the corporation to begin the building of a new debtors' prison. But it found — or rather endorsed Sir Jeremiah's finding — so many inadequacies and surviving abuses in the system as a whole that an Amendment Act was adjudged indispensable. When this was proposed by Holmes on 12 March 1787, the Commons readily agreed.[14]

The Amendment Bill was by no means the sole business of the gaols committee. It was also given the task of producing a new Insolvent Debtors Bill to help to re-clear the prisons, and thereby reduce both the chances of gaol fever and the accumulated mounds of human misery.[15] In another guise — as a separate *ad hoc* committee — it was charged on 27 March with discovering why the 1786 Act had not been applied in Dublin.[16] Driven by Blaquiere, it also pursued the metropolitan gaolers and bailiffs whose cruelties and extortions had been revealed in Fitzpatrick's 1786 report and, by implication at least, in the evidence of the Dublin witnesses; and eventually it saw to it that some were dismissed and even convicted.[17] In one matter, partly the consequence of Fitzpatrick's work, the committee split. This was the release of prisoners who had either been acquitted but still owed fees or else had not yet been charged. Crofton introduced and Blaquiere supported a Bill to halt what they spoke of as the liberation of hardened criminals to prey upon society once more; but Holmes, Griffith and another gaols enthusiast, Sir Charles O'Neil, joined the Secretary of State, Hely-Hutchinson, in resisting this attempt to turn the clock back.[18] Hard things were said on either side; but, remarkably, there was no lasting breach among the 'reformers' or between the two more reactionary members and Sir Jeremiah. Blaquiere in particular appears to have been ready to serve as a vehicle for carrying Fitzpatrick's notions into the Amendment Bill.

But though the committee was thus driven about in various directions during March 1787, its primary business remained the preparation of fresh legislation. It worked with extraordinary speed. We do not know when the Amendment Bill was introduced, but certainly the second reading took place as early as 27 March,[19] only fifteen days after the committee was asked to draft it. Of course, it had the recommendations of Fitzpatrick's 1786 report (presumably detailed and specific) before it when it began its work. It also called in Fitzpatrick as a witness or adviser on 14 March, and doubtless had him at hand in Dublin for informal discussions over the next week or ten days, so that the rapidity of the performance is perhaps not so astonishing as the mere chronology might suggest. None the less, it does testify to the sense of urgency which drove the members forward. One of them at least, Griffith, would have preferred the repeal of all prison legislation and the introduction of a new consolidation Bill. But even he realised that to attempt this so late in the session would merely destroy the prospect of any prison legislation at all in 1787, and he proposed that 1788 should be looked to instead as the year for such a major undertaking.[20]

By a lucky accident, both the Bill and Fitzpatrick's reputation came out very well from the second reading on 27 March. Apparently, some member or other was sceptical of the inspector general's evidence on the lamentable state of Dublin's gaols: he felt that so terrific a picture must be overdrawn. That afternoon Blaquiere, accompanied by the Chancellor of the Exchequer, Sir John Parnell, and Trench, the member for Maryborough, visited the Dublin Bridewell 'to satisfy [themselves] of the truth'. Fitzpatrick was gloriously vindicated in the House of Commons next day.

> Let any person he [Blaquiere] said, possessed of only the common feeling, picture, if possible, to himself a number of wretched and unfortunate females confined in a prison, without sufficient shelter to keep out the inclemency of the weather, (the window having no sash or glass, secured by iron bars, and constantly open) no bed, no covering, not even straw, but the bare cold flags to lie on; their support and allowance so very slender, of bread and water, as to be very insufficient for the support of nature for even a short time; and what is even more afflicting (if greater can be) all or the greatest part consuming with disease, without medical advice or assistance, the consequence of which is numbers have died, and are now dying.
>   He had viewed a place called the cell, a place wanting two inches of six feet in breadth, and about nine feet in length, where six of the unfortunate pitiable objects were lying naked, without even a blanket to cover them; nor, on enquiry, had there been any in the gaol for four years past; and were, in that situation left to perish without notice.[21]

Trench corroborated this to the full. He had gone to the bridewell expecting exaggeration, only to find 'that no painting, nor any power of words could convey an adequate idea of the place, or of the distresses of its inhabitants'.[22]

The upshot was the appointment of yet another committee (with Blaquiere, Holmes and Griffith in the lead) to report upon the City Bridewell;[23] further prison visiting by members; the more eager pursuit of vengeance by the House; and an atmosphere of the hottest sympathy for reform throughout the next crucial fortnight. No circumstances more favourable to the Amendment Bill could be conceived, and it passed swiftly and smoothly through both Houses, leaving the Lords on 19 April and receiving the Royal Assent in early May.

The velocity of conception, gestation and delivery notwithstanding, we should now pause and examine the new statute with some care. For the Prisons Amendment Act of 1787[24] anticipated – one is tempted to add the cliché, uncannily – the 'classic' first Amendment Acts of the 1830s and 1840s in various other fields of social reform. This becomes apparent once we arrange its clauses into their main executive elements.

First, the position and powers of the central authority – in this instance the inspector general himself was the effective central authority – were strengthened and consolidated. The Gaols Act of 1786 had, as we have seen, clearly envisaged the appointment as temporary, and the inspector general's task as the setting up of a system which would thereafter run itself without any special national supervision. Now the two-year limit on the office was abandoned, and it was rendered, at least potentially, a permanent post. Experience having already shown, the preamble ran, 'the further continuance of the said office will much contribute to effectuate the necessary reform in the management of gaols and prisons', its indefinite prolongation was left to the discretion of the crown. Moreover, the way of the inspector general was smoothed by a clause creating a new offence, that of hindering him in the course of his enquiries or visitations; for this fines of up to £50 might be imposed. The supremacy of his status within the new 'service' was also established by rendering the Dublin inspector unmistakably his subordinate. The 1786 Act had permitted the Dublin inspector to report directly to Parliament, as well as to the Court of King's Bench. But the Amendment Act, altering a few words, required him to submit his findings to the inspector general, who alone had the right and duty to deal with Parliament.

Secondly, the field to be controlled was extended 'laterally'. Fitzpatrick had had the insane in his charge from the beginning in so far as they were incarcerated, temporarily or permanently, in gaols or bridewells. But now the inspector general was empowered to visit all private as well as all public madhouses and places where lunatics or idiots were confined, 'as often as he shall think fit'. Thus the new activity was discretionary. But this does not mean that Fitzpatrick's authority here was weaker than that which he exercised over prisons proper. The contrary was probably the case. There were no local inspectors of madhouses, and Fitzpatrick was not required to report to anyone on his inspections of them. At the same time the madhouses were to be subjected to 'discipline' equivalent to that imposed upon the prisons; and the penalties imposed for impeding the inspector general in visiting them were exactly the same as in the case of prisons. An attempt was also made to remove the insane from prisons, and to locate them in hospitals instead — at any rate to do so for those who were paupers. Clause 8 authorised grand juries to present whatever sums were needed 'for providing and supporting a ward or wards [in the county infirmary] for the reception and support of such idiots and insane persons as shall be from time to time recommended by two or more magistrates of such county', the magistrates certifying both the fact of the malady and the fact that the recommended 'were destitute of support'.

Thirdly, existing regulations were intensified and rendered more exact. Perhaps the leading source of hardship for prisoners was food — its insufficiency and bad quality. For the more general injunctions of the 1786 Act, the Amending Act substituted precise and uniform requirements which would be comparatively easy to monitor and enforce. So that the prisoners might be reasonably well fed, each local inspector was to procure twice weekly such bread, potatoes, meal or similar provisions (the range had been widened) as would supply each person in gaol with food to the value of at least threepence (comparatively a large sum) a day. The food was no longer to be distributed by the parish clergyman, but instead by the local inspector. The days on which it was to be issued, Sunday and Thursday every week, were now specified. Also of critical importance for enforcement was the section prescribing the *advance* of the necessary monies to the inspector, with the expenditure to be accounted for by him later on. The weaknesses inherent in the existing system of reimbursement at assize times only may be readily imagined. Substantially the same form of advance payment was to be applied in madhouses, the purchase and distribution of the food being the responsibility of the surgeon of the county infirmary in this particular case.

Fourthly, a number of minor flaws in the initial legislation, which became apparent once the attempt was made to put it into force, were quickly removed. These all concerned the working of the Act in Dublin. It had been found, as we have seen, that the statutory limit of £50 per annum on expenditure on medicines in the capital was much too small, and the sum allowed was raised to £200. It was also found that the chaplain of the New Prison wished — or needed — to be paid quarterly instead of annually, and this was now sanctioned. The Dublin gaols were found to be too numerous for one man to supervise the prisoners' provisioning, and accordingly the city was divided equally for this purpose, between the metropolitan inspector and the New Prison chaplain. Most important of all, it was found that the dual process for appointing the metropolitan inspector — nomination by the grand jury and ratification by King's Bench — had not worked. An impasse had followed the rejection of the grand jury's nominee: thereafter no appointment was, or legally could be, made. The 1787 Amendment Act now required the grand jury to approve three candidates, one of whom King's Bench was to select; and if King's Bench determined that none of the three was worthy of appointment, the lord lieutenant was forthwith to nominate whom he pleased — a procedure strikingly (although of course accidentally) like that employed in Irish Catholic episcopal appointments, with the diocesan clergy, the provincial synod and the papacy filling, respectively, the three roles! Meanwhile the Act repaired, retrospectively, various pieces of damage which had followed from the absence of a Dublin inspector in 1786-7, such as the payment of the Dublin prisons physician's salary, although it had not been endorsed by the inspector, as the 1786 Act had prescribed.

The amendment of the Prisons Act of 1786 prefigures an important early and mid-nineteenth-century process of governmental growth. It would probably be too much to say 'pre-mirrored'. In terms of the nineteenth-century time scale, the earlier sequence foreshortened each development most sharply; and it inevitably included elements which were to disappear before 1815 and lacked others which had not yet taken shape. None the less the anticipation was remarkable, even startling. The four categories into which I placed the changes of 1787 represent four essential types or forms of the expansion of state power in the second and third quarters of the nineteenth century, and it is worth making the comparison, point by point.

The primary need of a governmental embryo was to ensure its own continuance. This generally meant that its nature had to be defined more clearly and its strength augmented. The 1787 Act may not have made Fitzpatrick's position permanent, but it took the first step towards doing so; and it also armed him with new powers and rights against persons and institutions hostile to the purposes of his office. If we examine the early growth of, for example, the coal mines inspectorate in Great Britain, we find essentially the same developments taking place in essentially the same sequence, albeit over a period of nearly two decades (1842-60) instead of twelve months. The three stages of Sir Jeremiah's acting as independent investigator, as official investigator-cum-arranger for a specific period, and as executive officer without limit to his term, are paralleled in coal mines regulation by the initial one- or two-man commissions of inquiry into particular events, the investigative inspectorate of Tremenheere from 1843 onwards, and the executive corps established in 1850 and gradually given more definite form and larger authority over the course of the next decade.[25]

Secondly – the progression is of course logical and not chronological, for the various transformations tended to be both simultaneous and interactive – the extension of prisons regulation to madhouses in the 1787 Act was typical of the 'lateral' expansion whereby the area of central government spread prodigiously and continuously in the nineteenth century. This sort of expansion derived from two main impulses. On the one hand, it might be felt that another field was so similar to that already undergoing regulation that it was meaningless to draw a distinction between the two. On the other hand, it might be felt that the evils against which regulation had been imposed in one field were so similar to those existing in another that the two should be regarded as on a par. In the case of the Irish prisons, the extension of the regulation to houses of correction[26] (which happened before 1786) was an example of the first category, and its extension to madhouses by the Amendment Act of 1787 an example of the second.

Factory legislation is perhaps the *locus classicus* of both types of development in the early and mid-nineteenth century. The regulation imposed only upon cotton mills and apprentice children in 1802 was extended step by step by the 1819, 1828 and 1833 Factory Acts to all other textile mills and to all factory children.[27] By a series of pieces of legislation, stretching from the Coal Mines Act of 1842 and the Print Works and Bleaching Mills Acts of 1843 to the Workshops Act of 1867, it was extended to cover practically all child labour in manufacturing industries, and to very small business, as well as factory, production.[28] Of course, the nineteenth-century processes of administrative growth under this head were much more lengthy and complex than their late eighteenth-century forerunners. But the difference is of degree not kind. Fundamentally, the respective patterns to be traced, and the reasoning or impulses governing them, would appear to be identical.

Thirdly, it was characteristic of the new branches of government in this sort of field to intensify their activity, in the light of the increased knowledge of need which practical experience provided. Let us take as an instance here one of the very subjects in which the 1787 Act itself exemplified the process of intensification, namely the greater specification of the amount and kinds of, and of the methods of paying for and distributing, food in prisons. The Passenger Acts and Passenger Amendment Acts from 1842 to 1855 followed almost exactly the same course in the matter of the sea-stock of emigrants from the United Kingdom to North America.[29] The general obligation placed upon shippers and masters of vessels in 1842 to furnish the emigrants with a set quantity of provisions was gradually refined, statute by statute, until by 1855 the amount and range of food prescribed had been considerably enlarged and the mechanism of distribution and quality control progressively improved. Again we find late eighteenth-century Ireland telescoping and concentrating a process which would become complex and protracted in early Victorian England.

Finally, the 1787 Act filled various gaps and corrected various mistakes in the initial legislation which had become apparent when the attempt was made to put it into practice; and cumulatively these minor changes tended to enlarge as well as define more exactly the area and operation of state intervention. Again this anticipated an important mode of nineteenth-century governmental growth. No field of Victorian social reform failed to manifest this mode of growth; but perhaps the most striking instances occurred, as we should expect, in the more technical and esoteric fields. The Alkali Acts of 1863 to 1884[30] and the Explosives Acts of 1860 to 1875[31] furnish good examples of the process of growth by correction and supplementation of an original statute. Of course, there were significant differences between the Irish prisons situation of the 1780s and its mid-nineteenth-century British counterparts. For one thing, amending legislation steadily became much more difficult to carry — at any rate, to carry quickly — as parliamentary time was competed for more fiercely; as it became customary to consult and if possible to compromise with hostile interests; and as the political parties boxed and coxed in office, with a corresponding turnover of ministers. Again, as subjects grew more technical and as the expert became lord of the field, there was a tendency to abandon change by amending legislation in favour of administrative discretions and delegated legislation, especially from 1850 onwards. None the less, these later developments were only refinements and logical extensions of a force for multiplication inherent in central government — the demonstrations of the inadequacy of the first legislation which invariably accompanied the earliest attempts to put it into effect.

III

As has been said above, the passage of the Prisons Amendment Bill through Parliament in March and April 1787 was accompanied by an extraordinary exposure of the evils of Dublin gaols. Blaquiere, the driving force of most of the inquiries, launched his campaign on 27 March with,

> it was of no consequence that regulations were made if the Corporation of the City of Dublin should, under the very nose of Parliament, presume to scorn the law; he wished to see who the offenders were, and why £200 was not levied upon them? He wished to know where the animadversion of the House ought to fall, for so many unfortunate wretches being suffered to rot in prison without a rag to cover them?[32]

The committee which Blaquiere secured to inquire into the Dublin Bridewell established that no body in the capital, whether corporation, mayor, sheriffs or grand jury, would accept responsibility for the gaols;[33] and after several snatches of debate it was resolved in the Commons on 3 April that the corporation and every other body appointing officers to gaols had the duty of superintending both their appointees and the places to which they had been appointed.[34] Otherwise, the committee found that the current scenes of horror at the City Bridewell had as their immediate cause the transference of forty prostitutes from the overcrowded house of industry. The police were guilty of moving them without authority, and indeed of incarcerating them without either charge or conviction. As Blaquiere put it, he

> did not know what crime it was for even a woman of easy virtue to walk the streets peaceably and quietly. In Holland, though they are rigid Calvinists, houses for their reception are legalized; and in the dominions of his holiness such establishments are permitted.[35]

The prostitutes were subjected to the same brutal neglect as the other inhabitants of the Bridewell — much worse indeed for all, now that this prison in turn was overcrowded and its bread ration still more precarious and inadequate than before. The crowning outrage was the discoveries that when after great difficulties a presentment for fuel for the Bridewell had been secured, the coal went to the gaolers', not the prisoners' use; and that a subscription Blaquiere got up with other members of the Commons to feed the prostitutes had ended in the keeper's pocket as fees! The keeper himself so prevaricated when examined by a committee of the entire House that by the speaker's (Foster's) warrant he was committed to Newgate on 30 March.[36]

So it continued, with scandalous revelation heaped upon revelation, while more and more members luxuriated in bursts of righteous anger. Meanwhile Sir Jeremiah was climbing still higher in the public estimation. Gaol fever having broken out in Clonmel prison at the end of March, he dashed there to stamp out the contagion, burning all foul straw, bedding and clothes, blasting gunpowder in every chamber, scrubbing and 'blanching' walls and ceilings, and creating systems of ventilation and sanitary order. In mid-April an anonymous Quaker wrote from Clonmel that 'his timely arrival . . . has, under Providence saved the lives of many', and that never before had he 'seen prisoners treated in that lenient manner which becomes the mild spirit of Christianity . . .' The Quaker went on to couple Howard and Fitzpatrick as the ornaments of the present age. Fitzpatrick's

> active genius and exquisite feelings for the distressed, and extensive knowledge in medicine, point him out as peculiarly qualified with the essential requisites to procure an alleviation of the miseries of the most wretched part of the community in this land.[37]

But even in this bright noon of reform the clouds were beginning to form. The viceroy, Rutland, died in April, and Orde, the champion of the prison reformers in the seat of power, was replaced as Chief Secretary.[38] Moreover, Orde's educational proposals,[39] introduced just before his departure, had produced a potentially dangerous polarisation. The Church of Ireland men were outraged, while the humanitarians, Holmes, Griffith, Blaquiere, Parnell and other supporters of prison reform were aligned with Orde and enlightenment — or irreligion, as Orde's enemies declared. The House of Lords was also showing some signs of restiveness. Although it offered no resistance to the prisons amendment measure, it so emasculated the 1787 Insolvent Debtors Bill that the Commons repudiated the new version indignantly.[40]

Most ominous of all however was the growing resistance in the metropolis. A resolution introduced by Blaquiere placing responsibility for inspecting the prisons of the capital squarely upon Dublin corporation, and laying down that 'any neglect thereof is highly criminal', was bitterly resisted; and only a watered-down version was eventually let through.[41] The powerful city interest was epitomised by Nathaniel Warren, brewer, alderman, MP and placeman, whom we have encountered already as an enemy of the 1786 Bill in its final stages in the Commons. Warren perfectly expressed the mixture of *amour propre*, love of patronage and jobbery, parsimony in responding to presentments, and repudiation of responsibility when things went wrong, which characterised the public bodies of the capital. Warren's own 'job' was the commissionership of the Dublin police. Although he could not deny that the inspection of prisons, one of the specific obligations of the police, had never hitherto been fulfilled, he blustered about their powerlessness to effect changes.[42] In fact, it proved an unlucky hour for prison reform when Blaquiere and others drew the police into their circle of condemnation. For from 1788 onwards the police commission, led by Warren, did inspect the Dublin gaols, and their anodyne reports[43] served, in effect, to block the way of improvement in the future.

Meanwhile, the Dublin opposition to prison reform grew more daring after the clashes in the House of Commons on Blaquiere's resolution. When gaol fever broke out at the City Marshalsea in June 1787 the high sheriff held Gamble and Scott, the metropolitan chaplain and physician, responsible as 'inspectors' for not informing him or the magistrate in time. He went on to describe complaints about the prison as much exaggerated, even if 'some of the persons confined had died'.[44] All this was either ill-informed or insolent. Dublin had no inspector, and Gamble and Scott had already pleaded in vain with various Dublin authorities for relief of one kind or another. None the less they were now openly vilified in the newspapers, and Edwards, the keeper of the City Marshalsea, warmly praised for his humanity and devotion. One letter to the press concluded,

> with what degree of reprobation must we behold the spurious ebullitions of a splenetic malevolent *bird of passage*, who before the public eye darkly endeavours to throw the slime of unwarrantable censure in his face, and that merely because Mr. Edwards does not to the office of Marshalsea Keeper add the learning of a Divine, or the medical knowledge of a physician[?][45]

Conceivably, Sir Jeremiah was the splenetic bird. But this is unlikely. All else apart, the City Marshalsea was not the subject of his severest strictures — he was probably out of Dublin at the relevant time. In fact, he spent the greater part of 1787 out of the capital, on inspection. During his tours of that year, which covered most of the kingdom, he examined and reported in detail on twenty-five of the thirty-two county gaols and five of the eight gaols in county boroughs. He also visited and reported on twenty provincial bridewells and corporation prisons, and five of the madhouses about the country. There were moreover thirteen prisons being built or rebuilt which he advised upon, and twenty others presented for, whose plans needed his close attention. Moreover, he had had, as we have seen, to fly to the help of Clonmel, and spend a considerable time at that gaol fighting the fever and reorganising the prison system. But this by no means completed his Herculean labours. During his spells in Dublin, he visited all the city's gaols and bridewells twice a week and applied — for the most part in vain — to the grand jury, the lord mayor and any other promising authority for relief of one kind or another. Meanwhile, reports, calculations and remonstrances poured from his pen.

Once again he was, according to his annual report for 1787, generally satisfied with the improvements in the provinces. Most grand juries were providing the money for building quite readily, as well as taking seriously their duties as superintendents of reform. Most local inspectors too were reasonably conscientious in trying to carry the particulars of the Prison Acts into effect. The progress over the preceding eighteen months had been quite rapid; and continued steady pressure should, he believed, gradually produce a more or less satisfactory working system. It was far otherwise with the country bridewells and town gaols, which Fitzpatrick was now inspecting regularly for the first time. Most of them provided no straw, coverings or fuel, and most starved their wretched inmates whose 'Fate depended on uncertain Charity'. In some the prisoners were even 'chained to Logs sunk in the Floors, also hand-cuffed and bolted whenever the Keepers considered their Prisons not sufficiently secured'.[46]

In terms of numbers, if not intensity of suffering, however, these constituted a minor problem. Ireland's crying evil was still the Dublin gaols. Despite the huffing and puffing of the city members and grandees, and the effusions of piqued or self-interested citizens, Fitzpatrick found that the Marshalseas (particularly the Four Courts) and Newgate were still in as lamentable a condition — but greatly magnified of course — as the worst of the village 'gaols'. It is true that on 23 June

1787, soon after the Amendment Act came into force, an inspector for the capital – Surgeon John Whiteway – had been appointed. But even on his own showing Whiteway appears to have been a poor creature, timid, passive and acquiescent. When for example he discovered that Newgate prisoners were being stripped of their clothes to pay for the now illegal penny-pot and garnish fees, he merely 'spoke to' the gaoler and turnkey about them; and on being defied, concluded lamely that 'he had no Power to redress these Grievances'. He reached the same conclusion about the filth and disorder of the prison infirmaries, and the want of blankets and fuel. When cross-examined after nearly nine months in office about other abuses, he replied in such terms as these:

> Witness has applied to Gaoler to have Prisoners, according to Act of Parliament, separated. Gaoler said he could not do it, that there was no Conveniency in the Gaol ... Has spoke to Gaoler about Spirituous Liquors being admitted into Gaol; has been answered by him that it was impossible to prevent it ...[47]

And that was that: a greater contrast to the pressing, indomitable Sir Jeremiah can scarcely be supposed.

Whiteway did not merely fail to produce changes in the prison administration of Dublin but he also, by his very occupancy of the post of metropolitan inspector, rendered it more difficult for Fitzpatrick, or even Scott or Gamble, to do so. Before the appointment, Fitzpatrick, by dint of pestering the corporation, had secured a handful of necessities such as the provision of wooden bedframes for the prison infirmaries – although typically, in the absence of effective surveillance, these were soon burnt by the prisoners for firewood.[48] Now his influence in Dublin was even weaker than before. Not only did Whiteway not do his own work, he also – however innocently – stood in the way of its being done by others. Thus Sir Jeremiah concluded that the Prison Acts, even with the additional powers and provisions of the 1787 measure, were still virtually ineffectual in Dublin.[49]

We know even less of Fitzpatrick's 1787 than of his 1786 report: only a handful of passages and general findings survive. His experience of the practical operation of the legislative amendments of 1787 is among the lacunae, although his general approbation of the local inspectors outside the capital may suggest that they worked tolerably well. In one case, however, we do have some positive evidence of success. When in July 1787 Fitzpatrick first tried to use his powers to inspect madhouses, Redmond Boate, the keeper of a private asylum at

Portobello, refused him admission on three several occasions. Fitzpatrick thereupon prosecuted Boate successfully, securing both admission and a fine of £20. This was regarded as a test case, with the threat of 'reiterated applications' by the inspector general, and of 'renewed fines' by the magistrates, to bring recalcitrant keepers to heel. It was certainly seen as a critical matter. As *Freeman's Journal* put it:

> The thousand arts made use of, both in England and Ireland, to remove wives, relations, and even children, in many families, in order to accomplish the purposes of vice, or obtain pecuniary gratifications, are too notorious. Many unfortunate beings in the perfect enjoyment of sense and reason, have been driven to real phrenzy by the cruelties practised on them in such mad-houses.[50]

Debtors on this day confined in the City Marshalsea.
March the 5, 1788

	Prison	Tabular Room	Wifes	Children	
Under 40 shillings	23	7	15	36	Note –
Under £5	13	9	8	19	the wifes and children
Under 10	14	10	10	35	of Tradesmen
Under 20	13	5	4	15	alone, are told.
Under 50	7	6	6	18	
Under 100	4	4	4	3	
Under 450	2				
Total	73	48	44	126	

By the above it appears that there are 50 persons confined for sums under £20 – of whom 36 are Tradesmen 33 of whom are married, and have 90 Children. – Many of the poor Brutes, are almost naked.

We also know that Fitzpatrick went on quietly supplying the politicians with ammunition and direction alike. For example, he furnished both Holmes and Foster with an analysis of the debtors in the City Marshalsea (see illustration) which established that the great majority had been imprisoned for very small debts (one-third for debts of under forty shillings) and that half were tradesmen, with an average of four dependants. Some owed almost as much in fees as the original debt; and in one case ('a journeyman Blacksmith — he lay on a Wisp of Straw on the damp ground, without a Blanket to cover him, fed by a charitable hand — and had a wife and three small children') the original debt of 8s had been immediately exceeded by the marshal's summons and warrant fees alone.[51] In his covering note to Foster, Fitzpatrick wrote, 'I know to a mind like yours I need make no apology, on this Occasion.'[52] Thus was he working out of sight, aiming to bring down his birds with shots to both wings, with flattery and sad, selected fact.

Notes

1. *Report of the Committee on Gaols*, 12 March 1787, *Journals of the House of Commons* (Ire.), vol. xii, p. dxxv.
2. *Journals of H of C* (Ire.), vol. xv, p. cccviii.
3. *Freeman's Journal*, 27-29 June 1786.
4. *Report of Committee on Gaols*, 12 March 1787, pp. dxxv-vi.
5. Ibid. I have been unable to locate the statute to which he refers.
6. Ibid., p. dxxx.
7. Ibid.
8. Ibid., pp. dxxviii-ix.
9. Ibid., pp. dxxiv-v.
10. *Journals of H of C* (Ire.), vol. xii, p. 153.
11. *Report of Committee on Gaols*, 12 March 1787, p. dxxiv.
12. *Parliamentary Register* (Ire.), vol. vii, pp. 420-1.
13. *Report of Committee on Gaols*, 12 March 1787, p. dxxx.
14. 27 Geo. III, c.29.
15. *Freeman's Journal*, 27-29 March 1787.
16. Ibid.
17. *Parliamentary Register* (Ire.), vol. vii, pp. 431, 440, 454.
18. *Freeman's Journal*, 3-6 March 1787.
19. Ibid., 27-29 March 1787.
20. Ibid.
21. *Parliamentary Register* (Ire.), vol. vii, pp. 425-6.
22. Ibid., p. 426.
23. *Journals of H of C* (Ire.), vol. xii, p. 246.
24. 27 Geo. III, c.39.
25. MacDonagh, *Early Victorian Government*, pp. 78-95.
26. 23 & 24 Geo. III, c.41.
27. MacDonagh, *Early Victorian Government*, pp. 22-34, 42-50.
28. Ibid., pp. 61-72.
29. MacDonagh, *Pattern of Government Growth*, pp. 147-8, 296-7.

30. R. M. MacLeod, 'The Alkali Acts Administration, 1863-84: the Emergence of the Civil Scientist', *Victorian Studies*, vol. ix (1965), pp. 85-112.
31. J.H. Pellew, 'The Home Office and the Explosives Act of 1875', *Victorian Studies*, vol. xviii (1974), pp. 175-94. For studies of similar developments, see R. Lambert, 'A Victorian National Health Service: State Vaccination 1855-71', *Historical Journal*, vol. 4 (1962), pp. 1-18; R.M. MacLeod, 'Social Administration and the "Floating Population": the Canal Board Acts, 1877-1899', *Past and Present*, no. 35 (1966), pp. 101-32; and 'Government and Resource Conservation: the Salmon Acts Administration, 1860-86', *Journal of British Studies*, vol. vii (1968), pp. 114-50.
32. *Freeman's Journal*, 27-29 March 1787.
33. Ibid., 29-31 March 1787.
34. *Parliamentary Register* (Ire.), vol. vii, pp. 453-4.
35. Ibid., p. 431.
36. Ibid., p. 440.
37. *Freeman's Journal*, 19-21 April 1787.
38. By A. Fitzherbert, later Lord St Albans.
39. *Parliamentary Register* (Ire.), vol. vii, pp. 486-96.
40. *Freeman's Journal*, 14-17 and 21-4 April 1787.
41. *Parliamentary Register* (Ire.), vol. vii, pp. 444, 453-4.
42. *Freeman's Journal*, 31 March-3 April 1787.
43. *Journals of H of C* (Ire.), vol. xii, p. dxliii; vol. xiii, pp. vii, cccx; vol. xiv, p. lvii; vol. xv, pp. xii, dxlv.
44. *Freeman's Journal*, 26-28 June 1787.
45. Ibid., 3-5 July 1787.
46. *Report of Committee on Gaols*, 3 March 1788, *Journals of H of C* (Ire.), vol. xii, p. dccxxxiii.
47. Ibid., Whiteway's evidence, p. dccxxxv.
48. Ibid., Powell's evidence, p. dccxxxv.
49. Ibid., p. dccxxxiii.
50. *Freeman's Journal*, 10-12 July 1787.
51. Fitzpatrick to Foster, 8 March 1788, Foster Papers, D562/8967A, P.R.O., N.I., ff. 491-2.
52. Ibid., f.490.

6 PROGRESS AND PENITENTIARIES, 1788-1793

I

With true eighteenth-century seasonality, the campaign for prison reform in 1788, as in other years, began with the opening of the parliamentary session. By the late 1780s the reformers, like a contemporary army on the continent, were emerging annually from winter quarters at more or less the same time, and conducting more or less the same initial manoeuvres. As usual, the House of Commons was at once addressed 'in a pathetic manner' by Holmes, introducing another Insolvent Debtors Bill and describing even more pitiful conditions than before because of the failure to pass any measure of relief in 1787.[1] As usual, too, an Acquitted Prisoners' Fees Bill was launched and fiercely opposed;[2] and the gaols committee was reappointed (technically, appointed afresh).[3] As in 1787 its first task was to receive and act upon the inspector general's report. The one novelty of the year was the receipt by Parliament on 18 January of a report on the metropolitan prisons from the Dublin commissioners of police.[4] But this was a sparse and futile document, the fruit it would seem of an afternoon's stroll about the city. For the most part it merely enumerated the numbers in the various gaols and bridewells, and in prison infirmaries. Otherwise it said little more than that the banisters and pump at Newgate had been repaired; that the women's hall there had been converted to 'an Hospital'; that the forty troublesome prostitutes had been moved from the bridewell to a temporary house of correction at Smithfield; and that the county prison at Kilmainham was 'in a very filthy Condition'.

The essential move was of course the reconstitution of the select committee once Fitzpatrick's report for 1787 had been submitted. Following the 1787 pattern, the 1788 committee used the report as the substance of the evidence before it, and called witnesses mainly to corroborate or elaborate its particulars, or to pursue the special abuses which it had disclosed. Sir Jeremiah's 'Attention and Accuracy' in his incessant visitations were warmly praised; his findings and recommendations were heartily adopted; and himself was judged to have 'executed the Duties of his office with extraordinary Zeal and Ability'. Again, both he and the committee regarded the progress of reform in the provinces as tolerably satisfactory overall. But again Dublin was found to be disgraceful. The preceding six years, the committee's report observed, had produced seven inquiries by the House of Commons and five Gaols Acts,

> for the avowed Purposes of conjoining the Exercise of Humanity with the Principles of True Police, the salutary effects of which already appear in most parts of the Kingdom; but in the City of Dublin, the Capital of the Kingdom, and Seat of Government, scarcely any useful Regulation has taken place.[5]

For the most part, the evidence and findings traversed all too familiar ground. But in respect to three of the evils, drunkenness, violence and neglect of duty by the metropolitan authorities, it dug much deeper than any of its predecessors, while it also pursued particular malefactors with a keenness and determination never known before.

Fitzpatrick's intervention in 1787 had checked the open sale but not the availability of liquor in Newgate. The turnkey kept a taphouse opposite the gaol from which, with the keeper's connivance, the prisoners were supplied. Even when, towards the end of the year, the inspector general's reforming pressure at last compelled the keeper to come into residence at Newgate and the turnkey to surrender his public house, mass drunkenness continued in the prison, for the keeper still 'tacitly authorized it [the sale of liquor] as a necessary Perquisite of said Turnkey's Office', while the turnkey simply switched the basis of his operations to tonnage paid by a 'front' publican. Drink was closely linked to violence. Drunken brawls and uproar abounded; in the affrays men were seriously injured; one was even killed. Moreover in the hunt for money for drink, new or timid or elderly prisoners were assaulted, robbed of what money they were carrying and even stripped, so that their clothes might be sold for whisky pence. The prison officers, who probably all stood to gain to some degree or other, turned a blind eye to the violence. In effect, the committee concluded, in Newgate as in the other Dublin gaols, they granted 'Impunity to every Species of Outrage and Disorder'. Nor were the officers' superiors, the various metropolitan authorities, much less culpable. The grand jury, the corporation, the lord mayor and sheriffs had all failed to intervene, even when called on to do so by Fitzpatrick, or by the chaplain or physician, Gamble or Scott. The latest lord mayor and sheriffs had shown welcome signs of a reforming disposition in their first months in office. But the corporation had effectively refused to recognise the responsibility for surveillance specifically laid upon it by the 1787 Amendment Act, while the grand jury not only failed to respond to urgent requests from Fitzpatrick and others for presentments for mandatory supplies desperately needed in the prisons, but were also already two years in arrears in presenting for the salaries of the prisons' physician, surgeon and chaplain and in paying the apothecary's bill. Even the coroners appear to have been remiss. A corpse lay five days in Newgate before one of them turned up to conduct an inquest.[6]

On this occasion, unlike 1787, Sir Jeremiah himself appeared as a witness before the committee. His further evidence about the particular evils of the day need not concern us. But his emphasis on the machinery of enforcement is worth attention. He was, with good reason, dissatisfied with the grand jury as the provider of money for necessities; and he despaired of gaolers and turnkeys as enforcers of the regulations. Nor, he continued, could the corporation be relied upon either to use its patronage responsibly in making appointments or to undertake the supervision of those whom it had appointed. Something might perhaps be hoped for from the sheriffs. But after all the gaolers were not under their 'Control . . . further than by keeping Prisoners in safe Custody'; and the former lord mayor at least had proved a broken reed when called upon to intervene. The obvious conclusion was to remove the business so far as practicable from elected bodies: 'without some strong coercive Inspection . . .', Sir Jeremiah concluded, 'the Gaols of Dublin will never be properly regulated'.[7] He did not expand upon this conclusion, at any rate in the portion of his evidence which was printed. But presumably he envisaged the enlargement of the powers of his own office in particular, and the addition to it of direct executive functions and discretions.

If this were the case, the select committee was not prepared to follow him immediately to such a length. It did resolve, however, that the power of appointment to and the superintendence of all Dublin prisons should be removed from the current authorities and vested in the lord mayor and sheriffs alone. This determination was flanked, on the one side, by a recommendation that the entire staff at Newgate be immediately dismissed 'and rendered incapable of being ever re-appointed', and, on the other, by a resolution that the city treasurer pay all arrears owed under the Gaols Acts forthwith, and in future conduct the prison business by advances to be accounted for when spent. All the committee's other resolutions, but one, dealt with some particular circumstance or abuse in the metropolis. The exception was the final recommendation that the inspector general's salary be increased at once, as his current stipend 'is not adequate for his Time and Labour, and the Expences necessarily attending the Discharge of his Duty'.[8]

Progress and Penitentiaries 129

This was indeed the case. Fitzpatrick's first year in office had cost him no less than £34, 'independent of all my own Expences, traveling thro' the Kingdom and residing in Town'. The wages of his clerk and groom accounted for almost £75. The four horses needed for his tours cost £18 each; the rent of rooms for offices, £45 10s; and postage, paper and the like, £35. In all the inspector general had spent £226 to maintain his establishment, receiving in return a net salary of £190 17s. Matters would be even worse in 1788 when, as Fitzpatrick himself put it, 'the Lunatic and Insane Inspection of the Kingdom, is added to the Office'.[9]

On 3 March 1788, just a fortnight after the committee was appointed, Holmes presented its report to the House of Commons. Immediately the introduction of another Amendment Bill was approved; and Holmes and Griffith were instructed to prepare it on the basis of the committee's resolutions – with one significant exception. The recommendation that the corporation and grand jury of the City of Dublin be stripped of their powers and (generally neglected) responsibilities under the Prisons Acts was disapproved:[10] members shrank from so audacious an assault upon the city interests. Within a week of receiving the commission, Griffith presented the new Bill. No copy has survived, and we can only infer some of the clauses and intentions from the proposed amendments and the recorded scraps of debate.

Vengeance upon the miscreant prison officers of the Newgate had to await another occasion. Griffith accepted the attorney general's protest against retroactive legislation, as contrary to constitutional convention; and the Bill was reintroduced without the original punitive clauses directed at the keeper, deputy-keeper and turnkey. Doubtless, the proposer was consoled by assurances from the floor that the matter was altogether one of abstract principle, and that the objection neither palliated the misdeeds of Newgate nor subtracted from the glory which the prison reformers had already earned.[11] We also know of three additions to the Bill while the House was in committee. New regulations to suppress drinking in the gaols were devised; at least one further salary was increased; and payment for the treatment of sick prisoners was facilitated. The main subject of debate and dispute in the lower House, however, was the clause doubling the inspector general's annual stipend, from £200 to £400. Not that the opposition to this was widespread. Sir Francis Hutchinson sustained the battle against Sir Jeremiah singlehanded. When he first objected, on 11 March, Hely-Hutchinson pointed to Fitzpatrick's train of achievement, including the 'many lives' saved by his intervention at Clonmel. He added that this exertion had been made almost at his own [Fitzpatrick's] private expense, for the trifling salary allowed by the public was scarcely sufficient to maintain the horses which carried him from one end of the Kingdom to the other.[12]

When Sir Francis Hutchinson renewed his opposition six days later, another privy councillor, O'Neil, replied that everyone who had troubled himself to follow the course of prison reform knew that Sir Jeremiah's zeal and diligence were unequalled in the entire public service:

to devote himself to his duty he had given up his profession, and he had trusted ... to the generosity of the public for such reward as his conduct might merit.[13]

The House of Commons generally agreed with O'Neil that the increase in salary was a basic act of common justice, and Hutchinson was easily overborne. The Bill was passed on to the Lords, without further change, on 20 March. None the less the tussles over Sir Jeremiah's salary were ominous. At precisely this time, the committee investigating the charter schools was in session, and Fitzpatrick was proffering his very damaging testimony. Sir Francis Hutchinson was both a member of the Incorporated Society's central committee and its main parliamentary advocate, so that we may safely ascribe some if not all of his opposition to the salary increase to revenge and pique. The Society had of course many more supporters in the upper House, and when the Bill entered committee there on 25 March, Carhampton opened his argument for rejection with an attack upon the proposed increase. The Lords' opposition to the measure was largely expressed (in almost early Victorian fashion!) in terms of over-government and over-expenditure in general. Perhaps these really were the governing sentiments. But the timing and the direction of the cavilling were such that it is difficult to avoid the conclusion that it was Sir Jeremiah's offence against the Society which was being punished. Evidently some attack against him had been expected, for his sole defender in the debate, Mountgarret, had the details of his 1786-7 expenditure (down to the charges for horses and for clerks used in the compilation of the annual report) at his fingertips. At any rate, when Earlsfort proposed the postponement of the Bill for six months — that is, effectively, its rejection — the Lords readily agreed, without a division being called.[14]

Next day, in the House of Commons, Holmes fiercely denounced this irresponsibility, in particular the treatment of the inspector general, to whom the public already owed an incalculable debt. He wished to move an address to make good the money lost to Sir Jeremiah by the action in 'another place'. But at that stage in the session the House was very thin and he appealed instead to the executive:

> the reward was a debt of justice to the merits and attentions of Sir Jerome; and as the House had acknowledged that debt, he doubted not that Government would act consonant to their intentions.[15]

Meanwhile Holmes secured the publication of the evidence before the 1788 gaols committee — 'such enormities as would astonish the public' — in order that the disgraceful conduct of the House of Lords might be exposed.

Although it was not apparent at the time, this was a climacteric in Irish prison reform. As has been said, we do not know the contents of the 1788 Bill, because it was never enacted. But we can fairly guess its substance from the committee's resolutions and the clauses which we know to have been withdrawn and those which we know to have been added. It seems clear that it was a typical second-stage amendment measure. Various further deficiencies in the working of the original legislation, and weaknesses in the inspectorial system, had been revealed, and given dramatic force by lurid testimony. Such, in the mid-nineteenth century, would form the prelude to another round of administrative and regulative changes, a second or third Amendment Act in a sequence joining one major statute to the next. But in the Irish circumstances of 1788 such a measure could fail for quite trivial or even personal reasons, despite the solid support of the executive and the House of Commons. The truth was that prison reform had had a very lucky run in the Irish Parliament. Now fortune turned; or perhaps we should say that the movement, in its parliamentary aspect, had become identified with an individual who had offended an interest with the power to block further legislative change. At any rate, the customary pattern failed. The gaols committee was reassembled comparatively late in the 1789 session, once Fitzpatrick's report for 1788 had been received; and Griffith reintroduced the Gaols Bill on 22 April.[16] But if the Bill did clear the House of Commons again — and even this is not certain — it failed to make its way through the House of Lords. Nor were the findings of the 1789 committee ever published. In 1790 the receipt of Sir Jeremiah's annual report for the preceding year was once more the signal for Holmes to move for the setting up of a committee to scrutinise the prison system.[17] But this committee never reported. A general election intervened and brought an early end to legislative business. It also cost Griffith his seat in the House of Commons. This was a serious loss for by now Griffith shared with Holmes the leadership of the prison reform lobby. The era of annual gaols scandals and annual gaols legislation had really come to an end in 1788. This was not only confirmed but also obvious by the end of 1790.

II

Although the process of government growth in terms of legislation had been halted, 'progress' did not cease on every point. Setting aside for the moment Fitzpatrick's day-to-day activity, and the never-finished business of insolvent debtors and salaries and fees, the provisions for transportation under the 1786 Act[18] are worth some attention. Broadly speaking, these empowered the Irish central government to send convicts to any part of British North America or to any other place outside Europe (this last provision being so formulated as to include the Barbary Coast among the possible destinations!). Before the American war, the individual Irish counties had been responsible for transporting their own convicts, which was done by sending them across the Atlantic one by one or in small handfuls on ordinary merchant vessels. The 1786 Act, however, rendered transportation a national business and envisaged large consignments sent on ships exclusively hired for convicts. But even in this the state was to be involved no further than to contract out the enterprise to private speculators for an agreed sum.

Although the British government began sending convicts to New South Wales in 1787, there was some doubt as to whether this recourse was open to the Irish; and in any event the cost, variously estimated at £60 to £100 *per capita*, was generally regarded as prohibitive. When the first two vessels from Dublin sailed in 1788, their destination — though a secret and the subject of wide-ranging rumour — was almost certainly Nova Scotia.[19] But wherever it may have been, it was never reached. One ship was seized by the convicts and headed towards France: several of the triumphant mutineers were soon back in Dublin. The captain of the other vessel unloaded 140 of his charges at New London, Connecticut, and others at Sandy Hook, New Jersey — in part because he was bribed, and in part no doubt because this saved time and trouble. Again, it was not long before the convicts began to trickle back to Ireland.

Despite the farcical conclusion of the 1788 ventures, two further shiploads were despatched from Dublin in June 1789. One ended up at

Barbuda, a tiny West Indian island with a population of only 1,500. The fate of the unfortunate transportees is — mercifully perhaps — unknown. The other vessel, the *Duke of Leinster*, was probably meant to reach Nova Scotia; but 'a kind of Spotted putrid Fever'[20] having broken out at sea, the captain dumped the convicts at the first land sighted, on the desolate coast of Newfoundland. Another tragicomedy then took place. Newfoundland was still primarily a summer fishing station, equally incapable of employing or of supervising the detention of the convicts; and after much confusion, indignation and alarm, most of them were rounded up and eventually returned to Portsmouth on a chartered vessel. This precipitated a major bureaucratic and even constitutional tussle between the British and Irish governments as to who should pay the bills and where the convicts should at last come to rest: at one point a revenue cutter was despatched from Dublin to intercept the transport carrying the convicts from Portsmouth and bribe its captain to stay at sea *pro tem*. Finally after nearly six months' journeying and the useless expenditure of a great deal of money most of the prisoners were back in Dublin's Newgate.

Fitzpatrick had played no part in the fiascos of 1788-9, although he had talked to many of the convicts on their way to transportation or after their return, surreptitious or enforced as this last might be. Clearly, the experiments in contracting out the business had proved disastrous; and in the autumn of 1789 he set about seriously considering how the problem of the long-term prisoner or habitual offender might be answered. His first step was a study tour of English workhouses and penitentiaries, in Shropshire, Oxfordshire, London, East Anglia and perhaps other regions. The workhouses yielded him nothing of value, apart from some organisational detail, for Ireland had no poor law. Much the same was true of the prison system in places such as Oxford, where the convicts were engaged on public works outside the gaols, for Ireland did not lend itself to such projects, partly because of the great cheapness of 'free' labour there and partly because of the want of appropriate employment. It was the penitentiaries of Norfolk, and particularly the first to be set up, Wymondham, which provided Sir Jeremiah with his models.[21] Wymondham was a small prison, the average number of inmates at a time being only forty. But its 'turnover' was very rapid. In the six years of its operation, to that date, over five hundred convicts had been discharged, many of them, it was claimed, to a life of usefulness or at the least of respectable labour. Like all penitentiaries proper, Wymondham was based upon isolation, silence, compulsory regular work and religious instruction and exhortation to effect the desired 'moral' change. Those who brought trades with them to the gaol continued to engage in them where practicable. The rest were taught (by a 'master') hemp and flax dressing or rope and cord making, or else set up as wood-choppers or sawyers. All might work over-hours, and receive payment *pro rata* on their discharge; and if their behaviour was satisfactory during their first year at large, they were given additionally the same sum from general prison funds. A further reward for diligent labour and conformity to the expectations of Wymondham might be commutation of sentence. On the other hand, idleness or recalcitrance were penalised by the withholding of these advantages. In short, it was meant to be a regime of carrot and stick or (in Sir Jeremiah's more elegant phrase) the wreath and the rod. Two other features of Wymondham appealed particularly to Fitzpatrick: first, it paid its way and, secondly, among its superintendent's qualities was 'humanity to pleas for the feelings of the sufferers', for 'by rigorous severity, the heart becomes hardened'.

Upon his return from England, Fitzpatrick dashed off a forty-two-page pamphlet, *Thoughts on Penitentiaries*. The dedication to Fitzgibbon (now Lord Chancellor and Lord Fitzgibbon) was more than formal. It both began and ended with a lengthy personal appeal for his intervention — and not without some ground for hope. Fitzgibbon had always been a friend, if a distant one, to prison reform, and he was at that particular juncture heavily and angrily involved in the current imbroglio over the *Duke of Leinster*. Sir Jeremiah struck at the transportation 'system' while this particular iron was still hot. Not that he believed it could be dispensed with altogether. There would always be an irreducible minimum of irreformables. But, resting on his long experience of Irish criminals, he concluded that they would probably average less than forty a year, only one-quarter or one-fifth of the number generally regarded as subjects for transportation. He excluded those whose death sentences had been commuted, arguing that if royal clemency had been exercised, either their circumstances or their qualities must be such as to raise the hope of reformation:

> If such should prove the happy consequence . . . the present age could have to boast of the beneficient acts, adding humanity to the liberality, useful improvements, and other splendid advantages of the 18th century.[22]

In fact, Sir Jeremiah, although he could not see his way to dispensing with it altogether, was generally inimical to transportation. He quoted with approval Burn's tart remark, in *Penalties*, that the community rather than the criminal suffered by this practice, in losing the fruits of all his future labours; as well as Beccaria's, that transportation sent the criminal from the country in which he had offended and where his punishment might serve as an example to one where he had never transgressed.[23] Fitzpatrick also discarded, as subjects for penitentiaries, the great mass of petty offenders, those who had merely broken some 'social contract' and whose crimes were too trivial to call for a change of heart or habit. Thus the body with which he was concerned was comparatively small: in his own words, 'the youthful, the giddy and the unthinking', those who were as yet but 'seedlings for the gallows',[24] and perhaps also some slightly more hardened offenders. The most promising category for reclamation was of course the juveniles. Several of the convicts on the *Duke of Leinster* were boys of twelve or thirteen years, and even younger children had been included among the other consignments of 1788-9.

Once more, Sir Jeremiah's essay was largely derivative, with much of the derivation handsomely acknowledged. Once more Howard was freely drawn upon, although in this case William Eden's *Principles of Penal Law*, published eighteen years before, was the more important source. In one vital respect however Fitzpatrick, tacitly at least, departed from the received model of the penitentiary. Religion, crucial in Eden's and Howard's schemes, played virtually no part in Sir Jeremiah's. Occasionally he sketched an obeisance in this direction, and it was of course never specifically repudiated or even slighted. But he clearly regarded it as a minor or negligible force in the reformative process. He seems to have taken it (*faute de mieux* perhaps) that solitude, silence and work would generally by themselves suffice. He did however lay more stress on the wreath and less on the rod than his English counterparts, and the sympathy and kindness which he looked for in the keeper (or 'governor') may have been seen, to some extent, as a sort of substitute for clerical exhortation. On the other hand, Fitzpatrick put less emphasis than the English upon the financial savings of the system. True, the expected economies (in the narrow monetary as well as in the general national sense) were deployed as a powerful argument in favour of the penitentiary in Ireland. But he warned against assuming that it would necessarily pay its way, let alone be profitable after the fashion of a Wymondham. Still, the penitentiary would always cost less than transportation, even if — as would be far from the case — there were no return at all from the prisoners' labour; and in any event, establishing a spirit of industry, reformation and obedience . . . being the intention of Penitentiaries, it is to be hoped, that the idea of profit will bear no competition.[25]

As ever, Fitzpatrick came into his own when he turned to the practicalities. Even his findings at Wymondham were translated into detailed tabulations, and his knowledge of the Irish convict 'system', extending to hundreds of individual Irish convicts and acquired over many years, gave great weight and force to his depiction of the problem and the choices. In proposing penitentiaries for Ireland, Sir Jeremiah set out the cases for and against the 'districtal' and the local plan. The 'districtal' or regional might consist of two, four or half a dozen institutions depending on whether the two largest cities (Cork and Dublin), the Irish provinces (Leinster, Munster, Connaught and Ulster), or the assize circuits were chosen as the basis. Such a system would have three advantages. It would offer economies of scale, very great economies of scale if only two penitentiaries were erected. It would also make it practicable to locate them only in major cities, where 'advantageous employ would be more readily found'. Most important of all, were the possibilities of specialisation:

> the improvements of mind and body (the great objects) would be more easily and systematically effected, in having fewer proper and intelligent keepers, instructors — in respect to labour or taskmasters to provide.[26]

But the financing of any regional scheme presented difficulty. The county was the basic unit of taxation and public expenditure, and counties varied markedly in resources. Should each county within a district be charged the same or charged *pro rata* according to its income? Moreover, the use made of the regional penitentiary by particular counties might vary prodigiously from time to time. The adjoining Munster counties of Tipperary and Waterford had had, respectively, 140 and 3 convictions during a recent circuit. Further, Fitzpatrick envisaged the stay in a penitentiary as comparatively short — prolonged solitude he regarded as psychologically dangerous, and he assumed that those who did not seem to be responding to the penitentiary treatment would be returned quickly to holding prisons. Thus any attempt to divide the expenditure on an individual basis, according to county of origin, would soon produce a hopeless administrative tangle. Sir Jeremiah glanced wistfully at the obvious solution, that the regional penitentiaries be paid for entirely by the state and not the counties. But this was too revolutionary a change in method and thinking to hold out much promise of success immediately.

The county plan would have of course weaknesses corresponding to the districtal advantages. But it had advantages, chiefly practical and and political, of its own. First, it might be fitted into the existing prison system with very little disturbance. Many counties and cities were building or about to build new gaols, parts of which might be readily converted to penitentiary use. The local inspectors already in office might extend their supervision to the new ventures, reporting annually upon them to the inspector general and twice a year to the judges of assize, as part of their regular obligations. Finance would create no administrative problems. The grand juries could either add the sum required for buildings, salaries and materials for the convicts' work to the ordinary prison presentment or set up a separate account to cover deficits in the penitentiary's working. Finally, local *amour propre* would be satisfied and power and patronage kept in local hands.

> The Grand jury, or Magistrates of the county would likewise have to appoint the Keeper, the Task-master or Instructor of Labour — all of whom would be under their absolute dominion, and of their special choice.[27]

Although he did not choose specifically between the two, it seems clear that, other things being equal, Fitzpatrick would have preferred the more centralised and sophisticated districtal form of penitentiaries. But he evidently believed that the local form had much the better chance of adoption, and devoted considerable space to anticipating and countering possible objections to it: these ranged from the number of cells needed to the unhappy 'precedent' of the existing Irish houses of correction. Overall, Fitzpatrick's handling of the organisational choices is most impressive work, a model — to look into the future — of the sort of brief 'situation paper' which an able upper civil servant might present to his political master today.

The pamphlet was published at the beginning of 1790, evidently with the blessing of the executive; and it was left to the chief baron, Yelverton, to carry the project forward. His first step was to submit it for comment to every grand jury in the country. Only ten, almost all from the north or west, replied. Of the rest, one answered that 'in the bustle of electioneering' it was impossible to give it due consideration, and doubtless the imminence of the general election explains other defaulters. All the respondent grand juries approved of the idea generally, if in some cases confusedly too. Two at least were inclined towards the districtal form. Cavan supported a regional penitentiary for each province, if it could be self-supporting, and Derry also favoured a provincial system, adding, as the alternative, that a national establishment some distance from Dublin might 'be attended with great advantage to the community'.[28]

Encouraged by these replies, the executive eventually in 1792 secured an Act permitting the commutation of transportation in penitentiaries.[29] But although a Penitentiaries Act was generally regarded as a rival to transportation, this was — as Fitzpatrick himself agreed — not completely the case. Most people accepted that there was a core of irreclaimable 'professional' criminals on whom it would be well worth spending even £70 each to be rid of them, in New South Wales, for ever. Accordingly an Act was rushed through, in the short parliamentary session of 1790, to authorise the transportation of Irish felons to Botany Bay;[30] and in the following year the first consignment of 147 was despatched.[31]

Meanwhile, well before the passage of the Penitentiaries Act, the first of these institutions was actually set up in Dublin by executive action.[32] There can be little doubt that Fitzpatrick was at work behind the scenes, bringing this about. In the first rehearsal of the subject in the House of Commons, on 15 February 1790, both Holmes and the Chancellor of the Exchequer, Parnell, were repeating his arguments and instances, though without attribution.[33] The *Freeman's Journal* seems also to have been a vehicle for Sir Jeremiah's opinions.[34] He was however aided in the campaign by the extraordinary overcrowding of Dublin's prisons during most of 1790, in part because of the re-incarceration of returned transportees of the 1788 and 1789 seasons and in part because of the failure of the Insolvent Debtors Bill of that year to clear the House of Lords before Parliament was prorogued. The overcrowding was of course accompanied by the usual alarms of gaol fever and gaol escapes.[35]

As early as June 1790, the decision had been taken to open a penitentiary in Dublin.[36] Three months later, on 12 October, the former St James's Street Bridewell was taken over for this purpose, and the first cartload of convicts carried there from Newgate: it included three boys of 11, 12 and 13 years respectively.[37] From the beginning of 1790, fears had been expressed that the penitentiaries would open up new mines for jobbery.[38] Perhaps it was for this reason that Sir Jeremiah himself took charge of St James's Street and that the undertaking was officially described as an 'experiment'. But he himself would certainly have welcomed both steps without any ulterior justification. He was always eager to direct affairs himself, and particularly anxious to exhibit the merits of the penitentiary system to the capital. The establishment, whose declared object was 'to receive . . . and put to hard labour such convicts as were considered capable of reformation', was small, with less than fifty inmates at a time.[39] Probably, though not certainly, the majority were boys or youths, being instructed by regular masters in shoe-making, ribband-weaving and similar trades. It is not clear whether the forms of 'hard labour' in which the adult prisoners toiled were more laborious or less skilled.

Whether or not the 'experiment' should be regarded as successful, in terms of Fitzpatrick's hopes, is difficult to say. In the first two years of its existence, only 79 convicts were admitted, some of them as young as nine years of age. Of these, nineteen had been returned to Newgate as irreformable, and thirteen pardoned, all of whom were subsequently reported to be conducting themselves 'excellently' as 'Tradesmen, Dealers & Servants'. Evidently no boys were among those set free in 1791. This seems a modest enough achievement. But when a House of Commons committee, chaired by Holmes, visited St James's Street at the beginning of 1793, it reported upon the penitentiary with the warmest approbation.[40] In particular, the committee was impressed by the quasi-apprenticeship system for the boys. It recommended the immediate enlargement of the building at St James's Street, the provision of more capital for materials so that the convicts could be constantly employed and (rather more ominously) 'above all, a sufficient Power to enforce and establish Subordination'. The committee was in no doubt that Sir Jeremiah's experiment had succeeded. But its enthusiasm should not perhaps be taken at face value. Through Holmes or otherwise, Fitzpatrick probably nudged it in this direction. In any event, it was clearly the fruit of an anti-transportation movement. The main recommendation of the report was that transportation should be abandoned altogether, and replaced by the penitentiary system all over Ireland. The committee argued that the expense of transportation — 301 Irish convicts had been sent to New South Wales in 1792 at a cost of nearly £20,000 — was insupportable. On the other hand, the recent improvements in county gaols, it was said, had rendered a local system of penitentiaries practicable, and grand juries should be empowered to present for them. Savings apart, such a change would be more equitable and humane. With these predilections, the committee was unlikely to have regarded Fitzpatrick's venture with a very critical eye.

Meanwhile early in 1791 Parnell had invited Bentham to submit a sketch plan for an Irish penitentiary — doubtless to be multiplied all about the country, if it were successful. Presumably, Parnell had learned of Bentham's interest in prison architecture through the arrangements which he was currently making for the publication of his *Panopticon* in Dublin. Bentham responded enthusiastically. But although his plan was approved by Dunn, the architect of the Dublin Newgate, Parnell was sceptical of Bentham's costings — a foreshadowing of the British government's later (and well justified) scepticism of the costings of his Millbank project. 'If you won't have a good and cheap prison,' Bentham replied angrily to the Irish Chancellor of the Exchequer, 'then have a dear and bad one.'[41] None the less, he went on with undiminished vigour 'to draw up specifications, suggest architects, and even draft an advertisement for manufacturers to undertake management of prison labour'.[42] The advertisement concealed the nature of the undertaking, merely announcing that the manufacture, engaging two to three hundred people, was 'to be carried out by new hands who will require to be taught the business'. But the Irish government had had enough of Bentham now, and withdrew their commission. Angrily he 'kicked the penitentiary business out of doors', taking some revenge however by charging Dublin Castle £92 for his expenses.[43] Fitzpatrick may well have had a hand in the rejection of the sage. Parnell and other members of the administration would probably have consulted him on Bentham's plans, and his particular admirer, Holmes, was very likely to have been involved in the negotiations. But there is no direct evidence upon the point.

The subsequent passage of enabling legislation for the development of the penitentiary system, and the appointment of the 1793 committee,[44] make it clear that the Bentham episode did not dampen the enthusiasm of the penitentiarites. But in fact no new penitentiaries were built in Ireland until after the Act of Union, and by 1794 St James's Street itself was half-empty. When war with France broke out, the convicts there were permitted to enlist, and to most of the men and youths the army represented an escape from servitude. Their director himself was, in effect, to follow their example before 1793 was out: by the year's end, Fitzpatrick had entangled himself in army medicine, and would never return either to the penitentiary or his larger prison duties. Meanwhile, the keepers of St James's Street decamped, carrying with them the proceeds of two years' hard labour by the inmates, a mere eighteen of whom remained with only bread and water for their sustenance.[45] St James's Street survived after a fashion;

and when at last, more than two years later, a successor to Fitzpatrick[46] was appointed, he struggled hard to set it upon its feet, as a national and not merely a Dublin institution. Despite the support of the lord lieutenant and chief secretary[47] of the day, he failed. The rebellion of 1798 intervened, and government and Parliament had much larger issues to engross them. But Sir Jeremiah's venture was not altogether fruitless. When in 1801 the next Irish penitentiary was established in Smithfield, Dublin, it was upon the St James's Street principle, and exclusively for offenders under fifteen years, all of whom were to be 'bred' to tailoring, shoe-making, comb-making or weaving. In 1808 it was pronounced by Fitzpatrick's successor to have proved remarkably successful;[48] and in its turn Smithfield was to serve as the model for other Irish undertakings. In his last years, Fitzpatrick himself was its benefactor, perhaps its only benefactor. He had always been concerned that children should be properly shod and clothed.

III

By a happy chance, the House of Commons committee of 1793, although concerned essentially with the substitution of penitentiaries for transportation, also reviewed the seven years of Sir Jeremiah's service and its effects.[49] This was fortunate because it could not have been foretold that this would be the last balance sheet to be cast, that Fitzpatrick was about to quit Irish gaols forever. He himself described in a bold, broad passage the change which the prison system had undergone in the past decade. In the early 1780s, he testified, violence, intimidation and extortion were rampant in the gaols. Rapes, robberies and even murders were commonplace, and committed, practically speaking, with impunity. Of course, intoxication, unchecked, was the ultimate cause of most of this internal prison crime. Disease and death reigned. Accommodation was generally filthy and airless. A large number of the prisoners were housed in damp underground cells. Almost all lacked bedding and even straw, and many had to lie on clay floors, wet and odorous. Food was bad, scanty and uncertainly distributed. Where the gaol construction was ramshackle and insecure the prisoners were so loaded with irons that they could scarcely move. The natural consequence of such a concatenation of misery was a succession of outbreaks of typhoid and other contagious diseases.

Most of this, Fitzpatrick claimed, had been swept away during the 1780s. Garnish and the other official extortions had altogether disappeared. He could not say quite the same for drunkenness, where the battle still continued. But by and large it had been checked. Cleanliness had been generally established, and the sick provided with hospital rooms and humane treatment. Food, bedding and ventilation were regularly and adequately supplied; and even periodic bathing was now practicable and compulsory in most gaols. Almost all too now segregated men from women, debtors from felons and – a new wartime problem, presumably – deserters from the rest. Of course, the necessary preliminary to these beneficent changes had been prison reconstruction and rebuilding. In the past four or five years, thirteen new gaols had been erected and four completely renovated; currently eight others were being built and three more being modernised; and several fresh ventures in one category or other were being prepared. Even the Dublin prisons, and even that former seat of evils, Newgate, had shown recently a most remarkable improvement. Sir Jeremiah modestly refrained from claiming much credit on his own behalf for this general transformation, preferring to praise Parliament for its humane legislation and the grand juries for their ready presentments. But his pride in one achievement, his earliest goal as inspector general, burst through the official decorum. He had almost eliminated the old practice of detaining prisoners indefinitely without charge. After his recent national tour of inspection, only a single person still remained in this unfortunate condition, and he was a lunatic in Cork city gaol 'into whose Condition and Cause of Detention an inquiry is now making'.

The picture was not, however, quite without shade. Although the majority of the local inspectors were reasonably diligent, some still were unsatisfactory – whether in enforcing the regulations or compiling the returns is not made clear. Not all the clerks of court were sufficiently timely or accurate in furnishing Fitzpatrick with the material on their assizes which the 1786 Act required, 'with corresponding deficiencies in his annual Reports'. Similarly, although gaolers and turnkeys conducted themselves with far more 'Tenderness' than before, 'a few Instances lately of their Cruelty are to be seen in his Reports'. This last was so serious a business that Fitzpatrick recommended that the local inspectors be required to add a section to their biannual returns evaluating the conduct of the keepers and deputy-keepers in their region. But much the worst feature of the current prison system, he reported, was the bridewells and corporation gaols. These had been subjected to the same regulation as prisons proper by the Amendment Act of 1787. But simply sweeping them into a net designed for larger institutions had not worked. Of the forty-five bridewells in the kingdom (several of them far removed from the county towns), only ten fulfilled their statutory obligation in providing bedding, and only three their obligation to furnish food. Fitzpatrick probably hoped that the select committee would recommend a further Prisons Amendment Bill to deal specifically with the bridewells and corporation gaols and with further surveillance of the keepers. Doubtless he would have liked some further means of compelling all local inspectors or clerks of court to perform their duties on pain of dismissal; but it was difficult to envisage any new step which grand juries would not resent and repudiate as an interference with their powers or patronage. But the committee's *idée fixe* was penitentiaries. It looked forward airily to 'complete reformation' of the ordinary gaols, in the light of the recent progress of reform, and it turned Fitzpatrick's evidence of the advances in prison building and segregation into a springboard for the launching of its darling schemes. None the less, for what it was worth, its report enthusiastically endorsed the inspector general's account of the improvements of the past decade, attributing them primarily to his incomparable 'zeal' and 'activity', and looking to these qualities as sufficient to maintain the current happy state, and to cross the few t's and dot the few i's which were still outstanding.

Obviously, the committee was an uncritical body, with its eye on other things. Its estimate of Sir Jeremiah's stewardship may have added little to his own, which should not, of course, be taken at its full face value. The reports of his successor as inspector general, the Rev. Foster Archer, made it clear that many prisons were in a deplorable condition at the close of the 1790s — insanitary, ill-kept, ill-disciplined, dirty and overcrowded.[50] How is the apparent discrepancy to be explained? Three rough bridges may be thrown across the chasm. First, almost a year elapsed before it was certain that Fitzpatrick had abandoned the inspector generalship; and almost three years elapsed between Fitzpatrick's departure and Archer's entry into office. In these intervals, prison regulation seems to have collapsed in many areas. The inspector generalship was the driving-wheel in the system developed in the 1780s; and it became clear that most local inspectors and most crown clerks — to say nothing of keepers and turnkeys — needed to be driven. Moreover, the inspector generalship had been designed for a quite extraordinary man, and Fitzpatrick's successor was a commonplace, untrained and unenthusiastic functionary, apparently appointed for political convenience[51] and without any prior knowledge of or interest in the gaols. There was little hope that Archer would make up the ground lost in

1793-6. Secondly, Archer's reports on Irish prisons describe conditions from 1797 onwards. Thus they relate to years when the gaols were overstrained by the wholesale imprisonments and cruel punishments which followed the disarming of Leinster, Munster and Connaught in 1796-7. Archer's darkest descriptions are in fact of Leinster prisons in the second half of 1798, when they were crammed with survivors of the Wexford rising awaiting bloody or other retribution. Thirdly, we should perhaps allow something for rising expectations. What would have passed without particular notice in the late 1770s might appal two decades later. Fitzpatrick's own work must have raised immeasurably the examination standard. Certainly Archer's accounts included no outbreaks of disease upon the old scale, no instances of violence and extortion, no chained and bolted men, no starving prisoners, no dungeons underground.

These considerations should modify scepticism — if much scepticism is felt — about Sir Jeremiah's achievement as depicted in 1793. Doubtless, there must be some set-off for self-satisfaction, long familiarity with the problems, administrative tactics and pride of authorship. But not much needs to be allowed. Serious crime was at a low level in 1791 and still lower in 1792, while transportation to New South Wales was already drawing those who were presumably the most 'intractable' prisoners in both these years. Fitzpatrick's depiction of 1793 was probably, then, close to the current actuality, especially in the terms in which he was asked to make it — the cumulative changes of a decade. The very little evidence to be found of his work during 1789-92 does suggest that he was moving on a tableland of moderate success. Dublin was perhaps the field of greatest triumph, not indeed in that it now led the way in reform, but because the gap between the conduct of the metropolitan and country prisons had almost been closed. In 1792, Cavan suffered the first large-scale outbreak of gaol fever since Clonmel's visitation in 1786; and Fitzpatrick, hastening there and taking command of all in the emergency, produced a similar transformation, with similar *éclat*. Perhaps the very fact that prisons descended, by and large, to the humdrum, and that the inspector generalship itself seems to have declined largely into a routine, was a measure of his success: happy is the regulation without a history. Certainly he retained his original pattern of surveillance, with a central office in Dublin, systematic tours on horseback and a clerk (sometimes two) for copying and statistical compilation. How this was paid for is unknown. In his last year in office he received something over £500, and possibly this had been the case since 1788 or 1789. His stipend was never raised above the original

£200 per annum, and the only record of a further payment to him in the parliamentary estimates is of a trivial sum in reimbursement of his hire of a 'nurse-tender' in Dublin.[52] One's best guess is that Dublin Castle responded to Holmes's appeal in 1788[53] and met the expenses of Fitzpatrick's office – as against his salary – from resources at the disposal of the executive.

By 1793 prison reform in Ireland had reached, and was held fast in, what may be regarded as the third stage of a species of administrative revolution – the first two being the initial intervention and its amendment and adjustment after the first shock of attempted enforcement. Doubtless the directions in which Fitzpatrick would have wished to advance were, first, further control over those who were effectively his subordinates, in short, further centralisation of authority; secondly, further lateral extension of the regulation, as with bringing the bridewells and town gaols up to the level of the rest; and thirdly, a more radical solution of the general problem, such as the widespread adoption of the penitentiary, with a corresponding diminution of the place which the traditional prison represented within the system. How things would have gone had war, with all its immediate and remote effects, not broken out, it is of course impossible to say. But further changes in the 1790s seemed unlikely. Despite the fervid recommendations of the 1793 committee, the instant multiplication of penitentiaries would have raised very great difficulties of money and management. As for the inspector general, all the indications are that he had reached his bourn – for a few years, at least – by 1790. The prospects of a further Prisons Amendment Act, upon which any significant advance in the powers or scope of the central authority depended, looked poor thereafter. Of course, the situation might have quickly changed, and in fact the crisis of 1797-9 might have provided Fitzpatrick with the opening for a further reorganisation of the entire system. But to one standing at 1793, the particular wave of change sweeping inwards since the early 1780s must have looked a spent force.

On the other hand, we should not forget that such a change as marked the 1780s had general social ramifications which took a considerable period to absorb. This is perhaps best illustrated in the two movements which had accompanied prison reform proper from the start. Acquitted prisoners' fees and insolvent debtors presented real problems of adjustment. In part the opposition to retaining in gaol acquitted prisoners was a disreputable desire to keep all who might be 'criminals' behind walls. But in part it sprang from the common eighteenth-century practice of organising occupations upon the basis of fees, not salaries. As in the case of gaolers and turnkeys, a fundamental change of outlook and new sources of remuneration were required for the transition; and these took time to come about or into being. Similarly, the opposition to the release of insolvent debtors was not entirely benighted and repressive. Baulked creditors might end as debtors themselves. Even more to the point, debtors flocked into the gaols and spunging houses on the whisper that a Bill indemnifying the incarcerated from liability for their debts was being prepared. In 1782 the Dublin prisons had been cleared completely of insolvents. In other years, lists were drawn up on various criteria — length of imprisonment, size of debt or friends in Parliament. To move on further to rejecting the entire notion of imprisoning insolvents, and arranging contractual relations generally upon some quite different basis, would involve a long and difficult journey. Here too society was at a half-way house at the close of the eighteenth century.

So it would not have been surprising if prison reform in Ireland came to a halt after its first hectic decade. The very idea of imprisonment for lengthy periods, and the very question, 'what was such a detention for?', were still comparatively new.[54] The wonder might rather be how much was done in half a dozen years. But all this is speculation. The essential fact remains, that although the *primum mobile* of it all set off in routine fashion upon his customary autumn tour in 1793, he was never to return.

Notes

1. *Parliamentary Register* (Ire.), vol. viii, pp. 150-1.
2. Ibid., pp. 347-8.
3. *Freeman's Journal*, 14-16 February 1788.
4. *Journals of the House of Commons* (Ire.), vol. xii, p. dxliii.
5. *Report of Committee on Gaols*, 3 March 1788, *Journals of H of C* (Ire.), vol. xii, p. dccxxxvi.
6. Ibid., pp. dccxxxiii-iv.
7. Ibid., p. dccxxxiv.
8. Ibid., p. dccxxxvi.
9. Foster Papers, D562/8967B, P.R.O. N.I., f.494.
10. *Journals of H of C* (Ire.), vo. xii, pp. 389, 397.
11. *Parliamentary Register* (Ire.), vol. viii, pp. 393-4.
12. Ibid., p. 395.
13. Ibid., p. 408.
14. *Freeman's Journal*, 25-27 March 1788.
15. *Parliamentary Register* (Ire.), vol. viii, pp. 425-6.
16. Ibid., vol. ix, p. 389.
17. Ibid., vol. x, p. 260.
18. 26 Geo III, c.24, clauses 64 and 66. Cf. *Dropmore Papers*, 7 vols. (Historical

Manuscripts Commission), vol. 1, pp. 546-8.
  19. For the 1788-9 transportations from Ireland, see J. [recte. G.] Martin, 'Convict Transportation to Newfoundland in 1789', *Acadiensis*, vol. v (1975), pp. 84-99.
  20. Letter from B. Lister, St. John's, C.O. 194/38, ff.89-90, quoted in Martin, 'Convict Transportation', p. 88.
  21. Fitzpatrick, *Thoughts on Penitentiaries*, pp. 22-9. For a study of similar endeavours in Gloucestershire, see E. Moir, 'Sir George Onesiphorous Paul' in H.P.R. Finberg (ed.), *Gloucestershire Studies* (Leicester, 1957), pp. 195-225. Among other magistrates and penal theoreticians and architects working or writing on penitentiaries in the period were Samuel Clowes the younger, Thomas Bayley, Sir Thomas Beevor, John Jebb, Jonas Hanway, George Moneypenny, James Blackburn and Robert Adam. (I am grateful to Dr J. Kerr for this information.)
  22. Fitzpatrick, *Thoughts on Penitentiaries*, p. 20.
  23. Ibid., p. 9.
  24. Ibid., pp. 38-9.
  25. Ibid., p. 34.
  26. Ibid., p. 37.
  27. Ibid., p. 36.
  28. This paragraph is based on H.J. Heaney, 'Richmond General Penitentiary, Dublin: the Failure of an Experiment' (MA thesis, Queen's University, Belfast), p. 18. He refers to CSO [Chief Secretary's Office] official papers, 2nd series, 508/17/4.
  29. 32 Geo. III, c.27.
  30. 30 Geo. III, c.32.
  31. T.J. Kiernan, *The Irish Exiles in Australia* (Dublin, 1954), p. 9.
  32. *Freeman's Journal*, 19-21 October 1790.
  33. Ibid., 13-16 February 1790.
  34. Ibid., 18-20 February 1790.
  35. Ibid., 11-13 March, 1-3 April, and 15-17 and 17-20 July 1790.
  36. Ibid., 10-12 June 1790.
  37. Ibid., 19-21 October 1790.
  38. Ibid., 22-24 June, 18-21 September, 9-11 December 1790.
  39. *Report of Committee on Gaols*, 11 July 1793, *Journals of H of C* (Ire.), vol. xv, p. ccccviii.
  40. Ibid.
  41. Bentham Papers, 117a/25, University College, London; quoted by Heaney, 'Richmond General Penitentiary', p. 20.
  42. Ibid., 117a/34, pp. 50-3.
  43. *Journals of H of C* (Ire.), vol. xv, p. 151.
  44. Heaney, 'Richmond Penitentiary', p. 21.
  45. Ibid.
  46. Rev. Foster Archer.
  47. Earl Camden and Thomas Pelham respectively.
  48. *Report of Inspector General of Prisons*, H.C. 1808, ix (239).
  49. *Report of Committee on Gaols*, 11 July 1793, *Journals of H of C* (Ire.), vol. xv, pp. ccccviii-ix.
  50. *Journals of H of C* (Ire.), vol. xvii, pp. cxcix-ccxiv; vol. xviii, pp. dlxxii-dclxxxiii; vol. xix, pp. ccxxxiv-cccxlviii; vol. xx, pp. dccxxxii-dcccxlix.
  51. See Inglis, *Freedom of the Press in Ireland*, p. 88. In 1794 Archer obliged the authorities by initiating a prosecution for libel against Denis Driscol of the *Cork Gazette*. 'The government tried to escape some of the responsibility' by this means.

52. *Journals of H of C* (Ire.), vol. xv, p. xl.
53. *Parliamentary Register* (Ire.), vol. viii, pp. 425-6.
54. R. Morgan, 'Divine Philanthropy: John Howard Reconsidered', *History*, vol. lxii, no. 206 (1977), pp. 392-4, 400-1. This paper also provides a valuable survey of late-eighteenth-century prison 'philosophies'. See also L. Radzinowicz, *A History of English Criminal Law and its Administration from 1750*, 4 vols. (London, 1948), vol. 1, pp. 151-6.

7 THE TRANSLATION, 1793-1794

If there is a pattern to men's lives, Fitzpatrick's was surely polygonal. The next change in the direction of his career, altering country and calling alike, would seem to have been altogether accidental. But with Sir Jeremiah chance had a habit of turning itself into opportunity on the spot. At any rate, the beginning point of this particular tangent was his arrival in Cork, probably in late November, in the course of his prisons tour of 1793. He was greeted with the news that the 'Philadelphian fever'[1] had broken out on board the transports of the 40th Regiment, then embarking at Cove[2] (half a dozen miles down river from the city) for Plymouth. As ever, he thrust himself into the hurly-burly.

> I waited on General Moucher, commander in chief at Cork & offered my services such as they might prove, which he accepted with marked thanks & accordingly by letter introduced me to Col. Bromfield, then on board the Pitt transport at Cove. On my arrival all was confusion and irregularity, the as yet healthful laying not only with the sick, but with the actually dying; and the former as were diseased continued in the very same berths, nearly as crowded (by what I hear) as the Guinea slaves, from which the tainted, putrid dead were the moment before removed; this the condition of the four transports, more particularly the *Whisk*.[3]

Sir Jeremiah's first care was to procure a hospital ship to house the infected. It took three days and Moucher's intervention to obtain the *Sarah* from the transport service. The *Sarah* was ill-suited for the purpose, being so low between decks that 'the height of the most lofty [berth] was but 2 feet', the sick were 'incapable on the necessary Occasions, of even going on their Knees', and Fitzpatrick himself had to be wheeled about on a chair when on his 'visits' three times a day.[4] Such as she was, however, the *Sarah* fell under Sir Jeremiah's total sway. The regimental surgeon was brushed aside, and relegated — literally — to the care of the well. As soon as a man fell ill he was transferred to the *Sarah* and Fitzpatrick's ministrations. But the same success did not immediately attend Sir Jeremiah's effort to secure the medicines, diet and drinks which he considered necessary.

According to army regulations, the private soldiers were placed under 'stoppages' once they were at sea. The 'justification' of this procedure was that it helped to clear off arrears of pay; and for the army being 'at sea' might include even weeks on end in a landlocked harbour, provided one was actually afloat. Stoppages were a serious matter for the sick at Cove. Their pay, which had to cover the cost of all food and drink other than King's rations, was reduced from twenty-one to eight pence per week. Fitzpatrick, to whom diet was of critical importance in the treatment of infection and in convalescence, 'prayed' at once for the restoration of the full 1s 9d weekly together with a *per capita* division of the proceeds of the ships' provisions which were to be put up for sale. He was disappointed. A transport service vessel for hospital use was all very well, but soldiers' pay encroached upon the colonel's own financial interests. In the end, it was agreed that the provisions should be sold, and the sum realised proportionately divided among the soldiers. But with malignant fever and dysentery abroad among the regiment, the price would be much depreciated. Fitzpatrick was furious. 'Your Lordship', he wrote later to Lord George Lennox, the Lieutenant-Governor of Plymouth, 'may well conceive what I felt on hearing such a declaration, Knowing that the most atrocious offenders in Irish prisons, when ill, are by our statute law, obliged to get every matter for their comfort and recovery.'[5]

He repaired to Cork and Moucher for the third time, once more successfully. It was not to be expected that Moucher would override Bromfield, the regimental commander, directly. But he did sanction Fitzpatrick's purchasing whatever he considered necessary for the sick, and guaranteed full reimbursement. With this undertaking in his pocket, Fitzpatrick had no further difficulties with the officers of the 40th in Cove. They complied with the great majority of his requests; and he himself paid for the remaining supplies with the promise of recompense once the ships' stores had been sold off, and Moucher's assurance that any shortfall would eventually be met.[6]

All this to-ing and fro-ing appears to have taken two to three weeks, and – prison inspection for the present, indeed for ever, quite set aside – Fitzpatrick spent at least three weeks more in attendance on the *Sarah*. When at last, in mid-January 1794, the regiment sailed for Plymouth, the flotilla included the hospital vessel, with Sir Jeremiah, having 'humanely volunteered the passage over in order to assist the sick',[7] still aboard. The 40th had spent nine weeks afloat in Cork harbour, and left forty of its men, nearly one-fifteenth of the whole, behind it, buried in Cove.

The transports – except for the *William and Mary* which became separated from the rest and ended up at Portsmouth – reached Plymouth on 20 or 21 January. In Fitzpatrick's eyes the passage itself provided a justification of his 'system', and of the dietary measures in particular. Although the *Sarah* carried, of course, none but infected men, only two had died aboard her during the crossing. The regular transports fared much worse. The *Whisk*, for example, lost four men on the voyage and landed no less than seventy sick. But the price of this gratification was further difficulties. In all nearly two hundred men were landed ill at Plymouth. Once more, Sir Jeremiah went straight to the top and showered the lieutenant-governor with requests for aid, medical speculations and ornate flattery. He proposed that the sick be sent at once to a shore hospital, that the convalescents 'and all suspicious persons' be separated from the remainder and that the fit men be removed from the vessels to barracks so that the ships could be fumigated and purified from stem to stern, and most of the bedding destroyed and the berths removed: 'Otherwise the infectious principle even at a remote day may, as by resurrection, live and rage.'[8]

We do not know fully what happened next. Certainly Fitzpatrick stayed for more than two weeks in Plymouth supervising the cleansing of the vessels and the transferences of the troops, and working at the isolation hospital with an army surgeon, Fleming, in whom he rejoiced to find 'not only medical abilities, but the essential qualification – humanity';[9] and certainly he won Lennox over altogether. Lennox was profoundly impressed by Fitzpatrick's charitable exertions and his expertise in treating infectious disease. Well into February two or three men were still dying daily of typhoid in the Plymouth hospitals, but Fitzpatrick was returning many more recovered patients to their companies. But of course Sir Jeremiah was not content with mere medical attendance and the improvisation of counter-measures. Within a few days of arriving at Plymouth he had composed a 'post-mortem', in more senses than one, upon the calamity which had struck the 40th.

The original cause, he found, had been 'the unwise conduct in sending several from the military hospital in Cork on board the transports as yet ill of the dysentery & malignant fever'. Equally unwise was the failure to land those who fell sick at once, or to seek a hospital ship before his own arrival at Cove. The transports themselves were grossly overloaded with men, women and children, their total tonnage, 1,034, being almost matched by the total number of passengers, 923.[10] Such a complement had been arranged on the mistaken assumption that crowding was a matter of small consequence on a short passage – as it happened, nearly eleven weeks passed between first embarkation and final landing in this particular case – and in any event no sea passage was so short that close packing might not produce disastrous results. Again, the intermingling of their families with the men aggravated the evils – many of the women, of course, being pregnant or lying-in; and the diet also helped to spread the infection as it consisted almost entirely of perishable food, 'kept pork, butter, cheese &c.'.[11]

All this Fitzpatrick regarded as the immediate chain of causation. The ultimate source of the trouble was the regimental commanders and surgeons. Many a colonel measured the strength of his regiment by its numbers (a very different matter, Fitzpatrick added, 'to its real efficiency, for altho' unacquainted with military matters, I should consider the hospital Tail the very worst that can follow either the camp or fleet');[12] and many a regimental surgeon from ignorance, timidity, or sycophancy pandered to his superior by passing the unfit as ready for service. Here Fitzpatrick was certainly putting his finger on a fundamental reason for the rapid spread of infection. In 1793 and early 1794 the government attempted to combine a hasty mustering of new troops with economy by defraying the cost of fresh levies through the sale of commissions. The officers had then to recoup themselves – or better – by trafficking in men. In April 1793, a lieutenant was already advertising in the London newspapers for one hundred recruits at a price of two thousand guineas; and, writes Fortescue, the system soon 'extended to the raising of a multitude of battalions which, for the most part, were no sooner formed than they were disbanded, and drafted into other corps'.[13] The net result was to raise the price of recruits and the value of those enlisted all round to anything up to £30 a head, depending on the time and place. 'Think of my bad luck about recruits', bemoaned Lady Sarah Napier, the sister of Lord George Lennox himself. 'If I had seen an officer one fortnight sooner who is here, he would have sold me 20 at 11 guineas per man. Is not that unfortunate; but they are now gone. My Dublin stock too, which was 40, has been reduced to 26.'[14] In such a military economy the pressure upon regimental officers and their medical subordinates to pass every man who could stand as active was very strong. In vain did Fitzpatrick now and on many later occasions point to the dreadful cost of the apparent saving: 'deprive an Army of Health and Spirits, what avails its Numbers? the Sick become an *Onus* in respect to their requiring protection, their Removals are expensive, and together with infecting others, they further injure the healthful by their consuming all the best Provisions'.[15] In this as in his analysis of the physical causes of infection, Sir Jeremiah wrote plain and simple sense. But the war department had so arranged the matter that the interests of the army as a whole clashed headlong here with the interests of its subordinate commanders.

Sir Jeremiah evidently drew up as well an elaborate programme of prevention and curtailment of infection among soldiers in movement, which cannot now be traced. But its substance is clear from letters which Lennox had asked him to compose, recommending a future course of action to deal with the infections which had plagued Plymouth ever since it became a major mustering point for troops from Ireland in late 1793. First, Fitzpatrick advised 'proper' military hospitals at Cork and Duncannon (the other troop embarkation point on the southern Irish coast) with responsible medical staff charged with certifying the fitness of the men before they were allowed aboard the transports. The Irish government could be relied on to assist in this although 'the fault by no means rests with [them] . . . of sending sick men on board, but with the regimental surgeons and commanding officers'.[16] Next, the casual arrangements for short passages should be abandoned. The standards of passenger space, provisioning and fittings should be brought closer to those laid down for regular ocean voyages, for the mere number of sea miles was no adequate measure of how much or how long the soldiers would have to endure upon the water. Moreover, when sailing was delayed, the soldiers should be disembarked 'or aired on shore every day', and the vital precautions of cleansing decks and berths, fumigation and blasting gunpowder repeated. Finally, women and children should not travel on the transports – certainly no woman should who was in danger of having to lie-in on board.[17]

Fitzpatrick had originally intended to return to Ireland within a few days of his arrival at Plymouth. But after a fortnight there he found – doubtless concocted – business to take him to London instead, and Lennox, who was now well on the way to regarding him as a *deus ex machina*, wrote to the Army Medical Board, enclosing copies of three long letters from Fitzpatrick to himself, and begging them to grant him an interview. This evidently went well, despite Fitzpatrick's tacit – and sometimes more than tacit – strictures upon army medicine. When later in the year references to Fitzpatrick began to appear in the board's correspondence, they were grateful, respectful and even deferential in tone. Far otherwise with Lord George himself. On 3 May he received from the board an insolent reply to his reiterated pleas for a permanent military hospital at Plymouth under some independent physician (he may well have had Fitzpatrick specifically in mind). The board told him that a large hospital would merely create overcrowding, the prime condition for infectious diseases, and that any hospital for soldiers must be in the charge of an army surgeon or physician.[18] Many months later Lennox told the War Office that he was so disgusted at the Medical Board's patronising, arrogant and complacent answers that he had washed his hands of the entire affair. After nearly two years of struggling for a permanent hospital (of course, he added, he knew very well that the infectious must be separated from the rest and did not for a moment mean them to be housed with the other sick), as well as the sight of men dying in the open because there was not room for them even in the stables commandeered for those in fever, he quite despaired.[19] But Fitzpatrick had meanwhile moved off upon another tangent, and this distanced him temporarily from Plymouth and Lord George.

Lord Moira's expedition to Brittany in December 1793 had proved abortive. It had, through no fault of his, sailed too late to be of use in the Vendée revolt, and the eight thousand troops had ended in the Channel Islands without ever having set foot in France.[20] There typhoid and dysentery had struck the transports, just about the time that it was striking the transports of the 40th in Cork. Many of Moira's troops were returned to Southampton, and dispersed along the Hampshire and Dorset coasts, and Moira himself had accompanied this portion of his force. Here was a new diversion for Sir Jeremiah. Close at hand to him at Plymouth was essentially the same situation as had first involved him in army medicine in Cork, except that the infected were being landed instead of embarked. It was also substantially the same sort of situation as he was currently embroiled in (or rather had currently embroiled himself in) in Plymouth. Moreover, Moira was an outstanding general officer, high in reputation and influence, and also Irish, perhaps even an acquaintance of Sir Jeremiah's in his parliamentary days in Dublin. Given all this, it is not at all surprising that Fitzpatrick proffered him his advice and assistance, probably in the course of his London visit.

The letter with which Fitzpatrick introduced himself to Moira was one of his most accomplished pieces of writing. Of course, it largely rehearsed yet again the sad history of the 40th, and the lessons to be drawn from their misfortunes. But practice had improved both the narrative and the analysis, and several additional matters were broached such as securing the personal cleanliness of the men, the freshness of their clothing and the diet of the sick. Moreover Fitzpatrick had now had some time to reflect upon the new field in which he found himself and in which, as things turned out, he was largely to work over the next

The Translation 155

nine years. Characteristic of his habit of trying to think a matter through to its foundations is the following passage, wherein he prefaced his preventive scheme by a consideration of the fundamental problems of the unmonied passenger in the days of sail.

— therefore it is My Lord, that without pointing at the conduct of any Individual, I consider it a Duty I owe the Government and Mankind, to point out what appears to me as necessary to avert the like Misfortune, as that which attended the 40th Regt in future; but before I come to make those Remarks, I beg to shew what occurs to me in respect to the State of the Sailor, and newly Embarked-Soldier.

— The former is by habit on his natural Element supplyed with sufficient Space, and with his accustomed Provisions: kept in a State of Activity, necessarily ventilated in the Shrouds, on Deck, and in Ships of War thro the Port-Holes, with his Hammock aired aloft in favorable Weather; whilst the Soldier, who in the first instance gets nauseated, of consequence has his Stomach and Bowels deranged, without the aid of the Officers Wine-Hamper or Chicken Coup, is thrown on Ships Provisions, widely Differing from his fresh Meat, Vegetables, Malt Liquor and Milk, his accustomed Cleanliness and Exercise are given over: the Space for his Existence is as it were sunk in the Womb of the Vessel — there crowded without the refreshing Streams of Air enjoyed thro' the Port-Holes or Cabbin-Windows: no possibility of airing, Hammocklike-his fixed Birth: the only accessible Spaces for Air, nearly covered with the Ships Boats when at Sea, and in rough Weather as completely closed as the fatal Hole at Calcutta: thus living on unaccustomed Food and deprived of accustomed Exercise, pure Air and Cleanliness — what is not to be expected? perhaps Your Lordship might Answer — Mortality — at least inefficiency on their landing, in place of necessary Alertness and Vigor.[21]

Fitzpatrick frankly confessed that he wrote in the hope of enlisting Moira's standing and influence in the matter; as ever he spoke of humanity and policy as working together, adding that Moira himself would appreciate both the ordinary soldier's sufferings and the economic and military waste in neglecting counter-measures. He put forward firmly but not immodestly his own claims to attention in this field. The medical problems were essentially those of gaol fever which he had been combating for many years and with such success in precautionary measures that there had been only two significant outbreaks in Irish prisons over the past seven years. Here he was indeed on strong ground. Both the regimental surgeon of the 40th and the Army Medical Board had concluded that it was gaol fever which had struck at Cove and Plymouth, and the same term was being employed for the affliction from which Moira's troops were suffering both in Jersey and Southampton. Fitzpatrick concluded by offering his services to Moira; at least his final sentence seems to mean as much:

> My Duty requires my immediate return to Ireland: but should any Endeavors of mine for the general Good of the State be considered of advantage, our Governments in essence being justly one and the same, I feel already an excuse, in obeying commands on this side the Water.[22]

In proposing further French leave for himself — he had already spent some three months away from prison inspection — Fitzpatrick may have felt justified in terms of 'war efforts'. Of course he had no administrative superior more specific than the Irish Parliament. He had no office routine. He arranged his own tours and determined his own duties. His only commitment in 1794 (which incidentally he never fulfilled) was to produce by March his annual report on the prisons in 1793. In this circumstance, he probably felt that he would be held blameless in Ireland for his temporary abandonment of the inspector generalship. The Irish House of Commons — to say nothing of Dublin Castle — was *en masse* decidedly 'patriotic' when it came to war with France, and both institutions must have been thoroughly familiar with the chaotic military improvisation, and the drifting and thrusting of helpful or unwilling amateurs into army business, which marked the first years of the conflict. At any rate, Sir Jeremiah was never reproached, let alone reprimanded, for his dereliction.

On the other hand, there can be no doubt that Fitzpatrick's inclination was with what he presented as a duty to humanity. He was by now passionately engaged by the new problems of army health. Immediately, it was diet and ventilation on the transports which struck his innovative mind as subjects for improvement.[23] For example, among the staple foods, the oatmeal used was, in his view, wrong in quality and poorly prepared. He at once altered the variety of oatmeal to be purchased, and prescribed a new method of cooking. So confident was he of the superiority of this method that he submitted it to the Navy

Board as well before he left Cork (perhaps the approach was made through Admiral Kingsmill, the naval commander at the station, whom he saw when trying to secure the *Sarah*). The Navy Board approved and adopted his proposal. Again, after the passage from Cork to Plymouth he devised, as he himself claimed, 'effectual, cheap and convenient Ventilators, and . . . Funnels or Transit-Air Holes, thro' the Decks', for use on the troop transports. As these examples indicate, Fitzpatrick was by now quite absorbed in fresh medical and mechanical questions. Doubtless, he had no particular eagerness to return to the grind of measuring cells and interrogating turnkeys.

Nor did he have to. Moira with 1,600 men ill in and about Southampton eagerly enlisted Sir Jeremiah. Moreover, the expeditionary force, now that intervention in France had ceased to be a practicable course, was destined for the war in the Low Countries; and Fitzpatrick was appointed also to supervise the fitting out of the transports and the care of the men's health generally. It is not clear whether Fitzpatrick was able to introduce the dietary tables and modes of cooking which he had by this stage elaborated. But he certainly established his sanitary regimen among the troops, and was given free rein for his gadgeteering on the vessels. Not only were the ventilators and 'Transit-Air Holes' introduced, but he also designed and had fitted arm racks and seats between decks for the 'Comfort' of the soldiers. Moira of course had supported him warmly, even issuing supporting general orders, 'Viz. that the Troops when on board should obey the rules proposed for their greater cleanliness, general ship Drills and regularity',[24] which last presumably included two of Sir Jeremiah's pet preventatives, daily airing ashore when afloat within the harbour and periodic changes of linen.

When the English-based section of Moira's force sailed for Holland in mid-June 1794 (the Jersey section sailed to rejoin them at the same time), Fitzpatrick may have accompanied the men as he had done in the case of the 40th on their passage from Cork five months before. At any rate, he served — or perhaps intruded himself — among the wounded at the rear of the British forces in Holland some time in the summer of 1794. He was of course soon noting, measuring, remonstrating, exhorting and complaining yet again. He found, for example, when he entered the ambulance wagons 'with some difficulty' to tend the wounded that the roofs were so low that he had to bend his head, though kneeling. The suffering of the 'poor wretches' packed into these shallow, foul-smelling vehicles under a burning sun was pitiful.[25] Fitzpatrick was driven to a mournful reflection often to be found later in his work, that was, that the solution, raising the wagon covering by two or three feet, was so simple that only the most hardened indifference to the pain of others could explain the failure to adopt it: 'Thus do great evils arise, and so easily might those be obviated'. The same applied to the careless pitching of tents, without regard to the surface of the ground

> notwithstanding the numerous declivities which it afforded, and which might be subserviant to carrying off the water after rain; or where the surface was completely flat, by sinking gradually the surrounding Tent Drain, so as to induce the water running from the Tents Sides to settle or pass off thro' the lower part of it the consequence of which neglect was, that after a heavy shower of Rain, many of the Tent Floors were so wet by the Water running in, that the Men could not lay down, and those who did, risked laying the Foundation of Rheumatism, or some Intermittand Disease, Cough &c – yet how easily prevented?[26]

However long he spent with the Duke of York's army in the Netherlands – and the comparative paucity of proposed reforms suggests a very brief visit – Fitzpatrick was back in residence in London by early September 1794, and struggling for a greater prize than any he had yet secured since he left Ireland. Moucher, Lennox and Moira were all by now behind him, none of them disenchanted by his work, certainly not Lennox and Moira, who wittingly or unwittingly were helping him in his advance. It is true that the 'gaol fever' had not been eradicated from Plymouth by the time of his departure (nor indeed for long afterwards) and also that Moira's army had brought it with them to Holland in June. None the less Fitzpatrick's claims to have reduced its incidence and the merits of his preventive methods were apparently accepted at full face value by both his English 'superiors'. At any rate, by now Sir Jeremiah had become known to the Secretary of War, Henry Dundas (appointed to this newly created office on 11 July 1794) and to his most important subordinates, Evan Nepean, the Under-Secretary, and William Huskisson, Chief Clerk.[27] Nepean in particular appears to have fallen under his spell, although Dundas was also to give him a remarkable measure of support in the coming months.

Again, the moment seems to have been right for Fitzpatrick. New brooms at Whitehall – at least new to the floors which they were to sweep – meant a willingness to innovate as well as a distrust of the established modes which were readily blamed for the current disasters.

The disasters in Holland seemed as much the product of disease and neglect of the sick as they were of French superiority. Fitzpatrick, with at least a decade's work behind him and a successful regime in Ireland, was at least a semi-professional in the vital field of gaol fever where all the remainder of the world seemed amateurs. Moreover, as he told Huskisson, his first pamphlet, the *Essay on Gaol Abuses*, was based largely on the work done in military medicine during the War of the Austrian Succession and the Seven Years War, on the principle that infectious diseases of the gaol and camp-fever type had substantially similar causes, courses and cures.[28] Thus, the wheel had come full circle and he could apply his 'learning' to army health, the field from which much of it had first derived. In addition his experience at Cove, Plymouth and Southampton, on troop transports and in Holland in 1794 had rendered him something of a professional in a complex of problems which no one had ever before looked at, or worked upon, in interaction.

By 13 September matters had sufficiently advanced between Sir Jeremiah and the war department for him to submit, in general terms, his ideas on what he termed a 'Commissary of Health' for the army. The duties envisaged were of course the sum of the activities which Sir Jeremiah had already attempted or glanced enviously upon. More interesting is his stress upon both the clear definition and the sufficiency of the powers of the future Commissary: clearly some recent painful *contretemps* explained the observation,

> new regulations, be they ever so proper, and the more particularly when recommended by a person not immediately connected with the different officers, whose concurrence may become necessary for their execution in the proportion to their novelty, because custom and prejudices are to be attacked [and] will ever meet impediment.[29]

Because Nepean was at this time seriously ill, Fitzpatrick had to forward his proposal to Dundas and the Cabinet through Huskisson. This made no difference. Within three days, Fitzpatrick had learned from Huskisson that the ministry had approved the scheme 'in principle' (one need hardly add that no eighteenth-century public servant penned this curious phrase: then, 'approve the idea and admit the necessity of' exactly and felicitously, if more lengthily, expressed the meaning).[30] Huskisson went on to ask Fitzpatrick to set out formally and extensively both the duties and the powers which he considered appropriate for the new office. In short, Fitzpatrick was being asked, for the second time in his career, to write his own orders. Few men would have responded more eagerly or confidently than he to such an invitation.

Despite a modest demurrer about his competence in draftsmanship, Fitzpatrick produced a very colourable imitation of an official commission.[31] Although untrained in law, his mind was lawyerly; he was doubtless experienced in drawing up prison regulations and perhaps even parliamentary Bills; and he was acutely conscious of the importance of defining the new officer's standing *vis-à-vis* other bodies with precision. First, the officer (name and title were as yet left blank) was to examine and adapt appropriately all troop transports including those used for the carriage of horses, stores or military material. He was to check the quality, quantity and storage of the water, and 'to order and direct the means for the cleanliness, better ventilation and convenient accommodation of all our troops ... so as to preserve them in a state of healthfulness, and contribute to their comfort and to the relief of all those who may be indisposed'. Secondly, he was to advise on the siting of hospitals, barracks and camps when called on to do so, and to advise and direct 'as to the proper and healthful mode of fitting up all such hospitals or barracks'. He was also to be enjoined to inspect the army hospitals and hospital ships, and to ensure that the sick and wounded were properly and humanely treated, in terms of attendance, accommodation, food and medicine alike. To render such a role practicable the officer was to be appointed to the army medical staff with a right of direct access to the Army Medical Board, with whom he was to arrange any matter tending to benefit the sick. Thirdly, he was to inspect all troops embarking for foreign service, and to keep ashore all those whom he judged to be unfit; and fourthly, to advise all commanding officers on the pitching of tents, making of huts and construction of ambulance wagons, and all other matters affecting the health of troops in the field. Finally, the officer was to keep complete journals of all those activities, from which he was to report to the government monthly, if not more often.

It is noteworthy that the areas in which Sir Jeremiah dared to seek absolute powers were the sanitary discipline, fittings and supplies on troop transports and the passing or rejection of men for service overseas. The remaining functions were essentially advisory in character, except that the selection and adaptation of vessels and the adoption of measures to alleviate the sick and wounded were left in a shadowy middle ground. The explanation of these exceptions was of course that Fitzpatrick wished to avoid direct challenges to the Transport and Army Medical Boards. The curious and unsatisfactory arrangement for joint determination by — and, as it were, equal status for — the officer and the Medical Board in hospital management told the story of early troubles; and indeed in his covering letter to Huskisson, Fitzpatrick observed that

> the alarm is taken by some medical gentlemen, who from the minuteness of my enquiries would be much better pleased [if] matters in future went on as formerly, than to be subject to any sort of report save their own too frequently attributing to unknown and latent causes what they know *I know* to have been the fault of several within the class and which I am inclined to think would not have happened were they sensible that from time to time genuine and impartial reports would be made on the general state of the hospitals and of the sick and wounded.[32]

A final curiosity of Fitzpatrick's draft is its anticipation in concept and even here and there in phrase of much of the work of Florence Nightingale and Sidney Herbert sixty-five years later, in the sanitary commission of 1859.[33]

In composing his draft, Fitzpatrick had virtually written his own orders. The substance was little changed in the official orders, and in several places even his very words were retained. There were one or two omissions. Some of the references to army barracks, for example, were quietly dropped. On the other hand, the commission exceeded even Sir Jeremiah in administrative exuberance here and there, as when the catalogue of what was to be provided for a corps embarking was ended with, 'in short, that nothing is wanting for the maintenance of the health or the comfort of the Indisposed'.[34] The awkward question of conflicting authority was avoided. Nothing was said of consultations between, or agreed decisions by, the Inspector of Health for the Land Forces (such was the title first fixed on, though 'inspector general' was commonly employed later on) and the Army Medical or Transport Boards. George III, in endorsing the proposal, had shrewdly observed that it might lead to jealousy and wrangling between the various services.[35] But in the end Dundas optimistically rested upon 'an equal reliance on your [Fitzpatrick's] experience and zeal, and on the readiness of the respective Departments with which you will be connected to afford you every Assistance and Facility'.[36]

Fitzpatrick's appointment was backdated by some two months to 8 September 1794, Dundas himself entering the day after an erasure. But this was evidently fixed on to correspond with Sir Jeremiah's formal abandonment of the inspector generalship of Irish prisons, and he actually began his new work as soon as Dundas endorsed the inspectorship, and before the king had signed the commission. This preliminary may be explained by the arrival in the Thames in October of several troop vessels from the West Indies, all with 'malignant fever' aboard. On at least three of them more than half the crew had died during the voyage. Huskisson, with the warm concurrence of the Transport Board, directed Fitzpatrick to deal with this emergency. The inspector-elect hastened to examine the ships down river, and ensure that they were kept below Deptford. He arranged for their fumigation, removed the bedding and bunks for cleansing and airing ashore and prevented the sailors from leaving for London immediately.

Of course Sir Jeremiah improved upon the occasion. He proposed to Dundas the establishment of a quarantine station below Woolwich for all troopships returning from the West Indies, with appropriate procedures for disinfection. He was also inspired to develop his ideas on passenger space at sea by measuring — perhaps for the first time — the vessels used by the army for ocean transport. The 'ill-founded general idea of *one and half* or *two tons* allowed to a man', on which the army worked in allocating numbers to ships, should, he concluded, be discarded. What mattered was not the tonnage but the space to be inhabited by the men. The common type of ocean troop transport was a vessel of 300 to 400 tons with only four to five feet between beam and deck. Many vessels with six to seven feet between decks were available just as cheaply; and Fitzpatrick argued that such ships, even if only 150-200 ton brigs, were preferable to the regular troop vessels. In these last

> it is impossible that men can continue in health who cannot allow the full extent to their muscles, either standing or sitting; and who, whether when in or out of bed, whilst in their allotted place below, unavoidably exist in and inspire back at every breath, their own exhalations;

whereas with over six feet between decks

> men can sit or stand at ease, and the tainted air have space to fly off yet their expense but half that of the former class, with an evident capability of containing in their berths an equal number.[37]

Fitzpatrick added that the adoption of the arm racks and 'trundle' type seating which he had designed for Moira's transports would add further to the effective room in the passengers' quarters. All this bore the marks of eminent simplicity and sense. More than half a century later the United Kingdom emigration officers were slowly groping their way towards recommending a change from tonnage to superficial deck space, and then from superficial deck space to the cubic space between decks, as the basis of setting limits to the number of emigrants whom vessels might carry.[38] Using specially designed furnishings as a means of creating more usable space between decks lay still further in the future. Meanwhile Sir Jeremiah set about rendering his ideas into ratios and scales, for submission to Dundas in the first instance.

Fitzpatrick was very soon obliged to set up offices in Deptford and London and to employ a clerk at Deptford. By mid-November he was considering the employment of a second clerk 'to see that the business is properly executed, and to collect my *Notes*, keep the journal, transcribe, etc.'.[39] The programme of action which he had drawn up for himself on 17 September set out as the first tasks the inspection of all troop transports being prepared in British ports (pointing out 'to intelligent carpenters the precise mode of fitting them up'); the preparation of hospital ships for the sick and wounded; and a visit to Holland to advise the commander-in-chief in the Netherlands, the Duke of York, on measures for the soldiers' health and comfort 'whether in the camp or in quarters'.[40] He had in fact thrown himself into the inspection and fitting up of vessels as soon as he was appointed. During November he visited Portsmouth three times, primarily 'for the regulation of the shipping there' but also to advise the local commander, Sir William Pitt, the latest of the generals to succumb to his eloquence and enthusiasm, on hospitals, barracks and surgeons at the port.[41] He had also secured two vessels from the Transport Board for use as hospital ships, and was supervising their internal reconstruction at Deptford. He had somehow found time as well to perfect his ideas on diet for the troops, especially those aboard the hospital vessels.[42]

Already there were signs that Sir Jeremiah was overextending his activities. I mean this not in the sense of the number or length of his labours (which although awesome were probably equalled by his volcanic energy), but in the sense of the growing multitude of other administrators with whom he had to deal. When, for example, he took up the general question of the troops' diet, he entered the sphere of Secretary-at-War, Windham, and of his Under-Secretary, Lewis, as well as those of Dundas and Nepean, on the one hand, and of the Commander-in-Chief, Lord Amherst, on the other. It is not that Windham or Lewis or Amherst was hostile to Fitzpatrick: Fitzpatrick may well have known Windham personally in the days when he was Irish Chief

Secretary in 1783. But the round of correspondence was being steadily widened, and the number of people to be persuaded and placated further increased. Moreover, as he reached higher in his ambition, he became more vulnerable to the counter-ambition of others. On 17 November he told Nepean, now restored to health, that 'a particular gentleman at a particular board' was putting forward, in conversation with Pitt and Dundas, Fitzpatrick's dietary scheme as if it were his own. The most likely candidate for 'particular gentlemanhood' here was Thomas Keate, one of the three members of the Army Medical Board. But the identification does not matter especially. What really counts is the signal that Sir Jeremiah had now reached the higher bureaucratic battleground. He attempted to take counter-measures. Nepean was asked to recommend to Pitt and Dundas, 'as if from yourself', that Fitzpatrick should be left free to cultivate by himself the fields proposed for him in his letter of appointment,[43] and also that he should be allowed to arrange things

> immediately thro' you [Nepean] and not indirectly thro' any board, for I find such a tenaciousness of *all-power*, of all direction, and self amongst certain men that I must beg to trouble those of whom I entertain a different opinion with the presenting of my ideas.[44]

At the same time Sir Jeremiah requested a formal interview with the Army Medical Board to discuss victualling on hospital ships, presumably in the hope of saving himself from being pre-empted by having *his* ideas put forward directly by the board.

The interview with the Army Medical Board on 20 November appeared to belie Sir Jeremiah's fears. The board not only approved his proposals for the hospital ships, but also solicited his opinion on dieting troops generally at sea. This was also gratifyingly received, and he went on to tell them his views on provisioning the army under ordinary circumstances, which he was then elaborating for Windham to submit to the Treasury. The Medical Board then raised the subject of the seven to eight hundred sick and wounded then 'in ill adapted Ships at Dort'; and Fitzpatrick characteristically rushed to proffer the two hospital ships which he had prepared at Deptford to bring back two hundred of the worst cases at once, adding 'that He if directed to do so' by Government, would take charge of the Undertaking, and see that the poor Men were (not as hitherto) comfortably brought home'. In reporting all this to Windham, he – again characteristically – proposed that the Transport Board be asked for some further vessels, which he had already marked down as both idle and suitable in construction; and also that himself be authorised to arrange immediately for a reception 'hospital' to be made ready at some convenient port: 'Sir Jerome begs to mention, that the sooner it is done the better − for Hurry is generally attended with irregularity and imperfection'.[45]

This happy bustle and restored serenity was continued in the report on army victualling which he completed and despatched to Windham on 24 November 1794, four days later.[46] Fitzpatrick had been asked specifically (ultimately by George Rose of the Treasury, and immediately by Windham) for his advice on the use of spirits on troop transports, but, confidently expansive, he swelled his reply into a document of nearly five thousand words. It was a most able piece. First, a generous foundation, selected from his experience, inferences and schematisations since his fateful arrival in Cork a year before, was laid. The soldier's health was presented as part of a much larger problem of health, that of all those who were institutionalised, confined and ordered in their movements by, and dependent for their diet on, some exterior authority. He quoted his own words on the contrasting circumstances of the sailor and the soldier at sea, carefully acknowledging his self-debt by inverted commas. However, 'the happy day is arrived' at last when the primary difficulties, unsuitable vessels and the lack of room and proper fittings for the troops, were being overcome; and 'it next naturally follows to enquire what the diet should be to combine the necessary strength, vigor and alertness to prevent disease, and tend to correct it, should it exist'. Fitzpatrick recommended, in the main, the substitution of farinaceous for animal products, partly on the ground of keeping to accustomed food, partly because of the dangerous deterioration and maggot-bearing to which meats were subject, but partly because of a curious belief (the remains of a pathology of 'humours') that what derived from animals heated the body and predisposed it to various infections. As well as oatmeal, barley and rice, Fitzpatrick urged the use of potatoes and onions, as 'keeping' vegetables, and of course 'sour Krout' as an antiscorbutic. When he finally came to answer the original enquiry, he pronounced decidedly against spirits, and even, except in rare and peculiar circumstances, against wine. Porter should be the standard drink on troop transports. Wine for the common soldiers was and always would be admixed and poor in quality,

> whilst the Malt Liquor equally a Restorer and a Resister of putre-

faction will not from its cheapness tempt the Adulterer; it will not in its consequences require more Stowage, because it will be used without the admixture of fresh Water, and further its cheapness, and being the produce of our own Country, may be of some Moment.[47]

By now, quite carried away, Sir Jeremiah went on to propose and elaborate two new reforms, the provision of a hospital ship to accompany every transport fleet, and of medicines and medical equipment for every transport vessel.[48]

Fitzpatrick's fortunes were however of dizzying variety at this stage. Within three days of his report to Windham, not merely his proposals on diet but his entire new career seemed to him in danger of collapse. The Army Medical Board had advised Windham on diet for the troops, substantially in the same terms as Sir Jeremiah. Moreover his report had been sent to them for comment. To the pangs of the robbed author was added the humiliation of being patronised by the appropriators, and over and above both the fear that he would lose control of the matter altogether, and that with it would disappear the hope of 'true improvement'. He began a letter of 27 November 1794 to Nepean (the words were to be used thriftily once more a year later):

> Almost every moment proves to me what this world is: men holding stations in office . . . trembling, fearful least the ideas or improvements of others should be adopted . . .[49]

Nepean was told, in the most passionate terms, that the crisis of the infant inspectorate had arrived already. Unless Dundas and he supported Fitzpatrick instantly and wholly against the numerous enemies of improvement in the public service, the office would fail and the customary evils triumph.

But there was to be no denouement — no immediate denouement at least. Whether with or without ulterior motive, the Medical Board had meanwhile taken up Fitzpatrick's suggestion of a week before that he himself might oversee the removal of the most seriously ill and wounded from Dort.[50] They even supported this proposal. Fitzpatrick needed no urging to go. It was not the case with him, as it doubtless would have been with many men, that he was taking, figuratively and literally, a way out of a difficulty which had come to seem almost insuperable overnight. His spirits were too mercurial and his temper too ardent for this. Moreover, he would always tumble in love with the untried task, and jackdaw-like be readily diverted by the more glittering bauble. In this case too he had planned from the beginning to visit Holland, and once there he certainly would not confine himself to Dort or to trans-shipping two hundred patients. He departed almost immediately, leaving behind him as open questions both the real meaning and the ultimate success of his instructions from Dundas.

The instructions are emblematic of the slapdash government which provided Sir Jeremiah with both the chance to rise and the likelihood of falling. War is the great agitator of bureaucracy, as of so much else. In this case there were the added disturbances caused by the lack of even the nucleus of a military organisation appropriate to the revolutionary circumstances, and the general upheaval in Whitehall which followed the intrusion of the Portland Whigs into the administration and the consequent division of departments. Again Dundas – and to a lesser extent Nepean – were bold, not to say reckless, ministers, Churchillian in their daring and distrust of the generals alike; and Huskisson was one of those talented amateurs who, in effect, suddenly find themselves civil servants in a crisis. No set of conditions could have been more favourable for Sir Jeremiah to find his way to and start to climb the great administrative ladder; and no mode of action could have been more congenial to his disposition.

At the same time, extreme bureaucratic 'flexibility' had the defects of its qualities: it is often forgotten that careers open to talent may be open at both ends. It was all very well for Fitzpatrick to go on perceiving needs, up to the point where they might be crystallised into the subjects of an official's business. He was not the sort of person who would cease to perceive needs once he became an officer. It was all very well for him to draw up, for all practical purposes, his own commission. It would not, in the nature of things, have occurred to him to consult all the organs of government which his commission would affect – not indeed that they would have paid him much attention so long as he spoke to them from outside the service. It was all very well for Dundas, Nepean and Huskisson to follow the same insouciant line as Fitzpatrick, and leave consultations with other agencies to the future and the outcome to the workings of a general goodwill. But government according to Pangloss could not succeed. It denied the iron laws of power- and function-distribution in the public domain. Fitzpatrick's virtual creation and definition of the office of inspector general of prisons in Ireland was only superficially similar to his virtual creation and definition of the Inspectorship of Health to HM Forces. In the case of the Irish prisons he was moving into almost uninhabited country, administratively speaking. But in Great Britain he was entering regions of long-settled, much-tangled and ever-bickering bureaucratic tribes, all suffering moreover from a recent and sketchy redefinition of their boundaries.

Aptly enough perhaps, Fitzpatrick himself paid the penalty for precipitancy and informality in government in the very matter of his own rewards. He received no salary as inspector general of Irish prisons for 1793-4, nor of course for 1794-5 or any subsequent year. Nepean had secured him an immediate payment of £200 in lieu in November 1794,[51] but six months later he was struggling hard for the balance of lost salary — £584, according to his own computation.[52] He based his case on the ten months' work from early November 1793 to early September 1794, first with the 40th, then in Plymouth with other troops as well and finally with Moira's army in and about Southampton and in Holland. All this was of course a retrospective claim. He had neither leave from the Irish government nor promise of remuneration from the British when he first set off for Cove, or probably at any stage over the next ten months. Meanwhile, when he did come to the British establishment, on 8 September 1794, he did so in characteristic confusion as to the terms of service. His stipend was clear enough, two guineas per day, the remuneration of an inspector general of army hospitals and other senior 'technical' officers. But what of his travelling expenses and the cost of the clerks and offices, so freely employed by him as need arose? Nearly three years later, this became a really critical question. Nothing had been set down in writing in 1794. Fitzpatrick asserted that he had been told that all his travelling and away from home expenses, at least, would be met. A War Office clerk who had been present at the relevant interview seemed to remember that an additional guinea a day for all expenses had been agreed upon. Meanwhile other War Office clerks had taken it that the payment of two guineas a day covered everything due to the inspector.[53]

All this encapsulates the sort of government by improvisation, word-of-mouth and gentleman's agreement which reigned in late 1794. Perhaps it would be too fanciful to say that it attracted Sir Jeremiah magnetically, and that he acted as a magnet for it in his turn. But certainly they fitted naturally. Equally certain was it that misunderstanding and disappointment must ensue. Such a system supplied at least as many snakes as ladders.

Notes

1. *Freeman's Journal*, 16 November 1793; A. King, 'The Relations of the British Government with the Emigrés and Royalists of Western France, 1793-5'

(PhD dissertation, London University), pp. 165-8.
2. Then named, in full, the Cove of Cork, renamed Queenstown in 1849, and now Cobh.
3. Fitzpatrick to Lennox, n.d. 1794, no. 2, W.O. 1/896, ff. 31-9.
4. Fitzpatrick to Moira, n.d. 1794, B.M. Add. MS. 37874, ff. 196-7.
5. Fitzpatrick to Lennox, n.d. 1794, no. 2, W.O. 1/896, ff. 31-9. The *Flying Post* (Exeter) greeted Fitzpatrick's arrival as follows:

It must afford infinite satisfaction to the public mind, to find that Sir Jerome Fitzpatrick has conjoined to his zeal for the wretched, medical abilities – hence the good that attended his accompanying the 40th regiment in all their misery from Cork here; and we have infinite pleasure in mentioning that he has not only laid the causes of their diseases before our Chief Governor here, Lord George Lenox, but has likewise made such general observations on the transport service, as will, in all probability, prevent the like misfortune in future. We find that he has visited the Mill Prison and our Marine Hospital, and have no doubt of great advantages from the observations he has made. 6 February 1794.

6. Fitzpatrick to Lennox, n.d. 1794, no. 2, W.O. 1/896, ff. 31-9.
7. Lennox to Army Medical Board, 4 February 1794, W.O. 1/896, ff. 11-15.
8. Fitzpatrick to Lennox, 23 January 1794, W.O. 1/896, ff. 19-23.
9. Fitzpatrick to Lennox, n.d. 1794, n. 2, W.O. 1/896, ff. 31-9.
10. Fitzpatrick to Moira, n.d. 1794, B.M. Add. MS. 37874, f. 196.
11. Fitzpatrick to Lennox, n.d. 1794, no. 2, W.O. 1/896, ff. 31-9.
12. Fitzpatrick to Lennox, n.d. 1794, no. 1, W.O. 1/896, ff. 27-9.
13. J.W. Fortescue, *A History of the British Army*, 13 vols. (London, 1906), vol. 4, pt. 1, p. 212.
14. Ibid., p. 215.
15. Fitzpatrick to Moira, n.d. 1794, B.M. Add. MS. 37874, f. 200.
16. Fitzpatrick to Lennox, n.d. 1794, no. 1, W.O. 1/896, ff.27-9.
17. Fitzpatrick to Lennox, n.d. 1794, no. 2, W.O. 1/896, ff.31-9.
18. Army Medical Board to Lennox, 3 May 1794, W.O. 1/896, ff.78-80.
19. Lennox to Windham, 7 December 1794, W.O. 1/896, ff.119-27.
20. Fortescue, *History of British Army*, vol. 4, pt. 1, pp. 154-6.
21. Fitzpatrick to Moira, n.d. 1794, B.M. Add. MS. 37874, f.198.
22. Ibid., f.200.
23. Ibid., ff.199-200.
24. Fitzpatrick to Dundas, 17 November 1794, W.O. 1/897, ff.49-50.
25. Fitzpatrick to Huskisson, 13 September 1794, W.O. 1/897, ff.9-16.
26. Fitzpatrick to Huskisson, 17 September 1794, W.O. 1/897, ff.20-1.
27. J.C. Sainty, *Colonial Office Officials 1794-1870* (London, 1976), pp. 8-9. See also J.C. Sainty, *Home Office Officials 1782-1870* (London, 1975).
28. Fitzpatrick to Huskisson, 17 September 1794, W.O. 1/897, ff.22-4.
29. Fitzpatrick to Huskisson, 13 September 1794, W.O. 1/897, ff.9-16.
30. Fitzpatrick to Huskisson, 17 September 1794, W.O. 1/897, f.17.
31. Ibid., ff.22-8.
32. Ibid., f.19.
33. *Report of the Commissioners Appointed to Enquire into the Regulations affecting the Sanitary Conditions of the Army, the Organisation of Military Hospitals, and the Treatment of the Sick and Wounded*, H.C. 1857-8, vols. xviii-xix.
34. Dundas to Fitzpatrick, 8 September 1794, W.O. 1/897, f.3.
35. George III to Dundas, 6 October 1794, no. 1134, A. Aspinall (ed.), *The*

Later Correspondence of George III, 5 vols. (Cambridge, 1963), vol. 2, p. 251.
36. Dundas to Fitzpatrick, 8 September 1794, W.O. 1/897, f.1.
37. Fitzpatrick to Dundas, 17 November 1794, W.O. 1/897, f.48.
38. Not until the Consolidating Passenger Act of 1855 (18 & 19 Vic. c. 119), more than half a century after the first legislation in this field, was the space allowed per passenger calculated, to any degree whatever, in cubic terms; even then, the main determinant remained surface deck area.
39. Fitzpatrick to Nepean, 17 November 1794, W.O. 1/897, f.44.
40. Fitzpatrick to Huskisson, 17 September 1794, W.O. 1/897, ff.29-30.
41. Fitzpatrick to Nepean, 17 November 1794, W.O. 1/897, f.44.
42. Fitzpatrick to Windham, 24 November 1794, W.O. 1/897, ff.61-72.
43. Nepean appears to have been more sympathetic and responsive to Fitzpatrick than any other person in the British administration. He was an extraordinarily conscientious and energetic Under-Secretary and later Minister. William Knox found him 'intelligent, attentive and obliging'; and Huskisson wrote on 12 September 1793, 'I have constantly met with the greatest civility from Mr Nepean the Under-Secretary, no less remarkable for his indefatigable attention to business than for his upright & honourable conduct', R.R. Nelson, *The Home Office, 1782-1801* (Durham, N.C., 1969), p. 29.
44. Fitzpatrick to Nepean, 17 November 1794, W.O. 1/897, ff.41-3.
45. Fitzpatrick to Windham, 20 November 1794, B.M. Add. MS. 37874, f.164.
46. Fitzpatrick to Windham, 24 November 1794, W.O. 1/897, ff.53-73.
47. Fitzpatrick to Windham, 20 November 1794, B.M. Add. MS. 37874, f.163.
48. Fitzpatrick to Windham, 24 November 1794, W.O. 1/897, ff.70-1.
49. Fitzpatrick to Nepean, 27 November 1794, W.O. 1/897, ff.75-9, see below p. 223.
50. Fitzpatrick to Windham, 20 November 1794, B.M. Add. MS. 37874, f.164.
51. Fitzpatrick to Nepean, 17 November 1794, W.O. 1/897, f.44.
52. Fitzpatrick to Huskisson, 9 April 1795, W.O. 1/897, ff.298-9; Fitzpatrick to J. Rudge (War Office clerk), 22 April 1795, W.O. 1/897, ff.313-14.
53. Fitzpatrick to Huskisson, 4 September 1797, W.O. 1/897, ff.559-60; Fitzpatrick to Huskisson, 30 December 1797, W.O. 1/897, ff.563-4.

8 THE LAYMAN WITH THE LAMP, 1794-1795

Sir Jeremiah arrived in the Netherlands on the eve of the final crisis for the Anglo-Hanoverian forces. During the summer of 1794 the French had broken through the Allied defences along the Scheldt and swept across Flanders.[1] As the reinforcements under Moira, whose fitting out Fitzpatrick had helped to supervise, were landing at Bergen-op-Zoom and other southern Dutch ports at the end of June, they were already being subjected to French bombardment. As autumn set in, the Duke of York fell back to a line of fortresses stretching eastwards from Bergen to Nijmegen. Mrs Harcourt, the wife of a member of York's staff, foretold that 'winter quarters on the frontier of Holland would ruin our army'.[2] But there were not even to be winter quarters in the new form of war fought by Revolutionary France. From September to November 1794, the attack upon the fortresses was unremitting. Bergen fell first, and Nijmegen finally on 7 November. The line of the Meuse had been lost, and the British and Hanoverian troops had been driven back to the north bank of the Waal. Meanwhile Prussia had concluded peace with France, the Dutch forces had virtually capitulated and the Austrians had retreated towards the Rhine. True, the Waal, a fast-flowing river, still constituted a formidable obstacle. But it would not do so once it froze over. This was the juncture at which Fitzpatrick landed at Helvoetsluys, the southernmost Dutch port still in British hands, on 9 December.

He was bound for Arnhem, where the headquarters and the main general hospital for the British troops was now located, but the sights and needs which met him at Helvoetsluys kept him there for five days. *En route* to England were 1,230 wounded:

> In so inconsiderate, and I may say in so cruel a mode, poor wretches were never sent on Board: In ships ill-suited and filthy, and although they [the wounded] had got some trifling supply of tolerably well calculated Food five days past at Schrevendale, yet on my visit, the unfortunate wretches altho' in putrid Fluxes and Fevers, had their tongues parched and shrivelled from want of common . . . Drinks, and on one scanty meal in twenty four hours.[3]

Characteristically, Fitzpatrick even noted the absence of salt and of candles 'from which they could receive in their Night-Sufferings a gleam of Comfort'.[4]

Within a day of his arrival, he had bought and in part distributed rice, barley, sugar, wine and tea, and arranged for bakings and the supply of fresh bread, at a cost of some £200. He had found — as was to be almost invariably the case in his military career — a sympathetic or compliant officer. Captain Craven, 'a man warm in humanity and zealous in forwarding the Service',[5] was harried into finding better temporary accommodation for the sick and into making good the shameful deficiencies in food and clothing on the transports which were to bear them to England. Already Fitzpatrick deplored his lack of authority to deputise — with such an authority, he wrote, he would have been able to leave Helvoetsluys almost immediately — but within four days of his arrival he had taken it into his own hands to direct Dr MacLueran, an army physician, to accompany the wounded back to Deal. He was well aware of his exorbitance: 'I consigned [him] (in as much as I had Authority; Yet I fear I had none)'. None the less he dispatched MacLeuran not merely with detailed instructions on providing for the sick but also with wide discretion as to purchasing further supplies and taking emergency actions — meanwhile deriving comfort from the fact that MacLeuran was dressed in the full-laced uniform of a staff physician and carried a letter of recommendation from Thomas Keate of the Army Medical Board whereby the innocent — and the guilty — might be overawed! By now, Fitzpatrick had received so many accounts of the chaos at headquarters that he was eager to leave at once for Arnhem. 'What my authority will be when I get there I know not', he wrote apprehensively to Dundas, telling him at the same time that unless he were given authority to deputise he could achieve comparatively little.[6]

On 14 or 15 December Fitzpatrick left for Arnhem, and traversed the Waal line of defence as he proceeded. The condition of the army was most pitiful. To the usual miseries of the eighteenth-century soldier was added, in most cases, near-nakedness: the customary meandering process of clothing a regiment, designed to enrich the colonels, had failed under the sudden pressure of raising new forces, and many of the men were despatched with only linen jackets and trousers for covering. To the usual miseries of eighteenth-century warfare were added a winter campaign, an unstable front line, a peculiarly bare and harsh land, a hostile civilian population and incessant wet and cold. Two major and general retreats in the autumn and early winter had quite broken down the military system.[7] Communications — in the unsure hands of the Royal Waggoners, a corps of released gaol-birds for the most part – fell into disarray. The troops on the Waal, hungry, ragged and ill-armed, lacked fuel and shelter, other than makeshift hovels of turf sods. Typhus and dysentery, brought from the Channel Islands and England with Moira's troops, were endemic; the few regimental (or 'military') hospitals could not cope with the rising numbers of sick; and the general (or 'public') hospitals to which most were forwarded were notoriously inefficient. 'The dreadful mismanagement of the hospital [departments] is beyond description,' wrote Colonel Craig, York's chief of staff, 'and the remedy beyond my power. Every branch and every fibre of every branch draws a contrary way.'[8] 'Ah, poor fellow, we shall see thee no more, for thou art under orders for the shambles'[9] was the soldiers' reaction to a comrade's being transferred to a general hospital. Both types of hospital, however, suffered from the retreats which demanded improvisation and ingenuity from a routine-ridden service, and which created new deficiencies and difficulties in supply almost day by day.

The Netherlands Campaign, 1794-5

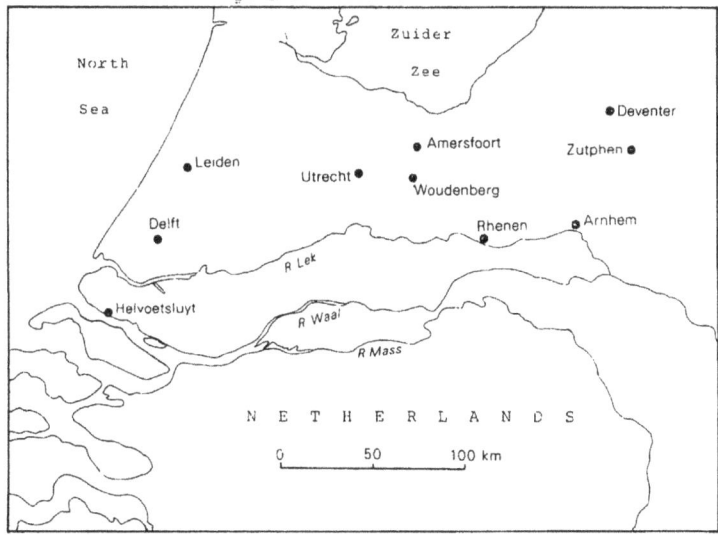

These were the scenes through which Sir Jeremiah travelled on his way to Arnhem. He spent a week on the journey, most of it apparently in inspecting and attempting to 'reform' the troops' condition of living and dying at or close to the front lines. But he began by examining the 'hospital' at Leiden in which the surviving Hanoverian sick in the west were housed — one might almost say, entombed: of 750 patients 417 had died already. Professor Burgmans, who held the chair of natural history at Utrecht (a 'humane and learned' man, according to Fitzpatrick), and was attending the Hanoverians 'out of charity', predicted 300 more deaths soon unless there were an immediate and radical change of system. Fitzpatrick found the remaining patients lying on straw with only 'one poor blanket' each, in smoke, damp and malodour from excrement left lying about the ward, and half-starved with only 'abominable' buckwheat bread and 'vile' broth for food. He did not blame the doctors for this tragedy — even the Hanoverian physician might have been a good man, 'for aught I know' — but instead the purveyors and army administration; and he reported to the commander-in-chief that the first and most necessary reform was to render the hospitals altogether independent of purveyors and hospital departments.[10]

Along the front, Fitzpatrick was immediately precipitated into action rather than recommendation. According to his own report,[11] he set about procuring hot food (with the quantity of meat for broth carefully specified and punch for the men on picket or night duty), and set up indoor kitchens where he could. Bread was once again a critical matter, and he turned his attention at once to the setting up or providing cover for the 'bakeries'. 'The poor soldiers have got better bread since my arrival.' Where huts had been hastily erected with the doors in the wrong situation, he got them changed from the north or east to the south sides of the buildings. Where the bare earth formed the floor, he arranged for hurdles or rollers to form the bases for the straw on which the troops lay. Where, as was very commonly the case, the private soldiers slept in hay sheds and outhouses, he 'recommended their being lodged in the Farmers' actual Houses, in place of the cold barns, and by calling on the Officers' Humanity, they have cheerfully in most instances made them the Partners of their Lodging Houses'.[12] Fitzpatrick added that Colonel Manners of the Guards had taken the lead in inducing the officers who occupied the farm houses to share their accommodation with the men. Blankets and winter clothing were 'in great want', and although Fitzpatrick managed to locate and secure some though an insufficient quantity of the first, the second proved impossible to find.

So far the work was simple in concept (though not in practice) and the obstacles merely material. But to go further enmeshed him in the purveying and medical systems, and brought him into conflict with their functionaries. Food and medicine being desperately short in the regimental hospitals close to the front lines, Fitzpatrick proposed that the regimental surgeons should be supplied weekly with both from the depots of the general hospitals at Arnhem and Rhenen. Such an intermingling of the two forms of hospital supply and management was regarded with astonishment. 'This was considered extraordinary but I replied that the situation was too extraordinary to allow fine spun distinctions between Regimental and Public [i.e. general] Hospitals.' Still greater offence was given by his attempts to intrude himself into the running of the hospitals and the treatment of patients.

He had already clashed with the 'faculty', to use the contemporary term for medical staff, both on the troop transports and at Helvoetsluys, for their refusal even to consider any alteration in the immemorial routine of army medicine. Now he complained again of the 'one *Jog-Trot* mode of treatment'. Whatever the disease or the patient's condition, 'purgative sugar' was — *à la* Mrs Squeers — indiscriminately prescribed. Whatever the need, the patients were visited only once or twice at fixed times during the day. Whatever the crisis, a patient was never visited at night; no drinks were prepared or warmed, no fires were kept up, no orderlies were in attendance after dark.[13] This account foreshadowed the crisis in Fitzpatrick's career as inspector general of health; this catalogue of humble but cruel inadequacies epitomised his charges against the military hospitals. Inevitably, these aligned him against the army surgeons and physicians, or many of them. His second report to Nepean from Holland had suggested what would follow. 'To have power, in a certain sense, is to have trouble' he had written on 13 December, 'I want it not; but there seems to be such a determination in severals of the Faculty . . . to jog on, not quietly but obstinately in their old Errors, that some persons not absolutely leagued with them appear necessary to see carried into effect rational improvement.'[14] Fitzpatrick was to continue to see his gathering conflict with the Army Medical Board and its officers in terms of 'rational improvement' struggling against the 'jog-trot'. To the board he would soon take shape as an ignorant and insolent intruder into its own established business.

Meanwhile the scene shifted from the front line to headquarters. On Christmas Day 1794, Fitzpatrick wrote to Nepean from Arnhem, where he had arrived on 21 December. He was, he wrote, benumbed by cold but so harassed by business that he had not sat for thirteen hours except to breakfast briefly with 'that very good man', Major-General Sir Ralph Abercromby. He had been appalled by the general hospital at Arnhem. 'Such misery and wretchedness as I found', he told Nepean, 'can scarcely be described: — an apparent want of everything, and a real want of many necessary Articles.' Once again 'several of the Faculty' had been astonished by his requests but not more so than the purveyor and commissaries. None the less he had achieved much by working through 'every Commanding Officer'. As usual, he found the colonels (following the lead, in this case, of Colonel Don) grateful for and eager to apply his regimen. But whether the new order would continue to be observed once he left for a further tour of the front line and base hospitals was another matter: 'there is no system yet established for continual regulation'. He repeated therefore, with doubled urgency, his request to Dundas for the power to 'deputize'. It was, evidently, ultimate authority which was to be deputised: 'Can I, or who is', asked Fitzpatrick, 'to recommend or appoint a proper Person to see actually carried into effect such Matters as I suggest − supposing them to be approved by the Commander-in-Chief here?'[15]

The cold which benumbed Fitzpatrick's fingers as he composed this letter − the handwriting bears witness to his misery − was also destroying the front line of defence. The Waal had frozen over at last, with the ice so thick that cavalry and the heaviest cannon could cross the river in security in many places. In the last days of 1794 a new British retreat began, and Fitzpatrick was diverted from inspection to improvisation. The retreat over the barren grey and white country was 'shocking beyond description', wrote Mrs Harcourt. 'No tree, no house was there to shelter our troops, nothing but wild heather, covered with snow, and the severest frost that was ever known.'[16] By the scores men fell out or lay down to die on the roadside, but the sufferings of the sick made their fate seem merciful by contrast. Piled into open carts, without blanket or cover, dying men were driven into and often abandoned in the barren waste.[17] Overwhelmed and disorganised, the 'faculty' at the general hospitals was evacuating the sick at random. Here was a new cause of conflict for Fitzpatrick. On 29 December he wrote from 'a Straw House near Rhenen, where I discovered a Treasure − fresh, dry Bedding for the Hospitals' that some of the 'medical gentlemen regard me as requiring too much, in point of their greater attention', and the same applied to the commissary and purveyors department, in point of further supplies.

> Be their opinions as they may, I am determined to go on in obtaining for the poor Men every possible Comfort and in having enforced by the Superior Authority here the fulfilling of every necessary Duty.[18]

Most of the remaining time which Sir Jeremiah spent in eastern Holland was taken up with preceding the sick wagons, and arranging accommodation ahead of the retreat — anticipating the system established in the Peninsula fifteen years later. But he was back in Rhenen on 6 January 1795, and intended to stay briefly at the general hospital there, partly because he was exhausted but mostly to prevent the sick and wounded, 'objects not describable, several of them appearing to have but a few hours to live', being despatched to — or rather towards — new hospitals which had been set up to the rear at Zutphen and Deventer, on the river Issel. Fitzpatrick's efforts were steadily resisted by the medical officers at Rhenen, who told him that they were strictly bound by general orders and the orders of the director-general of hospitals, Dr Smith. He appealed over their heads to Abercromby against the sick being sent off in the evening in open farmcarts to spend the night in the freezing air and probably end dead upon arrival.[19] 'To his honour' Abercromby intervened, and Fitzpatrick prevailed in this particular matter.[20] He also won a partial victory on an issue which he had first taken up at Arnhem before Christmas. The basis of feeding the British army was still — as it was long to remain — that the men should pay for what they ate; and the deductions (for being off duty) made from the pay of the sick, and still more of the convalescents, laid them open to near-starvation. Sir Jeremiah now succeeded in persuading General Woodward to order that convalescents receive sixpence instead of fourpence per day for diet: this put them on a par with the sick, even if it still left them without enough to eat.

Fitzpatrick had earlier supposed that he had secured the convalescents their full tenpence per day by an instruction from the Duke of York.[21] But York had left for England, and for some reason or other the instruction — if it ever was made out — was never executed. York's departure was generally bemoaned by Sir Jeremiah. Although Harcourt, of York's staff, did support him in some other minor matters, and was invariably 'human' in his responses, he told Fitzpatrick that he did not feel warranted in sanctioning large-scale changes in the absence of the commander-in-chief. It was most unlucky, Fitzpatrick wrote, that he should have just missed York at headquarters, for his power was necessary to rectify the ill-judged measures of the medical departments. As things stood, 'the Confusion, impropriety and Cruelty practised here [the Rhenen general hospital] — and with such a degree of indifference — is beyond description'. Even the sanguine Sir Jeremiah despaired. 'I having no sort of power to direct a single matter, and the Faculty so tenacious of their prerogative, that I often wish I was in England again.'[22] This conclusion contrasted sharply with that of his previous report from Rhenen, twelve days before, when after recounting all the difficulties he had encountered he had none the less ended, 'My heart rejoices at having come here . . . how necessary it was.'[23] The change is doubtless a measure of the despondency which the concomitants of the terrible retreat induced.

By now the scarcely remitting cold, which was gradually rendering all waterways and even the Zuider Zee iron hard, permitted the French to advance freely, not merely beyond the Waal in the interior but also northwards along the Dutch coast. The evacuation of the vanquished Anglo-Hanoverian forces would have to take place, for the most part, from the north-western German ports, and this was eventually and most painfully completed on 14 April 1795.[24] Meanwhile, in early January a western escape from the Arnhem-Rhenen area was still practicable, and within a day or two of writing his second report from Rhenen, Fitzpatrick left for the temporary capital, Utrecht. From there he reported to Nepean on the 9th that he waited on the British ambassador, Lord St Helens, whom he had known since he had served, as Alleyne Fitzherbert, as Chief Secretary in Dublin in 1787-9. Once again, Fitzpatrick was attempting to enlist 'Superior Authority' in his cause. Again he was pleased with his reception. Lord St Helens approved of his 'general mode of . . . management of the Sick, as to their movements, Diet and Covering'[25] being applied to the hospitals set up at Zutphen and Deventer in the east, and at Woudenberg and Amersfoort, near Utrecht. Whether the ambassador's fiat had any force in such a field and amidst such a headlong withdrawal all along the front is, of course, another matter. Doubtless Fitzpatrick was playing his last card before leaving the dreadful scene of battle, and making his exit to the coast. He intended to visit the sick at Delft on his way to Helvoetsluys, and St Helens asked him to call at Rotterdam as well to collect more wounded for repatriation. Like the pied piper, Fitzpatrick kept gathering the ill as he journeyed to the point of repatriation.

At Helvoetsluys once again, Fitzpatrick's last days in Holland were his happiest. He had supervised the removal from Rotterdam of 'all the patients who were fit in my opinion to be moved', leaving behind not only the dying but also about one hundred of the convalescents who might recover and rejoin the army falling back in the east. In the hospital at Helvoetsluys, he was in complete control. As a species of transit depot for the sick, it was not attended by army surgeons or physicians. Fitzpatrick congratulated himself on being so fortunate 'as not to meet with any of the *great Staff Faculty*'. He was equally fortunate, he wrote, in meeting for the first time willing and considerate purveyors. Interestingly enough, the wheel was coming full circle so far as his relative evaluation of army doctors and purveyors was concerned between his first and second stays at Helvoetsluys. In each successive report in the interval his criticism of the purveyors tended to slacken and that of the medical department to be enlarged. Now he was able to establish his own system of 'management' at the hospital. How it would fare after his departure – one thousand sick and wounded were to be embarked on the *Colchester* transport – depended on how closely 'the Medical and Surgical assistants attend my suggestions (for I can do no more)'. Fitzpatrick concluded his final report before his return to England with an urgent plea – or, more exactly, a reiteration of pleas which had begun at Rhenen – that no hospital reorganisation be 'concluded on' until he had had a full opportunity to present his views to Dundas.[26]

About 20 January Sir Jeremiah crossed to Deal. War had been left behind, but not conflict. His struggle with the military medical corps may have changed cockpits, but its intensifications steadily continued. He was as appalled by the state of the general hospital at Deal, to which the landed sick were transferred, as by any of the sights which had horrified him in the Netherlands. On 24 January he reported to Nepean:

> The Hospital Dept. here is shamefully attended to. You could scarce credit the irregularities and neglects. Unfortunately, the mode of remedying the flagrant errors is so *round about*, thro' different departments, and necessarily thro' the Medical Board, as matters now are conducted, and I merely having the power of suggesting ideas, that they must remain for some time irremedied; but I am decided on laying a plan before you for conducting the whole of what relates to the diseased, for Government's consideration, regardless of every man and body of men.[27]

On the same day the indefatigable Sir Jeremiah wrote three other letters, to General Smith, the commanding officer at Deal,[28] to the barrackmaster of Deal[29] and to the surgeon of the Berkshire militia,[30] who were stationed there. Between them, the letters indicted the hospital department for the neglect of the sick and the sparseness and meagre regularity of the medical attendance, for the failure to segregate the various categories of sick, for the absence of any sanitary regulation, the desperate shortage of 'utensils' and several other matters of this kind. Fitzpatrick had immediately proposed additions to the equipment, the setting aside of special rooms as wards, and the provision

180 *The Layman with the Lamp*

of new heating and ventilation. Even as early as the 24th, within a very few days of his arrival at Deal, he had had some success. As usual it was the commanding officer who had responded: General Smith had sanctioned some of the proposed changes and acquisitions at once. Fitzpatrick had justified his demands upon the ground that

> my Office impowers me to point out not only the situations best suited for all Military Hospitals, but their Constructions and the Modes of fitting them up.[31]

This well exemplifies Fitzpatrick's subtlety (not to say, cunning) in finding standing ground for his intervention, as well as illuminating the fundamental ambiguity of his administrative situation. What he evidently relied on here was a passage towards the end of Dundas's instructions to him of 8 September 1794:

> Lastly, when called upon at Home by the Commander in Chief, the Secretary at War, or the Army Medical Board, you are to give your Assistance and Advice in determining upon the proposed Spots, in regard to Health, for the Erection of Barracks or Hospitals, and that upon their Construction and Fitting up you are also required to visit occasionally the established Hospitals and Barracks; in order that it may be ascertained beyond a Doubt that in Point of Accommodation, Diet, Medicines and Medical Attendance, every Thing practicable is done that can contribute to the Preservation of Those who have devoted themselves to the Service of their Country.[32]

It was arguable, according to what he actually wrote to the various officers at Deal, that he was not pretending to possess larger official powers than in fact he did, but merely exercising his right to 'point out' the best or better 'constructions and Modes of fitting . . . up' military hospitals. But whether the officers whom he was pressing would, in the hectic circumstances of Deal, have grasped the full distinction between an advisory and an executive role may well be doubted. Sir Jeremiah was a master of the *suggestio falsi* in such conditions. The very clause on which he relied surely envisaged no more than recommendations as to the siting, planning and furnishing of new hospitals. Even less plausibly could he have claimed to have been called on 'by the Commander in Chief, the Secretary at War, or the Army Medical Board' to intervene at Deal. But again a shadow of justification could be conjured out of his vague roving commission to assist the

British expeditionary force, a suffering fragment of which he was now attempting to tend upon its shore of origin.

Two days later, on 26 January, Fitzpatrick wrote again to Nepean elaborating his difficulties and exertions at Deal, and begging again for a postponement of any decision upon the reorganisation of military hospitals until after he had had an opportunity to submit a full report and recommendation.[33] Later evidence suggests that he was already at loggerheads with the army surgeons and physicians at Deal.[34] But this conflict never developed into a full-scale confrontation, for at the end of January Fitzpatrick was despatched to supervise the embarkation of troops at Plymouth. He carried with him to the new arena the accumulating effects of all his earlier challenges to the Army Medical Board.

Sir Jeremiah's general report upon the army hospitals was never written. He was to meet his Waterloo at Plymouth before this could be done; and after his defeat such a composition would have been pointless. But we can confidently guess what its contents – or at least the bulk of its contents – would have been. During his first stay in Helvoetsluys, he had drawn up for General Woodward (who had promised to do his best to effect them) a catalogue of 'reforms' for hospital ships.[35] These included the sweeping and drying of the passenger decks and between-decks accommodation twice daily; the daily 'turning up' of beds and cleansing of the space between them; the immediate removal of excrement and soiled dressings; the immediate throwing overboard of all the bedding and clothing of men who had died; and the more generous supply of food and drink. The 'medical' recommendations were more bizarre. Presumably to expel or dissipate malignant atmosphere vinegar heated in tar-kettles was to be drawn round between decks, especially in the 'darkest and lowest spaces' every four hours, and pistols discharged frequently in the same places. Neither the oddity of the remedies nor the error of the miasmic theory of infection which they expressed should, of course, lead us to forget that the attack upon bad atmosphere was also, in part and in a sort of fortunate ignorance, an attack upon the disease. But in any event these were the minor recommendations. Hygiene was the centrepiece of Sir Jeremiah's preventive medicine.

The substance of all these proposals would certainly have found a place in any report of Fitzpatrick's upon military hospitals, and to them we may add with assurance a number of others which recurred in his writings from the Netherlands and other observations of 1794-5. Ventilation and heating, clean and adequate supplies of blankets and heavy clothing, fresh food (in particular, bread), segregation of patients according to the severity and the character of their illnesses, full payment of allowances for convalescents as well as sick, secure doors, roofs and windows, and night drinks were the common themes of his letters and reports. But perhaps the weight of his assault would have been on the medical and purveyors' departments. His basic objection to the current conduct of hospitals was that the doctors were committed, or committed themselves — out of fear of their superiors or from hope of promotion — to an unreasoning and cruel routine. This had manifested itself, in his eyes, at the general hospitals of Arnhem and Rhenen in the standardisation of prescription, in the few and fixed times of visiting the wards, in the absence of night attendance and indeed in the virtual putting up of the shutters in the hospitals once evening fell. It had shown itself in the preference for the convenience of the waggoners over the sufferings of the sick, and in the blind adherence to 'general orders' and Dr Smith's diktats from on high. The cardinal sin of the purveyors was not so much that they were brutalised routiniers as that they were inhumanely negligent and corrupt. Few knew their own business, and the business which many of them did know was skimming profits for themselves from the rations, allowances and comforts of sick soldiers. Grave deficiencies in beds, bedding, pots, pans, food, drink, shelter and carriage lay at the door of the purveyors' department.

It is much less easy to guess what new system of controls Sir Jeremiah would have proposed for army hospitals. He had certainly advised a change in either the person or the conduct of the director of hospitals. Currently the direction of hospitals lacked 'zeal' and enfolded and encouraged an unhealthy strain of ambition and self-seeking within the service. Fitzpatrick had also advised a greater degree of supervision of and intervention in the hospitals by the commander-in-chief.[36] But neither of these suggestions cut really deeply into the problem. Each was conventional and expected. The nearest we can get to a more thorough solution implicit in his informal reports is that his own inspectorship be rendered executive as well as advisory, in the sense that this new branch of government be empowered to reorder the equipping and management of hospitals and the transport to and from them. It is probably fair to speak of his having 'a branch of government' in mind: he believed that residential deputies for the chief inspector — in other words, subordinate inspectors stationed in particular places or areas — were needed to maintain the required standards. It would also be fair to say that he envisaged a separation between this inspectorate and the medical establishment. Although he was appalled by the current forms of attendance, treatment and prescribing in the hospitals, there is nothing in his writings to suggest that he had any designs on these affairs: rather he looked to a reform in the hospital directorate to reform them in their turn. Finally, Fitzpatrick was impatient with the distinctions between regimental and general army hospitals. Undoubtedly, he failed to realise upon what different and sometimes antagonistic principles the two systems were organised, or how revolutionary a move it would be to attempt to break down the barriers between them.

Had Fitzpatrick elaborated a complete scheme of reform upon the lines of his letters and reports from Holland, its centrepiece would therefore have been, in all likelihood, an independent army inspectorate of health with coercive powers in the areas of hospital administration and transport. In one sense, of course, this might be regarded as a bureaucratic commonplace. 'Reforming' civil servants naturally tend to see solutions to the public evils with which they grapple in the multiplication of themselves and the magnificence of their own authority, and Sir Jeremiah was certainly not above wistful glances towards omnipresence and omnipotence. On the other hand, he was capable of translating such impulses and aspirations into a practical, carefully articulated and effective inspectoral system: the inspectorates which he later projected for regulating the slave trade were thoroughly considered and imaginatively designed. Moreover, the need for change was truly desperate. By the time Fitzpatrick sailed from Helvoetsluys some 6,000 (or nearly 30 per cent) of the 21,000 Anglo-Hanoverian troops in Holland had died, over nine-tenths of them from disease rather than in or as a consequence of battle. One of the regimental surgeons serving there observed later that 'in the general hospitals, there was neither system, or control, or rule of management. As soon as circumstances pressed, every hospital consequently became a pest house – a deadly drain upon the effective strength of the army'.[37] Another regimental surgeon in the Netherlands, the young James McGrigor who was later to become Wellington's surgeon-general in the Peninsula and director-general of the army medical service, wrote that 'the want of system... and the inexperience of the medical officers were at this time striking', and that the general hospitals proved seed-beds of diseases, in particular, of typhus,[38] and like Fitzpatrick, McGrigor, a man of extraordinary courage and decision, had sometimes to break through the 'jog-trot' and take matters into his own hands in the emergencies of the campaign. And reaching the hospitals was as cruel an experience as being immured in them. A Dutch observer in Rhenen was horrified to find five hundred sick lying in the barges which had carried them from Arnhem 'under charge of a single surgeon's mate, without sufficient provisions, without even sufficient straw'.[39] They were awaiting room for them in the Rhenen general hospital. Meanwhile the corpses of the forty-two who had already died lay strewn along the river bank.

Thus, Fitzpatrick could certainly have pleaded the necessity of desperate remedies; and he could also have justified — at least subsequent events were to provide him with ample justification for — scepticism of the capacity of the army medical service of 1794-5 to generate any reform from within itself. Not until 1809 was there an effective response to the scandals of 1794-5, and even then the initiative came entirely from without.[40] The case for an independent paramedical inspectorate was therefore strong in the closing stage of the Dutch débâcle.

A final consideration in favour of Fitzpatrick's truth and sense in this particular excursion is the remarkable similarity between Florence Nightingale's experiences, findings and reactions in the Crimea in 1854-5[41] and Sir Jeremiah's in the Netherlands in 1794-5. *Prima facie* there are profound contrasts between the two, the earliest and most obvious of all being that between woman and (in so far as the term is apt for such a person as Miss Nightingale in 1854) nurse and man and physician. But even the earliest and most obvious of the apparent contrasts does not seem very deep once we separate the substance from the accidents. Initially Nightingale thought of her sphere in Scutari as the feminine, although she was quickly led by a variety of needs into moving well beyond the domestic economy of, and the service of mercy in, hospitals. But Fitzpatrick's sphere was also, in part, the domestic as mid-nineteenth century people tended to divide these things. Cooking, clothing, bedding, washing, fastidiousness, attendance and caring accounted for a substantial proportion of his concerns. In any event, whatever the labels contemporaries might have attached, or we might attach, to their respective engagements, the two people came rapidly to concentrate upon the same body of practical matters in the running of hospitals and the diminution of the sum of misery and pain.

Similarly, although Fitzpatrick was a physician, he had neither superior knowledge to nor *locus standi* against the military doctors; he never attempted, except in the most general of matters, such as the purblind uniformity of treatment or the neglect of the wards, to challenge the army physicians on their own ground. Practically speaking, he adopted as fully the layman's role in military medicine as Nightingale did (ostensibly, at any rate) sixty years on. Thus, beneath the variety of circumstances, background, time and persons there was an essential similarity of situation between the two. Each had, by one chance or other, become the protégé or protégée of a minister of war. Each had been despatched to the front with loose instructions and an indeterminate range of action and authority. None the less the assignment of the superintendent of nurses and of the inspector general of health alike might be roughly translated as a commission to aid and report upon the sick and wounded in army hospitals and transport.

The correspondence between the reactions of the two administrative adventurers to army medicine at war was also extraordinarily close despite the chasms of period and place. 'The root of the evils which have to be dealt with', wrote Nightingale's biographer in paraphrase of his subject's dicta, 'is *division of responsibility and reluctance to assume it*.'[42] This is, in a highly epigrammatic form, the substance of Sir Jeremiah's fundamental criticism of the system which he encountered. Moreover, not only were the two apprehensions virtually identical, but also each of the apprehenders was an instinctive unifier and centraliser in government, and a natural assumer of authority. If we examine the first five or six weeks of Nightingale's services in Scutari – a period corresponding to Fitzpatrick's stay in Holland – we find her discerning substantially the same evils as he had done, and even doing so in much the same sequence.

It was the deplorable conditions in which the sick were transported by sea and the deficiencies in supply which first caught her attention. On her very first full day at Scutari – Sunday, 5 November 1854 – Miss Nightingale encountered the problem of the sea transport of the sick from the Crimea. The surviving wounded after the battle of Balaclava, fought eleven days before, were still being disembarked at the Barrack Hospital. [43] It was essentially the same story as that of the ships and barges at Helvoetsluys and Rhenen in December 1794 – the mass of men, some dead already, packed on the open decks and between decks, the lack of medicine, food, drink and covering, the single surgeon tending hundreds, handing out the uniform placebo to the dying, the fevered and the injured indiscriminately. All that had changed was the early Victorian pills which replaced the purgative sugar and the like of the late eighteenth century.

In the Barrack Hospital itself food was the first deficiency, in both importance and the order of Miss Nightingale's response. Bread, beef and tea, all more or less badly prepared, were the only diet; it often took three to four hours to distribute them about the wards; and the portions of vestigial scraps hardened or putrefied under cots and pillows. Like Sir Jeremiah, Nightingale attempted to reorder the kitchens and meal distribution, to provide 'supplementary diet' and to enlarge and diversify the food allowances, as well as to relate them to the various needs of the different categories of sick. Again, like him, she was immediately appalled by the lack of night attendance by the orderlies as well as by the general lack of attendance by the doctors, but was powerless at first to do more than deplore. Next came the assaults upon dirt − the quick removal of the tubs of excreta, the clearing of accumulated filth from the space beneath the beds, the scrubbing and lime-washing of wood and walls, saturated with organic matter. Next, the cleaning of the men themselves, their flea-, louse- and maggot-ridden, blood-stained and mud-caked sheets and blankets, their beards, hair and bodies; then, the attempt to secure from the purveyors all that was needed for this task (as well as for the tasks earlier defined) − coppers and kettles, plates and mugs, knives and spoons, soap and basins, scissors and sacking, bedding and clothes, medical supplies. Finally, Nightingale was led like Fitzpatrick into the field of hospital extension and reconstruction. This is an epitome, somewhat artificially schematised though broadly in the sequence in which the subjects of 'reform' were broached, of Nightingale's first month or so in Scutari.

Thus essentially the same path in observation and attempted remedy was followed by Miss Nightingale sixty years after the original Dutch disaster. It would seem reasonable to conclude that Fitzpatrick's findings and actions in Holland were, respectively, true and rational in substance. The pattern of undesired but inevitable conflict with the purveyors, the physicians and the hospital administration underlay both episodes. So too did the pattern of appeal, on the one hand, for supplies or intervention, and on the other, to the supporting ministers in Whitehall. Even much the same emotional gamut was run. After some three weeks in Holland Fitzpatrick had 'rejoiced' in having come: 'how necessary it was'.[44] After some ten days in Scutari, Nightingale, despite all the blood and horror, echoed St Peter at the Transfiguration, 'It is good for us to be here.'[45] Fitzpatrick's 'holy' elation was followed by an inrush of despair as he found himself powerless to move the faculty; Nightingale's when she felt herself doomed to ineffectuality and confusion by the impending arrival of Mary Stanley's party. Content returned, to a greater or less degree, in each case when the reformer gained or regained the management of the relevant affairs of a hospital.

This protracted comparison is not meant to imply that Fitzpatrick was of equal or even nearly equal stature to Nightingale. Her intelligence was of the highest order, her energy bottomless, her will indomitable. In fact this is the point, precisely — that even a commonplace person could — and did — analyse the problems and compose the solutions (or rather countervailing expedients) in the same fashion as the most gifted. The real answer to the question, 'Why (relative to Nightingale) did Fitzpatrick fail?' must be sought elsewhere than in his own inferiority.

One of Nightingale's fundamental advantages was the possession of independent funds. This bought her subordinates, a separate organisation and a measure of control of her own undertaking. Fitzpatrick also had considerable strength in this respect. Just as Nightingale could furnish the 'supplementary diet' at Scutari from money under her personal command, he could buy additional supplies at the government's expense. Exactly how far he was authorised to purchase new goods or services is unknown. But evidently his discretion was wide: before he left Helvoetsluys he had already expended over £200.[46] After his return from Holland he wrote, 'The Moneys I laid out in the pressing necessities for the Sick was by order of Mr Dundas, with his hearty thanks, [he] in the name of the Service paid my Order, by Evan Nepean Esq his then Secretary.'[47] None the less, Sir Jeremiah's situation was very much the weaker. He was after all a paid official; he lacked assistants; he could buy neither labour nor services; nothing lay under his own control. Moreover, Nightingale's station and location were markedly more favourable. Her specific duty was to act where Fitzpatrick's was to investigate and report; she served with a victorious and not a defeated army; she had a safe and single base, he scrambled from place to place in the midst of a general retreat.

Worse still, Fitzpatrick lacked access to 'public opinion' and had to operate within a generally closed political system. The facts that Nightingale was a woman, a nurse and a Victorian does not, as I have said, serve to distinguish her role sharply from Fitzpatrick's. But it certainly helps to explain her comparative success. By the mid-1850s in fact — particularly in the breakdown of party in the mid-1850s when the House of Commons came closer than ever before or after to controlling government, and the newspapers came closer than ever before or after to dominating the House of Commons — 'popular sentiment' was master in Great Britain. Such a venture as Nightingale's in the Crimea could not have been more felicitously timed, in terms of the power which an extra-governmental and extra-political campaign might suddenly amass. The elements of the venture moreover could not have been attuned more sweetly to their day. The venture was modest, heroic, novel, merciful, protestant and patrician in its emanations. Above all, it was feminine, and at that so extraordinary a form of femininity that it struck responsive chords in male dominance and women's aspirations alike. The year 1854 represented a moment of equipoise in this particular thing, when the image of ministering-angel seemed equally satisfying to those who sharply divided the sexes' roles and those who struggled for parity between them. In short, Nightingale was a burning glass focused upon a second burning glass, massed opinion, which in turn concentrated the doubled power upon a third, the complex of metropolitan editors, publicists, preachers and parliamentarians which governed governments. By contrast, Fitzpatrick possessed no leverage whatever.

Finally, Nightingale had the supreme advantage of membership of the governing class. Fitzpatrick was, it is true, supported by Dundas during his career in Holland, at least to the degree of not being repudiated; and he said later that Nepean had despatched him to the front with adjurations to go forward in his reforming work.[48] None the less, his standing was precarious. As an outside and an *arriviste*, he lacked any hold over the men in office other than that which his personal persuasion could continue to provide. Nightingale's relations with Sidney Herbert, for example, were of a very different order from Fitzpatrick's with Dundas. They were underlain by long acquaintance, by networks of cousinhoods, by knowledge of the same secret social language. Fitzpatrick, an Irish soldier of fortune in government, was not only without the dominant caste but even lacked the partial compensation of a patron committed in any serious sense to his cause. This was a disastrous deficiency.

Notes

1. For the general setting and an outline of the campaign, see J.S. Watson, *The Reign of George III* (Oxford, 1960), pp. 363-70.
2. E.W. Harcourt (ed.), *The Harcourt Papers*, 14 vols. (Oxford, n.d.), vol. 4, pt. 2, p. 511.
3. Fitzpatrick to Nepean, 10 December 1794, W.O. 1/897, ff.91-3.
4. Fitzpatrick to Nepean, 13 December 1794, W.O. 1/897, ff.95-6.
5. Fitzpatrick to Nepean, 10 December 1794, W.O. 1/897, ff.91-3. Craven to Transport Commissioners, 10 December 1794, Adm. 108/34, 18 December 1794; Transport Commissioners to Craven, 18 December 1794, Adm. 108/34.
6. Fitzpatrick to Nepean, 13 December 1794, W.O. 1/897, ff.97-8.
7. R.L. Blanco, *Wellington's Surgeon General: Sir James McGrigor* (Durham,

The Layman with the Lamp 189

N.C., 1974), pp. 27-30.

8. Craig to Nepean, 12 August 1794, W.O. 1/169, quoted by Fortescue, *History of British Army*, vol. 4, pt. 1, p. 300.

9. Fortescue, *British Army*, vol. 4, pt. 1, p. 314; see also An Officer of the Guards, *An Accurate and Impartial Narrative of the War*, 2 vols. (London, 1785), vol. 2, p. 99, 'The general orders issued at this time for the removal of the sick; [sic] proved a death warrant for numberless helpless and miserable objects.'

10. Fitzpatrick to the aide-de-camp of the commander-in-chief, 21 December 1794, W.O. 1/897, ff.111-13.

11. 'Advantages Obtained for the British Army in Holland', December 1794, W.O. 1/897, ff.83-8.

12. Fitzpatrick to Nepean, 29 December 1794, W.O. 1/897, f.119.

13. 'Advantages Obtained for the British Army in Holland', December 1794, W.O. 1/897, ff.83-8.

14. Fitzpatrick to Nepean, 13 December 1794, W.O. 1/897, f.98.

15. Fitzpatrick to Nepean, 25 December 1794, W.O. 1/897, ff. 107-10.

16. Harcourt (ed.), *Harcourt Papers*, vol. 4, pt. 2, p. 386.

17. See Officer of the Guards, *Narrative*, pp. 99-100. 'Constantly removed in waggons, exposed to the intense severity of the weather, to drifting snow and heavy falls of sleet and rain; frequently without any victuals, till the *army halted*, and then but scantily provided; littered down in cold churches, upon a short allowance of dirty straw . . . it is no wonder they expired, martyrs to the most infamous and unpardonable neglect.'

18. Fitzpatrick to Nepean, 29 December 1794, W.O. 1/897, f.118.

19. See Officer of the Guards, *Narrative*, pp. 103-4, for a description of a family which had frozen to death.

20. Fitzpatrick to Nepean, 6 January 1795, W.O. 1/897, ff.121-3.

21. 'Advantages Obtained for the British Army in Holland', December 1794, W.O. 1/897, f.87.

22. Fitzpatrick to Nepean, 6 January 1795, W.O. 1/897, ff.121-5.

23. Fitzpatrick to Nepean, 25 December 1794, W.O. 1/897, f.110.

24. Fortescue, *British Army*, vol. 4, pt. 1, pp. 323-4; Blanco, *Wellington's Surgeon General*, p. 30.

25. Fitzpatrick to Nepean, 9 January 1795, W.O. 1/897, ff.129-30.

26. Fitzpatrick to Nepean, 13 January 1795, W.O. 1/897, ff.134-6.

27. Fitzpatrick to Nepean, 24 January 1795, W.O. 1/897, ff.142-3.

28. Fitzpatrick to Smith, 24 January 1795, W.O. 1/897, ff.149-51.

29. Fitzpatrick to Barrackmaster, Deal, 24 January 1795, W.O. 1/897, ff.157-9.

30. Fitzpatrick to Surgeon Newbold of the Berkshire Militia, 24 January 1795, W.O. 1/897, ff.153-4.

31. Ibid., f.153

32. Dundas to Fitzpatrick, 8 September 1794, W.O. 1/897, f.6. These instructions can also be found in *House of Commons Sessional Papers of the Eighteenth Century*, 100, Reports and papers 1795-6, Forces West Indies, no. 15, 67-8.

33. Fitzpatrick to Nepean, 26 January 1795, W.O. 1/897, ff.145-7.

34. Fitzpatrick to Dundas, 26 March 1795, W.O. 1/897, ff.261-2.

35. Fitzpatrick to Woodward, 12 December 1794, W.O. 1/897, ff.99-101.

36. Fitzpatrick to Nepean, 6 January 1795, W.O. 1/897, f.125.

37. Dr J. Borland's evidence, *Fifth Report of the Commissioners of Military Enquiry*, 1808, v (6), 160; W. Fergusson, *Notes and Recollections of a Professional Life* (London, 1846), p. 56, quoted by Blanco, *Wellington's Surgeon General*, p. 31.

38. J. McGrigor, *The Autobiography and Services of Sir James McGrigor Bart., Late Director General of the Army Medical Department* (London, 1861), p. 32. See also S.G.P. Ward, *Wellington's Headquarters: a Study of the Administrative Problems in the Peninsula 1809-1814* (Oxford, 1957), for McGrigor's later career.

39. Officer of the Guards, *Narrative*, vol. 2, p. 89. See also Fortescue, *British Army*, vol. 4, pt. 1, p. 314.

40. The Fifth Report of the Military Commissioners in 1808 led to the dissolution of the old Army Medical Board in 1809.

41. See Sir E. Cook, *The Life of Florence Nightingale*, 2 vols. (London, 1913), vol. 1, pp. 145-308.

42. Ibid., p. 179.

43. I.B. O'Malley, *Florence Nightingale, 1820-1856: a Study of her Life down to the End of the Crimean War* (London, 1931), pp. 224-64.

44. Fitzpatrick to Nepean, 25 December 1794, W.O. 1/897, f.110.

45. Nightingale to Bowman, 14 November 1854, quoted by Cook, *Florence Nightingale*, vol. 1, p. 184.

46. Fitzpatrick to Nepean, 13 December 1794, W.O. 1/897, ff.95-6.

47. 'Advantages Obtained for the British Army in Holland', December 1794, W.O. 1/897, f.88.

48. Fitzpatrick to Huskisson, 18 March 1795, W.O. 1/897, f.239.

9 WATERLOO, 1795

Fitzpatrick landed, and spent the last nine days of January 1795 at the Kent port of Deal. As has been said, it was Holland all over again. At once he attempted to reorganise and improve the temporary military hospital in which the sick and wounded troops from the continent were first lodged after evacuation. Again he was horrified by the dirt, disorder and indiscipline in the infirmary, and attempted to compel the hospital surgeons and other staff to mend their ways. Nine days were too short a time for even Sir Jeremiah to believe that he had achieved much good. But they were certainly long enough to do some harm – to himself. The resentment which his hectoring and intervention had aroused among the army doctors in the Netherlands was heightened and brought into focus by his continuance in the same course at Deal. Later he himself wrote of the episode at Deal as determining the fixed and unrelenting hostility of the Army Medical Board to himself.[1]

Once more, however, the denouement was postponed. Nine regiments had recently been embarked at Plymouth to sail with Admiral Hyde Parker's fleet as reinforcements for the West Indies; and malignant fever had broken out on board the transports. As soon as he was apprised of the disaster, Dundas urgently directed Fitzpatrick to cross from Deal to Plymouth. When he reached Plymouth on 2 February, Fitzpatrick found that three of the regiments were infected (the 38th Regiment having nearly one hundred men ill aboard, apart from its patients in shore hospitals), with the fleet on the point of sailing. Within forty-eight hours he had managed to disembark the obviously sick, to find transports to use as temporary hospital ships, and to arrange with Parker for these vessels to be convoyed later by a frigate to Torbay where Parker was to rendezvous with Admiral Howe. Fitzpatrick had made an excellent impression on Parker, whose pressure had soon brought a cavilling transport service officer to heel; and Fitzpatrick reciprocated warmly. 'Whenever I apply to persons who care more about the good of the service than their own self-importance,' he told Nepean, 'I succeed.'[2]

In fact storms kept Parker in Plymouth harbour for the next week. It was a week of incessant activity for Sir Jeremiah despite the fact that he himself contracted fever, even despite his heroic self-prescription of 'Hock, Cyder & Fruits'. He removed 111 men from the 17th

Regiment to two new hospital vessels, and began — doubtless more in hope than expectation — to plan what he said was really needed, the removal of all 10,000 (the average regiment slightly exceeded 1,000 in strength) troops from the infected vessels, so that these might be thoroughly purified and fumigated.[3]

Meanwhile he had fallen into a new scrape. While he lay ill in bed in his inn on 9 February, Murray, the colonel of the 96th Regiment, his surgeon and his major called to protest against Fitzpatrick's ordering sixteen of the men of the regiment to a hospital ship. In half a dozen cases, youth or old age was the primary reason given for the removal. Of course, the war department responded that the inspector's concern was 'how far the people were diseased — their time of life was no point for his consideration'. Equally of course Sir Jeremiah responded in his turn that the boys and ancients in question were 'diseased': one boy had curvature of the spine, while the removal of three 'diseased' men, aged 62, 65 and 67 years respectively, would still leave Murray with many fit greybeards 'who can relate the actions in which they bore a part in the years 1757-8-9'.[4] Fitzpatrick also worked out a scheme with Lord George Lennox, now as before his warm ally, for making up the numbers in the companies which had been reduced in strength through 'losses' to the hospital ships.[5] The inspector and lieutenant-governor were ordered to stick to their lasts, and in the event, Murray appears to have held his grip successfully upon the half a dozen in dispute by refusing them permission to leave their transports. But Fitzpatrick probably felt that the battle, which he kept up to the point of sailing, was well worth while. Colonels, he wrote, had a dreadful propensity to maintain the numerical strength of their companies by fair means or foul,[6] and would certainly capitalise on any weakening on the inspector's part.

As it happened, the colonels proved remarkably untroublesome. Fitzpatrick was unable to carry out his full scheme of landing all the fit men in rotation, inspecting them quickly ashore, furnishing them with clean linen, knapsacks and bedding, seeing that they were shaved and washed, and in the meantime fumigating the vacated vessels, one by one. Five of the regiments sailed with Parker for Portsmouth as soon as the storms died away, but the four suffering most from infection were allowed to remain at Plymouth, to be dealt with as Fitzpatrick proposed. He himself wished to pursue even the five healthiest regiments, and for a day or two entertained a madcap notion of posting across to Portsmouth to set up his 'system' there.[7] But he had more than enough to do at Plymouth. Treating four regiments and their shipping as he desired implied the provision of new accommodation for some 2,500 men (in round figures 300 ill, 200 convalescent and 2,000 in the course of being inspected), and the great majority of these billets would have to be newly found on shore. Moreover the entire operation would have to be complete within three weeks at the outside if the troops were to have any hope of catching Parker's fleet at Portsmouth or nearby; and, Fitzpatrick being Fitzpatrick, he heaped other labours on himself by pressing for changes in the ship's provisions and additions to their prophylactics, and by ordering special brewings and bakings in the town. Porter and bread of good quality, he argued, would prove a true economy in the long run for enfeebled men about to embark on active service[8]. Of course, Fitzpatrick intended to inspect each man himself, in addition to maintaining his daily torrent of correspondence, reports and journal entries.

On 19 February he began his task by supervising the conversion of the Mill Prison into both a convalescent hospital and a quarantine, and of a section of the New Barracks in another part of Plymouth into a second quarantine, through which the troops would pass before being permitted to re-board their transports. He spent the entire day, he told Nepean, with 'builders and workmen and carpenters', 'arguing and ordering'. But he hoped that within twenty-four hours, or at worst forty-eight, the buildings would be ready, and sufficient bedding on hand for 2,000 men.[9] In fact it was five days before the first two regiments, the 17th and the 31st, could be disembarked, but even this was a stupendous piece of work; and within four days more the remaining two regiments had been landed. Additional delays had occurred and fresh demands on space had been made because the colonels were unable to furnish second sets of clothes and knapsacks for their men. This Fitzpatrick graciously allowed to be a 'reasonable' objection to his scheme, from officers who were co-operating with him as best they could.[10] But it did mean that no man could leave shore quarantine until all his clothing, newly laundered, had been returned from the regimental ships, which were themselves being fumigated.

The bulk of this huge and multifarious work was done by Sir Jeremiah himself, flying from fever hospital to convalescent hospital, from hospital ship to regimental transport, from quarantine barrack to quartermaster's store, and from the lieutenant-governor's to the naval or transport service's offices. But he was swimming with the tide of general support and approval throughout February. The navy, from Hyde Parker downwards; the colonels, with the early exception of Murray of the 96th; and the transport officers, once Fitzpatrick had induced Dundas to order them on 6 February[11] to provide him with every possible facility, had all striven earnestly to help. But Lord George Lennox's backing towered over all.[12] He believed that he had found in Fitzpatrick the answer to the problems of death, disorder and squalor which had beset him at Plymouth for the past eighteen months. Not only did he endorse Fitzpatrick's various proposals, use his authority freely on Fitzpatrick's behalf, and virtually place his aide-de-camp, Colonel Sabine, at Fitzpatrick's disposal during the crisis, he even encouraged him in his exorbitance. Together they returned in late February to the task of culling from the remaining regiments those whom Sir Jeremiah regarded as unfit for service, whether or not they were suffering from a specific disease. This time the colonels did not resist, although no less than 530 men were eventually invalided, discharged or appointed to garrison duty. The folly of embarking 'absolute encumbrances, consuming food and space and contributing only to disease' had long been a King Charles's head for Lennox and Fitzpatrick alike.

Meanwhile, however, the two men were unwittingly laying, or helping to lay, the powder train for the explosion which wrecked Fitzpatrick's career at Plymouth. During his first weeks at Plymouth, Sir Jeremiah had been on almost as amicable terms with the army medical corps as with the other military and naval services in the port. John Boone, the chief army physician in Plymouth, could provide no beds in the three existing military 'hospitals' when Fitzpatrick first arrived; nor had he any medical staff to spare. He had seemed delighted when Fitzpatrick had procured and fitted up the first hospital ships, and found two surgeons of his own, Cambell and Donovan (the first, a surgeon in the artillery and the second, surgeon to a fencible corps) from among the guests at the inn where he was quartering. According to Fitzpatrick, Boone

> laid his hand on my shoulder, and said, it was a lucky thing to get them; and he desired that those Gentlemen should wait on him, to whom he not only gave Medicines, but the necessary sorts of Diet, Wine &c., and gave them power, by what I understood, to get whatever they wanted at his Druggists.[13]

This is likely enough. Boone was old, idle and negligent, as well as overburdened, and Fitzpatrick was taking off his shoulders the entire new burden which threatened to descend upon them. So long as Fitzpatrick possessed and was occupied by his own domain, the hospital ships, no difficulties arose. Nor did any difficulty of significance arise even after Fitzpatrick set up his own shore establishment at Mill Prison. Donovan took charge this, leaving of the hospital ship to Cambell; and Boone's purveyor, Fleming, the same surgeon whose humanity Fitzpatrick had praised a year before, attended both makeshift infirmaries daily to provide and authorise the supplies. Here there certainly was some friction, as we can infer from Sir Jeremiah's report:

> in all cases I took concern in seeing that every article intended for the Sick, and for which I am certain Government pays, was supplied and in readiness; and would not allow the hacknied apologies, of, *its being time enough* and that Matters were, *well enough*, and done and executed *as was usual*.[14]

But though Fleming may have been reluctant, he none the less complied.

But when it came to the disembarkation of the four regiments left behind in Plymouth, Fitzpatrick had considered using beds in the regular military hospitals under Boone's direction. Lennox, who had long been concerned by 'the daily mortality and criminal neglects' in these hospitals, had been urging Fitzpatrick to inspect them for some time.[15] But it was not until 19 or 20 February that he first did so. At once there was trouble. By the 22nd an inquiry had been held at the Friary hospital on Fitzpatrick's charges against three of the assistant army surgeons serving there: Boone and Sabine had joined with Sir Jeremiah to constitute an informal judicial body. The specific charges against the assistant surgeons were the insufficiencies of attendance, of prescriptions, of heating and of appropriate drinks, and failure to keep up the prescription book. According to Fitzpatrick, all the charges were admitted by the defendants, although they blamed the material deficiencies on Boone and Fleming, who had not provided enough supplies. Boone himself claimed that most of the trouble arose from the shore hospitals being grossly understaffed. But Sir Jeremiah added, in his report to Dundas, a root-and-branch condemnation of 'the Mansion of Misery' (as he termed the Friary hospital), from the broken windows, roofs and doors which exposed the eighty poor wretches immured there to the torments of rain and cold to the total lack of segregation according to ailment among the patients, and their being treated only during the doctors' set daily hour.[16] This was throwing down the gauntlet to the Medical Board, for it was their 'system' of regulating army hospitals which was being excoriated.

Hitherto Fitzpatrick had been comparatively cautious in his dealings with the medical corps. He had been careful not to prescribe himself nor to allow his 'own' surgeons to do so. Nor had he intervened in 'supplies' beyond pressing for the scheduled quantities and for what he regarded as worthy quality. Even now he rejected Lennox's offer to arrange for the three assistant surgeons to be court-martialled; and he attempted to forestall counter-action at the start by observing that everyone who was threatened would naturally work to persuade the government 'that I am troublesome rather than usefull' – with the rider, of course, that he would continue to perform his duty fearlessly.[17]

Despite all this Fitzpatrick had taken a fatal step in holding his inquiry into the conduct of the army surgeons and reporting upon it in passionate terms to the war department. He might determine to be cautious, but caution sat ill upon his shoulders. Even after the inquiry at the Friary hospital had been concluded, he could not resist taking Sabine about the wards and on finding a patient 'neglected' because it was not 'customary' for the medical staff to make morning visits, summoning a surgeon whom he 'rated' publicly.[18] But perhaps it was just ill-luck which rendered Fitzpatrick's step a fatal one. For this was the precise juncture at which Nepean left the war department to become Secretary of the Admiralty, and Huskisson was promoted to his place. It appears to have been Huskisson who forwarded, through Windham, Sir Jeremiah's letter of 27 February on the Friary hospital affair to the Army Medical Board, and thereby, in effect, ensured a declaration of open war. It may be that Nepean would have done the same. The holding of even an informal inquiry into neglect of duty may have rendered the action inevitable. For that matter, the army medical staff at Plymouth was bound to retaliate, and attempt to discredit Fitzpatrick whatever happened; and this might well have had the same effect. On the other hand, Fitzpatrick was Nepean's protégé and his relations with Huskisson were, and remained, correct and civil rather than warm and eager as with Nepean; and Nepean had never passed on to the Medical Board any of Fitzpatrick's savage criticisms of their surgeons and hospitals in the Netherlands or at Deal. At any rate, whether or not it had been inevitable from the moment that the letter of 27 February had been sent, the die was cast once it was forwarded to the Medical Board.

It was three weeks more, however, before Fitzpatrick received any inkling that he was launched upon a sea of troubles. Boone acquiesced in everything which he proposed at Plymouth, and Boone's subordinates were to all appearances cowed by the findings of the inquiry.

Fitzpatrick was still busy with passing the troops through his 'system'. But he now had a little more time for devising (for example, he fitted up a room in the quarantine for fumigating clothes once he knew that the regiments could not supply a second complete set of clothing for every man), for intervening (in the existing military hospitals) and for directing (the building of the new hospital, among other things). It was therefore with pained surprise that he received on 18 March a peremptory letter from Huskisson summoning him to London, and implying that his work at Plymouth was practically completed. Fitzpatrick began by attempting to dispel this last illusion.

> You seem to imagine by your letter that there is little at present to require my attendance here. I could wish that to be the case; and when Mr Dundas comes to know the difficulties I have to encounter, as well in the arrangement of matters in our new buildings with their necessary alterations to render them convenient and healthful, the hitherto unknown mode of conducting the hospital departments, with the prevention of abuses therein, and the manner of classifying the diseased and bringing the convalescents forward with safety to join their respective regiments, and holding those forward for actual service as men in their shoes. I flatter myself that he [Dundas] will be pleased with my conduct. I have an extensive field and am determined to weed and meliorate it. I will remember Mr Nepean's last direction — go on.[19]

He could not leave for London, he continued, unless he could procure Donovan as a *locum tenens*, at least for routine hospital and troop inspections, as well as the approval of Lennox and Boone of his temporary absence. He had no intention moreover of spending all his time with Huskisson on the defensive. In the notes which he prepared for his interview with Huskisson, Fitzpatrick reminded himself to ask to have a cutter and crew at his disposal, to include East India vessels among those to be inspected, to be specifically empowered to test the quality of ships' supplies and to be allowed to continue with his purchases of fumigation materials.[20] At the same time he was well aware that there were dangers ahead. On 22 March, the day he left for London, Lennox, doubtless by arrangement with Fitzpatrick, wrote to Dundas urging that he be speedily returned;

> unless he returns, in my opinion the result of all the good He has

been doing, will be useless Expence, & a compleat confusion in every Department that relates to the Sick, for it is impossible to be otherwise until He has had an opportunity of finishing his Work, of arranging his Plans & of forming the necessary Regulations.[21]

Lennox, having pointed out that 175 men had died in the past three weeks and that 6 March was the only death-free day in the preceding four months, concluded, 'I sincerely hope that there are not many places that require Sir Jerome's presence more than Plymouth.'[22]

Fitzpatrick's meeting with Huskisson was comparatively cordial, although colder in tone than his dealings with Dundas or Nepean. The basic complaint against him was of course his interference in the fields of others, in particular, the Army Medical Board.[23] But he was also in trouble with the Barrack Board. At the end of 1794, the War Office had suddenly responded to Lennox's year-long pleas for the institution of a permanent military hospital at Plymouth. Much to his annoyance, Lord George only learnt of this decision when General de Lancey, who was in charge of military construction, was actually in the town to select the site and prepare for building; and Fitzpatrick too was aggrieved — perhaps unreasonably, as he was then in Holland — because he was not consulted. When he discovered, after a few days in Plymouth, what was afoot, he rushed to the site and ordered various alterations in the buildings without securing the agreement of or even informing de Lancey.[24] The War Office had been at fault of course in proceeding quite independently of Lennox — and possibly at fault too in acting independently of Fitzpatrick in the light of the oversight of hospital building which had been awarded to him, however vaguely, in his original instructions. But Fitzpatrick himself had also been at fault; and the War Office being his master, this was the fault which counted. He pleaded that the alterations were the merest common sense, and that he had had neither time nor an address to reach de Lancey. None the less, he had been exorbitant and was in trouble on a second front.

Fitzpatrick readily agreed with Huskisson that he should communicate in future with the relevant authorities to explain his interventions and recommendations: it would prevent jealousy, possibly secure their aid and, in any event, permit proper budgeting. He had no satisfactory defence for — only a voluble elucidation of — his invasion of de Lancey's province. But the Barrack Board's expostulation was a mere matter of form: neither now nor later was there bad blood between this board and Sir Jeremiah. In the case of his real enemy, the Medical Board, however, he could plead the acquiescence of Boone in every action which he had taken. What matter that Boone was indolent and easily intimidated: 'if they do not choose to send on such Occasions a Man of Abilities and Vigilance the fault is not mine'. None the less, the future was frightening. It looked as if Fitzpatrick would be required from now on to obtain the sanction of the Medical Board before acting in many, if not most of his accustomed fields: 'the child of my affections and the adoption of Mr Dundas himself', he cried out, would thus be endangered. If he were forced to observe scenes of misery and cruelty, unable to act 'other than thro' the indirect road of the Army Medical Board', instead of delighting in his appointment, he should regret 'the Infant stabb'd in its Birth'. Instead, as Helvoetsluys, Rhenen, Deal and Plymouth had all shown, the vital thing was that there should be someone 'to take a part in favour of the poor unfortunate Soldiers', and that the Medical Board should be told firmly that this was Sir Jeremiah's appointed role.[25]

Fitzpatrick begged an interview with Dundas before fresh instructions were issued,[26] and he appears to have fared better there. In revising his commission, in a letter of 8 April 1795, Dundas agreed to his immediate return to Plymouth 'in order that the Improvements you have suggested in the Accommodation, Diet, and Medical Attendance of the Sick may be continued under your immediate Inspection'. On the other hand, the 'Misunderstanding' with the Medical Board and the Barrack Board would greatly damage the service, 'if not counteracted at its present Stage'. Fitzpatrick was told that if any of his proposed alterations or innovations were resisted by a local medical, barrack or transport officer, either because he disagreed with it or because he did not think that sanction for it lay within his powers, the plan was to be submitted at once to the relevant department and the local officer told that this had been done so that he too could write to his department.[27] What was to happen if the department rejected Sir Jeremiah's plan? Nothing was said of this, but obviously the department would prevail.

Dundas was placing his trust in the supersession of the politics of conflict by the politics of consensus. The government policy which had led to the creation of the inspectorship of army health, to forward 'whatever Arrangement can contribute to the Preservation of the Health, and to the Care, Comfort, and Accommodation of the Sick and Convalescents, in His Majesty's Forces', was unchanged.[28] But Dundas told Fitzpatrick that he was sure he could overcome the obstacles which he had hitherto encountered in pursuing it, by tact and conciliation. This of course passed over, in its hearty way, various immutable contrary traits in Fitzpatrick's personality. It also ignored the Medical

Board's enmity to him, which was already set, and the fact that, as Fitzpatrick put it, 'the Army Medical Board and I stand on very different Grounds',[29] with the one primarily concerned to defend its system and its men, and the other to discover the defects in both. Dundas's final paragraph epitomised his efforts to square the circle, to reconcile army discipline, administrative regularity and humane reform:

> I cannot, however, close this Letter without cautioning you against an Evil to which, from your Anxiety to promote the Public Service you might otherwise unwarily contribute. The Point I allude to is the dangerous Tendency of making Remarks, or entering into Explanations in Presence of the Sick, and particularly of the Soldiers embarked or under Orders to Proceed on Foreign Service. Conversations of this Nature, and especially if they are accompanied with any Strictures on the Conduct of the Medical or other Officers, to whose habitual Care the soldiers are committed, will, if disseminated, create Uneasiness and Discontent, and destroy the necessary Confidence which ought to be reposed in such Persons. It is far from my Intention to intimate by this that you ought to omit noticing any Instance which may occur of Neglect or improper Behaviour; but it will be your Duty, in all such Cases, to confine the Communication of your Observations to the Officer superior in Command to the Person on whom the Blame may attach, or to the proper Department in Town, who will, I am confident, pay all due Attention to your Representation. I can only add, that you will at all Times find me ready to give the most effectual Support to your unremitting Exertions for the Amelioration of the important Branch of the Public Service committed to your Care and Abilities, and to assist your laudable Efforts in promoting your beneficial Pursuits for the Health and Comfort of His Majesty's Troops.[30]

Despite the new restraints and the rebukes, Fitzpatrick had emerged from his first major trial remarkably well. Short of a direct challenge to the entire army medical service, which did not even come within his ministerial province, Dundas could scarcely have avoided an instruction to him to refer his hospital and sanitary plans to the Medical Board; and the rebukes were not only mild but also warmly tempered by praise and expressions of trust. Above all Sir Jeremiah had not been removed from Plymouth or even discouraged from instituting his 'systems' there. Nor had any of the Medical Board's complaints of his conduct in the town (except for what could not possibly be avoided, his dressing down of an army surgeon in a privates' ward) been so much as mentioned. Finally it seemed clear that Fitzpatrick still retained, substantially, Dundas's confidence.

He returned to Plymouth, more determined perhaps than chastened. New building was a straightforward enough affair. He briskly drew up a list of further 'necessary' improvements in the permanent hospital and also in the Plymouth barracks, and dispatched them to de Lancey. Characteristically, his glance at barrack building led him into a fresh field for reform. De Lancey had failed to secure the sites adjoining a new barrack being built in Plymouth, and now, unless the War Office paid exorbitantly to acquire them, they would probably be used, Fitzpatrick said, for brothels or tippling houses. With barracks going up all over the country, he wrote to Dundas, this was a large and general problem:

> it will little avail in many places, the proper choice [being] made of any situations, and those removed some distance from Towns, as well for the purity of air, as to prevent increasing intercourse or tippling of the soldiers in Dram-Shops and Night Houses, if some stop is not put to the construction or building of such Houses.[31]

Nor would things be much better if noxious trades — 'slaughterhouses, shambles, skinners, Glue Boilers Yards, Glass Houses &c' — were carried on adjacent to the barracks, contaminating the soldiers' air. Fitzpatrick proposed to Dundas the introduction of legislation authorising the barrack master-general and the inspector of army health, together, to disallow the use of buildings close to army barracks for purposes which they considered injurious to the interests of the troops; and also to empower them to acquire contiguous land compulsorily to set out adequate sewage systems. He could not resist dangling before Dundas a possible addition to the Bill (patently the child of some dispute with a contractor) to provide for on-site arbitration on the quality of materials used for army buildings. Even Fitzpatrick owned that the last proposal lay outside the scope of his office, and he played the usual card of the Georgian reformer with a feeble hand by talking loudly of the money it would save.[32]

All this, and the busy round of troop inspections, segregations and clearances which Sir Jeremiah took up again on his return were, however, the lesser matters. The vital subject was hospital reform. Immediately after his return to Plymouth, Fitzpatrick reported cheerfully. Two of the hospital surgeons did not merely acquiesce in, but were eagerly forwarding his ideas, and the remainder were passive, at worst.[33] But these days of hope were few. Within a week, reports that he had been reprimanded and humiliated in London were abroad in Plymouth. Boone and the entire body of army medical men in the town drew together, sensing that the kill was close. According to Fitzpatrick, they were set upon lowering his consequence. They freely predicted his dismissal and even his trial and imprisonment for unauthorised expenditure.[34] He judged the assault upon his standing to be highly dangerous, and he was right. Sir Jeremiah was (in the literal, not the pejorative, sense) a confidence man. So long as people believed that he had powerful patrons he was powerful, just as the rising financier could borrow without let so long as no one probed the limit of his assets. But once faith in his ability to draw upon the war department for support was shaken, his empire would crumble on every side. Instinctively, Fitzpatrick had recognised this himself from the beginning. Hence his incessant appeals to Nepean and Dundas, since the preceding November, for their backing; and hence, conversely, the paucity of his references to the formal powers set out in his instructions. It was the air and not the letter of authority which he must rely on.

Fitzpatrick was probably unaware of the full extent of his danger. At just this point, on 16 April 1795, the Army Medical Board launched an open attack upon him by telling Windham that his concern appeared to be, not the good of the service, but 'to criminate the Medical Department';[35] and he would not have known of this letter for some time. But even what threatened him immediately at Plymouth sufficed to drive him into counter-attack. About 20 April he asked Lennox to institute a court-martial, charging William Elliot, one of the assistant surgeons now posted to the Mill Prison hospital, with neglects of duty resulting in the death of Hugh McKay, a private soldier in the 32nd. Fitzpatrick made it clear to Dundas that he brought the case, not because of Elliot's negligence or McKay's death, deplorable though both were, but to beat down the opposition to his hospital reforms:

> when I find that there is an established system of Error persevered in, and that any ideas are not likely, except thro' public conviction to be complied with, I am drove to those means which alone are left me.[36]

As he expressed it later, he saw the case not as one between the prisoner and himself, but one between the entire medical staff and the body of the army.[37] Presumably Lennox agreed with this; his own earlier suggestion of a court-martial[38] was rather similar in motivation. At any rate, he sanctioned the proceeding.

The second arm of Fitzpatrick's counter-offensive was to prepare a detailed scheme of reform for army general hospitals, beginning with Plymouth, and to submit it not only to Boone[39] and the Medical Board (as the revised instructions of 8 April required) but also to Dundas and Windham in the hope that they might be brought into play should the medical corps reject it — or better still that the medical corps would hesitate to reject what Dundas and Windham might well approve. The first essential of Fitzpatrick's scheme was to 'methodize' (or classify) patients, staff and hospital accommodation according to ailment. Apart from the strict segregation of those suffering from infectious diseases from the remainder, medical, surgical, convalescent and quarantine cases were each to have separate wards, surgeons and orderlies assigned to them. Next, adequate medical attendance and supplies should be ensured. The head of the medical department should attend the principal hospital daily to oversee the general management of affairs; his deputy was to oversee the next most important hospital; and so on downwards until the chain of instruction and advice would be complete. All medical staff were to make morning and evening visits to the hospitals; and to facilitate this, as many of them as practicable should live near one or other of the hospitals. Fitzpatrick added that, if this were approved, he would apply at once to the barrack master-general to fit up contiguous doctors' houses. The third proposal reads curiously now, but would have seemed quite humdrum in a day when a 'ration' of wives was allowed to each battalion. Childbirth, Sir Jeremiah proposed, should not take place in the ordinary military wards, as was currently the case, but in some isolated room 'and attended as delicacy suggests'. Finally, Fitzpatrick submitted a *pro forma* patient's record to be entered up daily by the surgeon or assistant surgeon on duty at the time.

The first three recommendations were fairly direct and obvious responses to deficiencies which Fitzpatrick had observed in the hospital system over the preceding fifteen months, and in several theatres. They were certainly clear, rational and coherent. Perhaps they were facile in assuming, after the manner of paper schemers, that large numbers, quantities and amounts of staff, buildings and money might, and would, be provided. But so far the lesson of the war seemed to be that buildings and money were available *ad lib.*, even if securing them was often a confused, risky or protracted business. As to more surgeons, the

Fitzpatrick's *Pro Forma* Patient's Record

Regiment	Name	Rank	Date Visited	Disease or Symptoms	Prescription		Wine & Quantity	Entered	Discharged	Dead	Wants in Hospital	Conduct of Orderlies
					Morning	Afternoon						

Medical Board's own prejudices and system of procurement were probably the greatest stumbling block. As the board was discovering —[40] Fitzpatrick had briskly exploited it already at Plymouth — once the standard was 'lowered' to admit Scottish and Irish medical graduates, the available supply was large. Thus, Fitzpatrick's first proposals may not have been at all utopian. Intrinsically, they were logical and to the point.

It was the fourth proposal which was really original and arresting. The patients' record sheets were meant not merely to monitor the progress of the sick and the conduct of the surgeons and thereby ensure that the earlier recommendations actually took effect. They were also meant to lay the statistical basis for advances in army medicine. In the course of time the information gathered in the record sheets should throw new light upon the causes, course and treatment of disease in hospital. When two decades later, James McGrigor became director-general of army medicine, the starting point of his efforts at reform — not to add, one of the sources of his high renown during his early years in the office — was the systematic collection of medical statistics in the military hospitals.[41] Moreover, this paper of Fitzpatrick's was intended to be the first of three, the others to deal with diet and the purveyors' department respectively.[42] Doubtless he meant to gather further information methodically on standard forms, at least upon the subjects of diet and recovery or decline.

Boone received this document on 28 April with a request to tell Fitzpatrick immediately whether he would agree to institute these reforms ('in a manner I hope pleasing to the Government') or 'on what Principles their execution are [sic] disapprov'd of by your Department'. A copy of Dundas's instructions of 8 April and a threat to call on the war department to see that the system came into effect at Plymouth accompanied the 'request'.[43] Poor Boone seemed appalled. He tried to temporise. Perhaps, he pleaded, the matter was not so urgent now that the fever had somewhat abated. Perhaps Plymouth was not the best location for such pioneering work, for its hospitals were widely scattered. In any event he needed more time for consideration. His colleagues must be conferred with, and if he and they disagreed with Fitzpatrick they would have to compose a rejoinder to forward to the Medical Board.[44] Fitzpatrick was inexorable. He would allow but twenty-four hours more before calling on the secretary of state to intervene. Presumably Boone and his staff failed to meet the deadline. At any rate the entire correspondence soon reached Huskisson's desk at the war department.

Up to a point, Fitzpatrick's double counter-offensive had some immediate success. Generally, he was content with his progress at Plymouth during the first three weeks of May. The medical opposition to him was cowed, for the time being; and best of all the entire Plymouth corps was visiting patients and prescribing and providing with quite unprecedented frequency and promptitude. Even Boone, whose sole appearance in any military hospital for months had been in response to Fitzpatrick's summons to attend the inquiry at the Friary hospital in February, now made daily examinations.[45] Sir Jeremiah was doubtless correct in his surmise that the Army Medical Board had ordered this extraordinary bout of industry. The board had been gathering material from its Plymouth staff to meet Fitzpatrick's charges since mid-April; and it would naturally have told its doctors to minimise the case which could be made against them. But Fitzpatrick was probably also correct in believing that his own audacity was having its effect upon their conduct. Not content with the forthcoming courtmartial and the hoped-for support of Dundas and Windham for his hospital scheme, he was exposing the earlier neglects 'upon all occasions, even in the public papers'. He himself considered that this attempt to appeal to opinion at large — as nearly as he could manage it in all the circumstances — was not only chastening Boone's staff at that particular moment but would also produce more lasting good. 'Whatever the result might be of the court martial on Mr Elliot,' he told Lennox on 14 May, 'whether my charges might appear ill or wellfounded, trivial or of importance to the service, I am certain great advantage [will] arise therefrom to many wretched and neglected subjects.'[46]

He was wrong. His success depended on his standing, and he had put his standing to the hazard by both his hospital proposals and his charges against Elliot. Keate eventually dealt with the first by a few words of acknowledgement so rudely phrased that Fitzpatrick refused to write to him ever again unless explicitly directed to do so.[47] Meanwhile, neither Dundas nor Windham — that is, if Fitzpatrick's appeal ever got beyond Huskisson and Matthew Lewis, his counterpart at the War Office — would intervene, at least immediately. On 17 May Sir Jeremiah pressed both secretaries of state anxiously though vainly for an opinion.[48] He had more reason for anxiety than he knew. On the preceding day the Army Medical Board had reported at last on the complaints made in his letter of 27 February.[49]

Every member of the medical corps at Plymouth had contributed something to the rebuttal, which broadly speaking amounted to this:

that the Friary was up to the normal standard of general military hospitals; that its conduct was the best that could be achieved in circumstances of extraordinary pressure; that improvements were being made; and, finally, that economy had also to be studied. Some of the surgeons and assistants argued that classifying patients and keeping the prescription books up to date (or at all) were impossible at any time; others, that they were impossible in such a crisis as that of February and March in Plymouth. But the main 'defence' was an attack upon Fitzpatrick himself (and his assistant, Donovan) as altogether inexperienced in hospital management. The Mill Prison infirmary was denounced on all sides as grossly indisciplined and wildly extravagant.[50]

All this was writ large by the board itself, which coolly assumed the role of final arbiter. It found that Fitzpatrick had not made good his charges except in trifling instances which could, it observed, happen in the best run of military hospitals. Non-attendance of its doctors at the hospitals, even Boone's total absence, was slurred over. The failure to keep prescription books and other records was attributed to the need for haste. Despite the board's having infuriated Lennox a few months before by observing that he failed to understand that segregation according to ailment was an elementary principle of hospital management, the report went on, 'We do not approve of the Classing of Diseases, which cannot be reduced to practice.'[51] The supplies ordered by Fitzpatrick were described as absurdly lavish, while his 'Language to the Soldiers, and intemperate Conduct to Medical Persons in the hearing of Soldiers' fostered dissension in the service and discontent, if not actually a spirit of mutiny, in the troops.[52] The whole imbroglio, the Medical Board concluded, arose from Fitzpatrick's

> not having been bred, or accustomed to practice, either in Physic or Surgery in Hospitals of any kind; that he is totally divisted [sic] of any Idea of Economy . . . That owing to his gross and abusive manners, together with a determined ill Opinion of Medicine and Medical Persons, and his apparent deficiency in Professional Knowledge he [Dundas] should withdraw those Instructions which allow him to interfere with the Medical Conduct of Hospitals and to order him merely (for which purposes he seems alone to be fit) to superintend the Cleanliness and Ventilation of Prisons and Transports, and in this he may undoubtedly be of Service.[53]

Judicially considered, the report scarcely met Sir Jeremiah's case.

Although a few incidents were disputed, what he complained of was in general admitted, often openly. What the episode revealed rather was the vast gap between the respective expectations and concepts of normality of the antagonists. The Army Medical Board was complacent. Any deficiencies in their system were dismissed as trivial, temporary and the consequence of either extraordinary circumstances or occasional mistakes. They spoke of the sick as if of so much material to be processed. Sir Jeremiah, however, regarded the neglects and the suffering as intolerable, however they might be palliated or explained; and, as he repeatedly observed, he saw his own duty as that of reforming radically, and himself as the prescribed champion of a host of actual, wretched people, the soldier-patients. The imaginative worlds of the board and the inspector were poles apart. But there could have been no doubt even in 1795 as to which was self-serving, slothful and ignoble.

There were of course chinks in the inspector's armour; and these were well discovered. He had never served in a military hospital in his life; perhaps he had never served in any. He *was* immoderate in condemnation. In the flush of his self-righteousness and self-importance, he did trample blindly upon the sacred army principle of rank and order, as when he berated medical staff in the open wards and (apparently) in the newspapers. Even by the hobby-horsical standards of late-eighteenth-century medicine, he rode his hobby horses wildly. He was often reckless of the cost; pints of wine were ordered not by the dozen but by the hundred, for his own establishments. But even in these cases, Fitzpatrick was not without some defence. First, being 'bred' in a hospital meant more to the Army Medical Board than the words simply implied. It meant graduation from one of the ancient English universities and having 'walked the wards' (that is formed part of the student tail which followed the physician on his rounds) in one of the great London hospitals. Supervision of the army's general hospitals was reserved for army physicians; and army physicianships were not open to surgeons or apothecaries or Scots- or Irish-trained but reserved for Oxford and Cambridge graduates who had 'walked the wards' of St Thomas's or the Middlesex or Guys — an early instance in fact of the familiar socio-economic discrimination in English life.

It was of course true, as one critic observed, that 'to pass an examination, a man need only read in his chamber, but to be able to distinguish diseases he must have visited the sick',[54] and that, as another wrote:

> unless the Physician-General can satisfy the public that when a

student is entered in the books of the university, he is presented with a key or picklock for all science, I can see no reason why a young man who knows Greek and Latin, mathematics and logic, as well as a Cambridge student, should be qualified only for glysters, while Dr. ——'s principles [fit him to treat] all diseases.[55]

None the less, the management of general hospitals was the preserve of the university men, and the Army Medical Board would have liked even the subordinate surgeonships to have been the preserve of the English — as against the Scottish and Irish — colleges, setting aside as below consideration the mere continental schools. Thus the charge against Sir Jeremiah was as much that he was neither an Oxford nor Cambridge man as that he had never worked in a military hospital, for many an Oxford or Cambridge man had been appointed to an army physicianship without ever having set eyes upon such an establishment. Moreover, it should be remembered the major part of Fitzpatrick's 'system' was concerned with organisation rather than medicine. As Dr Johnson had once pointed out, 'Who rules o'er freemen should himself be free' was as nonsensical a dictum as 'Who drives fat oxen should himself be fat'.[56]

Secondly, while Fitzpatrick could certainly not have expected the army to acquiesce in officers being rebuked before the men, or the setting aside in various other ways of its hierarchy of authority, he had after all designed for himself a type of ombudsman function, which implied an avenue of appeal for the subject and of censure for the erring officer. Moreover, he was often dealing with the most immediate problems; and as he himself asked sarcastically:

> should I have the Misfortune to meet similar distress [to that in Holland or on the south coast], and at such distance as Plymouth or Helveotsluys are, am I for Etiquette sake, to remain inactive, no matter how pressing the Case, untill I can digest my Plan and wait for the Army Medical Board's approbation?[57]

Finally, even his more bizarre remedies (as they may appear to us) were not necessarily absurd in an age of *a priori* medicine, while the free hand with which he spent government's money might quite plausibly be defended as true economy. Where four deaths out of five among the soldiers were caused by disease instead of war, it was arguable that investment in the troops' health was incomparably the more effective expenditure.

This leaves the vilification of Fitzpatrick and the attempt to degrade his office to that of a cleanser and fumigator of ships. Perhaps the billingsgate in the Medical Board's rejoinder mattered more than any of the counter-arguments, for it signalled a depth of hostility to him across which no administrative bridge could be cast. For Dundas and Windham the fact of so bitter a conflict was bound to overshadow the rights and wrongs of either of the parties in the case. The maintenance of army discipline and official reticence aside, there was nothing in the counter charges against Fitzpatrick to cause either man to throw him over. As he himself pointed out, he had 'received thanks [from Dundas and Nepean] for my conduct at Helvoetsluys, although I was not warranted to do as I did';[58] and probably he was right in believing that a further encomium for his conduct at Plymouth was on its way before it was intercepted, just in time, by the revelation of the Medical Board's enmity. Not that Dundas or Windham could have regarded the board highly. The disaster in the Netherlands had shaken its general reputation, and its insolence, self-satisfaction and delays combined to infuriate its neighbouring departments.[59] None the less, it did engross army medicine, and, as the events in Plymouth showed, it could produce complete solidarity in the medical corps when it chose. No matter what the internal divisions and dissatisfactions might be, the doctors instantly formed an irrefragable *bloc* when they were threatened from outside. It was not likely that the secretaries of state would risk open conflict with their entire body of army physicians and surgeons (the regimental surgeons apart) for Sir Jeremiah's regulations, or indeed any other cause. It was true, as he had written earlier, that 'from the Mortar Boy in the Apothecary's Shop to Mr Keate (this I know) and I fear to the other Members of the Staff Faculty, my conduct as well here [at Plymouth] as in Holland [has become] obnoxious; for the Jog trot line was not my Road'.[60] But so long as the mortar boy, Mr Keate and the remainder hung together, this 'obnoxiousness' was probably sufficient in itself to ruin Fitzpatrick's hopes.

There was still a chance, however, that Elliot's court-martial might redress the balance, for in the eyes of Plymouth at least it had grown to the dimensions of a test case. But Fitzpatrick had chosen his ground badly for a major trial of strength. When the general court-martial began its hearing on 25 May, it broke down his charges against Elliot into one of 'flagrant neglect of duty' overall, and two of specific failures to ensure sufficient attendance for, and the administration of the prescribed medicine to McKay;[61] and it refused permission to Fitzpatrick to introduce any matter which might incriminate persons other than the defendant.[62] Thus was formed a very narrow salient for Sir Jeremiah's intended onslaught on the entire army medical corps, all the more so as Elliot, doubtless on somebody's good tactical advice, withdrew his entire body of witnesses rather than expose them to cross-examination.[63] At the same time, there was a sense in which the Army Medical Board (or at least its hospital system) was standing trial. For although it soon became clear that the utmost confusion reigned in the determination of responsibilities in the medical corps, and that McKay had been neither treated nor attended regularly, it simultaneously became clear that the case merely exemplified the ordinary course of things in army hospitals. But again Fitzpatrick had to fight his battle on unfavourable ground. For it was argued, successfully, on Elliot's behalf that it would be inequitable if one comparatively junior officer were to suffer for the general negligence, and for a system moreover which had been authorised by his superiors.[64]

Fitzpatrick, who took over the prosecution himself, was of course eloquent, passionate and indefatigable. His account of the last hours and death of McKay was truly moving, and his peroration in the high strain of the Bushes and Currans of the Irish bar. If, he told the court finally, 'the meritted Censure' were not administered, 'it will be proof positive to the crowding, anxious and interested members of the Faculty, who stand around your table, that Neglect and Cruelty may be exercised with impunity', for whatever excuse there might be for negligence on the war front overseas, there could be none at Plymouth 'in the day of peace, and the Lap of Means'.[65] But despite the court's initial admonition, Fitzpatrick persisted in declaring that the case was one against the entire medical staff rather than 'the prisoner' individually. In these circumstances, it was not perhaps surprising that Elliot should have been found not guilty on all counts.[66] An attempt was made to compensate Fitzpatrick for the failure. The judgement went out of its way to acknowledge his altruism and devotion to the troops:

> it has appeared to the Court from the proceedings that Sir Jeremiah Fitzpatrick, the prosecutor has been activated by the best of motives, humanity to the soldiers, and the general good of HM service. They feel it a duty incumbent upon them thus publickly to mention it . . .[67]

But this was cold comfort for Sir Jeremiah. As another of the great Irish advocates, O'Connell, was to put it, 'Ah, a speech is a fine thing, but the verdict is *the* thing.'[68]

212 *Waterloo*

Notes

1. Fitzpatrick to H. Dundas, 26 March 1795, W.O. 1/897, f.262.
2. Fitzpatrick to E. Nepean, 4 February 1795, W.O. 1/897, f.167.
3. Fitzpatrick to Nepean, 9 February 1795, 11 February 1795, W.O. 1/897, ff.169-70, 185-7.
4. Fitzpatrick to Nepean, 9 February 1795, W.O. 1/897, ff.169-83.
5. Fitzpatrick to Nepean, 3 February 1795, W.O. 1/897, f.164. See also, 'Sir Jerome Fitzpatrick, medical inspector of all the forces, notwithstanding the badness of the weather, continues, with unremitting assiduity, to inspect all the transports here with troops; he has already sent on those many melancholy objects; he has also got two hospital ships fitted up, for the purpose of separating the sick from those in health, which will be of great service; and is also indefatigable in procuring several necessary articles of diet, which will assist most eminently in the preservation of the troop; among them is an excellent preservative of health in long voyages; an extract or essence of malt, preparing by Mr Arthur, brewer, of this town, under Sir Jerome's inspection. He has sent on board, for the use of the sick, wine, sago, rice, and fine biscuit. In short, could Sir Jerome have been here sooner, there is no doubt from his regulations, many hundreds of gallant fellows who have perished thro' neglect, and sunk in an untimely grave, to say no worse, would have been preserved and done their country essential service', *Flying Post* (Exeter), 12 February 1795.
6. Fitzpatrick to Nepean, 9 February 1795, W.O. 1/897, ff.179-80.
7. Fitzpatrick to Nepean, 12 February 1795, W.O. 1/897, ff.190-3.
8. Fitzpatrick to Nepean, 22 February 1795, W.O. 1/897, ff.209-10.
9. Fitzpatrick to Nepean, 19 February 1795, W.O. 1/897, ff.200-1.
10. Fitzpatrick to Nepean, 25 February 1795, W.O. 1/897, ff.215-16.
11. Dundas to Transport Commissioners, 6 February 1795, *House of Commons Sessional Papers of the Eighteenth Century*, 100, Reports and papers 1795-6, Forces West Indies, 81.
12. Fitzpatrick to Nepean, 22 February 1795, 25 February 1795, Fitzpatrick to Dundas 27 February 1795, W.O. 1/897, ff.209-10, 215-16, 225-6.
13. Fitzpatrick to Dundas, 26 March 1795, W.O. 1/897, f.256.
14. Ibid., f.258.
15. Fitzpatrick to Dundas, 27 February 1795, W.O. 1/897, f.227.
16. Ibid., ff.221-6.
17. Ibid., ff.226-7.
18. Ibid., ff.225-6.
19. Fitzpatrick to Huskisson, 18 March 1795, W.O. 1/897, ff.238-9.
20. Fitzpatrick's notes for an interview with Huskisson, W.O. 1/897, f.241.
21. Lennox to Dundas, 22 March 1795, W.O. 1/897, f.249.
22. Ibid., ff.249-50.
23. Fitzpatrick to Huskisson, 4 April 1795, W.O. 1/897, ff.279-80.
24. Ibid., f.280.
25. Ibid., ff.278, 281.
26. These were subsequently printed in the parliamentary papers, *House of Commons Sessional Papers*, 100, Reports and papers 1795-6, Forces West Indies, 113-14.
27. Dundas to Fitzpatrick, 8 April 1795, W.O. 1/897, ff.285-90.
28. Ibid., ff.290-1.
29. Fitzpatrick to Dundas, 26 March 1795, W.O. 1/897, f.262.
30. Dundas to Fitzpatrick, 8 April 1795, W.O. 1/897, ff.291-4.
31. Fitzpatrick to Huskisson, 26 April 1795, W.O. 1/897, f.321.
32. Ibid., ff.322-6.
33. Fitzpatrick to Huskisson, 30 April 1795, W.O. 1/897, ff.329-32.

Waterloo

34. Fitzpatrick to Huskisson, 25 April 1795, W.O. 1/897, f.306.
35. Army Medical Board to Windham, 16 May 1795, W.O. 1/897, f.379, refers to the Board's letter of 13 April 1795.
36. Fitzpatrick to Huskisson, 25 April 1795, W.O. 1/897, f.305.
37. Fitzpatrick to Huskisson, 8 June 1795, W.O. 1/897, f.425.
38. Fitzpatrick to Dundas, 27 February 1795, W.O. 1/897, f.226.
39. Fitzpatrick to Boone, 28 April 1795, W.O. 1/897, ff.333-9.
40. Army Medical Board to Amherst, 3 May 1794, W.O. 7/101, ff.123-4.
41. Blanco, *Wellington's Surgeon General*, pp. 169-70.
42. Fitzpatrick to Boone, 28 April 1795, W.O. 1/897, f.339.
43. Ibid., ff.333-4.
44. Boone to Fitzpatrick, 29 April 1795, W.O. 1/897, f.343.
45. Fitzpatrick to Huskisson, 17 May 1795, W.O. 1/897, f.418.
46. Fitzpatrick to Lennox, 14 May 1795, W.O. 72/17.
47. Fitzpatrick to Huskisson, 11 June 1795, W.O. 1/897, ff.433-4.
48. Fitzpatrick to Huskisson, 17 May 1795, W.O. 1/897, f.418.
49. Army Medical Board to Windham, 16 May 1795, W.O. 1/897, ff.379-406.
50. Ibid., ff.379-402.
51. Ibid., f.404.
52. Ibid.
53. Ibid., ff.405-6.
54. Nathaniel Sinnott, *Observations Tending to Show the Management of the Medical Department of the Army* (London, 1796), p. 16, quoted in K.E. Crowe, 'The Walcheren Expedition and the New Army Medical Board: a Reconsideration', *English Historical Review*, vol. lxxxviii (1973), p. 772.
55. Robert Jackson, *A Letter to the Commissioners of Military Inquiry explaining the True Constitution of a Medical Staff: with the Best Form of Economy for Hospitals etc., with a Refutation of Errors and Misrepresentations contained in a Letter by Dr Bancroft, Army Physician, dated April 28th, 1808* (London, 1808), p. 9, quoted in Crowe, 'Walcheren Expedition', p. 772.
56. G.B. Hill (ed.), revised by L.F. Powell, *Boswell's Life of Johnson*, 6 vols. (Oxford, 1934-50), vol. 4, pp. 312-13.
57. Fitzpatrick to Dundas, 26 March 1795, W.O. 1/897, f.263.
58. Ibid., f.261.
59. N. Cantlie, *A History of the Army Medical Department*, 2 vols. (Edinburgh, 1974), vol. 1, pp. 178-82, 188-9, 227-9.
60. Fitzpatrick to Dundas, 26 March 1795, W.O. 1/897, f.267.
61. The official report of the proceedings of the court-martial held 25 May-3 June 1795, is contained in W.O. 71/170, ff.1-81.
62. Fitzpatrick to Huskisson, 8 June 1795, W.O. 1/897, f.419.
63. Ibid., f.420.
64. W.O. 71/170, f.79.
65. Fitzpatrick to Huskisson, 8 June 1795, W.O. 1/897, ff.425-6.
66. W.O. 71/170, ff. 78-81.
67. Ibid., f.78.
68. M. MacDonagh, *The Life of Daniel O'Connell* (London, 1903), p. 193.

10 THE AFTERMATH, 1795

I

On the first anniversary of the Glorious First of June a select party assembled near Plymouth for a celebratory dinner in the 'old English style', with 'smoking sirloin, British plumb pudding &c.', and no foreign foods or even wines. As the Exeter *Flying Post* reported it:

> G. Teaite, Esq. in the chair, Colonel Thornton, Sir Jerome Fitzpatrick (Inspector of Health to the Army), and several officers who shared the glory of the First of June, were present. Many loyal and constitutional toasts were given, some excellent songs sung, applicable to the glorious occasion of the meeting; and the company separated with regret after the celebration.[1]

This was in effect a feast before the funeral, a humble version of the Duchess of Richmond's ball. The court-martial declared its verdict two days later, on 3 June 1795, and Fitzpatrick immediately felt the effect. Work on a hospital ship, which had been almost fitted up, was halted at once because the Army Medical Board would not sanction the medicines, drink and diet which he had recommended. Men with fever were sent by the army surgeons to the overcrowded Friary hospital instead of to the half-empty and newly appointed Mill Prison hospital, which was still under Sir Jeremiah's control. Rogerson, an army physician just despatched by the board to take charge in Plymouth, seemed determined on Fitzpatrick's abasement. This Fitzpatrick discovered painfully when he visited the Friary hospital, where he found, incidentally, a gravely ill soldier unattended and the prescription book missing from its place. The assistant surgeon whom he sent for, Bragg, assailed him in the open ward as 'A Mean Dirty Lying blackguard' and a 'Lying blackguard and Scoundrel'; and when Fitzpatrick threatened to report such insolence to the department for war, Bragg replied that he was not that 'soft young man, Mr Elliot', but instead feared no one. Supported by the members of the hospital staff who happened to be about, Bragg followed the inspector general down the street crying, Fitzpatrick wrote, 'in a most insolent tone, I dare not meet him *like a Gentleman*'.[2] A few days later, having been sent by Lennox to report on convalescents in the Friary hospital, he was met by a party consisting of Rogerson,

The Aftermath

Boone, Fleming and the apothecary with a demand for written authority to enter. Rogerson informed him that he would need a separate note from Lennox or Windham or the commander-in-chief for every visit which he proposed to make to a military hospital. Clearly the Medical Board and their *alter ego*, the Plymouth staff, now reasoned that Fitzpatrick's new set of instructions rendered him dependent upon their concurrence with his proposals. Since they never did concur with them, he was powerless. And Bragg was evidently not the only bravo. Fitzpatrick ended the letter in which he described his reception by Rogerson and Boone with, 'I am obliged to carry Pocket Pistols – thus am I reduced to self-defence.'[3]

Fitzpatrick struggled to stem the contrary tide. He appealed repeatedly to both Dundas and Windham to intervene, or failing that to afford him an opportunity to plead his cause with them in London. He asked Dundas, with unwise rhetoric (for once there was a rapid reply from Whitehall), to consent to his publishing 'what must shock the human Ear'.[4] Most pressingly and pertinently of all, he proposed an independent inquiry into the system of military hospitals, and the appointment, not of an inspector like himself 'with his Hands tied', but of a director of hospitals with plenary powers.[5] He also told Lennox that, unless such conduct as Bragg's were punished,

> it will be impossible for me to discharge my *Duty*, if so *grossly & insultingly* treated, – the more particularly by those very *Persons*, whose *Conduct* towards *His Majesty's Soldiers*, I am to observe on.[6]

It was not all in vain. The Medical Board's hope that Fitzpatrick would be dismissed, and better still disgraced into the bargain, was disappointed. Lennox was quite ready to provide the necessary notes to open the army hospitals to him could he have borne with the shame of repeated applications. But in general he was met by silence or inaction, while the supportive recommendations of the court-martial that the Army Medical Corps be reformed gathered dust. He himself was aware that he had become a bore and a nuisance to the departments. Almost every letter of June contained some explanation of or apology for his enforced importunity. 'I fly to release myself', he wrote to Windham on the 20th, 'from torturing reflections [upon the soldiers' sufferings] by perpetually troubling you & Mr *Dundas*.' In the same letter he cried out that he could no longer bear the mounting daily insults of the medical staff and begged to be removed – or even, if need be, dismissed – rather than forced to connive 'at the greatest of Peculations – the robbing of the State of its honest deserving Subjects'.[7] After four months of futile struggle, 'Indeed, I am tired', he told Huskisson.[8] At last the end came, early in July. He was transferred to Portsmouth and Southampton, and left the field of his humiliation, Plymouth, never to return until his last inspections of all, in August 1802.

But the fact that he had been beaten from one battleground might not necessarily mean that he would fail elsewhere. It was some time before the full implications of Fitzpatrick's defeat became apparent — at any rate, to himself. His own buoyancy of spirit and diversity of interests, and the new challenges which he was to meet at Portsmouth, protected him immediately from such a knowledge. During June 1795, while still stationed at Plymouth, he visited London to direct Alexander Brodie, a metal worker whom he had engaged to manufacture a dozen 'airing & Baking stoves' for troop transports to his specifications. Sir Jeremiah wished to alter the design according to an 'improved plan' which he had devised. Later Brodie had to make 'many further expensive alterations . . . of the Stoves at Sir Jerem.'s desire'.[9] Doubtless such work as this distracted Fitzpatrick from the vendetta with the Army Medical Board; and as he was also supported in it fully by the patient Transport Office, his loss of influence may have been partly concealed from his own view. Not only was he by nature a most sanguine man, but also when he did reach Portsmouth in July he was immediately engulfed in fumigation and other preparations. Twenty-nine troop transports had been assembled there and at Southampton for Abercromby's new army of the West Indies.[10] As if this were not enough, nine vessels returning from the West Indies reached Portsmouth early in August having suffered heavy mortality during the passage and with numerous sick soldiers and soldiers' dependants to disembark. At the heart of these flurries, interspersed as they were with dashes to London or Greenwich for supplies or help, Fitzpatrick can have had little time to speculate upon his discomfiture at Plymouth.

In addition, he was soon embroiled in a fresh sanitary campaign. As the transport commissioners laconically summarised what was no doubt an eloquent appeal of his of 17 August 1795,

> says beds ought not to be given to a Soldier sleeping in a hammoc, as they generate disease, and retain infection, especially in warm Seasons, and Climates: — recommends, that only a hammoc & a blanket be allowed — Advises, where Births are used in Lofty ships, that Cases should be used filled with Straw, & Unquilted, to admit of emptying & replenishing — Says, present Bedding, filled with

flock, Rags &c never can be cleansed, or purified — Urges, as an essential Article for rendering his labors for preserving health effectual, that a commendable discipline be established; for a detail of which he refers to a letter to Genl. Pitt [the lieutenant-governor of Portsmouth] for perusal of H.R.H. of York &c.[11]

Fitzpatrick's principal object was the creation of more living space between decks and the eradication of as many sources of infection as possible by substituting hammocks for the fixed berths built in tiers. Having procured a team of naval carpenters from Greenwich under a foreman, Boyce — Sir Jeremiah's 'own men' being 'busy with cleansing, fumigation &c' — he set them to work to gut the twenty-nine transports of their below-decks cabins and other fixtures. So swiftly did the work of destruction proceed that when on 20 August Captain Patton, the transport officer at Portsmouth, awoke to what was being done, it seemed to him already too late to reverse the enterprise. 'Lamenting', as he said of himself, Patton proposed as a *pis aller* that the hammocks be slung much closer together.[12] The cause of his dismay was of course that Fitzpatrick's alterations would reduce the troop-carrying capacity of the transports — by how much was not revealed but presumably to a considerable degree. But the commissioners would not accept any reduction in numbers. They immediately ordered that all transports, '*malgré* Sir Jerem.'s instructions, must be fitted with the means of Stowing the greatest number of men & this, the fitting with hammocoes, however desirable, will not admit'.[13] Boyce was told that he had been sent to refit and cleanse the vessels, not to transform them, and asked severely on whose authority he had ventured to change their interiors.[14]

Boyce, thoroughly affrighted, pleaded that his intentions and exertions had alike been of the 'best'; and, as the commissioners must have known he would, he put forward written instructions from Fitzpatrick to justify his action.[15] He was then graciously absolved from blame — at any rate, from much blame — and ordered on 22 August to 'forward the immediate re-equipment of the transports so improperly altered', meanwhile calculating the useless expenditure involved as he went along.[16] Yet Fitzpatrick himself was not reproached. Nor was he at all abashed. So far in fact was he from contrition that when he discovered that his orders had been countermanded, he in his turn 'lamented' bitterly the consequent diminution of the comfort and health of the common soldiers:

when ships of only 5' 4" between Decks are fitted with two heights

The Portsmouth Inspectoral Region

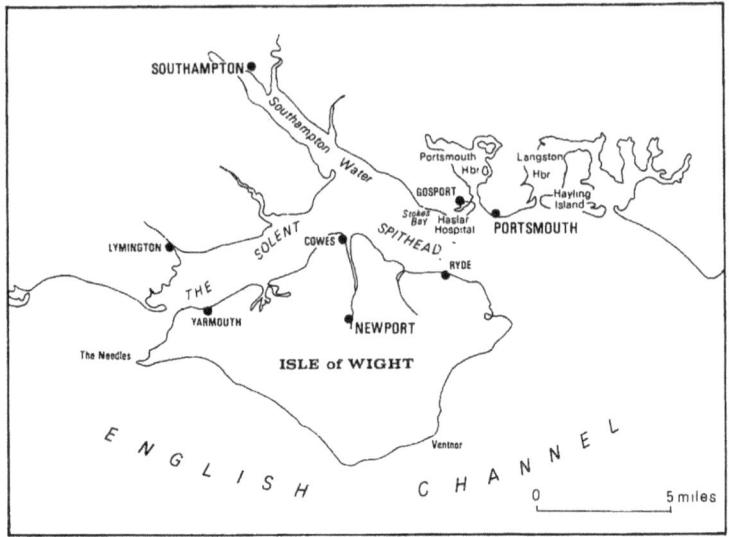

of Births, where men can neither stand, nor sit erect in them, the men must continually, with confined muscles, & contracted limbs, be imbibing their own morbid Exhalations!

Men, not 'inefficient Spectres', should be disembarked in the West Indies. '25,000 . . . crowded in a huddled way into transports, will only be on paper, that number; at the place of their destination not more than 15,000 of them will appear in their shoes.' But Fitzpatrick was never one merely to beat the air. Immediately he fell back upon another plan, that of laying loose boards upon the decks at night, on which the men might place their pallets and sleep, removing both boards and pallets in the morning and cleansing the decks thoroughly at once. He also 'entreated' that small low portholes be cut forward in the vessels to provide ventilation.[17] Whether or not either measure was adopted — no evidence survives upon the point — his intrusions and pertinacity did him no real harm at the Transport Office. The commissioners directed him to examine and pronounce on the adequacy of the medical stores and equipment on the two hospital ships at Southampton, already prepared by Dr McNamara Hayes, the chief medical officer of Abercromby's force, to accompany the fleet; and also to inspect the fittings and supplies on all the transports moored at Southampton.[18] True, a renewed plea of his for discretionary power over all matters of health and comfort was ignored by the commissioners.

On the other hand, they never upbraided him either for his original exorbitance or on account of the money wasted in dismantling and reconstituting the ships' interiors.

The West Indies fleet was much delayed and in time fell into the usual trouble. By mid-October dysentery had broken out among the troops and their dependants upon the transports, and Fitzpatrick was importuning Dundas for an affirmation of his right to land the sick and take his other customary counter-measures. Dundas having failed to reply, he wrote again to Huskisson on 25 October, begging that his original commission be confirmed 'that it may be made known anew by those Persons thro' whose power or authority matters are to be executed'. He had had some success. Perrier, the colonel of the Scotch Brigade which had suffered especially heavily from dysentery, Captain Shank, the War Office commissary at Portsmouth, and General Sir William Pitt had all proved helpful, and agreeable to Fitzpatrick's setting up a hospital ship for the sick troops. But the paper strength of the regiments remained the sticking point. Shank had told Fitzpatrick bluntly that he would consider it his duty to re-embark the sick of the Scotch Brigade and the other sick, when the fleet would sail, unless he were ordered otherwise.[19] Hence the urgency, in Fitzpatrick's eyes, of Dundas's intervention either to order directly the retention of the sick at Portsmouth or (better still) to support Fitzpatrick's right to make such a determination.

Dundas eventually replied, and although his letter has not survived, some of its contents may be inferred from a response of Sir Jeremiah's dated 14 November.[20] Dundas had evidently ignored or slurred over the critical question of whether or not the sick should accompany the army to the West Indies; but he appears to have suggested that Sir Jeremiah himself might sail with them, to get first-hand knowledge of the problems of army health at sea and to enforce a sanitary regimen upon the voyage. Possibly this was proposed as a method of getting rid – *pro tem.* at least – of an increasingly turbulent priest. But Dundas was deeply concerned about the appalling West Indian death rate; and he may well have genuinely desired an independent, 'expert' observation of conditions during the passage, as well as whatever general control Fitzpatrick might be able to exercise at sea. He had also asked Fitzpatrick to draw up fresh 'Instructions', presumably to govern the troops' health on the voyage. A caution to take regard of the susceptibilities of the Army Medical Board may have been appended to this request, for Fitzpatrick, in piqued terms, stressed the pains which he had taken to avoid offending the board, or laying down a 'system' to which the army doctors would pay no heed. 'I am actually set down', he added bitterly, 'either as a mere *Fumigator* or *Cleanser* of ships.'

The new 'Instructions' supplied by Fitzpatrick were never issued, and remain a mystery. It is difficult to see why Dundas should have asked for them at all when a departmental committee of his own at Portsmouth had already drawn up health regulations only six or seven weeks before,[21] while Fitzpatrick himself had already drafted a set for Sir William Pitt and the commander-in-chief during July. Perhaps Dundas meant merely to parry his troublesome inspector general, while leaving the frontier between him and the Medical Board as ill-determined as before. Meanwhile, if he really had wished Sir Jeremiah to sail with the fleet, he was to be disappointed. Fitzpatrick refused: he would be so harrowed and humiliated, he wrote, that the voyage would be unendurable. Instead he begged to be sent to Ireland to supervise the departure of that portion of the West Indian army which was being embarked at Cork.[22] Certainly he was needed there; the disorder and slovenliness of Irish embarkations were already notorious. But his plea, the first of many such, may also have sprung from a combined heart- and home-sickness of the moment.

For Fitzpatrick's fortunes since leaving Plymouth had been, though mixed, predominantly bad. Even at the height of his early busy usefulness at Portsmouth his standing in London was being undermined. During July the Army Medical Board had used the occasion of an earlier complaint of his that a soldier of the 32nd had been inhumanely treated at Plymouth to tell Lennox, ultimately for Windham's edification,

> As it is evident that Sir Jerome Fitzpatrick sends to the War Office exaggerated Accounts of transactions that occur without making due enquiry into their nature, so as to be accurate in what he writes, and which tend to give great Alarm, we hope Your Lordship will permit that we should also transmit to the Secretary at War a full Statement of this and other Matters.[23]

This was followed on 2 September by a report by Keate upon a recent visit to the Plymouth hospitals, in which he blamed the overwhelming numbers of the sick and the impediments thrown in their way by the local inhabitants for the disasters of the spring. Keate went on to assail Fitzpatrick and 'his Colleagues' for extravagance and the loss of soldiers for the front – two sure shots to fire within a military bureaucracy. Fitzpatrick's expenditure in setting up quarantines was, Keate wrote, worse than wasted money as it had produced 'less commodious and less wholesome' quarters; and between those of his staff who 'found an Interest in malingerers' and those who 'were easily imposed upon by the artful . . . upwards of 500 men have been lost to the Service, principally from this Cause'.[24] In both of these cases it was the Plymouth medical staff who had supplied Keate with the ammunition. But it can scarcely have been the less damaging to Sir Jeremiah for that, as he knew nothing of the investigations or report, and could present no counter-argument.

During the long delay of the fleet at Portsmouth and Southampton, he gradually felt the weight of the Medical Board's hostility. The Plymouth imbroglio had taught him that he was powerless 'in getting attendance for the neglected sick [in hospital], however great their suffering';[25] and he made no immediate attempt to re-engage in this particular battle. But he was on the water day and night visiting the transports, and on every ship he found something or other which he wished to remedy. Chief among the 'evils' was of course the presence of sick or incapacitated soldiers. He was no longer able to land these on his own authority, even in cases where the disease was infectious, or in one instance, where a man was blind; and no other medical officer at Portsmouth appeared to have been empowered to act in this 'essential Duty'. A little later he did succeed in getting an army physician, Dr Morris, to accompany him to one especially distressed vessel and to land the sick. But meanwhile a delay of ten days had occurred while Keate was arranging to send Morris down from London, and during this interval the number of those ill on board had trebled and the ship had become so infected as to need clearing and fumigation once again.[26] There were many lesser problems. For example, when Fitzpatrick argued against the troops being embarked in foul weather, with their clothes and baggage 'wringing Wet', he was 'desired to attend to the *cleansing* of my ships'. When he attempted to place his new ovens and baking troughs on the hospital ships, the Portsmouth 'Faculty' refused to allow them aboard — although in this particular case Fitzpatrick succeeded in overriding them in the end. When he pressed to get men and women trained in baking superior light bread for the sick, he was refused. When he took up the cause of diseased horses, suffering cruelly from glanders and spreading the disease throughout the horse-ships since July, he was told that it was none of his concern.[27]

Of course, it was not all rebuffs and failure. As he himself summed up his battered journey, 'I carry some points but not all, — nor scarce any in the way I like.'[28] He may have had considerable oblique success in less immediate matters. Early in September 'several Officers of Distinction' at Portsmouth applied to Dundas for permission to substitute porter for spirits and potatoes for other foods in the provisions of the West Indian army; and Dundas agreed.[29] Both of these were especial hobby-horses of Fitzpatrick, and he appears to have been on the same excellent terms with the generals and colonels at Portsmouth as was common with him elsewhere, so that in these cases he may well have been achieving his ends indirectly, through the military. It is difficult to believe that ordinary army officers, however distinguished, had proposed these dietary changes out of the blue. Similarly, when on 24 September Dundas set up a committee of regimental doctors and officers, who had served in the West Indies already and were now at Portsmouth, to advise him on the health of the West Indian army, its report resembled Sir Jeremiah's earlier recommendations most remarkably at many points. The committee may well have had the 'Instructions' which he had drawn up for Sir William Pitt and the Duke of York before them when they met. He may even have been interviewed by them. He certainly knew their chairman, McNamara Hayes, from inspecting Hayes' arrangements for medical supplies and perhaps earlier in Ireland, and had very likely met several of the other officers. At any rate, the committee echoed him exactly in setting the desirable height between decks for troop transports, and in pressing for 'Hammocks, which, with a View to Ventilation and Cleanliness, are greatly preferable to Standing Births'. The same was true of their recommendations for soldiers' clothing (wet uniforms meant disease); for wind sails and scuttles; for porter as liquor, and potatoes and vinegar as antiscorbutics; for cereal instead of 'animal' foods, such as cheese and butter; for port wine, rice and 'moist sugar' among the medical supplies; and for various other lesser requirements.[30]

Of course there was an element of the commonplace — quite how much it is impossible to say now — in some of these findings and proposals. But *en bloc* they repeat Fitzpatrick's urgings so closely and minutely as to suggest a measure of inspiration by him, or even a measure of collusion — all the more so as in some instances the recommendations ran counter to what the Army Medical Board had already advised or the department of war already practised — *malgré* Sir Jeremiah. Finally, Fitzpatrick seems to have been able to take charge of the landing of the sick from the Hanoverian regiments when they reached Portsmouth in November with infection on the transports.[31] The explanation of this 'success', one suspects, is that the unexpected arrival of so many Hanoverian sick created a medical vacuum into

The Aftermath

which he could rush.

Thus Fitzpatrick was not without his consolations in the late autumn and early winter of 1795. But his was not a nature to rest in consolations so long as several of the objects for which he was battling were slipping from his grasp. An ardent disposition rendered unendurable the thought of his inability to disembark the sick from the transports, or to save the well from 'wringing Wet' clothes and baggage or overcrowded quarters, while they were still before his eyes. Not that his was a nature to despair, either. As he told Dundas in his letter to him of 14 November, although his health had worsened and his heart felt almost broken, 'yet, such is my disposition, that I rally in the face of neglect and opposition, even to carry inferior Points'. He merely redoubled his imprecations to Dundas 'to say whether I am to exercise the Word or Spirit of your instructions of the 8th September 1794'.[32] But, like Huskisson, Dundas remained impervious to these appeals. Playing his last card, Fitzpatrick turned to Nepean, who had left Dundas's department almost nine months before. Perhaps this final fling is to be regarded as a cry of despair, a welling-up of resentment and anguish, rather than a real plea for aid. Perhaps also an exhausted spirit and body were calling for relief after more than twelve months of frantic labours in Ireland, England and the Netherlands, in Greenwich, Helvoetsluys, Rhenen, Deventer, Deal, Plymouth and now the Solent.

At any rate, the letter to Nepean, written on 26 November 1795, opened thus:

> Almost every Moment proves to me what this World is: Men holding Stations in Office evidently for the sake of Emolument, and others existing on the *Cloud* of vain Glory; fearful least the improvements or Ideas of others should be adopted, whom they apprehend will be considered by the rational as supported on a better *foundation* than themselves, such become envious and, Assassin-like, stab in the Dark; how otherwise reconcile the fear of some Persons, respecting the powers granted me by Mr Dundas in his Instructions?

This preliminary was succeeded by a cannonade of rhetorical questions, vibrating with Ciceronian scorn and encompassing the whole field of his adopted duty — the selection of vessels; their fitting up, their provisioning and watering; the rejection of unfit troops; advice on health and on the comfort of the sick; choosing the sites and furnishings of hospitals and barracks; inspecting and improving accommodation for well and sick alike; and above all seeing that what was ordered and meant by government was executed. Each angry paragraph began with 'Is it wrong . . .?', or 'Is it error . . .?', or 'Is it criminal . . .?'. Typical of all the headlong expostulation was Fitzpatrick's philippic on troop inspection:

> Is it proper to have a Person regardless of the frown or favour of the Commanding Officer, or even of the Colonel of a Regiment; and superior to the temptation of a Bribe, to become a check over the common Inspector of Recruits or over the Surgeon who is the creature of the Regiment, and scandalously permit improper subjects, real Objects of Misery, from age, infirmity and insanity, then possessed of the capability of discharging their allotted duties; so deceiving the govt, loading and infecting the shipping, crowding the hospitals on their arrivals and disappointing the generals?[33]

Of course Fitzpatrick ended by calling upon Nepean for support, and issued the nearest thing possible to an ultimatum which was open to him. If Dundas's instructions to his inspector were, upon consideration, to be regarded as too large, let them be abridged. But in this case let not the inspector be held responsible; let him not be blamed if he became 'less fervent'; and whatever the case, let him at least know the precise limit of his field of action. What it all signified, in Fitzpatrick's eyes, was that the cause of 'the wretched, and Sick and Wounded' was being in part abandoned, and that if there were a 'victor' in this squalid, sad campaign, it was the army medical establishment and its creatures.

II

If Fitzpatrick were in the habit of reading the bluebooks thirteen years later, he might have enjoyed a sweet revenge. In 1808, some of the fruits of a protracted inquiry into the conduct of the medical department of the army were at last published in the parliamentary papers. These certainly vindicated Sir Jeremiah's criticisms of the Army Medical Corps, and of the behaviour of army surgeons and physicians, during the Dutch campaign of 1794-5. James Borland, who had taken part in the campaign and was by now a distinguished physician, testified that many of the hospital staff had been inexperienced and ill-disciplined, contributing through neglect and mismanagement to a very great number of the soldiers' deaths. Still more to the point, however, the fifth

The Aftermath

report of the commissioners of military inquiry exposed Boone and part at least of the Plymouth medical department as negligent and corrupt, and Keate himself as negligent and unscrupulous, to put it at its lowest.[34]

Boone, a protégé and almost certainly also a friend of Keate's, had been placed in charge of the Plymouth hospital and sick camps during the summer of 1793; and one of the first acts of the newly formed Army Medical Board was to re-employ him, on 22 February 1794, to deal with the typhus epidemic among the 40th Regiment there. Not only was Boone old and idle, he was also grasping and venal. He appears to have delayed taking up his duties for as long as possible; and when he did get to Plymouth at last, to have neglected his military commitments in the interests of private practice. This last was dealt with fiercely by Lewis at the War Office, so far as hot words on paper could check Boone's wayward course. But if Boone was in fact checked here, he soon found means of compensating himself; possibly he had been using the same means during his first term of service in 1793. In 1804 the commissioners of public accounts discovered that over the preceding eight years £23,000 had passed through Boone's hands for which he could produce receipts for only £8,000; and even so, many of the receipts produced were not for the period in question. The modes of fraud were very crude – to judge by his sole surviving letter, Boone was an unsophisticated, not to add a scarcely literate man.[35] For example, he simply put down twice the same sum of £2637 3s 4d for medicines for the period March-June 1796. He even altered (or rather re-altered) the figures in tradesmen's bills, most profitably to himself, as the following short extract from the sequence of his small bills account for January 1796 reveals:

Tradesman	Charged by Dr Boone	Charged by Mr Gibbons to Dr Boone	Charged by Tradesman to Mr Gibbons
Mr Husband, Ironmonger	£4 16 1½	£0 16 1½	£0 16 1½
Mr Carlogan, Stationer	£3 4 6	£2 4 6	£1 7 0
Mr Lumpin, Cheesemonger	£6 6 6½	£5 5 6½	£4 5 6½
Mr Doidge, Repairing Instruments	£3 11 8	£0 11 8	£0 11 8
TOTALS:	£17 18 10	£8 17 10	£7 0 4

Over one two-year period Boone charged the War Office £740 for small bills for which Gibbons had charged him £428.[36] What Gibbons, who was clerk at the Plymouth general hospital, paid the tradesmen over the same period is unknown; but if the relativities of the sample apply it would have been something in the region of £350, he being much the more modest swindler. It is clear, from Gibbons's complicity, that the fraud in the hospital was both systematic and continuous. Whether or not Fleming, then assistant purveyor, or (perhaps less likely) the hospital mates were involved is unknown. But it does seem unlikely that imposition on such a scale over many years could have been confined to two of the members of the staff. At any rate, there can be no doubt that Sir Jeremiah's cries that the soldiers at the Plymouth general hospital were being robbed of food, drink and medicine − paid for in part from the stoppages from their pay − were being retrospectively authenticated. His various innuendoes that the conduct of the hospital staff was systematically fraudulent were to be regretted only in that they had never progressed to the accusation direct.

Keate was revealed by the commissioners of military inquiry as next only to Boone in turpitude. Although it was widely rumoured that he was corrupt − that he demanded and received bribes for appointing men to army surgeoncies and physicianships[37] − there is no evidence that Keate profited financially from Boone's misdeeds at Plymouth. But as inspector of regimental infirmaries, it was his business to examine and approve every item in hospital accounts; and he had endorsed all Boone's expenditure down to the time of his being uncovered by the commissioners of public accounts. Keate defended his own negligence, first by striving to bluster and hector his way out of the difficulty; then by attempting to transfer the responsibility to the clerk or auditor who checked the arithmetic; and finally by asserting the reasonableness of his assumption that men whom he knew to be officers 'of great respectability' would be altogether honourable in their public dealings.[38] But he had written earlier that 'in no case are there Accounts laid before the Comptroller until every possible means have been made use of to ascertain the propriety of the Expenditure'; and of one sum of £8,200 advanced to Boone and practically unaccounted for, he had testified that he was 'perfectly satisfied that it had been, from time to time, properly and advantageously expended for the use of the Sick'.[39]

The commission of inquiry not only swept contemptuously through these cobwebs of defence, but also made it quite clear that Keate was both a pluralist and a nepotist − perhaps his acceptance of bribes to appoint to office was not sufficiently established, or the offices themselves insufficiently sacred, for it to have added simony to the catalogue of guilt! In addition to £730 per annum (£2 per diem) as inspector of regimental infirmaries, Keate received £100 p.a., with a house, light, heating and other benefits, as surgeon to the Chelsea military hospital; an average of £60 p.a. (on 'doubtful authority') for the 'expenses of his Table when absent from London on inspectorial duty'; over £280 p.a. for maintaining an office; and three separate additional salaries as inspector of the National Cow-Pox Establishment, surgeon to St George's Hospital and examiner to the College of Surgeons.[40] All this was augmented by his very considerable private practice – possibly we should say that it was an appendage to it. As to Thomas Keate's nepotism, he was not called upon to exercise it on behalf of his most celebrated nephew, the ferocious 'reforming' headmaster of Eton; but he certainly brought it into play in the interest of John Keate's brother, Robert, who was apprenticed to him as an army surgeon in 1792. As the commission of inquiry noted, Thomas Keate soon employed Robert as deputy inspector of regimental infirmaries,[41] and this was but an early instance of his preparing him to step into his shoes in various of his Pooh-Bah roles, most important of all perhaps, that of surgeon by appointment to members of the royal family.

What the report did not, and doubtless could not, say clearly was that Keate was, besides, irascible, ruthless and a bully. His very first letter after joining the Army Medical Board contains not only a violent assertion of his own authority, but also a savage and mean-spirited personal attack upon the unfortunate physician who had questioned his powers as inspector.[42] It may be that he was 'an excellent surgeon', and he obviously conformed in several respects to the *beau ideal* of the pre-Listerian operator, the man who was bold, rough, careless of others' pain, 'powerful, quick, energetic and a master of anatomy'.[43] It may also well be true that he was a more lively and effective member of the Medical Board than his colleagues, Sir Lucas Pepys and John Gunning. But he was in addition – as Sir Jeremiah discovered – an ill-conditioned, unscrupulous and dangerous enemy within the administration. Even without any such depiction of Keate, however, the commission of military inquiry condemned him and his regime implicitly. It is no surprise that he and his fellow board members were, upon the publication of its findings, placed on half (or, exactly, two-thirds) pay; nor was it out of character that Keate should have then complained loudly, though vainly, that 'he was the poorer by several thousand pounds because his public duties [had] interfered with his private practice'.[44] What was revealed in 1808 was quite enough to vindicate Fitzpatrick's stand against Keate in 1795. Whether there was by then anybody left who bothered to recall, or cared about, the Plymouth scandals of that year is of course another matter.

It is true that many late eighteenth and early nineteenth-century men would not have used such terms as 'pluralism' and 'nepotism' to describe Keate's activities, or even perhaps have thought of Boone's activities as especially corrupt. The Grenvilles were still accumulating sinecures and offices beyond number; Addington as Prime Minister appointed his own twenty-one-year-old son to the clerkship of the polls, at £3,000 per annum, in 1802;[45] and it was not very long since Hastings had been acquitted at his impeachment. There is no need to rehearse the familiar *rationale* of Georgian political habits in terms of the inadequacy, or sometimes absence, of pay for the work actually done; the need to support the caste system in general; the view of stipends as property, even assignable or devisable property; the want of pensions; or the rudimentary character of life assurance. All this is valid enough, but still quite inadequate as a final comment on behaviour of the Boone-Keate type. The very protests of Fitzpatrick in 1794-5 evidenced a totally different view of appointments for familial and even less reputable reasons, and of the malversation of public funds and soldiers' stoppages; and, in his later strictures on the conduct of the convict department of the Home Office,[46] Sir Jeremiah spoke of the convict officials, physicians and contractors as being bound together in a network of favours and defalcation. For that matter, the commissioners of military inquiry took it quite for granted that the abuses of the army medical department were 'intolerable' corruption.

Nothing could be more misleading, then, than to dismiss the whole proceedings at Plymouth in 1795 as a simple expression of the accepted conventions of the day. Some contemporary departments, for example the Transport Board constituted by order-in-council on 4 July 1794[47] and the Alien Office which gradually took shape in 1793-4,[48] followed a very different course of conduct from that of the Army Medical Board. The Transport Board and Alien Office are good subjects for a comparison, for they were formed at virtually the same time as the Army Medical Board, and for essentially the same reason — the pressures of war with France. They were also similar in being rearrangements of older bureaucratic forms, the Transport Board conflating duties formerly performed by the Navy Board, Ordnance Board and Treasury; and the Alien Office harking back to expedients adopted in earlier wars and crises. Moreover, the Transport and Army Medical

Boards were identical in being composed initially of two 'professional' members and one 'civilian'. Yet both the Transport Board and the Alien Office were well-ordered, economical, rapid in business and resourceful, whereas the Army Medical Board maintained most of the worst bureaucratic features of the *ancien régime*.

Clearly, part of the explanation of the discrepancy was personal. Keate and Pepys were poor choices for the board, and the 'civilian', Gunning, was apparently a nonentity. Part may have been the sprawling and unco-ordinated character of army medicine, with regimental organisation practically unrelated to general, and a confused medley of appointing authorities for staff. Part was certainly the independent power base or bases which the medical 'profession' possessed. But it must also be remembered that 'reformed' and 'unreformed' branches of the administration co-existed during the Revolutionary and Napoleonic wars. The Pittite type of administrative modernisation and efficiency was not pressed as a general model upon the public service. Pitt was much too dependent upon royal favour and factional support in the House of Commons to attempt a universal reform, even if he had desired it. Nor should we regard the co-existence of characteristically early Georgian and characteristically early Victorian forms of central government in Hegelian terms of dying and emergent types. Rather should we look upon them as, say, Braudel looks upon the simultaneous presence of long-distance trade and high capitalism and subsistence economies in medieval Europe.[49] That is to say, we should see them as different contemporaneous levels of bureaucratic life rather than as a plain and open struggle between old and new. Thus the English clerkly world in which Sir Jeremiah moved was not simple but complex, with marked variations in norms and attitudes from part to part. He was unlucky, in entering the *imperium* of the Army Medical Board, to encounter a hostile authority which, although only two years old, was impregnated by Walpolean abuses and practically immovable and irreformable until long after he would have to quit the scene.

Notes

1. *Flying Post* (Exeter), 4 June 1795.
2. Fitzpatrick to Lennox, 16 June 1795, W.O. 1/897, f.448.
3. Fitzpatrick to Huskisson, 24 June 1795, W.O. 1/897, ff.456-8.
4. Fitzpatrick to Huskisson, 10 June 1795, W.O. 1/897, f.428.
5. Fitzpatrick to Huskisson, 8 June 1795, W.O. 1/897, f.424.
6. Fitzpatrick to Lennox, 16 June 1795, W.O. 1/897, f.449.
7. Fitzpatrick to Windham, 20 June 1795, W.O. 1/897, ff.442-4.

8. Fitzpatrick to Huskisson, 8 June 1795, W.O. 1/897, f.424.
9. Brodie to Transport Commissioners, 2 May 1797, Adm. 108/46, 15 May 1797.
10. By early August 130 troop transport, escort and other naval vessels had been assembled at Southampton — 'more than was ever seen here at a time', *Hampshire Chronicle*, 10 August 1795. By the beginning of October the number had risen to almost 200. 'There was never seen, by the oldest man living, so much hurry and bustle as this town [Southampton] has experienced for the last two days: boats full of troops going on board the transports, and others returning from them, together with near two hundred sail of vessels moored off the quay, formed an entertaining spectacle', ibid., 3 October 1795.
11. Fitzpatrick to Transport Commissioners, 17 August 1795, Adm. 108/36, 18 August 1795.
12. Patton to Transport Commissioners, 20 August 1795, Adm. 108/36, 21 August 1795.
13. Transport Commissioners to Patton, 21 August 1795, Adm. 108/36, 21 August 1795.
14. Transport Commissioners to Boyce, 21 August 1795, Adm. 108/36, 21 August 1795.
15. Boyce to Transport Commissioners, 22 August 1795, Adm. 108/36, 22 August 1795.
16. Transport Commissioners to Boyce, 22 August 1795, Adm. 108/36, 22 August 1795.
17. Fitzpatrick to Transport Commissioners, 26 August 1795, Adm. 108/36, 29 August 1795.
18. Transport Commissioners to Patton, 29 August 1795, Adm. 108/36, 29 August 1795.
19. Fitzpatrick to Huskisson, 25 October 1795, W.O. 1/897, ff.459-62.
20. Fitzpatrick to Dundas, 14 November 1795, W.O. 1/897, ff. 468-74.
21. *House of Commons Sessional Papers of the Eighteenth Century*, 100, Reports and papers 1795-6. Forces West Indies, no. 23, 91-6; cf. Sir John Dalrymple's memorandum of 2 February 1793, Melville Papers GD 51/1/597, S.R.O., f.597.
22. Fitzpatrick to Dundas, 14 November 1795, W.O. 1/897, ff.472-3.
23. Army Medical Board to Lennox, 3 July 1795, W.O. 7/102, f.13.
24. T. Keate to Windham, 2 September 1795, W.O. 7/102, ff.23-4.
25. Fitzpatrick to Dundas, 14 November 1795, W.O. 1/897, f.470.
26. Fitzpatrick to Huskisson, 2 February 1796, W.O. 1/897, f.485.
27. Fitzpatrick to Dundas, 14 November 1795, W.O. 1/897, ff.468-70.
28. Ibid., f.471.
29. Dundas to Lords Commissioners of the Treasury, 3 September 1795, *House of Commons Sessional Papers*, 100, Reports and papers 1795-6. Forces West Indies, no. 19, 84; Dundas to Transport Commissioners, 24 September 1795, *House of Commons Sessional Papers*, Forces West Indies, no. 20, 86.
30. *Report of the Board appointed by Sir Ralph Abercrombie, to Consider of Regulations for the Better Preservation of the Health of the Troops on the Voyage to the West Indies, and on Service There, House of Commons Sessional Papers*, Forces West Indies, no. 23, 91-6.
31. Fitzpatrick to Dundas, 14 November 1795, W.O. 1/897, f.474.
32. Fitzpatrick to Dundas, 14 November 1795, W.O. 1/897, ff.470-3.
33. Fitzpatrick to Nepean, 26 November 1795, W.O. 1/897, ff.476-7.
34. *Fifth Report of the Commissioners of Military Enquiry, Army Medical Department*, H.C., 1808, v (142), 73-7.
35. Ibid., 261.
36. Ibid., 75-7.

37. Cantlie, *History of the Army Medical Department*, vol. 1, pp. 188-9.
38. *Fifth report of the Commissioners of Military Enquiry*, H.C., 1808, v (142), 75, 77.
39. Ibid., 75.
40. Ibid., 7-8; Cantlie, *Army Medical Department*, vol. 1, p. 178.
41. *Fifth report of Commissioners of Military Enquiry*, H.C., 1808, v (142), 260-1.
42. Army Medical Board to Amherst, 29 March 1794, W.O. 7/101, ff.44-8.
43. A.J. Youngson, *The Scientific Revolution in Victorian Medicine* (Canberra, 1979), p. 218.
44. Cantlie, *Army Medical Department*, vol. 1, p. 190.
45. P. Ziegler, *Addington: a Life of Henry Addington, First Viscount Sidmouth* (London, 1965), pp. 141-2. Pitt, Addington's predecessor as Prime Minister, told him on 29 July 1802, 'I rejoice most sincerely that you have found it practicable to dispose of the Pells as you have done.'
46. Fitzpatrick to King, 21 November 1797, B.M. Add. MS. 33105, ff.242-3.
47. M.E. Condon, 'The Administration of the Transport Service during the War against Revolutionary France' (PhD dissertation, London University).
48. K.M. Berryman, 'Great Britain and the French Refugees, 1789-1802' (PhD dissertation, Australian National University), ch. 2.
49. Fernand Braudel, *Capitalism and Material Life 1400-1800* (London, 1973), pp. xii-xiv.

11 A SORT OF TABLELAND, 1796-1802

I

Fitzpatrick recovered his balance quickly after the outburst of November 1795. As early as 2 February 1796, he formally acquiesced in the government's decision (or decision by default) that he should not re-enter the arena of army hospitals.[1] But this was the limit of his withdrawal. He was far from reconciled to surrendering his claim on, for example, the sending of unfit soldiers overseas. In the same letter of 2 February he reported critically upon the composition of the Royal Garrison Battalion, then being embarked for Gibraltar. Many of them were, he wrote, 'absolute objects', pitiable and altogether unfit for 'any sort of Soldier-like Duty', even that of a hospital orderly. He asked his usual question: why send out men who would never be capable of discharging a military or even a quasi-military function? Of course, he knew that he would be answered, 'They make up the numbers.' But this still seemed to him an inane response. Embarking the ruptured, consumptive, lame and aged meant a squandering of lives and money, the spread of infection to the well, a brake upon military movements, a waste of transport, and sooner or later bonfires of clothes and bedding. He had no intention of yielding here.

Nor was he reconciled to his powerlessness in landing the sick from the waiting transports, even though it was this which had set off the chain of events ending in the Plymouth disaster. The sick could not be tended as they should on shipboard; the between-decks was a hothouse for disease; and vessels could not be kept clean, or recleansed, unless the immediate sources of typhus and dysentery were removed. Again he had no intention of quitting this field, although in the spring of 1796 he again failed to intervene successfully here,[2] as he had failed to intervene successfully in the embarkation of the unfit.

A third disputed area in which he soon showed that he maintained his claims was diet at sea and in service in the tropics. He seized on an outbreak of dysentery aboard the West Indian fleet in 1796 to press again the dietary 'system' which he had expounded in 1794 and which the Portsmouth committee had endorsed substantially in October 1795. The epidemic was laid at the door of 'putrisible' foods such as butter, meat and cheese, and he urged once more the substitution of farinaceous for 'animal' provisions, with the contrast drawn again between the navy's ready adoption of the change and the army's general neglect of this advice.[3] In this particular note, Fitzpatrick displayed considerable knowledge of, and dexterity in deducing from, contemporary chemistry and biology, partly no doubt to demonstrate (as he said himself) that he could advise on such a matter 'without trespassing on the *Drug prescribing* province of the Medical Gentlemen'. But this did not restrain him from attacking the profession as the blind enemy of innovation, wedded to 'the jog-trot of Centuries' whether from interest, idleness or *amour propre*.[4] There could be no doubt that this was another battle which Fitzpatrick intended to continue.

II

His basic work, the supervision of embarkation for the main theatres of land war in 1796-1802, the Caribbean and Mediterranean, was soon running smoothly. The only difficulties here arose from extraordinary hurry or the simultaneous preparation of vessels in several ports. Even Sir Jeremiah was bounded by time and distance. In such crises, he flew from ship to ship across the crowded harbour, or attempted to find a substitute for the port which he would never reach in time; and of course he complained in either case of the insufficiency of the inspection. But even the complaints — as in the case of the rushed embarkation of the 29th Light Dragoons at Portsmouth in March 1798, to take one example — struck a cheerful, busy note. Sometimes there was positive exhilaration or even complacency in the reports. The detachments which followed the 29th from Portsmouth in June 1798 sailed, wrote Fitzpatrick, in health and spirits, with the commanding admiral attentive to his every suggestion for the passage.[5] When, four years later, the 29th sailed again from England, bound this time for Halifax, he told Hobart, Dundas's successor, that they left 'with such a degree of Health, as would have delighted your Lordship to have witnessed',[6] even though the vessels had had to put back to port three times and the men had been on board already for nineteen days. Such was the fruit of 'the most exact attention to Discipline'.[7] Bustle meant happiness. On 13 August 1799, Sir Jeremiah told Dundas that for day after day, from 5 every morning, he had been working with the West Indian fleet, passing from ship to ship, arranging its cleanliness and ventilation; and now with the vessels luckily becalmed, he meant to stay afloat instructing the officers, ship by ship, in sanitary discipline until the very last, when a sloop would take him off.[8] It was the same when a fleet was held in port by foul instead of windless weather. Fitzpatrick put each hour's delay to use, more perilously and much more painfully, but with equal interior satisfaction.

His staple work appears to have become steadily more pleasing and systematic. In the last full year of his inspectorate, 1801, he wrote of his 'suggestions' as generally successful; hardly a week passed without some cause for congratulation in applying them. The credit belonged, he continued, primarily to Dundas who had

> afforded me increasing opportunities of preventing Disease and of alleviating misery & wretchedness, thereby adding strength and vigor to His Majesty's Arms: objects I am fully convinced could never be accomplished, was I ever so capable or zealous, did he not decidedly and uniformly support the word and spirit of His Majesty's will as stated by him in my Instructions.[9]

In the same year, the transport commissioners made it clear to a new under-secretary at the Home Office that, so far as they were concerned, 'the Inspection of Troops, under orders for Embarkation, respecting their Health, is particularly committed to Sir Jerom: Fitzpatrick';[10] and to judge by their acquiescence in his unauthorised replacement of cabins on a transport in 1798,[11] they had long given him a free hand in this commission. As a final instance of the administrative serenity of 1801, we may note Fitzpatrick's promise to attend the embarkation at Woolwich of an artillery detachment, bound for Martinique: 'I will recommend as usual every necessary supply for them, which is always concurred in by the Honorable the Ordnance Board.'[12]

Even the crises appear to have produced little opposition and no marked defeats. After the disastrous failure of the British-Russian expeditionary force in Holland in the autumn of 1799, Sir Jeremiah had to set up emergency reception centres for the sick and wounded. He spent the last fortnight in September planning, ordering and exhorting feverishly in Colchester, Harwich and Yarmouth. In Colchester where 800 men were shortly to be landed he arranged for the worst 150 cases to be sent to the military hospital, and found 'tolerably good' accommodation for the remaining 650 in a barrack from which the militia were to be dislodged. Next day he set off for Harwich where some of the most gravely ill were to be lodged, and from there to Yarmouth to seek more hospital space along the east coast 'in case it may be required suddenly during winter or spring campaigns'.[13] All this was accomplished without any of the old contention or imprecations. His choices of accommodation were supported by the barrack-master, Col. Frederick, and even by his late antagonist, Keate. True, one small contest between Keate and Fitzpatrick did occur. But this was almost a battle of courtesies! Keate approved of houses picked out by Sir Jeremiah at Yarmouth for the use of sick troops, but demurred at asking their owner to turn them over to the army. This Sir Jeremiah dismissed as 'delicacy' − a rare charge against Keate, no doubt. His own view, on which he promptly acted, was that 'any friend of Government' should be given the chance to demonstrate that friendship.[14] The unlucky landlord appears to have succumbed without a fight.

Similarly, Fitzpatrick seems to have met little resistance to using the fruits of his gadgeteering and minor inventiveness after 1796. In the 1799 crisis, for example, he devised a set of alterations to hospital cot frames to render them more serviceable for the sick to be landed at Colchester, as well as a plan to diminish their sufferings upon disembarkation. The Colchester hospitals were four miles distant, by rough cart track, from the landing place. Fitzpatrick immediately perceived that, instead of being jolted cruelly in wagons, the sick could be carried by small boats at flood tide to within three-quarters of a mile of the town, and the worst cases borne thence on a sort of litter or stretcher, which he set to to have 'knocked up' by the carpenters from cot frames.[15] Some of Fitzpatrick's exercises in ingenuity were of course more sophisticated. He prided himself especially on his invention in 1798 of a new type of illumination to replace candles on troop transports and in hospital wards. This was a closed lantern, run on oil, with mica reflectors and an earthen pan, perforated for ventilation. Sir Jeremiah believed that it answered many of the problems of crowding at night in cramped quarters. Candles consumed much of the oxygen, and men used them to light their pipes, thereby increasing the respiratory problem. Moreover, the lanterns gave, he claimed, a much brighter and more constant light.[16] Again all appears to have gone well with his venture. The lanterns were first installed on a convict vessel in the following year,[17] and presumably used increasingly thereafter.

The comparative tranquillity and success of Fitzpatrick's later years in office derived − though by no means solely − from his good relations with authority, in its various forms. The favour of Dundas was, as he himself testified, the most critical of all. Sir Jeremiah, volatile and fulsome, can never be taken *au pied de lettre* when he speaks of others. But it does seem clear that Dundas supported him to an extraordinary degree and with extraordinary consistency. Fitzpatrick was officially rebuked on only one occasion between 1796 and 1802. In July 1800, according to his own account, he proffered a Russian general, whom he had met casually, his help in fitting out a hospital ship for 265 Russian wounded. The general however denounced this as 'dictation' and 'interference', and Fitzpatrick was, to his deep mortification, censured publicly by Huskisson and told that foreign troops were none of his business.[18] But obviously the censure had more to do with Anglo-Russian diplomacy than with Sir Jeremiah's officiousness *per se*; and no other transgression of the limit of his 'sphere' during his last years as inspector was even officially noticed.

But this is not to say that Fitzpatrick was backed by Dundas, let alone Huskisson, whenever he sought to break out of his ordinary round of work. Nor is it to say that either was ready to devote time to him or his ideas except in the most pressing of cases. He had evidently been warned in 1795 or 1796 against pestering his superiors: he often pleaded thereafter that the diminution in his correspondence and requests was the best proof that he had taken such an instruction seriously. A note of 13 January 1797 written to Huskisson from the lobby of the War Department well illuminates the new relationship. Fitzpatrick begged that a message be sent down by porter fixing a time when Huskisson would see him. He apologised for the 'prolixity' of his first submission. But it was essential that he explain clearly what was wrong, and why it was wrong, before proposing his several reforms: 'It is impossible for me to state them [the arguments] in that brief manner suited to your very few hurried moments.' The note ended with a sly reassurance, which in itself told a tale of Fitzpatrick wearing out the patience of his masters,

> I know your extreme busyness but do not be alarmed – The Heads of what I have to propose shall be *Aphorisms*, without any Complaints against Individuals nor other the Lamentations of Jeremiah, than for the Good of the Service & the Honor & Happiness of Government.[19]

Thus, the support of the war department had decided limits. But within these limits, it appears to have been constantly supplied, at any rate while Dundas remained in office.

Of nearly equal importance in keeping the administrative waters smooth in this last phase was Fitzpatrick's continued success with the higher military officers. His relations with the successive lieutenant-governors of Portsmouth, Sir William Pitt and Major-General Whitelocke, were almost as warm and free as those with Lord George Lennox had been at Plymouth. Two other generals commanding in the Isle of Wight, Don (an old friend from the Netherlands days) and Stephens, appear to have been particularly sympathetic, and various other senior officers, among them Colonels Douglas and Gordon, were singled out by Sir Jeremiah for special praise. There were, it is true, several 'Battlings' with regimental commanders[20] and the index to War Office correspondence contains a reference — alas, no longer traceable -- to Fitzpatrick's 'injurious representation of Lt. Col. Fraser'.[21] But all the discoverable cases, and very likely the same would be true of Fraser's, had the same old bone of contention - whether or not those whom Fitzpatrick regarded as too ill or old or young or infirm to serve abroad should be removed from their regiments. This was, however, disputed ground, if not certainly outside the agreed field of the inspector general. So long as he stayed within normal duties, there were no quarrels whatever with the army proper. Regimental surgeons and the staff of the military hospitals were, of course, another matter. Here there was intermittent warfare. But after 1795 the conflict was never general or truly open, and it would not have occurred at all had Sir Jeremiah been able to resist all temptations to sally out from his established base and go over occasionally to the offensive.

Direct challenges to the Army Medical Board itself were of course out of the question; and, as we have seen, even Keate might prove amiable and amenable enough when the Board's toes were not being trodden on. With the main subsidiary of the War Department with which he had to deal, the Transport Office, Fitzpatrick's relations remained remarkably good, and he was by no means pegged by them within the strict boundaries of his authority. Occasionally he protested, as in his letter to Huskisson of 4 March 1798, that if only the Transport Office would instruct their agents to 'allways pay some reasonable attention to my suggestions (which I confess they sometimes have done) . . . the Service would profit & Expense be saved'.[22] But these shortcomings betokened not ill-will or sloth but lack of resources or prodigious pressures upon the transport agents and their staffs, especially in Portsmouth, during 1796-1800. It was rather that Sir Jeremiah was insatiable when it came to vessels and material than that the transport officers failed to help him, even in his 'extra-territorial' excursions, as best they could.

Sir Jeremiah's own 'office', after 1796, presented a corresponding picture of modest scale, moderate success and a tolerable degree of harmony. From mid-1795 he was based in Portsmouth although he appears to have spent almost as much time in London as in Portsmouth after 1799. He certainly maintained an office and a clerk at his base, and almost certainly a second office in London during the final years. A good deal of his time was spent away from either office, at Southampton, Deal or various embarkation places on the Isle of Wight or along the Thames estuary, or on forays such as that to the east coast ports in 1799. He also spent much time upon the water, moving from vessel to vessel in the crowded roadsteads. In addition to carriage hire and other minor expenses of his land travel, all this activity cost some £650 per annum.

As has been indicated above, the question who was to pay for it emerged in the most luxuriant confusion during the second half of 1797. Fitzpatrick had assumed originally that his actual office and similar expenses would be refunded, and by August 1797 he had received £587 on this bases. But the costs even to the end of 1796, he claimed, amounted to £1,505, 'for my *Clerk* [and in times of great business he had employed a second], *Postage, Stationery, Office,* Boatage &c &c monies actually expended in the discharge of my Duties'. There were various vague official recollections of the original agreement with Fitzpatrick, but nothing to the point in writing in any department. Huskisson proposed to allow him a flat £500 annually, but this was before he recalled – if he had ever known – that Fitzpatrick was being paid £2 per diem as a salary.[23] The matter dragged on for months, and we do not know certainly when or how it was ended. But it does seem to have been settled at last at £1 per diem for all contingent expenses, retrospectively as well as prospectively. There was no apparent diminution in Sir Jeremiah's activity – his claim to have paid for some things from his own pocket may well have been justified – but it must surely have destroyed any hope which he may have had of enlarging his establishment.

There is no evidence that Fitzpatrick ever toyed with the notion of setting up a subordinate inspectorate of health with branches in the various embarkation centres, although when two or more sets of embarkations were taking place at once he had sometimes to delegate his work to his clerk or a doctor or even leave one set of inspections neglected. It was certainly not because he could not elaborate an inspectorial scheme or project such an organisation that he failed to put forward any such proposal. The simple truth is, very probably, that the early euphoria and expansiveness in the war planning was short-lived. The open hand of 1794-5, in terms of both money and new powers and fields, was soon changed into a very tight fist. If Fitzpatrick

could not get fully recompensed for even the administrative Dotheboys
Hall which he was conducting, there was no chance whatever of its
being enlarged and improved considerably. What he himself felt most
deeply in the constraints which eventually applied to his expenditure
was the lack of authority to hire boats – as against carriages – freely.
He needed, he said, a pinnace of his own at Portsmouth, but short of
that he needed at least the power to call on boats, day and night:
'otherwise I must consider myself at my now advanced Stage of life,
most unfortunate in not possessing a Necessary and Honest discretion'.[24] But for whatever reason locked in the heart of bumbledom,
water remained distinguished from land, so far as payment for Sir
Jeremiah's journeyings upon it was concerned.

Fitzpatrick's Area of Operation, 1795-1802

III

It need hardly be said that Fitzpatrick was not the man to rest contented with his regular business, or to cut down work because of the
meagreness of resources. From first to last, he sought to move into
other areas as fresh problems crossed his path. Generally, the extension
or attempted extension was lateral or tangential. The plight of Irish
soldiers' and sailors' dependants was related to foreign service; both
convict transportation and the slave trade involved essentially the same
difficulties as sending troops on long ocean voyages overseas; and, as

we shall see below, Fitzpatrick's interest in these three fields grew 'naturally' out of his current work. There were however more direct augmentations, whether of the *pari passu* or the system-completion type. An instance of the first was foreign troops landing at or embarking in England. In terms of 'health and comfort', there was no distinction to be drawn between them and British soldiers. All had to eat, drink, sleep and dress; all were open on the same terms to infectious disease. Sir Jeremiah certainly disregarded all differences of nationality or command — at any rate until July 1800, when his attempt to subject the Russian sick being re-embarked at Portsmouth to his usual sanitary regimen provoked the outraged response from the general, and in turn Huskisson's rebuke. Sir Jeremiah had then responded with awful irony, 'my Reason no doubt . . . will preponderate over my Zeal on future occasions';[25] but whether in fact he kept his hands off all foreign troops who came within his reach during the next two years may well be doubted. Occasionally even civilians were on a level with soldiers in these matters, and Fitzpatrick became similarly involved. When, for example, a party of French *emigré* priests reached Portsmouth from the Channel Islands in September 1796, with several ill or dying from an infectious disease and the mayor refused to allow any to disembark, he took up the cudgels on their behalf. In the end, he induced Portland to intervene to save them.[26] As things turned out, the Home Secretary's intervention proved unnecessary. By the time the instruction reached Portsmouth, the mayor had already capitulated before Sir Jeremiah's onslaught.

But much the most important extension of the *pari passu* type was his bringing the East India Company troops into his purview. He had noticed their suffering in a fleeting, glancing way in the autumn of 1795, but was then borne away by the press of other business. But when there were large-scale embarkations for the East Indies at Portsmouth in the early summer of the following year, he turned the full force of his energy upon them. Even without formal authority or backing from the War Department, he achieved much. Captain Coggan, the Company's shipping agent, proved persuadable and kind. He agreed to all Fitzpatrick's proposals for whitewashing, fumigation and ventilation. He agreed to the supply of water purifiers, and to clearing the orlop decks, where the troops were 'stowed', of gear and cargo. Fitzpatrick was equally successful with the ships' masters whom he induced to fit new valve-type air tubes in the bows, and seats designed by himself, to save the men from having to lie on bare decks by day. He was moreover ready to act himself without any authorisation, as when

A Sort of Tableland

'Coggan told me he had no Portable Soup for them, I took it on myself (several of the men having bowel complaints) to supply them' — even if the burnt child's memory of the fire seems apparent in his anxious assurances to Huskisson that he had kept all the necessary copies and receipts on this occasion, and that he had adhered as scrupulously as possible to an accepted soup ration, that already laid down for voyages to the West Indies.[27]

But all this was not enough. Coggan made it clear that there were limits to the concessions which he might make off his own bat, or permit Fitzpatrick to make off his. Yet light and ventilation were, Fitzpatrick wrote, still inadequate, and in particular the naval space allowance of six feet by fourteen inches for a hammock was inhumane for landsmen who would have to spend much of their time between decks.[28] He set off immediately for London, and not only broke through to an interview with Dundas but even persuaded him to put the necessary pressure upon the Company. He had meanwhile elaborated a detailed scheme to submit to the Company's committee of shipping, as well as a confident plea for the retrospective blessing of all that had been done so far at Portsmouth. He had no doubt that the committee would recompense the shipowners for the alterations to their vessels, the expense being — Sir Jeremiah's inevitable word in all such cases — 'trivial' in comparison with the gains.[29] Apparently, his interview with the Company's shipping director, Thomas Chapman, which Dundas had arranged, went well; and on his return to Portsmouth he was emboldened to propose that one of the chartered vessels, the *Princess Charlotte*, be discarded altogether as a troop carrier. Certainly the case was a desperate one. The average height of the passenger space, 'for the Men to move or rather Creep about' in, was only 4ft 2¼in; it was impossible to provide them with light or air except through the hatches, which must be battened in bad weather; and even air tubes from the gun decks would have been worthless as these decks lacked ports. Almost jauntily, Fitzpatrick concluded his report with an expression of confidence in the Honourable Company, as too humane to send soldiers thousands of miles in such a vessel, or indeed to use it for anything other than a supply ship.[30]

This settled the East Indies question substantially for almost three years. There were occasional indications that Sir Jeremiah wished to push his frontier a little further forward; and in August 1798 he called on Dundas to intervene once more, principally to insist that the orlop decks be prohibited for troop accommodation on all East Indian vessels, and that certain types of ships' provisions be eschewed as unwholesome. Such were his relations with the Company by this time that he could assure Dundas that a line from him to the East India Board would suffice to win a ready compliance;[31] and so indeed it proved. Within a few days, Fitzpatrick reported that the chairman of the East India Board had seen to everything in a truly 'splendid' fashion: 'my mind is now at ease, and in justice to Mr Coggan, he has acted the Man of Humanity and the friend of the Service'.[32]

But this harmony ended with the preparation of the next East India fleet early in the following year, 1799. The root of the trouble was extraordinary haste in the fitting out, and repeated eleventh-hour additions to the troops embarked. Coggan and the ships' masters were exempted from all blame, and several of the regimental officers were singled out for high praise by the inspector general. But of what use was anybody's zeal or tenderness when all was irremediably confused, and slapdash from want of planning? Fitzpatrick was 'agonized' that vessels should sail so ill-found and unsuitable, with cargo and provisions jumbled together even in the troops quarters:

> to have stowed *396* Men, with a proportion of Women and Children, independent of the Crew, on board the *Carnadic* so incumbered, and 411 on board the *Taunton Castle*, was one of the most unreasonable acts ever committed, and would have been better classed with those of darkened Ages, than those of the enlightened 18th century.[33]

Such a number of passengers meant that the vessels were carrying at least one person for every ton burden. But even this gave an inadequate conception of the overcrowding, according to Fitzpatrick. In the system of calculating measurements and troop accommodation which he had drawn up for the East India Company in 1796 and which Dundas had induced the Company to adopt, Sir Jeremiah had proclaimed again his golden rule, that the crude passenger-tonnage ratio might be most misleading, and that it was the cubic area clear of all encumbrances and modified appropriately by the construction of the particular vessel, which should determine the permissible complement. In the helter-skelter of February 1799 this rule had been ignored, and Fitzpatrick beseeched Dundas to ensure that his 'true space' system was restored. He also begged for notice of the taking up of ships or tonnage so that he might have an opportunity to make the necessary space calculations, as well as to see that the vessels were adequately provided and fitted out.

A Sort of Tableland

It is at this moment the more particularly necessary as the conveyance of Troops is principally by *Freight Ships*, the chief principle of whose Owners, I am sorry to say, is gain; but as his [Dundas's] [aim] must be Justice of the Nation and Humanity to the Soldier, I already feel his compliance.[34]

Evidently, the East India Company also felt the weight of Dundas's compliance, for Fitzpatrick was happy with the measure of control which he was able to exercise for the remainder of 1799 and 1800. In 1801 and 1802, however, the contrary pressures mounted once again and Fitzpatrick complained that there was a marked deterioration in the space allotment on the East Indies vessels, in fittings generally and in the sanitary appliances such as water purifiers, not to add a return to using orlop decks for troop accommodation.[35] But since no barrage of protest reached the War Department during these years, and since these complaints were embodied in a general letter to a new Minister, Lord Hobart, begging for his support on all fronts, we may discount Fitzpatrick's jeremiad to some extent. Doubtless, he was in a period of greater difficulty, as was likely to occur from time to time in such undertakings. But overall he seems to have brought the East India Company's troop movements effectively and reasonably successfully into his domain during 1796-1802.

Other attempts at lateral extension of the field of action fared worse. In 1799, and probably on various unrecorded occasions, Fitzpatrick tried again to give horses a protection equivalent to that for humans, arguing his case in the familiar terms of reducing physical suffering, saving money and avoiding the folly of sending an evergrowing body of ineffectives overseas. But he never received authority to inspect or deplete the horse transports. Similarly, he failed time and again in his efforts to control or even influence the embarkations of troops for overseas from Irish ports. Nor was he ever allowed to undertake what he termed the 'humane & political act' of planning an Irish system there similar to that which he had set up in England. It was in April 1798 that he pressed for this most strongly, claiming that 'everyone' agreed on the necessity, ease and cheapness of the reforms which he had secured at Portsmouth, and on the readiness with which they could be translated to Dublin, Waterford and Cork.[36] But as ever Dundas turned a deaf ear to the Irish argument.

IV

A troop-inspectoral system for Ireland can be categorised as an attempt at 'parallel' or *pari passu* government growth, essentially of the same type as had brought the East India Company's vessels into the net. But there was also the matter of moving troops about in home waters to the mustering points in southern England; and this really involved something different in kind, an intensification, for it was an effort to press the regulation back to an earlier stage in the entire process. Passages from Ireland or the Channel Islands to the southern English ports were still regarded as 'a short Run', for which troop transports required little special equipment or fittings, and on which the soldiers might be crammed aboard virtually without regard to numbers. Fitzpatrick's initial experience in 1794 was enough to teach him the folly of these assumptions. Even the 'short Run' might turn to a week or more at sea, given persistent contrary winds.[37] Still worse, cross-channel voyages were preceded by assemblages of troops at the original port, Cork or Dublin or St Peter Port or St Helier, where infectious disease might take root, to flourish evilly before Portsmouth or Plymouth was reached. Again, *experto crede* for Sir Jeremiah. Thus a minimal standard sanitary regime in the Irish and Channel Islands ports, and health and safety measures for the cross-channel passages, had been persistent objectives of his, almost from the opening of his British career.

In the course of 1798 all these troubles came to a head at Portsmouth. First, early in March four transports carrying almost 1,100 men, women and children (their combined tonnage was only 1,300) arrived from Guernsey to join a fleet bound for the West Indies. Fitzpatrick reported the vessels to be in a filthy and disorderly condition, but that he was practically powerless to reorder them 'under the present restrictions [under] which I labor'. Yet, he continued, he could prepare the vessels fully within four days were he unequivocally authorised to do so for 'the proper mode of doing business is as evident as, that two and two make four'. The military bureaucracy, however, had planned the junction of the Guernsey vessels with the rest, without arranging for Fitzpatrick's 'system' to be applied to the new arrivals; and for all his fretting and fuming, it would seem that he had to let the Channel Islands detachment sail in the end 'in some ill-fitted dirty Ships with latent Disease'.[38] Meanwhile, further troops for the West Indies had arrived from Ireland. Fever had raged on board during the crossing, and over 100 men had to be removed from one transport, the *Calcutta*, during her few days at Portsmouth. Several of them died ashore.

Fitzpatrick could do little immediately, as he was then working day and night preparing vessels for the East Indies; but when the *Calcutta* and another Irish transport were moved on to Chatham for a thorough cleansing and fumigation, he followed them overland on the same day. He proposed — the regimental commander and medical officer meekly agreeing — to disembark all the men at Chatham and find an agreeable quarantine for them there where they might be thoroughly bathed, furnished with new uniforms (every piece of old clothing having been destroyed), disinfected and, where necessary, hospitalised.[39] He would meet the ships coming round the Head, and if there had been further deaths and sickness since leaving Portsmouth, order them to carry on to Deal, where the sick could be dealt with more easily.[40] The last precaution proved unnecessary, but more than two weeks' work was required at Chatham to get the vessels and their complements fit for the ocean passage.

The return passage to Portsmouth had its own difficulties, as the following summary of a letter from Fitzpatrick indicates — providing incidentally a powerful impression of its author's indomitable and infuriating zeal:

SIR JEREM. FITZPATRICK (Chatham 11th [April]) says that the CALCUTTA, perfectly purified, sailed Yesterday from Little-Nore but Capt. Poulden previously sent his 1st Officer Mr. Dunn, abd. ye PRINCE OF WALES (whose Master was in London for Hands) to conduct her to Portsmouth — for, with her Mate & Crew, all has, for two Days, been Intoxication & Irregularity. — Says that at 3 o'clock this Morning (she being Completely fitted & fumigated) he sent Lime, Copperas & Brushes aboard, as into the other, that she might be white-washed while sailing to Portsmouth. — says that at 3 o'clock to day, P.M. when he left Sheerness, she had not sailed, thro Delay, as he supposes, of the Pilot; but having met the Master (CODY) here, & hurried him to proceed immediately, he concludes she will quit the Nore early tomorrow morning. — says that he waits here to Complain to Genl. Fox of the Gross-Misconduct of putting infected Men into Transports.[41]

Fox, who commanded at Chatham, soon received not merely a complaint, but also an impassioned plea to take a hand in ending the errors and miseries of the Irish embarkations. For within four days of his galloping about the headlands, Fitzpatrick had composed a masterly little report, some 4,000 words long, upon the cross-channel passage.[42]

The men to be embarked at Irish ports were, he wrote, hurried out of tenders, prisons, hospitals and the other confined places in which they had been lodged for security against desertion. Their clothing was already 'poisonous', and their management in the hands of recruiting officers, often sergeants, who, bribed or indolent, made no attempt to control them. If they were accompanied by a surgeon, he had never been to sea and was rarely firm enough either to reject the unfit or to ensure that bedding and other necessaries were tolerable. He and the other officers would probably be as seasick as the rest. Even if they did wish to exercise any discipline they could not do so because they were as ignorant 'as the very recruits' about what needed to be done on ships.[43] There followed Fitzpatrick's familiar analyses of the nature of infectious diseases, the causes of their dispersion and the precautions and modes of conduct necessary to prevent or check them. The report ended with the elaboration of an inspectorial system both at the embarkation ports and on the transports, based upon Sir Jeremiah's own experience. Perhaps all this had been sent to Fox to facilitate another siege upon Dundas. At any rate, copies of everything were sent to the Secretary of State on 27 April, together with the usual trefoil of appeals, to heart, head and pocket. Humanity aside, 'Government's real Friend, *Health*, Man's greatest blessing, and the Essential of an Army' was at stake − to say nothing of the continual destruction of beds, clothes and fittings which the reform would obviate.[44]

Fitzpatrick was not long back in Portsmouth before the problem manifested itself again when the 61st and 81st Regiments arrived from Guernsey, carrying infection with them. Worse still, other regiments were embarked at once for the Cape of Good Hope on the very transports which had served the 61st and 81st, and, while delayed in port, these regiments in turn suffered a very heavy death-rate. Then in April 1799 the Irish cycle of misery recurred. When Colonel Ogle's regiment reached Chatham from Dublin, it had already suffered badly, probably from typhus. Fitzpatrick, who set off for Chatham at once, greeted the news with uncharacteristic *sang froid*, or even cynicism. What else could be expected, he asked, until a proper system of troop transport from Ireland was established? Without it − or, more plainly, until Dundas stirred himself to order its institution − the miseries 'which early in the War were too often witnessed by Lord George Lennox at Plymouth, & latterly by General Fox at Chatham' would recur each season. Last year's tragedies had already dropped out of mind; so too would this year's − until the next dreadful chastisement: 'the conduct of Col. Ogle was, the routine of *Irish-Recruit-Exportation* − there is

A Sort of Tableland

radical Error'. Fitzpatrick scorned a compromise proposal then being aired at the war department that two special transports be set aside for the transfer of troops from Ireland. Even twenty, he declared, would make little difference without the specific pre-embarkation and passage regulations set out in his report to Fox of 16 April 1798; and these in turn needed an experienced medical officer in the Irish port, and a 'steady' military officer and marine party to supervise the crossing, for their execution.[45]

Sir Jeremiah never came so close to rebuking Dundas as in these complaints. But it was all in vain. He could and did influence the counter-flow to Ireland or the Channel Islands. In April 1799, for instance, he persuaded General Stephens to add a third transport to ferry the 55th Regiment from Portsmouth to Guernsey. But he remained powerless so far as the extra-English embarkations were concerned. Occasional wild prayers to be sent even for a short time to the Irish ports, or sour or sad comments on the consequences of non-intervention, were the only outlets for his wounded feelings.

At a tangent to all this, however, Fitzpatrick was ultimately successful in one particular. In the end he did extend the limit of his activity a little by securing a permanent accommodation hulk and hospital ship for Portsmouth. The hulk and ship were not, of course, required solely for the cross-channel arrivals, but the problems which these created were certainly a great part of the difficulty. Almost as soon as he took up his station at Portsmouth, Sir Jeremiah had pointed to the inconvenience, or worse, of having no regular depots or sick bays in which to place troops while their vessels were being prepared or re-cleansed, or when sickness broke out between the inspection and the final sailing. But the gashes left by Plymouth were still too raw for him to press this hard at once; and for three years he made do with what Captain Patton, willing but generally short of spare vessels, could provide. But his experiences in 1798, both with troops crowding in from Ireland and Guernsey and with other regiments mustered at Portsmouth for the West Indies, evidently decided him to agitate in earnest. On 12 November he applied formally through the lieutenant-governor, Pitt, to the commander-in-chief and the war minister for a permanent solution. Pitt, like Patton, had long been sympathetic. 'You Sir', the application began, 'have been frequently pleased to say . . . that you saw the Evil, and was concerned at not having it in your power to remedy it.'[46] There was a military hospital at Gosport, but sending sick troops there from the transports created various problems, including those of victualling, desertion and the introduction of infection to a new place — Sir Jeremiah tactfully refrained from adding his own bad relations with the army medical department to the list. Still worse, at least in scale, was the absence or insufficiency of transfer vessels wherein the healthy troops might be quarantined or lodged. The answer was one or two large hulks at Spithead, Motherbank or Stokes Bay for the use of troops for short periods, primarily to secure health, but secondarily to facilitate the issue of clothing and provisions, to familiarise landsmen to life on water and to enable the women and children attached to the army to enjoy some measure of decency and comfort while still in port.

Fitzpatrick had appealed specifically to Pitt as one interested, compassionate and influential — he had been in attendance on George III — and evidently he had not called in vain. Almost eighteen months, and doubtless much ink and paper, were spent before the scheme materialised. But on 14 April 1800 Sir Jeremiah reported to Huskisson that the hospital ship to be stationed at Portsmouth was most commodious and suitable, with almost eight feet in height between decks. A second hospital ship had been procured for Deptford; and though neither as spacious (the between-decks height was six feet — 'however she is well aired') nor so forward in her preparation as the Portsmouth vessel, she too satisfied the exacting Fitzpatrick. Moreover, the original request for a hulk or 'floating-Barrack' at Portsmouth was well on its way to fulfilment. It had been long delayed, the Navy Board told him, because the Admiralty had not yet forwarded its formal sanction, and the board asked to have the approval sent directly to Portsmouth, with 'Instructions to have the vessel fitted up on Sir Jerome's principles, connecting the extent of her accommodation with her healthfulness'. Fitzpatrick urged Huskisson to stir Nepean to have the Admiralty order sent at once; 'when Disease or Inconvenience sets in, the means of preventions comes too late'.[47] Thus Fitzpatrick finally won the support-system needed to make his ordinary inspectorate fully effective — at least in Portsmouth and London, by now his main centres of operation. Clearly, he had a free hand in preparing the auxiliary vessels, and probably also in their general management, so long as he acquiesced in the Army Medical Board's dominion over staff and treatment.

Possibly emboldened by this success, he went on to attack his medical enemies in one of their own camps, the Gosport military hospital. The real *causus belli* was an old one: the army doctors' returning men to their regiments whom Fitzpatrick considered insufficiently recovered or unfit for foreign service. But in his letter of complaint (after what he termed 'unceasing pains' and 'Battlings' at Gosport) he also accused the hospital of supplying the men with bad provisions and deplorable accommodation.[48] On this occasion he won a military inquiry, although the inquiry, naturally enough, confined itself to measurable and material inadequacies, not venturing into the minefield of disputed professional opinion. Sir Jeremiah was at least partially justified by the findings. General Whitelocke told him, some time in the summer of 1801, that the court had condemned the hospital provisions, some of them being at least five years old.[49] As Fitzpatrick had predicted, the purveyor and his assistants were found guilty of negligence. This may have given him some modest satisfaction, but his principal concern, the embarking of sick, infected and incapacitated men, had been ignored.

Fitzpatrick never solved yet never abandoned the struggle to solve this problem. It certainly appears to have diminished in scale. After 1795 he rarely complained of the physique of the troops being sent to the main foreign theatres of war or the East Indies. But it was quite otherwise with those despatched to Gibraltar or the Cape of Good Hope. Possibly the explanation is that the quality of recruits, overall, improved markedly after the disastrous consequences of the early methods of enlistment had been revealed. At the same time, boys continued to be taken in and old and infirm soldiers were never disbanded. Thus while the fighting troops might have been generally fit, there would have been a residue who might be packed off to perform what were essentially garrison duties at places such as Gibraltar and the Cape.

At any rate, Fitzpatrick repeatedly denounced the inhumanity of shipping such soldiers as were being sent to these stations. On 31 December 1800, for example, he reported that the condition of those whose embarkation for the Cape he was supervising at Chatham was truly 'pitiable'. Of sixty 'men' in one vessel, forty-one were under eighteen years and eleven under fifteen. On another, there were a hundred boys or youths. None of the young soldiers, who amounted to two-thirds of the entire detachment, possessed great- or watch-coats, and cold and wet threatened all of them with disease.[50] For the conditions under which the Cape troops sailed matched their calibre. Only three vessels had been provided for 1,500 men who had been despatched there earlier in 1800, at very little above one ton per passenger, with no hospital quarters on any of the ships, and none of the ordinary health precautions taken. Fitzpatrick was told that the improvements would be made *en route*. '*Post mortem Medicus*', he noted savagely.[51] Next year he improved upon the news of heavy mortality on troopships to the Cape – which he had not been able to examine before they sailed from Deal — by observing that it demonstrated the necessity of a powerful inspectorate.[52] He must have made some headway over the years in his struggle to determine the fitness of the men for foreign service. One of the bitter questions with which he greeted news of his enforced retirement in August 1802 ran

> Who will [now] regardless of the frown of the Cols. or other Officers, or the trouble of the Surgeons, in the General Hospitals, keep Men from accompanying their Regiments or Detachments abroad, when found unfit to proceed, & only to establish an *Inefficiency* swell the Ranks, and deceive the Government, General &c?[53]

But whatever he gained was won by cajolery or bluster. He was never empowered to judge soldiers' fitness for their duty.

A final large field into which Fitzpatrick tried again to intrude was the planning of military hospitals, and even to some extent military barracks. His instructions of 1794 had constituted him an adviser, at least on the first; and five years later he wrote that he never understood why he had not been consulted on the site, construction or arrangements of the many barracks and military hospitals which had been built since the beginning of the war. He added that he understood that De Lancey, the general in charge of army building, would have been glad of his views.[54] This must have been disingenuous. He could not but have known that letting him loose on hospital construction would have precipitated a battle royal with the Army Medical Board; and De Lancey had certainly not welcomed his unheralded interference in the building of the hospital at Plymouth in 1795. Still he did possess some paper powers, which had never been withdrawn.

Characteristically, his later attempts to realise them derived from the chance discovery in 1799 that a new barracks was to be built on the Isle of Wight. He at once showered long and detailed proposals upon General Don, with whom his relations continued to be cordial. The proposals were accompanied by detailed sketch plans, with costings, of the military prison section. In these, the cell size was double that of the original, and sewers, water supply, light and ventilation (including a species of exhaust fan) were all laboriously considered.[55] How much, if any, of these amendments eventually found their way into the Newport barracks is not known. But Fitzpatrick's attempt to use his intrusion to revive his claims as adviser on hospital building failed altogether. He had sent copies of his letter and submissions to Don to the war department, in the forlorn hope that Dundas might recover his early

A Sort of Tableland

enthusiasm for some outside surveillance of hospital and barrack planning. It was painful, Sir Jeremiah wrote, to have to stand by, watching 'Error every day, which might with more Ease, and less Expence, be avoided than executed — doing due Justice to the Age of Improvement'.[56] But Dundas and the department were unresponsive. If Fitzpatrick could persuade senior officers to listen to and follow his advice, they would not intervene against him; but that was as far as they would go. As was the case so often, he was left adrift, to rely entirely on his own wits, luck, persuasiveness and gall.

V

In February 1801 Pitt's ministry fell, and Fitzpatrick lost his patron, Dundas. Huskisson and Windham also left office, and although Nepean survived into the next regime as under-secretary to the Admiralty, he had long ceased to have any influence upon Sir Jeremiah's career. Dundas's successor, Robert (now Lord) Hobart, took up his duties on an auspicious day, 17 March 1801. He had belonged to the Irish administration during the decade 1784-94, at first as Rutland's aide-de-camp and MP for the government borough of Portarlington, and later as chief secretary under Buckingham and Westmorland; and he had known Fitzpatrick and his work during these years. But though he was not unfriendly, he gave Sir Jeremiah no particular support, and he lacked the creativeness and enthusiasm, as he also lacked the administrative ability of Dundas. His under-secretary, John Sullivan, was also a newcomer to the department. He appears to have found it difficult — and who can blame him? — to understand the inspector general's role.

Fitzpatrick anticipated that there might be difficulties in continuing an appointment so intertwined with and dependent on Dundas, once he was out of power. In fact, it even seemed possible at one stage that he might have to leave office when his superior did so — the line between politics and the civil service was still ill-drawn. He therefore begged Dundas in the interval between his resignation and his departure 'to devise some means of rendering my office independent'. It was not, Fitzpatrick continued, that he had any reason to suppose that he would not receive 'the like enlightened, liberal protection' from Dundas's successor; nor were his motives personal.[57] But a service which had proved so necessary should be rendered permanent and secure. Doubtless Dundas agreed. He did not however take any steps, if there were any which he could have taken, to attempt to bind his successor.

In fact, Fitzpatrick's situation was not altered by Hobart's arrival. It was the coming of peace with the Treaty of Amiens signed on 27 March 1802 which undermined him. At first, the inspectorate seemed safe. The business did not fall away at once. The only early indication of trouble was the increased use of ordinary trading vessels instead of regular transports to send troops overseas, signifying perhaps a new passion for economy and certainly reflecting the sharp reduction in army numbers. By June or July 1802, however, Sir Jeremiah was sufficiently apprehensive to sound out such 'members of government' as he could lay hands — or rather voice — on as to the prospects of his office. Whether to escape his solicitations or not, he was assured by everybody that 'its notorious utility would warrant at all times, its continuance'.[58] Then on Saturday, 30 July, the blow fell with sickening suddenness. Fitzpatrick was informed by letter that his inspectorate was to be wound up and himself placed on half-pay.

Sir Jeremiah laid siege to the war department in the next few days. But his anxious hours in the vestibule failed to win him an interview with Hobart. He had been attending Canadian embarkations at Plymouth when the fatal letter came, and had to return there to supervise new sailings; so on 3 August, as a last fling, he sent Hobart up 'Humble Queries . . . in giving up Inspector of Health's Office', with a desperate plea for a few minutes of his time, that he might be persuaded to 'introduce my prayer to Addington as Dundas did to Pitt on my arrival here from Cork in 1793'.[59] Few would have discerned humility as the special quality of the 'Queries'. Who, they demanded, would now see to the health, convenience and happiness of the 'living freight' on troopships? Who would inspect the embarking, and strive to wrest the unwell and the diseased from the hands of army and regimental surgeons bent on supplying some mere number of human shapes? Who would look to the quality of the sea stores, the purification of water, the medical supplies, the sanitary precautions, ventilation, fumigation and the rest? No other person or department had made this a special study. Surely, when government 'reflect on the manner that every matter was carried on before the year *1794*, as well in Transports as Hospitals, they will not forget the friend to the Soldier'.[60] Hobart made no response, and a day or two later (probably on 5 August) Sir Jeremiah composed his final appeal in the hall of 10 Downing Street where Hobart was doubtless attending a Cabinet or on other business (one hesitates to add 'pleasure' to the choices) with Addington. The note was wavering and uncorrected, barely coherent and desperate in tone.

I must humbly entreat the honor of an Interview even for a few Minutes, let the result be what it may, it will set my Mind at Rest — & I flatter myself that your Lordship will consider yourself well compensated by the information you can only truely receive for [sic] the Pract[iti]oner if candid, and the Opportunities you will daily have in the exercise of the true policy and benevolence of your great trust [and] Station.[61]

On this the curtain falls upon the inspector general.

It is not difficult to suggest reasons for this downfall. Fitzpatrick had ever been eccentric and troublesome as a public servant, and he had lost his protective shield when Dundas departed. We do not know his age or remaining strength, but within the past three years he had spoken of himself as declining in both years and health. He had besides, as we shall see, fallen into another scrape at Portsmouth earlier in the year — and that of a dangerous kind: he had harangued common men in public on the inhumanity of the government.[62] But all this merely rendered him and his office the more vulnerable. It was almost certainly the Treaty of Amiens which gave the *coup de grâce*. Addington was set upon cutting the armed services and reducing the cost of the surviving military force.[63] The inspectorate of health and its bizarre incumbent were not likely to stand long in any economising gale. In the superficial view, moreover, it might have seemed enough that a 'system' of preparing and supplying troopships had been laboriously worked out, and a steady routine established — all the more so as York's general army reforms had by now taken root and raised the levels of health, discipline and organisation markedly. It was in vain that Fitzpatrick pointed out that peace would not end the movement of soldiers across the oceans, or that the substitution of merchantmen for transports to carry soldiers created new problems or revived many of the old, or that the East Indian arrangements lacked a secure foundation. It was in vain that he pressed — prophetically in terms of the nineteenth-century experience — the critical view that constancy of inspection was indispensable if a regulation were to be carried continuously into force. Such ulterior implications and such distant effects of reducing the public service and state expenditure were not likely to thrust themselves on run-of-the-mill ministers and under-secretaries in 1802.

The war was not resumed until 17 May 1803, some nine months after Fitzpatrick departed. Even when arms were taken up again, the regular army was not much enlarged immediately; Addington's ministry relied heavily on the militia and fencible corps instead. Moreover,

Addington's 'strategy' was defensive, concentrating his forces upon Fortress Britannica; and Bonaparte lacked the means to challenge him in theatres overseas. The resulting conflict between whale and elephant was the type least likely to need the old inspectorate of health for troopships. By the time Dundas (now Lord Melville) returned to office, Sir Jeremiah was about two years in retirement; and Melville went to the Admiralty instead of the War Office, into the bargain. Fitzpatrick importuned him at once,[64] of course, but equally of course in vain. There was no hope that the clock could be now turned back.

Seven and a half years elapsed between the winding-up of his office and Fitzpatrick's death. His half-pay life is almost as obscure as his pre-official one. We know that he lived in Dublin from 1807 to 1809 and that he died in London. We know that her husband had been restored to the 'Lady Elizabeth' – surely a Penelope, if one ever was! – in Dublin by 1807, and that she died some time before 23 July 1809. Occasionally, Sir Jeremiah's spirit flashes into view in these last years, as he takes up an old cause such as an Irish poor law[65] or a new one like Catholic emancipation.[66] But these are but gleams of mica on a stone. For the historian, this life ends almost as tracelessly as it began. There is a particular sadness in the waters closing so silently, and for so long, over one whose passion was the fame of well-doing. But he would have been pleased with the lapidary tribute, the fall of the elegiac compliments, of one obituary notice:

> Sir Jerome Fitzpatrick, knt. M.D. many years Inspector of Health to the British Army; a gentleman from whose eminent skill, extensive knowledge, and indefatigable activity, the Service derived the most signal advantages in his department. He was not only in a conspicuous degree the Soldier's Friend, but the zealous advocate of suffering humanity in our Prisons and Hospitals, where his benevolence procured for him the appellation of a second Howard: in him his country has lost a friend, and his profession an ornament.[67]

The friend of the soldier, the friend of his country: at the last God had given him the gift of others seeing him as he saw himself.

Notes

1. Fitzpatrick to Huskisson, 2 February 1796, W.O. 1/897, f.485.
2. Ibid.
3. Fitzpatrick to Dundas, 2 January 1797, and Victualling Commissioner, 9 March 1797, W.O. 1/897, ff.509-29.

A Sort of Tableland

4. Ibid.
5. Fitzpatrick to Huskisson, 12 June 1798, W.O. 1/897, ff. 607-8.
6. Fitzpatrick to Hobart, 3 August 1802, W.O. 1/897, ff.821-2.
7. Fitzpatrick to Hobart, 12 July 1802, W.O. 1/897, f.814.
8. Fitzpatrick to Dundas, 13 August 1799, W.O. 1/897, ff.721-2.
9. Fitzpatrick to Huskisson, 18 February 1801, W.O. 1/897, ff.789-90.
10. Transport Commissioners to J. Sullivan, 22 June 1801, Adm. 108/20, f.99.
11. Poulden to Transport Commissioners, 27 April 1798, Adm. 108/53, f.70; Bentham to Transport Commissioners, 29 April 1798, Adm. 108/53, f.70; Transport Commissioners to Bentham, 30 April 1798, Adm. 108/53, f.70.
12. Fitzpatrick to Sullivan, 2 September 1801, W.O. 1/897, ff.793-5.
13. Fitzpatrick to Huskisson, 18 September 1799, W.O. 1/897, f.728.
14. Fitzpatrick to Huskisson, 30 September 1799, W.O. 1/897, ff.933-6.
15. Fitzpatrick to Huskisson, 18 September 1799, W.O. 1/897, ff.725-30.
16. Fitzpatrick to Huskisson, 4 March 1799, W.O. 1/897, ff.653-6.
17. The convict ship was the *Earl Cornwallis: The Times*, 31 October 1800.
18. Fitzpatrick to Huskisson, 13 July 1800, W.O. 1/897, ff.753-60.
19. Fitzpatrick to Dundas, 13 January 1797, W.O. 1/897, ff.502-3.
20. Fitzpatrick to Sullivan, 2 July 1801, W.O. 1/897, f.782.
21. Index to correspondence, 1792-6, W.O. 2/1 refers to Letter Book 10, p.256.
22. Fitzpatrick to Huskisson, 4 March 1798, W.O. 1/897, f.573.
23. Fitzpatrick to Huskisson, 19 August 1797, W.O. 1/897, ff.645-8; Fitzpatrick to Huskisson, 4 September 1797, W.O. 1/897, ff.559-60; Fitzpatrick to Huskisson, 30 December 1797, W.O. 1/897, ff.563-5.
24. Fitzpatrick to Huskisson, 13 July 1797, W.O. 1/897, f.544.
25. Fitzpatrick to Huskisson, 13 July 1800, W.O. 1/897, f.759.
26. Adm. 108/38, 14 and 15 September 1796.
27. Fitzpatrick to Huskisson, 13 May 1796, W.O. 1/897, ff.488-90.
28. Ibid., ff.491-2.
29. Fitzpatrick to Chapman, 22 May 1796, W.O. 1/897, ff.493-5.
30. Fitzpatrick to Coggan, 6 June 1796, W.O. 1/897, ff.497-8.
31. Fitzpatrick to Dundas, 1 August 1798, W.O. 1/897, ff.611-13.
32. Fitzpatrick to Dundas, 11 August 1798, W.O. 1/897, ff.619-21.
33. Fitzpatrick to Huskisson, 6 February 1799, W.O. 1/897, ff.637-8.
34. Ibid., ff.646-7.
35. Fitzpatrick to Hobart, 12 May 1802, W.O. 1/897, ff.800-1.
36. Fitzpatrick to Dundas, 27 April 1798, W.O. 1/897, ff.587-90.
37. Fitzpatrick to Moira, n.d. 1794, B.M. Add. MS. 37874, f.197; Fitzpatrick to Lennox, n.d. 1794, no. 2, W.O. 1/896, ff.38-9.
38. Fitzpatrick to Huskisson, 4 March 1798, W.O. 1/897, f.569.
39. Fitzpatrick to Huskisson, 25 March 1798, W.O. 1/897, ff.577-80.
40. Fitzpatrick to Huskisson, 26 March 1798, W.O. 1/897, ff.585-6.
41. Fitzpatrick to Transport Commissioners, 11 April 1798, Adm. 108/53, 12 April 1798, f.37.
42. Fitzpatrick to Fox, 16 April 1798, W.O. 1/897, ff.591-604.
43. In a similar vein, Fitzpatrick to Huskisson, 22 April 1799, W.O. 1/897, ff.657-61.
44. Fitzpatrick to Dundas, 27 April 1798, W.O. 1/897, f.587.
45. Fitzpatrick to Huskisson, 22 April 1799, W.O. 1/897, ff.657-60.
46. Fitzpatrick to Pitt, 12 November 1798, W.O. 1/897, ff.689-90.
47. Fitzpatrick to Huskisson, 14 April 1800, W.O. 1/897, ff.749-51.
48. Fitzpatrick to Sullivan, 2 July 1801, W.O. 1/897, f.782.
49. Fitzpatrick to Huskisson, n.d. (probably mid-1801), W.O. 1/897, ff.786-7.

256 A Sort of Tableland

50. Fitzpatrick to Huskisson, 31 December 1800, W.O. 1/897, ff.766-7.
51. Fitzpatrick to Whitelocke, 5 January 1800, W.O. 1/897, ff.745-9.
52. Fitzpatrick to Sullivan, 2 July 1801, W.O. 1/897, f.781.
53. Fitzpatrick to Hobart, (probably 3) August 1802, W.O. 1/897, ff.825-6.
54. Fitzpatrick to Huskisson, 22 April 1799, W.O. 1/897, ff.701-2.
55. Fitzpatrick to Don, 29 March 1799, W.O. 1/897, ff.705-19.
56. Fitzpatrick to Huskisson, 22 April 1799, W.O. 1/897, ff.701-2.
57. Fitzpatrick to Huskisson, 18 February 1801, W.O. 1/897, f.792.
58. Fitzpatrick to Hobart, 3 August 1802, W.O. 1/897, f.820.
59. Ibid., f.819.
60. Fitzpatrick to Hobart, (probably 3) August 1802, W.O. 1/897, ff.825-6.
61. Fitzpatrick to Hobart, (probably 8) August 1802, W.O. 1/897, ff.829-30.
62. Graham to King, 17 January 1802, *Historical Records of New South Wales* (hereafter cited as *HRNSW*), vol. iv, pp. 678-9.
63. By May 1803, the regular forces had been reduced to 95,000.
64. Fitzpatrick to Dundas, 3 August 1804, Melville Papers, National Library of Scotland, MS.1041, f.22.
65. Fitzpatrick to Hardwicke, June 1805, B.M. Add. MS. 35760, ff.174-5.
66. See Chapter 1, pp. 31-2.
67. *Gentleman's Magazine*, vol. 80 (1810), p. 187.

12 SERVICE AND SERVITUDE, 1796-1802

Three of Fitzpatrick's later 'extra-mural' activities extend — or so at least it is hoped — our knowledge of *homo gubernatorius* in the 1790s. The first, concerning soldiers' dependants, illustrates both the simplicity and informality of bureaucratic systems of the day, and the great difficulty of the search for the lever which would bring them into play, the effective patron. The second, concerning transported convicts, illuminates the problems of reforming an established governmental machine. The third, concerning the slave trade, is by contrast speculative. It is an essay in large-scale administrative planning, although rooted in perceived specific needs, and deliberately pragmatic rather than deductive or *a priori*.

I Soldiers' Wives Have Skilly*

The problem of maintaining the families of soldiers serving overseas was a peculiarly Irish one. In the case of English troops at least (the case of the Scots may have been different), if the army did not pay the travel costs of their wives and families from the departure camp or embarkation port to their homes, they might be passed on from parish to parish until they reached their native habitations. Once there the poor law would — or was supposed to — take care of their maintenance at £6-8 per annum for the women, and £3-4 per annum for each child. But there was no equivalent to the English poor law in Ireland, and no mode of transferring the Irish poor from one part of the country to another at the public expense. Hence, although it was very rare for the families of the English troops to do so, the families of Irish soldiers accompanied their men overseas — even to the East or West Indies — wherever possible. But because there was an 'accompaniment ration' of dependants for each regiment going on foreign service, and also because of the limitations (often unpredictable up to the end) of the shipping available, there were always some Irish wives and children who were left behind. They often learned of this fate at the eleventh hour. One such happening was described thus:

*The piece of doggerel verse which accompanies the 'Officers Mess' call runs, 'Oh, officers' wives have puddings and pies, but soldiers wives have skilly', Eric Blom (ed.), *Grove's Dictionary of Music and Musicians* (5th edn, London, 1954), vol. v, p. 778.

> on Saturday night last, at a very late hour, by what I heard, after the ships departure, ten women & several children who came round from Chatham [to Portsmouth] in the *Harriot*, bound for Hallifax, being more than the compliment allowed were sent [back to Ireland] in their Lamentations on board the *Howard*.[1]

The desperate suffering of the abandoned appears to have gone unnoticed until Fitzpatrick stumbled across it in Plymouth in the spring of 1794. He wrote at once to several 'government men' in the Irish House of Commons – probably Dublin Castle placemen with whom he had worked as inspector general of prisons – begging that provision be made for such unfortunates in the next estimates. Two of the members callously replied that the Irish soldiers' dependants were no worse off than tens of thousands of other Irish destitute, adding, with the arresting but characteristic Anglophobia of so many of the Anglo-Irish office-holders of the day, that the soldiers were fighting Britain's battles, not theirs, and should accordingly look to Britain, not Ireland, for support.[2] A third Irish office-holder shrewdly observed that the Irish Parliament would only act in such a matter if directed to do so by the British government.[3] This advice Sir Jeremiah was to recall when the plight of the soldiers' wives and children next pressed itself strongly upon him, during the preparation at Portsmouth of Sir Ralph Abercromby's army for embarkation for Santo Domingo in the later months of 1795.

On 8 December 1795, Sir Jeremiah opened up the subject to Dundas,[4] economically prefacing his letter with the same antique and ornate flattery with which he had introduced another subject of reform to John Foster more than ten years before:

> To make an apology to a mind like yours for an attempt to do good would be, to presume a doubt where none should exist, and as the intention will plead the best excuse, that apoligist, alone I appeal to.

Already three transports were about to leave Portsmouth for Cork with complements of Irish soldiers' families who had been left behind, and there were also numbers

> of the like wretched Beings who must on the embarking of the Troops at Cork endeavour to return to their once homes (for now they have none altho on their Native Soil) there to become common beggars: the only means of their support being hurried to fight the

Countrys Battles.

Fitzpatrick wished Dundas to see to it that provision for these unfortunates was made by the Irish Parliament. He had evidently come to agree with his anonymous correspondent that much more was to be hoped from College Green if the proposal were known to have emanated from the British government (or its *alter ego*, the Irish executive) than if it were introduced by some Irish member independently. Ireland was, Fitzpatrick asserted, the disgraceful exception among European nations in making no provision for the dependants of the common troops in war. But, he continued (with conscious or unconscious irony), it surely needed only the 'recommendation' of the British Cabinet 'to persuade a generous senate to grant, without hesitation the trifling means of Assistance' required.

He eschewed proffering any plan until his 'Idea' in general was approved. But, of course, being Sir Jeremiah, he could not end without revealing a great deal of the cat already in his bag: at least three guineas per annum for the wife and at least one guinea each for the children of an Irish soldier, so long as he served out of Ireland, and provided that she and they returned to the parish of marriage; the same to continue until death for the widow and the orphans if the soldier died overseas; a proviso that only pre-enlistment marriages should qualify for these payments, 'as nothing should be done to encourage the Soldiers marrying afterwards'; and the money to be raised by county presentment or, less tardily and uncertainly (Sir Jeremiah was obviously recalling the difficulties of his prison inspection days), by parliamentary grant. Characteristically, Fitzpatrick paraded a number of prudential arguments in support of his scheme. It would increase recruiting and reduce desertion,

> for what man be his resolution ever so heroic, can leave the partner of his Bosom and his Orphan Children to become certain Beggars dependant on, an uncertain Charity.

It would also avoid 'the Misfortune (for by that Epithet I call the sending Women and Infants on board the Transports) and the expence of sending such Numbers abroad'. But as even the phrasing of these appeals to the politic indicate, the motor of his 'Idea' was 'feeling', even down to the final, sentimental request for a decision before 25 December so that 'the poor Women and Orphans' could look forward to 'a most equitable, just and delightful Christmas Gift'.

Fitzpatrick had too long and painful an experience of Dundas's waywardness in replying to trust to this letter alone. On the following day, he sent a copy to Windham, explaining that, if Dundas were too hard-pressed to take the question up at once Windham might wish to do so: after all he and Dundas were 'embarked in the same bottom' and joined in a 'congeniality' of humane feeling.[5] In the event neither was involved, as Dundas turned the matter over to the Duke of Portland, who as Home Secretary and former Irish Lord Lieutenant was best placed to bring pressure to bear on Dublin Castle. Meanwhile, Sir Jeremiah adopted other approaches for the most immediate problems. He secured from Captain Patton the best fitted transports available to transfer the women and children to Cork; and this was the beginning of many years of helpfulness by Patton in procuring passages to Cork or Dublin for the dependants. He also persuaded Abercromby, with whom he had already worked cordially in the Netherlands a year before, to grant two guineas to every soldier's wife and a half guinea to every soldier's child – Irish or English indifferently – to pay for the journey, from Cork or Portsmouth as the case might be, to their native parish.

Portland's reply of 18 December to the original letter to Dundas was replete with feeble good will and blockheaded misunderstanding. Profuse in recognising Sir Jeremiah's pity for the unfortunate and in pleading his own, he went on to argue that the existing provisions sufficed to carry families to their homes; that Fitzpatrick's proposed annual gratuities might last beyond one year, even perhaps into widowhood; and that payment to the Irish dependants would simply raise a clamour for payment to other dependants, for it was not to be expected that British troops would appreciate such niceties as the existence or otherwise of a poor rate.[6] Promptly and patiently Fitzpatrick pointed out, in his turn, that the arrangements for Abercromby's troops were *ad hoc* and in no sense to be relied on as an 'establishment'; that annual gratuities were indeed meant to last beyond one year – but also to be needed beyond one year; and that if the matter were properly explained, no one could fail to see the difference in situation between women and children with a poor law to fall back on, and those without any safety net whatever.[7] Doubtless Fitzpatrick triumphed dialectically. But it was a barren victory as Portland made no further response.

As the correspondence proceeded, Fitzpatrick was casually – almost absent-mindedly, it would seem – adding details to his scheme. In the day's interval between writing to Dundas and to Windham, he had calculated the maximum number of Irish families who might apply successfully at 1,400, and the maximum liability at £14,200 per annum.[8] By the time of his reply to Portland, two weeks later, he had concluded that the two-guinea journey gratuity to Irish women should be held back until they had been landed at Cork (otherwise not 'one farthing of that sum' would remain), and that, for the continuing endowment, dependent girls should be supported to the age of 18, and boys until they were 21.[9]

The return of newly widowed Irish women and their newly orphaned children from Santo Domingo nine months later led Fitzpatrick, on 13 November 1796, to renew his appeal to Portland in the most impassioned terms.

> Were the Irish Government and its Parliament only to have Witnessed with me this last Month at Spithead, the Number of Lamenting Widowed Wretches and the pitiable Orphans who returned from the West Indies, severals of the Infants Motherless as [well as] Fatherless, I feel they would not, nor could not defer the beneficent and just Act one single hour; the few English Women and their Infants were immediately sent at the public expence to their Parishes ... but the Unfortunate Irish Woman (who has cause to regret being Irish) has no asylum to return to ... the only portion for the latter, being itinerant Beggary, hence are the Sea-ports of this Country with its Capital crowded with the begging Widows of Irish Soldiers and Sailors.
>
> The hireling Hessians Wife and Children are always provided for, it is so in Siberia, & Ireland alone of all the Countrys in Europe has hitherto neglected the great good and just Act ... The Family of the Militia Man remaining in his Native Country, Ireland, in great measure in a comparatively pampered State, and risquing little or no danger, has by its Parliament provision made for it, but none for the disconsolate family of him who is sent by his King to meet Toil, Danger and Death.
>
> I entreat that I may be excused for *any indiscretion in any mode of expression – the Picture* with its mourning Drapery is so strong before me, black to the Heart, needing no lacquering, that, I am impelled, altho incapable, to attempt the representation of its faint Shade.[10]

This effusion concerned the bereaved of Santo Domingo, but Fitzpatrick also seized the opportunity to raise again the larger question of continuing allowances for wives and children. A new fleet of transports was

262 *Service and Servitude*

being prepared for the West Indies, and the Irish Brigade as well as many Irish soldiers in British regiments were embarking for Martinique. The usual wash of misery was to be expected when they sailed. Fitzpatrick not only rehearsed the humanitarian case on its behalf, but also expanded the prudential argument to point out that the cost of a wife accompanying a soldier overseas was at least £25 per annum (with a corresponding expenditure on children), to say nothing of the additional pressures on space at sea and on land, and upon supplies and the medical services.

At the same time, he attempted to open up another line of attack by writing to Nepean,[11] in part because he had always found Nepean the most sympathetic of the British politicians, and in part because he had now extended his proposal to include the wives and children of Irish sailors, and Nepean, as Secretary of the Admiralty, was the man to carry this into effect. Nepean, however, made no reply. Yet another avenue seemed to open up soon afterwards. In the next month, December 1796, Pitt introduced a new poor rate Bill in the House of Commons. Few would have seen this as in any way a hopeful circumstance for Sir Jeremiah's purpose. But his was a most sanguine – or perhaps a desperate – eye. He wrote to Pitt (through George Rose of the Treasury) pointing out that Ireland lacked altogether that public provision for the poor which Pitt was now striving to render more generous and humane in England. There followed the usual elaboration of his 'idea' and imprecation to direct the Irish executive to introduce the necessary legislation, with a particular stress on this occasion on the utility of the measure in terms of the war effort:

> were Justice and Humanity out of the question, it might not prove unworthy the Kings friends, to take concern in the crying concerns of his Army; in so doing, the Transports and Hospitals would have been less crowded during the War, the enormous expence of lodging and their Supplies, would have been in great measure lessened, and this Country at this Moment, by being released from Thousands of Irish Beggars would profit in proportion equal, to the Justice done, to the hitherto neglected Irish.[12]

The fruits of Fitzpatrick's third campaign, of the winter of 1796-7, were meagre. Portland did forward his request to Camden, the then Irish Lord Lieutenant, in January 1797, but apparently without much accompanying pressure and certainly without a favourable result. When the next 'embarkation season' came around the following October, Sir

Jeremiah's immediate ambitions were more modest. He applied to Crosbie, general officer commanding at Portsmouth, for assistance for two Irish families sent ashore because one of the troop transports bound for the West Indies was already overcrowded. He asked for the same gratuities as had been made by Abercromby to the soldiers' dependants in 1795, taking it as a matter of course that they would be provided and suggesting that these grants be set upon a regular basis and paid at the embarkation ports instead of by the agents of the various regiments in London. Fitzpatrick's letter made it clear that there would be many similar cases of hardship before the fleet sailed.[13]

He was unpleasantly surprised. Instead of acting on his own initiative like Abercromby, Crosbie sought directions from the Horse Guards, only to learn that

> as there is no fund for relieving their [the Irish families'] distress, H.R.H. [York, the commander-in-chief] can only commisserate this distress . . . the continuing such a Gratuity in all cases would be attended with a very considerable Expence, and would likewise operate as an encouragement to follow Soldiers from the greatest distance.[14]

The rationale behind (or even the precise meaning of) this last observation may be difficult to arrive at, but the burden of the whole was a decided negative. Fitzpatrick was forced back upon his last resort. 'I was necessitated', he wrote later,

> to apply to the humane at Portsmouth and its vicinity, and obtained thro Charity the means of covering some whose apparel was realy scanty and deficient, and distributed amongst them the little fruits of my collection, and the like I have been in the frequent habit of doing.[15]

In the end, however, Fitzpatrick's persistence carried some part of the day at least. When the troop transports for the West Indies and for Sir James Poulteney's army for Ferrol (largely Irish in composition) sailed from Portsmouth and Southampton in July and August 1800, the Duke of York consented to a gratuity of 26s (a guinea and a crown) *per capita* being paid to the wives and children who were not being embarked;[16] and he also agreed that this should be distributed through the commanding officer at the embarkation port instead of through the regimental agents in the capital. At roughly the same time, Sir Jeremiah also found a way at last into the higher reaches of the Irish executive. His channel was Castlereagh, now Irish Chief Secretary, whom he had probably known as a young member of the Irish House of Commons eight or ten years before. Through Castlereagh's exertions, Cornwallis, the next Lord Lieutenant, was induced to grant an additional one and a half guineas to each dependant of an Irish soldier serving overseas. This sum was to be paid by the local commanding officer as soon as the returning women and children disembarked in Ireland.[17]

It had taken some six years for Fitzpatrick to attain this position. During that time he had importuned Dundas, Windham, Portland, Nepean and Pitt (at the heads respectively of five British departments of state); his friends in Dublin Castle, and Castlereagh; Generals Abercromby and Crosbie, and probably also Whitelocke and Poulteney and the commander-in-chief; the Transport Office; and *in extremis* 'the humane' of Portsmouth. He was of course not satisfied with once-for-all grants (although amounting together to £2 17s 6d each), and free return passages to Ireland, for the Irish dependants. He had by now come to the conclusion that no Irish dependants should be allowed to leave Ireland at all unless they were guaranteed passages in the transports sailing overseas,[18] and he pressed this vainly on the Horse Guards. He also continued to urge, even with the most meagre of openings, his scheme for complete and continuing maintenance. Thus when advising the commanding officer at Cork on 12 February 1801 of the complement of the *Prescot* transport (385 Irish dependants being returned from Portsmouth and Southampton), he attached a 'statement' setting out

> 1st *Regmt*. 2nd Column [sic], the Womens Name & Christian Name of Husband; 3rd her Age; 4th Children with her here; fifth X Pregnancy; 6th Post Town or, Parish in the County. This intended in Case of any future Provision to be made for the poor deserving objects to lead to a knowledge of where they may be found & to prevent fraud on their parts . . .[19]

The labour and ingenuity required for the composition and completion of these tables (see illustration) testified to his indomitability. So too in its way did his pursuit of the Earl of Hardwicke, when he in turn replaced Cornwallis as Irish Lord Lieutenant. Hardwicke was practically badgered by him to ensure that the additional Irish guinea and a half from the vice-regal privy purse would not drop away with the change in office-holders.

Regts	Name, Wife of —, and Age Years	Number of Children	Pregnant	County Town or Parish
64th	Betty Boyle, Bartley 26	1	-	Castlewillen Co. Down
	Sarah Nicholson, John 20	2	-	Ballyshaning [non] Co. Fermanagh
	Hannah Landrigan, Will. 20	1	..	Dungiven Co. Derry
	Mary Ryan, Will.m 21	..	..	Dungannon Co. Tyrone
	Sarah Money, Edward 24	..	X	Newry
	Ann Armstrong, Robt. 21	1	..	Dublin
	Ellen Jordan, Thomas 22	1	..	Ballinrobe Co. Mayo
	Ellen Sheridan, Patt 21	1	..	Multifarnam Co. W.meath
	Mary Gavagan, Patt 20	1	..	Bandon
	Ann Nellis, Peter 24	..	X	Castlefin Co. Donegall
	Jane Crawford, James 21	1	..	Belfast
	Mary Toole, Charles 30	2	..	Lugall Co. Armagh
	Elizabeth Owens, Peter 21	..	X	Dublin
	Mary Bawmer, Ross 26	1	..	Ennis
	Mary Hall, John 40	1	..	Kilrikel Co. Galway
	Hannah York, Henry 29	..	X	Manafelt Co. Derry
	Mary Gafney, James 30	1	..	Newry
	Rose Gardiner, No Husband but two Sons in the Regmt.			Banbridge Co. Down
	Nancy Bond, Charles 30	1	..	Balruddery Co. Dublin
	Mary Cannon, James 20	1	X	Clerain Co. Antrim
	Kitty Feeny, Matthew 30	..	X	Ballymahon Co. Longfo.
	Peggy Hawthorn, John 29	..	..	Carlow
	Mary Kenny, Edward 24	1	..	Mullingar
	Elinor Nelly, John 22	1	..	Naconara Co. W. Meath
	Peggy Cavanagh, Patt 27	2	X	Ballina Co. Mayo

Of course, Fitzpatrick cuts an absurd figure in this affair, in certain respects. Dunning the unresponsive (and doubtless irritated) great is never a dignified proceeding; and the rhetoric of 'feeling' rings repellently, not to say ridiculously, in modern ears. What would we now make of

When I consider the state of the poor in that my Native Country, and their condition in this neglect – there [,] fosterage here, I wish, except for the opportunities I have of representing their grievances to those who may have power and inclination to Alleviate them that, my Mother had not been disburdened of me on that side of the Water.[20]

Could such bathos have been read without derision even in 1797?

But however monstrous his inflation of language and sentiment, the fact remains that Fitzpatrick, alone and in the face of all discouragement, had uncovered and doggedly assailed, a poignant if 'small' social evil. Although the personnel varied constantly, thousands of women and children were suffering in consequence of official ignorance, brutishness and inefficiency. It was not as mere classes that Fitzpatrick pitied them. Images and stereotypes (at any rate, if their 'purpose' was to depersonalise the unpleasant) were foreign to his mind. He pressed individual cases as urgently as the categories of wife or child. He insisted, in season and out, that sorrow and sensibility transcended class and culture: 'poverty', as he wrote to Portland on 13 November 1796, 'will not extinguish the sensation of heart felt anguish.' From 1795 on he even translated his own 'feeling' for the miserable soldiers' dependants into an annual donation of £50, although he was comparatively a poor man for his station.

Moreover, the administrative response which he proposed was at once simple in the extreme, and adequate and economical. The very tables which he devised bear these marks. Neither one item less of information, nor one item more, was needed to effect his scheme; and only a single element was missing from the detail of the 'Idea', as he incidentally revealed it. This, the distribution of the funds in the home parishes, was inherently most difficult. There was obvious objections to using the parson or the priest or the dispensary doctor or the local magistrate in a country where many, perhaps most, parishes lacked one or other or even all of these persons, and where the religion of the few was established and its rival still part-proscribed.

As to Fitzpatrick's solitary tactic of redress, the pursuit of the powerful, he knew no other system of effecting regulative changes; nor is it easy to think of one which would have had the smallest prospect of success in the 1790s. This dictated the tone of his campaign. Occasionally, Swiftian irony seems to glimmer in a passage of a letter. So, too, 'regulated hatred' seems to break through momentarily here and there, as when he speaks of the poor troops 'hurried to fight the

Countrys Battles, thereby [to] protect the rights [of] and enrich by their Conquests those who remain at home; from whos Doors . . . they may be spurned with disdain'.[21] But generally Sir Jeremiah is respectful, unctuous and tireless in his long courtship of the mighty. Dulcification and docility were, doubtless, necessary concomitants of such a pursuit. Even Burke once pandered thus to Rockingham:

> I have gone further than I intended in a matter on which I am but indirectly concerned, and of which I am but an indifferent Judge; But your Lordship has often with great Goodness borne the imprudent officiousness of my Zeal.[22]

Similarly, self-importance and insensitivity to the reactions of others may have been necessary to sustain Fitzpatrick in the chase. They should, however, count for little, given the plain good end in view. Even if, bored or mocking, we counted them very heavily, they would still be ultimately outweighed.

> This Jack, joke, poor potsherd, patch matchwood, immortal diamond
> Is immortal diamond.

II The Convict Ships

How Fitzpatrick took to the inspection of convict ships is uncertain. Two were being fitted out at Portsmouth soon after his arrival there in July 1795. As the supervision of the fitting out was formally the business of the transport service, it would not have been surprising if Captain Patton had asked him to extend his current work on troopships to convict ships — or (still more likely) if he had persuaded Patton to let him do so. He cannot have done much with the first ship, the *Marquis Cornwallis*; that vessel was bound for Cork to take Irish convicts aboard, and only the preliminary preparation would have taken place at Portsmouth. But his work with the *Indispensable* may have been considerable, as she did not sail until late October 1795, and it was at Portsmouth that she was fitted out and that her complement of 133 women convicts were embarked.[23] All we know is that he inspected both vessels, and that by 1796 he had made himself effectively inspector of all English convict ships, and had developed various schemes for improving this unhappy service.

Forty vessels had already carried convicts to New South Wales — a voyage of six months or more — before Fitzpatrick took a hand in the business. The character and fortunes of this involuntary emigration had varied widely. The first fleet which had sailed in 1787 had been largely equipped and managed by the navy, with very remarkable success in terms of one crude but important measure, mortality and health. Only twenty-three of 759 convicts embarked died at sea, and almost all the survivors were landed well at Port Jackson; and on only one vessel, the *Alexander*, 'where many of the convicts were embarked from the different gaols with malignant disorders among them',[24] was the death-rate considerable. This comparative good health was attributed — and, after the important factor of good luck, fairly attributable — to naval control. Long experience of very protracted voyages, of carrying large numbers of men in cramped quarters, of furnishing and provisioning troopships and of sanitary discipline at sea had rendered the Admiralty pre-eminent in this field. In particular, naval surgeons subject to navy training and regulations were easily the best superintendents of health on such a lengthy and difficult passage.

Unfortunately, because of mercantile pressure and seeming cheapness, the British government reverted thereafter to the practice of using private contractors to transport convicts overseas. The second fleet, which had been contracted out to speculators, bore sad testimony to the consequences of this inhumane departure. 'Would I could draw an eternal shade', wrote Captain Hill, an army officer who sailed with that fleet,

> over the remembrance of this miserable part of our voyage — miserable, not so much in itself, as rendered so by the villainy, oppression, and shameful peculation of the masters of two of the transports. The bark I was on board of was, indeed unfit, from her make and size, to be sent so great a distance; if it blew but the most trifling gale she was lost in the waters, of which she shipped so much; that, from the Cape, the unhappy wretches, the convicts, were considerably above their waists in water, and the men of my company, whose berths were not so far forward, were nearly up to the middles. In this situation they were obliged, for the safety of the ship, to be pen'd down; but when the gales abated no means were used to purify the air by fumigation, no vinegar was applied to rectify the nauseous steams issuing from their miserable dungeon. Humanity shudders to think that of nine hundred male convicts embarked in this fleet, three hundred and seventy are already dead, and four hundred and fifty are landed sick and so emaciated and helpless that very few, if any of

them, can be saved by care or medicine ... The slave trade is merciful compared with what I have seen in this fleet; in that it is the interests of the masters to preserve the health and lives of their captives, they having a joint benefit with the owners; in this, the more they can withhold from the unhappy wretches the more provisions they have to dispose of at a foreign market.[25]

Some corrective came with the introduction in 1792 of a bounty for each convict landed in good health.[26] This was certainly superior to the contract based on a flat payment for each convict embarked, although the incentive to treat them humanely on the voyage was still much weaker than in the earlier North American transportation, when the masters of the vessels could in effect sell the labour of the landed convicts to the highest bidder. The charter-parties drawn up by the Navy Board also provided a degree of protection, for they were extremely detailed and based upon as exact a knowledge of needs as was possessed by any body in the 1790s.[27] But the absence of effective superintendence during the passage, and the failure of enquiries in New South Wales to secure the punishment of ill-doers, meant that these precautions were partly wasted. They did however provide a point of entry into the affair for the naval agents, and eventually Fitzpatrick. Not only could they dispute the quality and quantity of the many items specified, but they could also render the later charter-parties more precise or full.

Sir Jeremiah began his work on the *Ganges*, being prepared for convicts at Portsmouth in August 1796, by requiring new 'Air Machines'. But he soon progressed to arranging for separate quarters for the women accompanying their convict husbands ('their merit in a conjugal sense being nearly unparalleled') to protect them from the 'insults' of the ship's crew and military guard, and for separate quarters for a ship's hospital. Water-purifiers and fumigation and medical supplies were his next care; and he attempted to ensure that the *Ganges*' brief call at Cork would be used to land the convicts for air and exercise, to add fresh meat and vegetables to the ship's provisions and to re-strain the salted meats, lest scurvy or dysentery develop later. 'I earnestly beg', he ended wistfully,

> to suggest ... (altho' I fear it will be considered irregular by the agent at Cork and am sensible the ship's steward will consider it troublesome) that the allowance or diet for the women and infants, in place of common ship's provisions, be inter-changed for a like

270 *Service and Servitude*

value of tea, cocoa, sugar, barley, raisins, and well-baked white biscuit.[28]

The second vessel on which he worked at Portsmouth in 1796, the *Britannia*,[29] was to embark Irish convicts at the Cove of Cork so that he could only supervise the preliminary fitting out, and pray that the necessary structural changes – not to add, the more refined improvements he had tried to secure for the *Ganges* – would not be neglected in Ireland.

All this was characteristic of Sir Jeremiah's early intrusion into a new field. So too was his rapid devising of a programme of reform. He had already found John King, Nepean's successor as under-secretary at the Home Office, sympathetic and helpful in the case of 'a poor miserable convict'; and he told him on 23 October 1796 that he would discuss with him shortly the convict question, together with 'another of my hobby-horsical subjects'[30] (possibly allowances for soldiers' dependants). This probably signalled the emergence of Fitzpatrick's scheme for an inspectorate of convict transportation which was to be fully developed in the following year.

In three letters of November and December 1797, addressed to King for Portland's consideration, Fitzpatrick set out his proposal. Its essential justification was the venality, sloth and callousness which he had encountered in the contract, prisons and medical departments of convict administration:

> that the Doctor will ever state his own neglect or mismanagement of his Patients, or that Keepers will state the exercise of cruelties or severe treatment, often produced to deter, as a substitute for the necessity of due vigilance, which is always considered troublesome; that those who supply Diet or Cloathing should be expected to report these Matters, other than of good Quality, or that the general Managers should criminate the Persons who may deserve it, but who are more or less within their own Appointments, surely is not to be expected.[31]

Fitzpatrick pointed to the Irish experience of prisons wherein magistrates, sheriffs, grand juries and local inspectors all had specific statutory obligations, which were yet generally neglected until an exterior central superintendence was imposed upon them all. As to the convicts:

> to furnish Articles whether of Accommodation, Diet, Medicine,

Cloathing &c &c — without proper inspection, is next a kin to the Expectation of receiving true and punctual Payments of Revenues or Duties from those, who should actually pay them, without the interference of inspecting or collecting Officers.[32]

The first duty of the proposed inspector was to examine all convicts quarterly and to classify them in terms of their suitability for transportation or hard labour or no labour at all. Currently, no distinction was made 'between the Labor of the Ruptured, the Dropsical, sore-legged, the Asthmatic, Epileptic &c &c'. The 'charts' on which this advice would be regularly set out would enable the Home Office to choose only the healthy and active for New South Wales, as well as to maintain an overview of the convict population in general. The inspector should also advise, on the basis of his visits, 'on Lodging, Air, Exercise, the nature of Labor, Modes of Shackling, Cloathing, Diet and Medical Attendance', which last Fitzpatrick had found to be universally neglected. The selection and fitting out of convict ships, and the supply of full and sweet provisions and water, and clothing and shackles as convenient as circumstances allowed, was the next responsibility. Finally — a vital matter — he should select adequately trained ship surgeons, and supervise the provision of medical supplies, quarters and equipment.[33]

King (and presumably Portland) were unresponsive. But whether or not as a *pis aller*, Fitzpatrick was supported to a surprising degree by both the Home Office and the transport service in the day-to-day business of his informal inspectorate at Portsmouth. To appreciate the significance of this it is necessary to enumerate many minute and apparently mundane details for it was on these that the chances of reducing the load of convict misery and holding back death at sea ultimately rested. Fitzpatrick's 'inspection' of the *Barwell*, which was fitted up for convicts at Portsmouth in the autumn of 1797, provides a good illustration of this point. First, he redesigned the hatchways to allow more ventilation and proposed privies for the orlop deck instead of the prevailing 'bucketed up . . . tubs'. He also pressed for an additional air machine for the between decks, and four 'close stools' with pewter pans for night use, to be built by the ship's carpenter to his specifications. It is a sad comment upon the convict vessels that Fitzpatrick could argue that the first two of these 'improvements' had already proved themselves on slave ships — *experto crede* again, for it was (he said) on his own recommendation that slave ships had come to adopt them.

Secondly, he proposed considerably more extensive prophylactic and medical supplies, including two large water purifiers and a supply of charcoal to refresh the casks periodically. The medicines were to be ordered under the supervision of the Apothecaries Hall; and the ship's surgeon was to be instructed in the principles of fumigation and other preventive measures. Fitzpatrick stressed moreover the importance of delaying the embarkation of convicts until almost the moment of sailing to reduce the danger of infectious disease taking hold in the stationary vessel.[34] Thirdly, he asked

> that Lights should be burn'd in Lanthorns on the O'erlop Deck for Convenience of the Convicts — that they should be allowed Soap to promote their Health & Comfort — & Frieze, with Sundry other Articles, for widening their Breeches, which may then be taken off at night notwithstanding the men are double bolted —also Saucepans to prepare Diet or Drink for the Diseased & articles out of which they may take Food or Medicine.

Practically, this involved a request for 3 horn lanterns, 112 lbs of candles, 600 lbs of soap, 12 yards of frieze cloth, 12 dozen horn buttons, 2 lbs of thread, 100 needles, sundry two-gallon and half-gallon saucepans, 2 dozen pannikins and 2 dozen pewter spoons.[35]

Such a catalogue may make very tedious reading, but it was just such petty particulars which rendered this 'inspection' administratively significant. Systematically considered, Fitzpatrick's proposals represented attempts to advance sanitation, preventive medicine, medical treatment and health, and to reduce the accumulation of miseries among transported convicts. Individually considered, they were remarkable for their ingenuity, practical imagination, and painstaking bureaucratic workmanship. Grotesque though they might seem, the cases of the close stools and the widened breeches provide excellent instances of Sir Jeremiah's skill and care. The materials and dimensions of the stool pans which he designed, and the tight fitting of their lids, were to him critical affairs — and rightly, for on these depended the smell between decks and the slopping over of urine and excreta as the ship heaved. Similarly, upon such trivia as the quantity of the cloth and thread, or the number of needles and buttons (for side-buttoning instead of seamed trousers were essential to the scheme), depended his way around the superficially ludicrous but truly poignant difficulty of men conjoined in irons, unsupervised, undressing.

In proposing these changes in the system, Sir Jeremiah urged, after the fashion of the defence in a defamation action, that the cost would be small and that, even if it were not, the government should not permit 'a paltry Saving to stand in Competition with the Lives, or even Comforts, of the unfortunate, ill-fated Wretches'.[36] But for once he succeeded almost effortlessly. With the exception of candles and lanterns (it being the contractor's business to supply lights), the Transport Office soon sanctioned all his modifications and requests and directed Patton at Portsmouth to provide all items not already in stock.[37] Emboldened by this, Fitzpatrick added various new recommendations for the *Britannia*, the next convict vessel which he was preparing: among these were the fourfold segregation of the convicts according to their previous behaviour and good health, and arrangements for protecting 'female delicacy', as both men and women convicts were to be carried on the ship. He also added clothing bags, tin mugs and tea kettles to the list of equipment;

> he relies upon the Board's providing these various Articles, from a Knowledge that is the Wish of the Duke of Portland, & a Persuasion that it is equally the Desire of Transport Board, that the Voyage of these unhappy Wretches should be rendered as Comfortable as possible.

True to form, Fitzpatrick included candles and lanterns among the items which he 'relied upon' the board to supply.[38] He could not wrest what he wanted from the contractor, but the state was to prove more malleable in this instance. By 1800 he had so far succeeded that special lamps of his own design, together with the necessary sperm oil and wicks, were being sanctioned by the Transport Board and paid for by the Home Office.[39]

His gradual expansion of 'requirements' for the convict ships did meet one serious check. When the *Hillsborough* was being prepared in October 1798, Fitzpatrick was refused various items which the contractor had already supplied, although of course not to Sir Jeremiah's satisfaction. He was told that

> all the Necessary Utensils are by Charter to be Supplied by the Owner & unless a special Complaint is lodged against him for Deficiency in those Articles the Board cannot interfere − ... [and] that any New Thing which he would recommend, should be proposed to the Master who will doubtless furnish it, if he be convinced of its being Matter of real Accommodation and that it will prevent a

Demand for some other Article.[40]

But this was an isolated effort to stem the tide of requests. Thereafter, as before, the Transport Office generally acquiesced in his demands, even if, as was often the case, he had already gone ahead and ordered or devised some new or 'improved' fitting or utensil.

In two other areas the history of Fitzpatrick's endeavours in convict transportation is essentially the same: an initial unauthorised intervention, an attempted check by his superiors and an ultimate acceptance of at least the substance of his proposal. The first was a species of 'payment by results', or rather bonus on results, for the ships' surgeons. In 1796 or 1797 Sir Jeremiah won some form of general agreement from Portland to his scheme for paying a *per capita* 'bounty' for each convict landed in New South Wales in good health.[41] Apparently specific sums and conditions were not settled. Apparently too, Portland conceived of this as being a charge upon the contractor, not the Home Office,[42] although doubtless the contingent liability was to have been taken into account when the tenders were being drawn up. At any rate, before the *Barwell* sailed in 1797 Fitzpatrick had agreed with her surgeon, J.T. Sharpe, that he should be paid half a guinea for each convict who was disembarked in a satisfactory state of health.

Only nine lives were lost on the passage, and Sharpe claimed not only for the 287 convicts but also for the 31 soldiers who were certified as well upon arrival at Sydney Cove. The ship's broker offered him a mere £7 per month of passage; he took only £5 per month, in the expectation of receiving the bounty later; the Transport Board refused to pay him anything because it was no party to the agreement; and Sir Jeremiah was faced with a demand from Sharpe that the promise made 'on the day of our sailing (as otherwise I should not have gone)' be made good.[43] Voluble pleas from Fitzpatrick eventually secured a grant of £50 by Portland[44] from Home Office funds; and thereafter the bounties appear to have worked on a settled and regular basis. Meanwhile, a similar problem had arisen in the case of the *Hillsborough*, which had sailed in 1798, before Sharpe had returned to England. Fitzpatrick had made the same agreement with its surgeon, J.W. Kunst, as he had done shortly before with Sharpe.[45] How this case ended is not known. Possibly Portland made another *ex gratia* grant of a sum below the full demand. But since the death rate on the *Hillsborough* was, partly through Kunst's ineffectuality, extraordinarily high,[46] it is unlikely that Fitzpatrick supported or the Home Office acceded to Kunst's claims.

The second disputed field was Fitzpatrick's right to land and replace convicts whom he considered too ill to be embarked. The problem did not arise, at any rate in an acute form, until the sailing of the *Hillsborough* in 1798. Gaol fever was abroad at the time of her preparation, both at Newgate prison in London and in the hulks at Langston near Portsmouth, from both of which transportees were to be drawn. The London convicts were embarked at Gravesend, under Fitzpatrick's supervision, before the vessel proceeded to Portsmouth. Despite his re-landing some of the Newgate convicts at Gravesend, fever broke out on the short passage to Portsmouth; and this was compounded by the addition of infected men from Langston. For nearly six weeks the vessel (already much delayed in London) was held up at Portsmouth while the sick were being replaced, the vessel cleared for re-fumigation and new beds, bedding and clothes provided. During this period some thirty convicts were removed from the vessel by Fitzpatrick, and several of them died ashore. There were also deaths aboard.

Fitzpatrick had in fact objected from first to last to any of the Langston convicts being sent on the *Hillsborough*, 'as the jail fever had raged there [Langston] with much violence, and he was fearful the infection remained latent in their [the convicts'] blood'.[47] But as the weeks went by the Home Office (and King in particular, it would seem) became increasingly impatient with the apparently endless postponements of casting off, and the repeated cycles of fever, landings, replacement of materials and vessel-cleansing. In the end, one of the clerks in the department was sent down to Portsmouth to report on the affair, and his representations, together with those of a Mr Groundwater, the surgeon employed by the contractor, appear to have been decisive in inducing – or perhaps we should say, facilitating – the Home Office to sanction the sailing of the *Hillsborough* at the end of December 1798, with some 150 convicts from Langston among her complement.[48] In short, Fitzpatrick had been overruled.

The voyage of the *Hillsborough* was the most disastrous in the entire history of transportation to Australia.[49] Ninety-five of the 300 convicts aboard died before reaching Sydney; several others died almost immediately ashore; and the lieutenant-governor of New South Wales, Hunter, described the survivors as 'the most wretched and miserable convicts I have ever beheld, in the most sickly and wretched state'.[50] Part of the tragedy may be attributable to a harsh master and a weak surgeon. William Noah, one of the convicts aboard, observed in his diary of the voyage,

It was, one would think, enough to soften the heart of the most inhuman being to see us ironed, handcuffed and shackled in a dark, nasty, dismal deck, without the least wholesome air, but all this did not penetrate the breasts of our inhuman captain, and I can assure you that the doctor was keep [sic] at such a distance, and so strict was he look [sic] after, that I have known him sit up till opportunity would suit to steal a little water to quench the thirst of those who were bad, he being on a very small allowance for them.[51]

But the prime cause of the great mortality was the gaol fever which the transportees, in particular those from Langston, had carried with them to the ship.

This was established at the inquiry into the disaster conducted in June 1800. The *Hillsborough* was roomier and better found and supplied than any earlier convict ship, yet before she reached even Table Bay one-third of the prisoners were suffering from gaol fever. Fitzpatrick, of course, blamed everything on the embarkation of the Langston convicts 'contrary to his wishes', and he was probably right. Yet the Home Office could have made out a case of sorts on its own behalf. It was all very well for Sir Jeremiah to say that no one should be taken from Langston 'be the inconvenience what it may'.[52] If this advice had been followed to the letter, either the *Hillsborough* would have sailed half-full or she would have missed the convoy, which could delay no longer. It might be months before another convoy might be joined and who could tell whether she might be in a better condition even then? To organise a sailing of transportees was a most laborious and expensive business, and once the date contracted for had passed, the government was liable for demurrage. Fitzpatrick might look to health alone, but for Portland and King the decisions were much more complex and difficult, and until the calamity of the *Hillsborough* actually occurred, they had no compelling reason to trust Fitzpatrick's judgement blindly with so much at stake.

Later in 1800, after the transportees had been put aboard the convict ship *Earl Cornwallis*, at Portsmouth, dysentery broke out amongst them. Fitzpatrick and the ship's surgeon were at one in their handling of the epidemic, and their counter-measures were evidently successful. But when they were called on to explain the delay in sailing, they pointed to their lack of power to land 'diseased' convicts without applying first to Whitehall. Fitzpatrick seized on the occasion to rebuke the Home Office:

as it is the bounden Duty of Men, as well to guard against every possible Injury which may afflict our fellow Creatures as to improve on Improvement, I hope on future Embarkations of Convicts in the first Instance to be heard and attended to.[53]

In future, he was not only 'heard' but also given, in effect, a completely free hand in landing sick convicts and choosing others for their place. The lessons of the *Hillsborough* had sunk in. Before the next convict vessels sailed, the Transport Board received this instruction from the Home Office:

No Convicts to be received from the persons in whose charge they may be brought, until fully examined by Sir Je. Fitzpatrick or some experienced Surgeon; and declared in perfect health & fit to undergo the Voyage.[54]

Fitzpatrick was even granted the power to determine the number of convicts which a vessel might carry when in the spring of 1801 his recommendation of a reduction in the complements of the *Nile* and the *Coromandel* was accepted, virtually as a matter of course.[55]

But a still more striking triumph and vindication was to follow when the Home Office issued new instructions to the masters and surgeons of convict ships on 10 June 1801.[56] The secretary of state,[57] 'entertaining a just Opinion of the Judgement and capability of Sir Jerh. Fitz Patrick Inspector General of Health', required these ships' officers to adhere strictly to the regulations which he had drawn up for the passage, and to 'minute their observance' in log-books to be delivered to the governor of New South Wales, and (in the form of certified copies) to the Home Office. There could be no doubt of the provenance of the regulations. Only one pen would have opened the catalogue with 'You the Surgeon are ever to keep in Memory that, Cleanliness is the Parent of Health'. The substance of the instructions, too, revealed Sir Jeremiah's hand.[58] In the most specific detail as well as the most grandiloquent of official prose, rules were laid down for the regular sweeping and scraping of the between-decks, washing down of berths and airing of bedding on the deck; for the trimming of the wind sails, the working of the air scuttles and air machines and the use of the water purifiers; for the treatment of the sick, their food, drink, hospital requisites and furniture, and disinfection upon recovery; the daily airing and exercise of each prisoner, their personal cleanliness – soap, combs and razors being supplied – and the daily fumigation of their quarters; and the variation of their diet as their well-being required, from the 'large supply of Lemon Juice, Sugar, Sago, Rice, Oatmeal, Peas, and Bread' which Fitzpatrick would prescribe for the vessels. This represented the apotheosis of Sir Jeremiah's career as a regulator of health on transports. Never before had he had such liberty in preparing them for the voyage, or in laying down the mode of their sanitary government on the high seas.

But Fitzpatrick was far from satisfied with the painful successes which he had achieved, for at best they covered only transportees, and even at that, only from the time of their embarkation at London or Portsmouth to the time of their departure for Australia. Since 1797 he had been struggling vainly to interest King in the larger issues:

> The principal Matter herein alluded to is, the criminal neglect, and I may say, for I could have proved it, the Cruel treatment of the Convicts, with the most inconsiderate and expensive Modes of producing anything from their Labour, the Errors in Dieting, Cloathing, and Lodging them, of treating them when diseased; – of conveying them to their allotted Banishment; of not supplying them, when that Period terminates, with the proper means of returning; in short, with deficiency in almost every Matter concerning them.[59]

On 16 April 1800, he made a final desperate appeal to King. At first, he wrote, he had not been too cast down by the departure of Nepean ('whose heart was in unison with my warmest wishes') because of King's high reputation for beneficence and his supposed influence over Portland. But King would never see him, not even during his long and bitter resistance to the embarkation of convicts from Langston on the *Hillsborough*.

> I flattered myself . . . [that this] would have induced You to demand an Interview with me – for when I speak to Mr Baldwin [the Home Office counsel for colonial business] – to whom I am much obliged, – he is pleased to say, he has not the Powers relative to the Convicts which You possess, and refers me to You; but unfortunately when I applied to You for nearly three years past – crowded as You have been with business, You never have been able to hear me.[60]

But King – in fact, a self-important *fonctionnaire*[61] – remained silent and unmoved, and Fitzpatrick could do no more than await a more favourable season. His one attempt to bypass King — by proposing a scheme for collecting criminal statistics to Portland early in 1798[62] — had proved quite fruitless; and his efforts to work through Baldwin later in the same year and in 1799[63] had met the fate already indicated in his letter.

He did think that his moment might have come when Pitt's ministry fell and Pelham, whom he had met as Irish chief secretary in Dublin in 1783-4, succeeded Portland at the Home Office on 30 July 1801. An interview was arranged for mid-August, but this fell through, and for the next two weeks Pelham was bombarded with letters from Fitzpatrick, one pursuing him even to

> his country residence which, Sir Jerome is sensible, should merely be devoted to Relaxation. This however is caused by fears that, unimportant as they may appear, compared to the Matters which crowd upon his Lordship at the Office, that Attention which His Humanity would be Solicitous to pay to the Subject, might not be possible there.[64]

In part, Fitzpatrick was so urgent because two convict vessels were then being fitted up in Cork, and he wished Pelham to authorise his temporary transfer to Ireland to supervise the preparation: for long and with good cause, he had deplored the neglect which attended the shipment of Irish convicts. But the main reason for his importunity was that Pelham represented a prospect of escape from the frustrations of the past four years. Headlong, Sir Jeremiah poured out the history of his endeavours to persuade 'someone of power & influence' to interest himself in the grievances of convicts; and marvelled at the callousness of men who could assign the infirm and diseased, even blind men and cripples, to hard labour and the hulks. But his anger burned hottest when he turned to the cruelty and corruption of prison hospitals:

> from all I could ever discover, more irreligious Neglect and more improper treatment, altho' I visitted Prisons and Hospitals in various parts of Europe, I never discovered, in short My Lord, the representations which I could have made in respect of their Laying, Drinks, Diet, the intermixture of the malignantly diseased, the putrid convalescent; . . . their being put on a common coarse Convict-Diet before their Stomachs were capable to digest it, the nature of the Food of the healthful, & samples of which I often brought to town,

the worst I ever saw; their bad and filthy bedding, some not having half the covering of their Bodies; the privation of the nutritious part of their Diet, by scumming the Fat off their Brooths; the defect of their clothing in the most intense cold; the indiscriminate application of their Labor, whether with complete and painful *Testicular Ruptures*, hanging towards their knees without trusses, yet in company yoked in the Carts; . . .[65]

The whole ended of course in an elaboration of the need for a general convict inspectorate, for which Fitzpatrick presented a thorough and well-articulated scheme.

Pelham's immediate reaction is not known, but the letters evidently took effect in time, although not perhaps quite the effect that Sir Jeremiah had intended. Either at the very end of 1801 or the very beginning of 1802 Pelham appointed an inspector of convicts. But it was one A. Graham, and not Fitzpatrick himself, who was appointed.[66] Possibly Fitzpatrick had not expected to occupy the office, if it were set up. But this would have been out of character for him, as well as difficult to reconcile with his rehearsing, in several of his requests for its setting up, the circumstances of his becoming inspector general of prisons in Ireland and 'Inspector General' of health. But by now he was an old man; and doubtless he had long ago been ticketed at the Home Office as a partisan, firebrand, spendthrift, eccentric and traverser of administrative order. He himself may have been surprised that he was passed over. But we may well doubt that many of the officials who had had to deal with him on government business would have been.

We do not know certainly that Sir Jeremiah felt aggrieved. Apparently, his old powers over transportation were left, essentially if not formally, intact. When the *Perseus* and *Coromandel* were being fitted out as convict ships and filled at Portsmouth early in 1802, and the problem of fever at Langston presented itself once again, Fitzpatrick was given a free hand in dealing with the epidemic, and Graham backed him altogether in his re-landing of the embarked sick and his selection of their replacements.[67] Similarly, when Fitzpatrick advised against allowing two wives of free settlers, far advanced in pregnancy, from embarking, Graham supported him and endorsed his arguments wholeheartedly.[68] On the other hand, Fitzpatrick had now someone unpleasantly close to being his 'superior officer' overlooking his work at Portsmouth; and it was soon clear, first, that Graham was expected to expedite the sailings of the convict ships, and secondly that, unlike his 'subordinate', he would manifest the due discretion of a civil servant. For example, when it was discovered that the contractor's agent for the *Perseus* and *Coromandel* was swindling the sick convicts of their food and 'necessaries', Graham spinelessly concluded, 'if it were not for fear of creating an alarm, which perhaps, had better be avoided, I would not hesitate to indict him'.[69]

On 17 January 1802, Graham ended his report from Portsmouth with this passage:

> I have been obliged to talk very seriously to Sir J. Fitzpatrick, in consequence of his haranguing people at taverns upon the state of the convicts, whose friend he styles himself. I told him if he had any complaints to make, he should do it in writing to you; that he might take his own method (having regard to the new contract) to cure those who are already ill, and to prevent by fumigation or otherwise an increase of the disorder on board La Fortunée [a hulk at Portsmouth], and I would answer for all the extra expence attending it; but that if I heard any more reports of his public conversations upon the subject (which cannot fail to have a mischievous tendency), I should feel it my duty to represent the matter in a formal manner to Lord Pelham.[70]

Possibly it was resentment of Graham's appointment which led Fitzpatrick into taproom oratory. But whether or not this was so, such a dressing-down must have been bitterly resented. Yet there was no official friction, and Graham, as we have said, supported Fitzpatrick fully and to the end, in both his recommendations and particular actions. Nor did Fitzpatrick continue to pursue Pelham or even to raise again any of his old King Charles's heads. On the contrary, he set out immediately to find another patron and to take up fresh causes of reform. On 30 January, he asked Hobart, secretary of state for the newly created Office of War and the Colonies, and yet another former Irish secretary whom he had known in Dublin in his prison inspection days, for an interview.

He may well have tackled Hobart before this. On the very day of Fitzpatrick's letter from Portsmouth, Hobart asked the Home Office to secure from him a detailed certification of the health of the individual passengers on convict vessels for use, if need be, later on in prosecutions of masters or surgeons for negligence during the voyage[71] — a proposal which smacks strongly of Sir Jeremiah! However that may have been, the letter of 30 January to Hobart proposed that any married convict who behaved well for two years after arrival in Sydney should have the right to have his wife, or her husband, and children − 'the deserted and despised innocent sufferers' − join him or her in the colony, with the free passages and all the other privileges of free settlers. The supporting arguments were family ties, sound morality and above all the security and solidity of the settlement in New South Wales, 'that extraordinary colony (there being none who please that do not acquire property there)'. Fitzpatrick sought an immediate answer so that he could hold out this rich prospect and inducement to the convicts of the *Perseus* and *Coromandel* before they sailed. One need hardly add that there was a postscript on another tack. Sir Jeremiah sought to use Hobart's well-known interest in Ireland to palliate the evils of the Irish transportees, of which he had so long complained. Copies of the instructions of 1801 to masters and surgeons in convict ships were enclosed to throw the contrast between English and Irish practice into higher relief. Possibly Fitzpatrick had an Irish appointment as inspector in mind, for he ended, 'your Lordship's knowledge of mankind will induce you to doubt their [the regulations'] acception without zeal, probity, and understanding, even supposing them directed'.[72] But no such appointment was made; and by the time the next convict ship was being got ready at Portsmouth, Fitzpatrick had been on half-pay for a year, and he was not called forth from his retirement to inspect it. That he was by then altogether resigned to his supersession − and perhaps also that he resented it deeply − was indicated by his submission at the end of 1802 of a claim for remuneration for the extra services performed in the inspection of fifteen convict vessels and 2,646 convicts since his first venture into this field on 27 June 1795.[73]

In certain respects, Fitzpatrick's inspectorate of convict ships was his most complete achievement. By 1802 he had established virtually full control over the fitting out and supply of the vessels, over the selection of transportees (at least in the negative sense of being able to reject the unfit), and even over health at sea, so far as surgeons' bounties, shipboard regulations with some check on their observance, and records of the conditions of the passengers when they embarked, could achieve it. Equally remarkable perhaps was the success of his proposal for an English convict inspector, for Graham's appointment might be regarded, technically at least, as a triumph of a sort. True, a further scheme of his for the return of convicts who had served their sentences, as well as his scheme for the settlement of convicts' spouses and their families in New South Wales, did fail. But these really opened into quite other fields. In terms of his original task, he had in general succeeded − granted that by modern measurement his achievements were pitifully small, in fact, difficult to perceive at all. For example, to secure the substitution of chains for bars in the prisoners' fetters certainly rendered their life between decks more bearable. But it is hard to speak of this today as a humanitarian advance (as Fitzpatrick, quite rightly and proudly, did) without sounding either satirical or brutalised. Again, it took more than three years of wrangling and petitions for Fitzpatrick to gain the type of small water keg which he desired for the between-decks. The difficulty was that water supply was the contractors' business, and contractors would not bring upon themselves the cooperage costs and general nuisance of installing containers of the right size. Yet, Fitzpatrick argued, this was a vital matter because water was the convicts' only drink and without small kegs and spigots (and the pannikins which he early gained, as they were technically 'equipment' rather than 'supply') they could not get it at will or at any time they wished.[74] Once more, it is difficult to realise this as an advance. Once more, the gap is great between what was a grave matter in the 1790s and what the 1980s can envisage in such terms.

Nevertheless, it hardly needs saying that Fitzpatrick's work must be measured in terms of the parameters of his time. To pursue the example of chains, fetters would have seemed an absolute necessity in such a business to late-eighteenth-century men. On almost half of all the convict ships of 1795-1802, the prisoners made attempts to seize the vessels.[75] The utmost hope was then that the fetters might be altered, never that they might be dispensed with. But the mere abandonment of bars represented an immense liberation in the convicts' capacity to move. Similarly with the second example. The convicts would have been waterless for twelve hours a day, and even longer in bad weather, had they relied upon it being served by others and from an upper deck. Thus, our minute, scarcely-perceptible gradations were their big matters, in terms of relative suffering and distress. Moreover, the rough but fundamental test of mortality provides some more general evidence that Fitzpatrick's system worked. There was, for example, only one death from disease upon his *Coromandel* in 1802, and all the other passengers reached Sydney healthy. Yet, on the two convict vessels which sailed from Cork late in 1801 (the two which Fitzpatrick begged Hobart vainly to let him supervise), almost one hundred of the convicts died at sea, and about the same number were ill upon disembarkation.[76] But most important of all, the regime which Fitzpatrick established was at or close to the border of what was administratively possible during the period 1795-1802. It covered the entire span from arrival at Portsmouth to landing in New South Wales. It embraced every known precaution and device for preserving health. It multiplied the checks upon the conduct of the superintending officers. It even softened, so far as one minor officer on the fringes of the business could do so, the pitiful life of the 'poor wretches' chained between decks.

But though his work in this field was remarkably comprehensive in the end, it had accumulated in a most *ad hoc* and even haphazard fashion. Not that the individual pieces of administrative design were slapdash. Like Arland Ussher's Irishman, Sir Jeremiah here amalgamated the precisionist and the marplot.[77] Meticulous planning interspersed the blundering tirades. Moreover, the crablike progress and incremental method were, to some extent, forced upon him. The contractors were, by the very nature of their interests, hostile to improvement; the transport service was generally amenable but also generally anxious to pass the buck; the Home Office blew hot and cold. But it was not all exogenous. It was also characteristic of Fitzpatrick that he should have taken up issues impulsively, opportunistically and with little apparent co-ordination. This was, however, his inveterate bureaucratic style; and it had, to say the least, the qualities of its defects. We may put down to its credit his passionate pursuit of an immediate end, his capacity to become engrossed in particulars and to work them through meticulously, and the fact that in his ranting, sprawling and ungainly way he often did build up — eventually — systematic and all-embracing answers to the problems.

III The Slave Trade

There was, however, one case in which Fitzpatrick was drawn into a field of reform, not by direct experience, but by projecting a scheme from without; and in the same case his 'idea' was developed as a coherent programme, all at once, instead of by gradual accumulation. This enables us to explore his administrative thought at a different and perhaps deeper level.

In 1797 he published a substantial pamphlet, *Suggestions on the Slave Trade*, in London. What led him to take up this subject? He may have actually examined vessels employed in the slave trade because some of these were later used for the transportation of East Indian troops or convicts. He claimed, as we have seen,[78] to have procured the alteration of the interior fittings of slave ships to procure more light and air between decks, although it is difficult to say when or how this might have happened. He was, we know from his many references to contemporary parliamentary debates or executive proposals, a close reader of the politics of the day; and Wilberforce's vain attempts of 1796 to carry through the abolition of the slave trade,[79] and that failing, to regulate the trade by relating the numbers to be carried to tonnage,[80] must have attracted his attention. There was no 'humanitarian' subject under the sun in which he was not ready to interfere; and it is quite possible that he saw himself as one of the inspectors — perhaps the chief inspector — whom he projected in his pamphlet. These seem to exhaust even the guesses which we can make as to his motivation.

Fitzpatrick was of course an outright opponent of slavery and the slave trade. But he did not regard this as absolving him from the attempt to ameliorate them. Although he looked forward to their ultimate disappearance, he saw this as both comparatively distant in time and requiring careful and graduated preparation. The interest of the slave-holders was still powerful in Great Britain; many influential and respectable persons were still persuaded by their case; and the sugar colonies were still a leading source of British wealth and still essentially dependent on slave labour. Moreover, he believed that, whether slave or not, African labour was the best suited to the West Indian climate and style of life, and would have to be continued.[81] For Sir Jeremiah, these constituted the ineluctable facts of the case. His scheme had to be worked out within the boundaries to action which they set.

The first step, he argued, was to reduce the demand for labour in the sugar industry. This should be done by a system of bounties and penalties designed to encourage the more economical working of the plantations and the increased use of more effective 'implements of husbandry' — the contemporary equivalent, more or less, of mechanised farming. In other words, capital-intensive cultivation was to be rewarded, and labour-intensive cultivation to be penalised. Here Fitzpatrick looked back to Irish precedents of the mid-eighteenth century when both the Royal Dublin Society and the Irish Parliament had proffered bounties to modernise agricultural techniques, especially those which were labour-saving, while at the same time statutory fines were imposed for backward or cruel modes of husbandry.[82] Secondly, Sir Jeremiah aimed at increasing the indigenous negro population in the West Indies by the reduction of infant mortality. In turn, this involved cutting the workload of the women slaves when they were pregnant, a rudimentary form of maternity leave; and a network of lying-in hospitals scattered through the islands, to be paid for by the proprietors through the local rates.[83] The hospitals proposal was developed with Fitzpatrick's usual eye for detail and concern for the actual carrying-out and sustaining of the measure.

Of course, the fundamental objective of both these features of the project was minimising the need, and the incentive, to import fresh labour from West Africa. The second also envisaged a start to the replacement of slaves by free negroes in the Caribbean, because the infants born in the lying-in hospitals would not be in a state of servitude. But Fitzpatrick had no hope that new African labour could be dispensed with altogether — at least immediately. This led him to take up, next, the improvement and control of the slave trade itself. He deliberately restricted himself to regulations which Britain could actually enforce. Thus no direct interference with slave trading or slave dealing in the African interior was proposed, although some indirect control — through, for instance, the refusal of licences to vessels with wounded or maimed Africans aboard or where families had been broken up — might be exercised. Given his concern for enforcement, his main interest was naturally the vessels and the passage; and for these he planned a triple inspectorate, in Britain, West Africa and the West Indies.[84]

It scarcely needs saying that the tasks set out for the British inspector closely resembled those of the current inspector of army health and convict ships. The British inspector was to satisfy himself as to the dimensions, carrying capacity and construction of the vessels employed in the slave trade, and to ensure that they were fitted out 'in accordance with the principles of health, convenience and security'. A plan of each vessel specifying its allotted 'passenger' space and prescribed fittings was to be entered in the ship's register, with heavy penalties to be imposed if there were any subsequent deviation from what was registered. Provisions and water for both slaves and crew were to be inspected and approved before the vessel sailed from Britain — better still, Sir Jeremiah added, if the contractor were wise enough to seek and follow the inspector's advice upon provisioning! Finally, the inspector was to ensure that the vessel carried sufficient medical equipment and cleansing and fumigating equipment.

All this is familiar enough; but Fitzpatrick's discussion of the principles of measuring passenger space is much fuller than in any other of his writings. As usual, he argued that neither tonnage nor height between decks was adequate as the basis of calculation, and that 'air volume' or clear cubic space was decidedly the superior criterion. The argument was reinforced by his setting out the dimensions of two troopships currently in use. By the standards then employed each might carry precisely the same number of men. But one of them would have its complement reduced by no less than 30 per cent, if measured by the effective living area which she could afford.

The second inspectorate was to be dispersed about the major West African ports, with a chief inspector at the main station. Using interpreters as need be, the local inspectors were to examine each vessel on arrival from Great Britain, and to inflict summary penalties for breaches of the regulations, to ensure that the ships were cleansed and whitewashed before slaves were embarked; to reject any slaves who had been procured by 'cruel' means; and to forward a complete report on each vessel to the chief inspector or local governor. They were also to 'advise' on all provisions being taken aboard locally. The vessels were then to proceed to the chief inspector's own port for further inspection and final clearance, and there too the senior ship's officers were to sign an oath to observe 'their duties to the slaves' during the passage. This deposition was to be transmitted to the port of destination, and later verified there – where defaults were to be heavily punished, even by transportation in the graver cases. This last was of course the responsibility of the third inspectorate, in the receiving ports of the West Indies, who were charged with the ultimate enforcement of the regulative code.

Fitzpatrick saw the role of his slave trade inspectorates as threefold. First, they would constitute a source of expert advice to those who were being inspected. He presumed that the inspectors would be or would soon become specialists in the business. Secondly, they would constitute a source of information for the government, and in time their experience and reports would form the basis of more refined and effective regulation. Thirdly, they would see to it that the law was enforced – at home, in West Africa and on disembarkation. Although he allowed that the navy alone could provide any measure of control at sea, Sir Jeremiah again argued strongly against relying on unprofessional authorities to execute legislation. Whether in the West Indies or in Ireland, he wrote, the gentry, the magistrates, grand juries and the like would simply neglect any extraordinary duties laid upon them. For this reason, not only should the special corps of officers have entire control of the affair, but they should also be paid for by Great Britain so that the colonies should have no shadow of excuse for not enforcing the regulations.

Finally, Fitzpatrick proposed what amounted to a gradual abolition of slavery,[85] although he was careful to avoid saying so directly. Each newly imported 'slave' was in fact to be a servant indentured for seven years, and free thereafter. Meanwhile, one-seventh of the existing body of slaves in the West Indies was to be liberated annually, and the newly-born were, as we have said already, to be free from birth. Thus, curiously enough, Fitzpatrick anticipated something quite like the apprenticeship system of 1833-40. He also bravely attempted to anticipate and provide for the difficulties in his main proposition. What would become of the old and infirm slaves after their emancipation? His answer was almshouses, provided for them and paid for from the rates on the plantations. Would not the limitation of the period of servitude diminish the value of the slave, and consequently prevent the African merchant from obtaining the best labourers in the market? The answer was British bounties to indemnify the merchant from loss — and (killing two birds with one stone) also to calculate these according to what Fitzpatrick called the 'aerial space' allotted to each person for the passage. What of the disruption of African society and the unsettling of West Indian by the unfortunate continuation of the traffic, even if it were transformed into one of indentured labourers? Both might be mitigated to some extent by prohibiting merchants from buying any member of a family, without purchasing and bringing away the entire unit.

Of course, all this laid Sir Jeremiah open to the charge of irresponsible speculation. Half a century later, a tart assistant under-secretary at the Colonial Office, faced with a systematic colonisation scheme, was to put the bureaucrats' case against external planners as follows:

> When a projector gets a plausible notion into his head and can continue to hitch in the government as an agent in his plot, he seems to think himself exempted from computing the power of his machinery — ships, money and men being all forthwith ready at his bidding, to any extent.[86]

Perhaps money to regulate the slave trade in 1797 would not have been so difficult to find as money to promote systematic emigration (or almost anything else) in 1847. Parliament would probably have paid heavily for any mode of escaping the total abolition of the trade, which the House of Commons had earlier recommended. 'Men' might well have been a harder nut to crack. Possibly a British inspectorate might have been recruited readily enough; possibly customs officers might have served the purpose in the West Indies, although Fitzpatrick would rightly have been unhappy with any such *pis aller*. But surely a West African corps, on the scale and of the type proposed by Sir Jeremiah, was quite chimerical. There was moreover a Heath Robinson quality about the intricate chain of communications between the inspectorates which he envisaged.

In July 1797, the *Monthly Review* greeted Fitzpatrick's pamphlet as a 'singular performance . . . an ill-digested plan', unlikely either to check 'the enormities perpetrated on the coast of Africa' or to remedy the evils of slavery. Yet – whether consistently or not – the *Review* also judged the scheme to be 'well designed'.[87] The balance seems reasonably fair. Fitzpatrick had no direct knowledge of the trade in West Africa or the operation of the plantation system in the Caribbean, and in both cases, and particularly the first, his scheme seems farfetched, even bizarre. But the gaucheries were essentially mechanical defects arising from ignorance, which he would doubtless have corrected, or at least palliated, had he the same experience in these fields as he had gained in the fitting out of vessels in Great Britain. The basic design of the plan was powerful and ingenious.

We must bear in mind that Fitzpatrick started with the assumptions that there was no immediate prospect of abolishing either the slave trade or slavery in the West Indies, and that there was no practicable alternative to negro labour – with fresh importations, at that – for working the sugar plantations. His first objective was therefore comparatively modest, to limit the extent of the problems. The encouragement of capital-intensive and 'modern' modes of production, and the increase of the indigenous negro population in the West Indies by maternity and infant care, were directed to this end. Next, he sought to end slavery not by a direct assault upon the institution but by circuitous methods which would have the additional advantage of gradual preparation for full emancipation. Thus, the newly-born 'Africans' in the West Indies would be reared in freedom, the newly-arrived would be indentured for seven years at most, and within seven years all those currently in slavery would be liberated. But liberation without the power to labour might be merely an exchange of miseries. Hence the necessity to supplement indirect emancipation by a species of poor law to provide the basic securities for the old, infirm, sick and incapacitated. Similarly, bounties would have to be employed to ensure that the substitution of short-term indentures for slave labour would not diminish the quantity or quality available.

In the third place, if the trade in Africans had to continue, the change in the status of its victims from slave to indentured would certainly not *per se* secure any improvement in their conditions during the voyage. Hence the necessity for a protective inspectorate, which would moreover have to be multiple because the vessels were prepared and furnished in Great Britain, yet filled some two thousand miles away, while the conduct of the passage could only be checked finally in a third continent. Certainly, the details of the regulation which Sir Jeremiah proposed diminished in precision and realism as it moved further from Great Britain, but the concept of a triple inspectorate was altogether apropos. Finally, the causes of both elementary personal rights and social stability as Sir Jeremiah understood them were to be served by measures to restore marriage and the nuclear family unit both in the West Indies and among the new arrivals from West Africa. All this was a rational and comprehensive mental construction. The proposals were clear; they formed a whole; they were logically consistent. Means were resourcefully and imaginatively deployed to reach the stated ends. 'Well-designed' was well-justified, on the whole.

Quite as striking as the power of synthesis demonstrated in the essay is Fitzpatrick's grasp of the bureaucratic process as a whole. As we have seen, he specifically divided the functions of inspectorates into three. First, they are coercive in the sense of being charged with the execution of the law. This also implied professionalism, for as ever Sir Jeremiah argued that enforcement required special officers: neither the gentry nor other services in government could be counted on to stir a finger. Secondly, inspectorates have an advisory role to perform. It is not to be assumed that all those subject to regulation will be, at all times and in all things, antagonistic to the state's officials. They may sometimes accept or even seek the guidance of those whom experience has rendered expert. For example, the choice of vessel, or health or provisioning at sea, might well be fields in which the more intelligent members of the trade would see a common interest with the inspectors. Finally, inspectorates are, or should be, creative. They should afford both regular and precise information on the actual state of things, and truly informed guidance on the changes needed in the regulation to effect what the legislature originally intended, and perhaps more. All this is a remarkable anticipation of the workings of the early Victorian inspectorates in the first two or three decades of their existence, all the more remarkable because no one during the period 1830-60 either foresaw or marked these developments very clearly: they simply grew out of the daily circumstances of governing on the spot.

The pamphlet also provides the fullest and most coherent exposition of Fitzpatrick's philosophy of pragmatic administration. Not only does he try to fit his plan to the current political realities as he saw them, and to undermine and circumvent rather than assail directly, but also he

Service and Servitude

draws heavily upon his own experience, generalising from specific problems which he, or those whose works he had read, had encountered in other areas. He sees administration as a process rather than an action or a structure. Here too he is prophetic, even if his prophecy was rooted in retrospection. Once more he comes close to discerning, roughly at any rate, the shape of things to come.

Notes

1. Fitzpatrick to Hardwicke, 22 June 1801, Hardwicke Papers, B.M. Add. MS. 35729, f.65.
2. This information is contained in an appeal by Fitzpatrick to Pitt for aid in securing such a measure. Fitzpatrick to Pitt, 11 February 1797, and enclosure, Fitzpatrick to Dundas, 8 December 1795, Anglesea Papers T2627/1/4, P.R.O., N.I.
3. Fitzpatrick to Pitt, 11 February 1797, Anglesea Papers T2627/1/4.
4. Fitzpatrick to Dundas, 8 December 1795, Anglesea Papers T2627/1/4.
5. Fitzpatrick to Windham, 9 December 1795, Anglesea Papers T2627/1/4.
6. King to Fitzpatrick, 18 December 1795, Anglesea Papers T2627/1/4.
7. Fitzpatrick to King, 25 December 1795, Anglesea Papers T2627/1/4.
8. Fitzpatrick to Windham, 9 December 1795, Anglesea Papers T2627/1/4.
9. Fitzpatrick to King, 25 December 1975, Anglesea Papers, T2627/1/4.
10. Fitzpatrick to King, 13 November 1796, Anglesea Papers T2627/1/4.
11. Fitzpatrick to King, 15 November 1796, Anglesea Papers T2627/1/4.
12. Fitzpatrick to Pitt, 11 February 1797, Anglesea Papers T2627/1/4.
13. Fitzpatrick to Crosbie, 25 October 1797, Anglesea Papers T2627/1/4.
14. Brownrigg to Crosbie, 28 October 1797, Anglesea Papers T2627/1/4.
15. Observation by Fitzpatrick, September 1800, Anglesea Papers T2627/1/4.
16. Ibid.
17. Cornwallis to Fitzpatrick, 30 September 1800, Anglesea Papers T2627/1/4.
18. Observation by Fitzpatrick, September 1800, Anglesea Papers T2627/1/4.
19. Fitzpatrick to the general officer commanding at Cork, 12 February 1801, Anglesea Papers T2627/1/4.
20. Fitzpatrick to Pitt, 11 February 1797, Anglesea Papers T2627/1/4.
21. Fitzpatrick to Dundas, 8 December 1795, Anglesea Papers T2627/1/4.
22. E. Burke to Marquis of Rockingham, 7-8 September 1770, *The Correspondence of Edmund Burke*, 9 vols. (Cambridge, 1958-70), vol. 2, p. 156.
23. Charles Bateson, *The Convict Ships 1787-1868* (Glasgow, 1959), p. 101.
24. Hill to Wilberforce, quoted in Hill to Wathen, 26 July 1790, *HRNSW*, vol. 1, pt. 2, p. 367.
25. Ibid.
26. A contract made in 1792 with William Richards, Jun., provided £17 for each convict embarked and £5 for each one landed in satisfactory health. Later contracts provided for similar amounts. See Bateson, *Convict Ships*, p. 20.
27. Ibid., pp. 12-15.
28. Fitzpatrick to King, 23 October 1796, *HRNSW*, vol. iii, pp. 161-3.
29. There were two ships called *Britannia*. The first (referred to here) arrived in Australia in May 1797, the second in July 1798. See Bateson, *Convict Ships*, pp. 139-40.
30. Fitzpatrick to King, 23 October 1796, *HRNSW*, vol. iii, p. 163.

292 *Service and Servitude*

31. Fitzpatrick to King, 21 November 1797, B.M. Add. MS. 33105, f.242.
32. Fitzpatrick to King, 12 December 1797, B.M. Add. MS. 33105, f.260.
33. Ibid., ff.260-1.
34. Fitzpatrick to Transport Commissioners, 15 August 1797, Adm. 108/48, f.207; Fitzpatrick to Transport Commissioners, 3 September 1797, Adm. 108/48, f.25; Transport Commissioners to Fitzpatrick, 4 September 1797, Adm. 108/49, f.25.
35. Patton to Transport Commissioners, 24 October 1797, Adm. 108/49, f.395, transmitting a copy of a letter which he had received from Fitzpatrick.
36. Fitzpatrick to Transport Commissioners, 15 August 1797, Adm. 108/48, f.25.
37. Transport Commissioners to Patton, 25 October 1797, Adm. 108/49, f.395.
38. Fitzpatrick to Transport Commissioners, 26 January 1798, Adm. 108/51, f.231.
39. King to Transport Commissioners, 30 August 1800, C.O. 324/112, f.445; Parke to Transport Commissioners, 2 October 1800, Adm. 108/68, f.5, enclosing a letter from Fitzpatrick; Transport Commissioners to Parke, 3 October 1800, Adm. 108/68, f.5.
40. Transport Commissioners to Fitzpatrick, 1 November 1798, Adm. 108/57, f.138.
41. King to Transport Commissioners, 19 March 1800, Adm. 108/66, f.313, enclosing a letter from Fitzpatrick. Fitzpatrick to Lindsay, 30 July 1801, Pelham Papers, B.M. Add. MS. 33107, f.201. This scheme had been partially in operation since 1794. See Bateson, *Convict Ships*, pp. 20-1.
42. Fitzpatrick to Portland, 14 December 1799, C.O. 201/15, ff.200-2.
43. Sharpe to Fitzpatrick, 5 December 1799, C.O. 201/15, ff.210-11.
44. Portland to Transport Commissioners, 1 May 1800, C.O. 324/112, f.376.
45. Kunst to Transport Commissioners, 19 May 1801, Adm. 108/69, f.298. Transport Commissioners to Kunst, 22 May 1801, Adm. 108/69, f.298.
46. Bateson, *Convict Ships*, pp. 150-2.
47. Fitzpatrick to Baldwin, 18 November 1798, B.M. Add. MS. 33106, f.138.
48. Ibid.
49. Bateson, *Convict Ships*, pp. 167-9.
50. Hunter to Portland, 27 July 1799, *Historical Records of Australia* (hereafter cited as *HRA*), series i, vol. ii, pp. 376-7.
51. W. Noah, *Diary*, quoted in Bateson, *Convict Ships*, p. 151.
52. Fitzpatrick to Baldwin, 18 November 1798, B.M. Add. MS. 33106, f.138.
53. Fitzpatrick to Whitehead, n.d., Adm. 108/20, f.76.
54. Hatton to Transport Commissioners, 22 April 1801, Adm. 108/69, f.241.
55. Fitzpatrick to Transport Commissioners, 11 May 1801, Adm. 108/69, f.274; Transport Commissioners to King, 11 May 1801, Adm. 108/69, f.274.
56. Instructions for the masters and surgeons of the *Canada, Minorca* and *Nile* convict ships, 10 June 1801, C.O. 201/20, ff.239-43.
57. These instructions are signed 'by the Secty of State' but the preamble says that the instructions were given 'at the request of the under Secretary of State by the order of Lord Pelham'. This is inconsistent with the date on the instructions (10 June 1801) as Lord Pelham did not become Home Secretary until 30 July 1801. The under-secretary mentioned at the end of the instructions is Sir George Shee, who did not take up this office until 18 August 1801. But in a letter to Hobart written on 30 January 1802 Sir Jeremiah refers to 'the instructions which I pointed out for the surgeons and masters of those ships, at the request of Lord Pelham' (*HRNSW*, vol. iv, p. 683). However the Transport Commissioners, when sending these instructions to the surgeons of the *Perseus* and *Coromandel* said, 'We have received from His Grace the Duke of Portland,

One of His Majesty's Principal Secretaries of State, a Paper entitled 'Instructions to the Surgeons of Convict Ships" ', 5 January 1802, C.O. 201/23, f.93.
58. Sir Jeremiah's authorship is stated on one copy of the instructions, C.O. 201/23, f.94.
59. Fitzpatrick to King, 16 April 1800, B.M. Add. MS. 33106, ff.362-3.
60. Ibid., f.363.
61. Nelson, *The Home Office*, pp. 34-5. W.M. Pitt, MP for Dorset, who had come to the Home Office for a passport in May 1794, wrote later to Nepean, 'I found so much difficulty in procuring even a *short off-hand* and apparently doubtful answer from the *great man* [King] in your *outer room* yesterday that I am obliged to trouble *you*', H.O. 1/2, 25 May 1794, quoted in ibid., p. 35.
62. Fitzpatrick to Portland, 5 January 1798, B.M. Add. MS. 33105, ff.325-6.
63. Fitzpatrick to Baldwin, 18 November 1798, B.M. Add. MS. 33106, f.138.; Fitzpatrick to Baldwin, 8 January 1799, B.M. Add. MS. 33106, ff.162-3.
64. Fitzpatrick to Pelham, 3 September 1801, B.M. Add. MS. 33107, f.412.
65. Fitzpatrick to Pelham, 25 August 1801, B.M. Add. MS. 33107, ff.343-5.
66. Fitzpatrick to A. Graham, 17 January 1802, *HRNSW*, vol. iv, pp. 678-9.
67. Transport Commissioners to Sullivan, 27 January 1802, Adm. 108/20, f.120.
68. Graham to King, 25 January 1802, C.O. 201/23, f.42. The date on this letter may be wrong, as Sir Jeremiah's letter to Graham on the subject of the two pregnant women is dated 26 January 1802.
69. Graham to King, 17 January 1802, *HRNSW*, vol. iv, p. 679.
70. Ibid.
71. Hobart to King, 30 January 1802, *HRA*, series i, vol. iii, p. 367.
72. Fitzpatrick to Hobart, 30 January 1802, C.O. 201/23, ff.64-7.
73. *HRNSW*, vol. iv, p. 787.
74. Fitzpatrick to Transport Commissioners, 31 October 1798, Adm. 108/57, f.138; Fitzpatrick to Transport Commissioners, 2 November 1798, Adm. 108/57, f.146; King to Transport Commisioners, 18 August 1800, C.O. 324/112, f.437; Transport Commissioners to Rains, 7 December 1801, Adm. 108/70, f.323.
75. Bateson, *Convict Ships*, pp. 131-68.
76. These two ships were the *Hercules* and *Atlas*. See Bateson, *Convict Ships*, pp. 160-6.
77. A. Ussher, *The Face and Mind of Ireland* (New York, 1950), pp. 174-5.
78. See above p. 271. Adm. 108148, f.207.
79. *Annual Register*, 1796, p. 73; *Parliamentary History of England*, vol. xxxii, 15 March 1796, pp. 901-2.
80. 37 Geo. III, c.104; 37 Geo. III, c.118.
81. Sir Jeremiah Fitzpatrick, *Suggestions on the Slave Trade for the Consideration of the Legislature of Great Britain* (London, 1797), pp. 4-7.
82. Ibid., pp. 53-4.
83. Ibid., pp. 37-8.
84. Ibid., pp. 10-25, 46-7, 56-7.
85. Ibid., pp. 30-46, 48-55.
86. Minute of T.F. Elliot, C.O. 384/80, 199 Emigration, 10 February 1847.
87. *Monthly Review*, vol. 23 (July 1797), pp. 347-8. See also the notice in *Gentleman's Magazine*, vol. 67 (1797), p. 862.

13 MEANINGS

I

Among the many dissimilarities between the present author and Byron is waking up one morning to find himself infamous. Not long after the publication in 1958 of my paper, 'The Nineteenth-Century Revolution in Government: a Re-appraisal',[1] it was assailed, first from one quarter and then another, until it presented — and doubtless still presents — a St Sebastian-like appearance, with the arrows angled from widely different directions. One critic argued that it was a Tory tract, partly it would seem because it attacked the Whig interpretation of British administrative history — forgetting no doubt that Butterfield's 'Whig interpretation' was not at all about Whigs as such, but about the cast of mind which glorifies particular historical sequences leading to the present. Another argued, incontrovertibly no doubt, that in the field of motivation it is impossible to prove a negative, in particular that one can never prove that men were not influenced in their actions by this or that belief, even if those actions could be satisfactorily accounted for without such a reference. Some raised the cry of 'taking the ideas out of history', others that of diminishing the role of the individual, and yet others the cant of 'explaining the how but not the why'. The paper was attacked for erecting a single instance into a general law; for confining doctrinal membership to those who openly expressed their adherence to a doctrine; and even for not being applicable to a period which it specifically repudiated. Perhaps Dr Valerie Cromwell was right when she said that the paper's leading cause of offence was its supposed attempt to devalue the contribution of the utilitarians, and especially of Bentham and his immediate disciples, to English social reform and the general liberal achievement.[2]

Like the cuckolded husband, the misunderstood author is not a grateful character to play. Friends may present him with long faces, but usually only to his own. Nor is the part of controversialist much happier or more profitable to perform. It may help in the building of one of those academical set pieces which, like the syllogistic exercises of the medieval schools, provide gymnasia for undergraduates. But unless the case is one of misused or neglected evidence, historical 'controversies' seem inherently prone to end in thickets of definition and counter-definition, and in the imputation of unstated stances.

Rarely is light increased, sweetness never. Sooner or later, the world at large wishes a plague on both houses, and moves on to other fields; and the ultimate consequence may be a halting rather than an advance of knowledge and interest alike.

At any rate so it seems to me; and instead of attempting to explicate and defend the old, this book has tried to improve upon it by carrying its concepts on to fresh ground, in the double hope of refining the first and mapping some little of the second. This appears to be all the more sensible a course because most of if not all the real points at issue in the 'debate' are extra-historical, being either epistemological or more generally philosophical. At the same time, it will surely not void a self-denying ordinance to outline the argument of 1958. For one hopes that the readership will be by no means confined to those who have the article at their fingertips, while one fears that many have 'read' it only at second-hand.

What did 'The Nineteenth-Century Revolution in Government' (or better still the paper as qualified and elaborated in the last two chapters of *A Pattern of Government Growth*)[3] actually say?

Its first concern was to make clear that such a revolution had taken place. Doubtless, the increase in state activity appeared very small when regarded retrospectively from the mid-twentieth century. Relatively, however, the growth from 1801 to 1900 had been prodigious. But it was the qualitative rather than the quantitative changes which were presented as revolutionary. It was the rapid transformation of central government from 'antique' to recognisably 'modern' modes and conduct which earned the change so drastic an appellation. Further, it was assumed that this change was concentrated into the half-century, 1825-75, and the subsequent attempt to construct an explanatory sequence was limited to these specific years.

No one in 1958 would have disputed that national government altered profoundly in the nineteenth century. But at that time the alteration had been little considered in its own right by historians. To notice and to name it seemed in itself worthwhile. Moreover, in so far as it had hitherto been analysed, this was mainly in the work of A.V. Dicey, a lawyer and student of political ideology and *mentalités*, whose terms of reference were almost exclusively ideas, sentiments, statutes and legal decisions. Such factors as industrialisation, urbanisation, developments in science, technology and medicine, the recruitment and procedures of the civil service, the relationship of political and administrative 'reform', or the influence of Irish or Indian precedent, had received small attention. Not least, the interior momentum of bureaucracy, once launched upon a particular course of social 'betterment', had gone virtually unrecognised.

The article attempted to draw these additional factors (and especially the last) into the definition and general description of the 'revolution'. In particular, it tried to arrange and evaluate them by means of a 'model'[4] of the process of governmental growth. The 'model' (clothed in protective inverted commas!) was not of course meant to be of either the predictive or universal type, but rather a heuristic device. It did not necessarily describe any specific — let alone all — administrative development. But it was hoped that by abstracting and ordering the most general tendencies of the day, a means of measuring the particulars might be provided. It was meant to be an historical tool, not an historical template. But historians as a class are not to the forefront in distinguishing the tin-opener from the contents of the tin: hence, many of the essay's later troubles. At any rate, what the 'model' set out was a logical five-stage sequence of development, applicable to the period 1825-75, which provided an account of and reasons for the revolutionary change.

First came the revelation of a state of things which appeared to be 'intolerable' to public opinion.

> Sometimes, the exposure was sudden and catastrophic, the consequence of an epidemic, a mine explosion, a railway calamity; sometimes, dramatic in another sense, the revelation of a private philanthropist or of an altogether fortuitous observer. On the whole, exposures were, so to speak, exogenous. Rarely were they, in this first instance, the fruit of the practice of administration or regular inquiry. Nor was sensationalism unimportant, for exposures were effective in so far as they directed public or parliamentary attention to particular dangers, suffering, sexual immorality or injustice. Once this was done sufficiently, the ensuing demand for remedy at any price set an irresistible engine of change in motion.[5]

The demand for remedies was in effect also a demand for prohibitory enactments: the instinctive reaction was to legislate the evil out of existence. There might be opposing interests, compromise and emasculation of the initial proposal. But no matter how weak the eventual legislative measure, it established a precedent, and meant that a responsibility had been assumed.

The second stage began when it was disclosed, whether gradually or abruptly, that the prohibitory legislation had made little or no difference to the actual conditions in the 'regulated' field. Generally, the draftsmen and politicians had no real knowledge of the field which they were entering, and a poor grasp of both the practical needs and the concrete problem of enforcement. Sooner or later, the original act came to be seen as but the expression of good intentions; and the answer to be, in part, the provision of special legal processes, but mainly the appointment of special officers to see that these were carried into action.

The establishment of an inspectorate, however rudimentary or haphazard in intention, was a step of immense if unforeseen consequence.

> As a rule, this meant some measure of regulation where before there had been none. It also meant a much fuller and more concrete revelation, through hard experience and manifold failures, of the very grave deficiencies in both the restrictive and executive clauses of the statute; and this quickly led to demands for legislative amendments in a large number of particulars. These demands were made moreover with a new and ultimately irresistible authority. For (once again for the first time) incontrovertible first-hand evidence of the extent and nature of the evils was accumulating in the officers' occasional and regular reports; ... Finally, side by side with the imperative demand for further legislation, there came an equivalent demand for centralization ... both for the definition of law and status and for protection and support against the anarchic 'public'. Moreover, centralization was quickly seen to be required for two other purposes, the systematic collection and collation of evidence and proposals for reform and the establishment of an intermediary or link between parliament and the executive in the field. Sooner or later, the pressures born of experience succeeded in securing both fresh legislation and a superintending central body. The point at which they did may be taken as the culmination of our third phase.[6]

The essence of the fourth stage was a change in attitudes in the administrators, the field inspectors and central officers alike. Gradually it was borne in upon them that continual amendments to the legislation and regulations in the light of experience, even where they could be secured intact and quickly, were not a fully satisfactory solution. Possible evasions, and the practical effects and judicial interpretations of clauses, could not be altogether foreseen; and the understanding of what could and should be done might change almost year by year. This led to a shift in approach whereby the administrators ceased to regard their problems as ever resolvable once and for all by some grand measure or reconstruction, and instead 'began to see improvement as a slow, uncertain process of closing loopholes and tightening the screw ring by ring, in the light of continuing experience and experiment'.[7] In short, a dynamic concept of administration gradually replaced a static one, and a growing sense of expertise led in time to an impatient desire for more autonomy.

The last stage in the 'model' is represented by the working out of these new concepts of government. Administrative discretions were sought, and to some extent won; and these might even include the imposition of penalties and the framing of by-laws sanctioned by mere ministerial order. Investigations tended to become not only more systematic but also more truly statistical and experimental. New techniques, and foreign practices which might be imitated, were positively sought; and the natural and mechanical sciences and medicine called on for answers to intractable difficulties in composing or enforcing particular preventive measures. As administration became more technical and authoritative, so the pressure for administrative autonomy and delegated legislation, and for fluidity and experimentation in the regulations, increased. In the more 'scientific' fields at least, a new sort of state was being born, as government took on a dynamic role within society.

It remains to measure Fitzpatrick's career against all this, and to evaluate the significance of the correspondences, variations and discontinuities. The remainder of this chapter will consider, in turn:

the degree to which his work in Ireland matches the mid-nineteenth-century 'model';
the differences produced by the change to military government, to closed as against relatively open bureaucracy;
the contextual differences (in this case, between Grattan's Ireland and Victorian Britain) as bearing on government growth;
the problem of similar development without a similar institutional framework, in particular, the absence in the 1780s of centralised departmental government;
the inspectorate, its permanent character and the shape given it by its temporal setting;
and finally, briefly, Fitzpatrick's part.

II

In Irish prison reform, there was no lack of detonators. The most important was gaol fever which, because of the nature of the legal procedures, might affect not only the prisoners and their custodians but a whole range of middle- and upper-class people from tipstaffs and jurors to barristers and judges, and through them society at large. To what extent typhoid actually spread beyond the gaols, it is impossible to say. The reports of mortality were often prospective and almost invariably general, without enumeration. But the important thing is that the alarms were practically annual, and the pictures of impending disaster horrific and directly terrifying to the powerful. A second cause of perturbation was gaol escapes, attempted or realised. Again these were frequent, and, as reported by the newspapers, frightening, though in rather unspecified ways.

Less craven and more worthy manifestations of the 'intolerability' effect were the repeated revelations of the miseries of incarcerated debtors, and after 1780 of other types of prisoner as well. Of course these were not absolutely distinguished from the infectious diseases and security factors. But in the main the response to them was commonplace humanitarianism. Again, there were bound to be regular detonators here during our period. Every parliamentary session brought, and had to bring, the insolvent debtors to the fore – if only because of prison overcrowding and the patron-client relationships between MPs and bankrupts. After Howard began his visitations, and still more after Fitzpatrick's had begun, it was certain that the most distressing accounts of squalor and suffering in the prisons would assail the public, year in, year out. There were, therefore, four powerful forces in operation to set off remedial endeavours.

Of course, in the case of Irish prisons the stages of sensational disclosure and gestural, ineffective legislation did not follow each other chronologically. Doubtless they had done so once; but by the time this book takes up the story, they had long fallen into a sort of systole-dyastole repetition. Some of the earlier statutes were remarkably practical and well-conceived. The Prisons Regulation Act of 1763, with its clear and pertinent set of gaol rules and local 'inspectorate', is a case in point. Yet in the absence of central surveillance and control, and of any full-time and professional supervisor or superior authority, Act after Act remained more or less a dead letter. At last, in 1780 or 1781, the dreary sisyphean rhythm was broken when Fitzpatrick, although not yet an official, became effectively a crown officer – at least in the investigatory sense but probably also with some extra-legal executive force. Perhaps we should add the simultaneous emergence of Holmes as a tireless parliamentary campaigner, for obviously much depended upon the interaction, and joint action, of the two.

Thus with Irish prisons the third stage, generally signalled by the establishment of a centralised executive corps, does not await such a formal institution. Fitzpatrick quickly assumed many of the functions and characteristics of an inspector general well before this specific office was set up. Similarly, other features typical of the third stage, such as the executive officers' findings in and reports on the field, or the parliamentary inquiries which they precipitated, preceded the formal office. In effect, Fitzpatrick's South Leinster tour and metropolitan investigations of 1783 (to take one instance) were inspectorial work, and his evidence before the Irish House of Commons committee of the same year constituted at once a report and a 'direction' as to the type of reform which experience and exact observation dictated. It was a close counterpart of, say, the Factory Act Select Committee of 1840-1,[8] following the revelations of the factory inspectorate of 1833, or of the Coal Mines Regulation Committee of 1852,[9] following the first disclosures of the coal mines inspectorate of 1850. In each of these cases, the evidence of the newly appointed inspectors was decisive in three respects. It established a new, and much deeper and more detailed, level of knowledge of the actual conditions obtaining in the field; it demonstrated the failure of the initial regulation to achieve most if not all the hoped-for ends; and it led on to a major reforming statute based on the findings of those who might most plausibly claim 'expert' and 'neutral' standing.[10]

Approximately, this describes the development of the prison question in Ireland during the period 1782-6. The 1784 Gaols Act was not a major reforming statute, but a first groping in this direction. Fitzpatrick's evidence coloured the legislation, in places quite deeply, but did not determine it as a whole. Moreover, he himself was still comparatively a novice in the field, and as yet lacked authority at all equal to, say, that of Howard. But his intensive and exhaustive investigations of the next two years, 1784 and 1785, during which he visited every prison proper in the kingdom at least once, increased his stature immensely. At the same time, he was forging or strengthening his links with the executive, while the 1784 Act was revealing itself in practice as, at best, an ineffectual interim measure.

Thus the 1785 Prisons Select Committee and the Prisons Act of 1788 completed and rounded off what the 1783 Committee and 1784

Act had commenced, in a tentative and uncertain fashion. Through all the inquiries and legislation of the period 1782-6, the 'inspectorate', in the person of Fitzpatrick, was steadily laying bare the evils and problems of Irish prisons and the failure of the law, as it then stood, to master them, and laying the foundations of a new, reforming statute.

It is true that this statute as enacted in 1786 had two uncommon features. It instituted the central inspectorate at the same time as it garnered the first great harvest of the work of a central inspector; and it partially exempted the metropolis from the operation of the new system: Dublin was treated in an ill-co-ordinated fashion which owed little to Fitzpatrick's revelations and a great deal to traditional city pressures and intrigue. But the creation of the office of inspector general was little more than the formalisation of an established arrangement. For more then three years, Sir Jeremiah had been performing most of the new statutory duties. It is true that the office was initially limited to two years in duration. Not only however was this soon altered, but it was also clear from other important features of the 1786 Act that some such office would have to be permanently established if the various centralised functions of information gathering, surveillance of the local inspectorate, prosecutions, uniform interpretation of regulations and national policy formulation were to be carried through. Correspondingly, the different treatment of the capital was not really much at variance with the mid-nineteenth-century patterns. In the field of public health alone, ranging from water sanitation to slaughterhouses, and burial grounds to dispensaries, London was treated exceptionally — and often for political rather than technical reasons — during the mid-Victorian years.[11]

Next comes the process of transition from a static to a dynamic conception of reform, the gradual abandonment of the belief that one grand once-for-all consolidation and reordering of both the legislation and the executive corps will resolve the difficulties. One aspect of this development was successive amendments of the 'master' statute. As we have seen, the Irish Prisons Amendment Act of 1787 certainly fits this pattern. The powers of the centralised inspectorate were enlarged, and its status improved, in the light of the inadequacies which were quickly apparent once the 1786 Act was in force. Some provisions of that Act were rendered more precise, and others more severe, in accordance with the lessons of experience. The inherent bias towards *lateral* extension manifested itself in the absorption of madhouses into the field of central inspection. All these are characteristic of the fourth phase of government growth. So too, is the fact that these changes, in their turn, soon seemed to be insufficient. In the very next session of Parliament, yet another Select Committee was constituted and yet another Amendment Bill introduced.

It is here that we run into difficulties of interpretation, for not only was the 1788 Bill rejected by the House of Lords – almost certainly for extraneous reasons – but we are also left in ignorance of its text. However, the few clauses which we can guess at, either because of the committee's resolutions or from amendments proposed in the debates, do suggest a continuation of the momentum of 1786-7 – strengthening the inspector general's position, closing loopholes newly apparent, and responding coercively to particular abuses demonstrated by the inspectorial reports. We know still less about the Amendment Bills of 1789 and 1790. Possibly they were mere reintroductions of the 1788 proposal, possibly they attempted to carry the regulation further forward in response to Fitzpatrick's latest annual reports and evidence before the Commons committee. At any rate, they suggest most strongly that the impulse to improve and extend the controls in the light of systematic observation was still struggling for practical expression.

There are a few indications of the changes for which Fitzpatrick was pressing in his later years in office. Clearly, he favoured increasingly a transformation of the entire prison system by the widespread use of penitentiaries. He had also considered carefully how this might be fitted into the existing inspectorial arrangements, and how the central administration might supervise its management. Moreover, he had further lateral extensions in view, in for example the area of bridewells, corporation gaols and houses of correction; and this in turn was leading him into the larger field of a general poor law. Again, he had some further intensifications in view, for example the better surveillance of and checks upon the conduct of the prison officers. Thus, in the end Fitzpatrick himself was certainly operating – or attempting to operate – a dynamic system of state regulation; and Holmes's committee of 1793 suggests that such a concept may also then have been abroad in the House of Commons.[12]

Whether or not Sir Jeremiah was consciously moving on to the still later stage in which the dynamic concept of government is institutionalised by administrative discretions, delegated legislation, internal control of appointments and the like, is another matter. *A priori*, we can take it that moves in such directions would have been his natural bent. It is also clear that he had much less need to press for these powers than

Meanings

his nineteenth-century counterparts. He could act extra-legally much more freely and safely than they; and in so far as he had any superior it was, by and large, his own compliant friends in the House of Commons or Dublin Castle. Even so, he was trammelled to some extent; and his evidence before the 1788 Select Committee, brief and cryptic though it is in the printed summary, does seem to indicate that he had reached the point where he would have welcomed the substitution of administrative discretions and autonomy for the difficult and doubtful course of repeated parliamentary interventions. But the whole process of change was so arrested in 1788 that speculation on the likelihood or otherwise of a 'fifth stage' developing, had no such check suddenly taken place, is fruitless.

Overall, however, the case of prison reform in Ireland in the twenty years 1775-95 conforms closely to the 'model' of governmental growth. Before 1783 the first two stages of the 'model' succeed one another several times: so to speak, the ignition key is switched on and the engine turns over repeatedly before the motor starts. Formally speaking, the third stage gets under way before instead of after the institution of a national inspectorate. The fourth stage remains incomplete, or at any rate executes only a single cycle; and only a shadowy outline of the fifth is discernible before the entire undertaking comes to an abrupt halt. But these variations are no more than one would expect in matching an actual course of events to a stylised and logical abstraction.

It is also true that the Irish prisons case was extraordinarily dependent on one person. Even Major Majendie, who towered over the development of explosives regulation in the United Kingdom in the last decades of the nineteenth century,[13] did not work quite as singlehandedly as Fitzpatrick. Certainly it would be wrong (to apply a phrase of E.P. Thompson) to rob Fitzpatrick of the dignity of an agent and replace it by the passivity of a vector of impersonal forces. As ever, Mrs Micawber is not to be gainsaid: 'things cannot be expected to turn up of themselves. We must, in a measure, assist them to turn up'. None the less, the strong lines of the pattern show through unmistakably. The process and movement underlying much — just how much we cannot know until the appropriate questions are asked of the material — nineteenth-century governmental growth is here prefigured with (if the jumbling of time will be allowed) a marvellous fidelity. Without some such heuristic device as the 'model' a great deal of the meaning of late eighteenth-century Irish development, and its anticipation of the later rhythms, might remain undisclosed.

III

In transferring from civilian to military work, Fitzpatrick entered quite a different administrative order. In certain respects, it was much easier to achieve his ends in the war sphere; in others, much more difficult. By the end of 1795, his basic military task had settled down to the inspection of troop transports for the regular army. Within this area, his duty was comprehensive, including the preparation of the vessels for health and accommodation; the inspection of food and water; ventilation and sanitation; medicines and prophylactics; mechanical devices, clothing and furnishings; quarantine and hospital quarters; and disciplinary codes to maintain fitness on the voyage. All this he had devised himself, much of it at the beginning, some from the harvest of his experience at Plymouth. It was not always possible to carry his 'system' into practice. It depended on his own presence at the embarkation – or at the very least the presence of an instructed deputy – and at busy seasons some vessels had to sail uninspected or ill-tended. It depended also on the degree of hurry and the scale of the embarkation, and often upon the chances of wind and weather. Finally it depended upon a jumble of little factors, such as the disposition of the regimental officers, the availability of a pinnace, the pressure upon the resources of the Transport Office or the Navy Board, or the speed of the London-Portsmouth coaches and hauliers. But given reasonable fortune, the task might be reasonably done.

Two directions towards which this work naturally spread were barred by powerful counter-interests. The early diagnosis and treatment of infectious diseases and other ailments was often critically important, later on, to health at sea. But any move by Fitzpatrick to enter this field, or the connected field of military hospitals, was resisted fiercely by the Army Medical Board and its local networks. Secondly, it was, if not a necessary corollary, at least an easy transition for Fitzpatrick to move from attempting to ensure health to attempting to exclude unfitness, whether it arose from extreme youth or age or from infirmity or disability. But this brought him into conflict with the regimental colonels, and their often servile surgeons, who had a vested interest in maintaining the troop numbers, so hardly won. Regimental interests were not so formidable as military-medical. They did not form a bloc; some commanding officers acquiesced in or even sympathised with Fitzpatrick's concern to reduce suffering and waste; and the war departments and commander-in-chief were much readier to override colonels than physicians. All the same, Sir Jeremiah was generally hemmed in upon this front, too.

A third confining factor was different jurisdictions. All attempts to duplicate the inspectoral arrangements in Ireland or the Channel Islands failed. So too did even the attempts to control the cross-channel traffic, although this bore directly upon the problems of inspection in the southern English ports. One plain reason for the failure was the difficulty of working through other governmental systems and by means of a much lengthened and more uncertain chain of communication. Ireland in particular was regarded as administratively troublesome, and avoided whenever possible by Whitehall. Moreover by the time this outer ring came under discussion the early fire and recklessness had died away in the war departments, and the prospect of entering new commitments whose limits could scarcely be guessed must have presented a chilling prospect at headquarters. Thus in three connected regions of great importance, bureaucratic counter-forces held back the growth of the inspectorate.

Such a man as Fitzpatrick was bound to press also for lateral extensions of his regulation in his new field. Two of these were bruited even before his office was authorised. The design of army barracks and army hospitals had an obvious bearing upon the health of the fit and the recovery of the sick and wounded, respectively. Fitzpatrick's Irish prisons experience and role would in any event have turned his eyes in this direction. Accordingly, in drawing up his own instructions, he tried to ensure that the new inspector of army health would play a leading part in the preparation of plans for military buildings. But though he did succeed in staking a claim in this area, it was only that he was to be consulted on the designs; and the instructions failed to lay down any set procedure for consultation or any clear division of authority between the inspector of health and either the barrack-master's department or the Army Medical Board. Thus, despite fitful efforts by Fitzpatrick to insert himself into the matter, the instructions proved more or less barren so far as barrack and hospital construction went. Several reasons for this failure can be readily adduced. The relevant established sub-departments were not apprised of his 'powers' or 'rights' beforehand, or possibly at any later stage; one of them at least, and probably both, would have strongly resented and resisted any attempt at intrusion; he was never free enough of other pressing business to try to mount a serious challenge on so large an issue; and neither Dundas nor Nepean ever showed any sign of special interest in or understanding of the matter. At any rate, whatever the explanation, only three instances of attempted interference by Fitzpatrick are recorded.

The second early projected enlargement of the office was still more sketchy as a proposal and never attempted in practice. It was natural enough for Sir Jeremiah to wish to extend surveillance of army transport from water-borne to land-borne carriage, particularly in the case of the sick and wounded. At the least, he regarded such matters as the design of ambulances as properly within his province. Similarly, he believed that the location and form of temporary encampments, huts and tents, bore directly on army health; and in this he was of course reinforced by the findings of Pringle and others that poor and ill-placed accommodation was the major precipitant of infectious diseases in armies in the field. But though Fitzpatrick pressed initially for powers in both these spheres, he failed to pursue either demand after his second return from the Netherlands, early in 1795. His chances of making headway on such points were probably very small: he would doubtless soon have found himself entangled with the Waggoners Corps, the commissariat and the engineers, to say nothing of the medical departments. But in any event it was out of sight, out of mind. Once removed from the campaign, Sir Jeremiah was immediately swept away in other directions, never to return to these issues except briefly and indirectly in preparing for the reception of the sick evacuated from Holland in 1799.

Other lateral extensions of his authority kept presenting themselves to Fitzpatrick in the course of his career as inspector. For example, to carry forward his inspection of transports from troopships to horse ships was a logical step to take — or rather to aspire to — for *mutatis mutandis* the cases were much the same. Again, to carry forward his designs on barrack-building to the elimination of noxious trades, brothels and gin shops in the immediate environs of the barrack was, if not a strictly logical progression, at least an imaginative and rational extension. We can readily accept Sir Jeremiah's argument that, in the large view of the matter, these were truly part of the essential problem of ensuring that the men's living conditions were healthful.

These two schemes were stillborn. But when Fitzpatrick sought straightforward extensions of his basic work of preparing transports and inspecting for health at sea he was generally successful. The East India Company's forces and (with the exception of the Russian repulse) foreign troops embarking or disembarking in England appear to have fallen readily enough under his sway. So too did civilians using military transports. Convict vessels represented an altogether new area of operation. But they involved few new techniques, and afforded Sir Jeremiah a much freer hand. The support of the soldiers' dependants who failed to secure places on the troopships really was a different kind of issue. True, where the dependants were to cross the Irish Sea, the passage had to be prepared for. But the prime concern was money for their sustenance; and Fitzpatrick had corresponding difficulties in this particular campaign. Still, even here, he eventually succeeded in establishing a system of allowances of a sort. There was thus a modest list of credit items to set against the major failures to expand beyond the character of 'mere cleanser and fumigator'.

How are we to explain the successes and defeats? Three general factors told against Fitzpatrick, and would have told against anybody who was appointed inspector or inspector general of army health late in 1794. Expenditure upon the forces was relatively open-handed and uncalculated early in the war. But this changed rapidly, and by the end of 1795 proposals for fresh types of spending would have met strong resistance. Secondly, men like Dundas and Nepean, whose support was vital to such an administrative venture as the inspectorship, could not long maintain their initial level of interest in the work – let alone strive for its multiplication – in the midst of all their other, and often overwhelming, difficulties. Thirdly, in an appointment like Fitzpatrick's, the lack of any clear definition of its limits or its relationship to other branches of the service may have been an advantage at the start. But sooner or later challenges to the inspector's authority were bound to come; and in the long run the lack of definition worked in favour of a minimal interpretation of powers and functions.

More particularly, the army health inspectorate was never well-considered. It should not have been impossible to set out a general justification for its institution and development. For example, it could have been argued that the Army Medical Corps was essentially concerned with diagnosis and treatment, but virtually ignored preventive medicine, which the new inspectorate would make its special business. This might have served as the basic distinction between the two arms of military health. It is true that the spheres overlapped, and influenced each other, and that there would always have been disputed no man's land. None the less such a broad division of responsibility and function does not seem inherently unworkable. But so far as we can tell Fitzpatrick never addressed himself to the fundamental questions of what the Army Medical Corps was meant to do, and what it made no pretence of doing. Instead, he recklessly invaded its specific areas of work whenever he scented 'inhumanity'. Moreover, he wrote or acted on some occasions as if he were a species of ombudsman, on others as a deputy *en mission*. Further, he never really developed a scheme for a general inspectorate of army health, as against a particular office for himself. He was, as we have seen, quite capable of elaborating a complex inspectorial system. He had even considerable experience of a rudimentary form of national regulation through a network of local subordinates in the case of the Irish prisons. But for whatever reason – distaste for delegation, incessant pressure of work or the patent hopelessness of the cause – he did not apply these ideas and lessons to the health inspectorate. The consequent limitation of the regulation, more or less, to what he could manage and enforce himself was stultifying.

Thus Fitzpatrick must take blame for not considering how his office might be developed into an executive corps. In turn, his various further ambitions might have seemed less chimerical had he had even a small staff at his command. But no matter what foresight had been exercised or what fortune enjoyed, late eighteenth-century army administration would have presented peculiar difficulties to the social reformer. True, there were favourable elements. For one thing, the British army in the 1790s appears to have had relatively few boobies or brutes in its upper ranks. At least, Sir Jeremiah encountered none. On the contrary, he had a remarkable run in converting lieutenant-governors, generals and colonels to the support of particular humane measures. This was the happy aspect of military administration for the reformer. If authority could be enlisted, one's purposes might be carried into effect with a speed and thoroughness inconceivable in civilian government. *A fortiori*, a writ from a Dundas or even a Huskisson might run fast, far and true.

On the other hand, the bureaucracy of the armed services was vast, complex and deep-rooted. Fitzpatrick had to deal with no less than four departments of state, the commander-in-chief, six separate military and naval boards, and numerous regimental organisations – to say nothing of their counterparts in the East India Company. The *vis inertiae* inherent in the system was immense: hence, for example, the great difficulty of procuring even so small and simple an innovation as separated dependants' allowances – at least as a regular and general award. Immediately it ran up against the two outmost bureaucratic defences – that it was unprecedented and that it might open a door to further demands – at the Horse Guards. Moreover, the fissiparation and quasi-autonomy of the branches of military administration gave them immense repellent power. This was especially the case where, as with the Army Medical Board, it comprised a professional caste and could lay claim to a particular expertise. In contemporary France, traditional medicine was being overthrown in the name of equality, and the undifferentiated and often unqualified 'health officers' were replacing the old medical corps in the armed forces. The immediate cost in lives and suffering was prodigious. But the resultant *tabula rasa* made radical reorganisation possible in the end.[14]

Britain 'escaped' any such gales of change, and the army there escaped even the lighter breezes. It remained substantially a state within a state — bureaucratically and not politically, of course. Thus, while innovation might be remarkably easy in the interstices of army government because of the relative simplicity and force of military decision-making and discipline, it might be remarkably difficult where it encroached upon an existing substructure of command and responsibility. It was not of course that army and civilian bureaucracy were absolutely different. But in the army the channels for governmental development were either much freer or practically stopped.

Moreover, military administration was in general a closed system. In ordinary circumstances, it was sealed off from either parliamentary interference or public scrutiny. It is true that gross, well-publicised military bungling or disasters, or large-scale peculation, might in the end produce a newspaper furore and a select committee of inquiry. But these were comparative rarities before 1805, requiring some extraordinary concatenation of revelations or peculiarly powerful party advantage. At the level and in the period in which Fitzpatrick worked, there was virtually no hope of appealing successfully to outside opinion or the politicians in opposition for aid in carrying forward a checked reform. For all practical purposes, failure to achieve an end within the system meant failure absolute.

This is not to say that the forces operating in civilian reform were absent. Clearly, Fitzpatrick's history shows, as much inside the services as without, evidence of governmental momentum and tendencies towards expansion and intensification. But the pre-existence of elaborate administrative structures and the lack of anything resembling parliamentary and legislative processes ensured that they could not operate in the same fashion. The truth would seem to be that military administration involves a natural history of its own, and that it belongs rather to the genus of autocracies than to the family of normal instruments of management in its society and state. But for all that it has its own revelations to make to the perceptive student of the patterns of government growth.

IV

In the middle quarters of the nineteenth century, social reform often depended, especially in its initial stages, on a nexus of newspaper publicity, the literate public's 'opinion', parliamentary questions and advocacy, and the select committee or royal commission. Sometimes, pressure groups, formal or informal, also played a part. To what extent did the Ireland of the 1780s, in which Fitzpatrick had to work, provide a counterpart?

While there can be no doubt that gleams of each of these Victorian factors can be seen in the earlier period, their extent, role and operation show interesting differences. Comparatively speaking, the Irish scale of things was minute. The telling debate and action was concentrated to an extraordinary degree in the metropolis. Provincial opinion was ill-formed and derivative; few members of the Irish Commons, other than the more or less hereditary county representatives, were returned for their own localities; and in any event members were loyal to Ascendancy *en bloc* rather than their region of origin. It is true that Dublin was then one of the largest of European cities, and the second largest in the British Empire. None the less its population did not exceed 200,000 and its circumference was a mere seven miles.[15] Moreover, its politically effective society was a very small proportion of the whole. Even the solid and upper bourgeoisie, the commercial, manufacturing and professional (the bar excepted) classes, constituted quite feeble interests, all the more so as their considerable Catholic elements were still politically impotent.[16] Essentially, power and decision lay in the hands of a few hundred noblemen, landed proprietors, ecclesiastical dignitaries, judges, leading counsel and officials, who were — or might be — remarkably impervious to outside influence. The crisis of 1780-2 had doubtless shaken the confidence and modified the exclusiveness of this élite; and in certain respects, the loosening may have facilitated social reform. But we must remember that the agitation had virtually died away by 1783 and there is little reason to suppose that social evils were more widely canvassed outside the charmed circle than within.

The Dublin press did not ignore social issues in the late eighteenth century. As we have seen, the *Freeman's Journal* seems to have conducted a short campaign for prison reform upon its foundation in 1763. But this was not repeated; and even the individual editorial pressing for some piece or other of amelioration was comparatively rare. It was by and large as a medium of reporting scandals or calamities, and of broadcasting correspondents' letters, that the newspapers made a contribution to beneficence. But circulations were tiny (probably none exceeded 2,000 copies in the eighteenth century),[17] and sooner or later all editors were brought to heel by Dublin Castle through advertising revenue, secret pensions or ruinous prosecution, or a judicious combination of the three.[18] There were simply no equivalents in the Dublin of the 1780s to *The Times* or *Morning Chronicle*, or the quarterlies or weekly magazines or great provincial dailies of Great Britain in the 1830s. Generally the Irish press printed what governments told it to print rather than told government what it ought to do or jockeyed government into action by its disclosures.

The press then, though not altogether negligible, was as minor a force in Ireland in the 1780s as extra-parliamentary opinion (in the special sense of the opinion of those outside the little knot which constituted the parliamentary class). On the other hand, the House of Commons petition, essentially a variety of the client system, was of far greater significance then than its counterpart at Victorian Westminster. Many of the Irish committees of inquiry, and even legislation and some direct parliamentary action, derived immediately from petitions. Paradoxically, the closed system of the Ascendancy was quite penetrable by individuals with a grievance and a patron, the ultimate explanation being of course the smallness of society and the security and easy self-gratifying condescension of the powerful.

In a somewhat similar fashion, the very parliamentary processes of the late eighteenth century were in several respects more favourable to social reform than their nineteenth-century successors. Quite commonly, a committee might be immediately appointed upon the introduction of a petition drawn up two or three days before; it might meet half a dozen times in the succeeding fortnight, and report within three weeks; a Bill might be presented almost at once and even find its way through both Houses and receive the Royal Assent in six to ten weeks more. Such an entire proceeding was often completed within a single, short parliamentary session. Occasionally, parliamentary time ran out upon a particular measure. But this was almost always because its introduction had been delayed until the fag-end of a sitting. In general, one could feel secure, if one had a modicum of support, in carrying a proposal into legislation within any three or four parliamentary months.

All this was a far cry from the British House of Commons sixty years hence. The major reason for the difference was of course the far greater pressure of business, which imperial as well as domestic responsibilities, and the rapid increase in both the volume and complexity of legislation, entailed. But there were other factors. Social legislation (in fact almost all legislation except that relating directly to the executive functions) was a matter for individual members rather than governments before 1825. There were no vedettes of departmental officials or Cabinet entanglements to be negotiated before a Bill might be presented. Correspondingly, individual members drew up their own proposals. They did not have to await the pleasure or leisure of parliamentary draftsmen: Holmes's maddening experience of 1784-5 when the judiciary was allotted this role by the House of Lords and failed to produce any Bill whatever in nine months was happily unique. In short, one consequence of the mid-nineteenth-century systematisation was to add months or even years to the legislative process, especially in the case of amending statutes.

To this list of late-eighteenth-century advantages, we might add the virtual absence of an adversary system. The general lack of organised pressure groups was matched by a lack of organised counter-groups. Not only did this render easier the carrying of measures, but it also avoided the long delay which set-piece battles, even if victorious for the 'reformers', inevitably involved.

Thus we should by no means assume that Fitzpatrick's task with prisons in the 1780s was at all points more difficult than, say, Sir John Simon's with public health in the 1860s.[19] There were of course serious drawbacks in the mid-Georgian disorganisation. It was haphazard; it depended heavily if not altogether upon the chance of individuals' interest and energy; it was prone to crudeness and partiality in both the form and content of regulation; and it is at least arguable that it was inherently ephemeral. But by the test of the ease, speed and single-mindedness of administrative innovation or correction, late-eighteenth-century Ireland was decidedly superior to the United Kingdom in the mid-nineteenth century.

To return to our initial point, the fundamental explanation of all this would seem to be the minute extent of politically effective society in the 1780s[20] and its compact physical compass in the capital during the parliamentary season. Fitzpatrick was probably acquainted personally with all the leading Anglo-Irish politicians in office — undoubtedly with Foster and Fitzgibbon, and almost certainly with Beresford and Hely-Hutchinson. We have his own testimony that it was Hussey Burgh who launched him on his reforming career. Moreover, quite apart from his possible relationship, blood and otherwise, with Richard Fitzpatrick, he appears to have come to know each of six succeeding Irish chief secretaries, W.W. Grenville, Windham, Thomas Pelham,

Orde, Fitzherbert and Hobart. As it happened, he encountered five of the six, either in person or in official correspondence, after his translation to Great Britain – a revealing indication of the interlinking of high politics in the two kingdoms, as well as of the extreme smallness of this conjoined group. Of the lords lieutenant, he certainly met one, the Earl of Westmorland, and possibly also Portland, who had re-entered his official life as Home Secretary by 1794. All this is not to suggest that Sir Jeremiah was on close terms with the mighty, although there is evidence of a fair degree of intimacy and confidence in certain cases, such as those of Orde and Foster. But it is clearly a most significant contrast with later days that a man of Fitzpatrick's rank should have been able to gain direct access to so very many of his political superiors and potential patrons.

More important still, Fitzpatrick had warm allies among the members of the Irish House of Commons who were most committed to prison and similar reform. There is no evidence that Blaquiere was especially his friend, although neither is there anything to suggest lack of cordiality between them. But Holmes and Griffith were particularly intimate associates, and other members on the fringes of the reform interest spoke as if they knew him tolerably well. Sir John Barrington has written of the extraordinary clubbability of the old Irish House of Commons.[21] Not only was faction left aside at the doors of the dining rooms, but the small body of active members (ordinarily only a hundred or so in number) were intimate, freely exchanging political and other gossip. Thus even those who had not met a man of Fitzpatrick's comparatively modest station and local fame would probably have learned a good deal in a casual way about his character and doings.

But this concentration and informality had extra-personal implications for government. It meant for example that the factor of 'intolerability' – the sense that a state of things, suddenly disclosed, was so abhorrent that counter-action must be immediately taken, come what might – could operate most powerfully in support of social reform. When in 1787 Blaquiere took into his head (or had the notion implanted there) to see for himself whether Fitzpatrick's descriptions of the Dublin bridewells and debtors' gaols were over-coloured, and a couple of the members to whom he spoke decided to accompany him, he and they were so worked upon by what they saw as to carry the entire House of Commons with them next day in proposing both punishment and reform, and even in getting up a subscription for the immediate relief of the unfortunate. A similar expedition by Lord Earlsfort in the same year had a similar effect, although of course much more muted in the case of the stonier-hearted peers. Again, in the Irish circumstances it was possible for a committee of inquiry to decide, virtually on the spur of the moment, to visit some site or institution in the city, or to call up even country witnesses, provided they lived east of the Shannon, within two or three days. This gave extraordinary elasticity and potential range to parliamentary investigations. Often they moved in directions which no one could have predicted at the outset. Sometimes a committee changed its very nature, in effect, during its deliberations; or else the same members or nearly the same members might be reassembled under another name.

Such a fluid and casual system greatly favoured the private member with a hobby horse − a type who would find it very hard to make his way later in the British House of Commons. On the other hand, it worked against regular and orderly procedure. The leading parliamentary protagonists in Irish prison reform might all be presented, in their respective ways, as stock characters: Blaquiere, the *bon viveur* and Tory humanitarian; Parnell, the rough squire, unexpectedly high in office; Holmes, the respected, middle-range professional with a worthy *idée fixe*; Hely-Hutchinson, the self-aggrandiser adopting philanthropic celebrities; and Griffith, the young, 'generous' liberal with causes. It would of course be shallow to suppose that people can be encapsulated in a smart phrase; in particular, it would be outrageous to fix their motivation in such mean and claptrap terms. None the less, these are not unfamiliar types in the parliamentary history of betterment. What distinguishes them from others of their kind is a special sort of political milieu, and House of Commons practices which rewarded their efforts extraordinarily.

They were favoured by three further factors. First, they were working in a self-conscious age of reform, with all the consequential confidence and *élan* which that afforded. In this regard, the 1780s in Ireland resembled the 1830s in England and Wales. In fact, the impression was both more powerful and more practically effective in the first case. In Ireland there was less conflict over the meaning of reform and much less systematic opposition to the social-reforming proposals of the day. Secondly, one type of prison reform, the relief of insolvent debtors, had, in curious and ironical fashion, become enmeshed in the gaiety of the Dublin season. For more than half a century charities, and chief amongst them debtor relief, had served as pretexts for public balls and concerts. The world's first public performance of Handel's *Messiah*, which took place at the Fishamble Street Music Hall on 13 April 1742, may have been for the benefit of the capital's insolvents.[22]

Meanings

Thus by a lucky chance one form at least of mitigating the miseries of incarceration was a traditional and familiar 'good cause' in leading circles long before Holmes took it up practically in Parliament. Finally, the House of Commons reformers were not merely favoured but also harnessed to the production of actual and systematic change by the presence of Fitzpatrick, a master (in contemporary terms at least) of both the facts of the problems and the remedial administrative means. Without such a man to define, draft, translate into bureaucratic machinery and act, much of their effort would have constituted a mere writing on the water.

By no means do all these particulars exhaust the contextual variations between Grattan's Ireland and Victorian Britain. But they should suffice to indicate the practical importance of the differences. They also show that the balance of relative ease in achieving concrete change is far from easy to cast. Each era and place had its own particular advantages, and otherwise. Moreover, the same forces, the press, 'opinion', Parliament, official inquiry and even the dedicated private member, had different relative strengths and modes of operation. On the other hand, there can be no doubt of the broad and fundamental similarity of the two phases of administrative development, all the more remarkable because there was virtually no continuity or connection between them. In fact, so powerful were the pressures making for this sort of change from the later eighteenth century onwards that they could produce a governmental revolution without the prior existence of what we might assume to be indispensable governmental instrumentalities. This is worth exploring in its own right, in a single leading instance, before returning to the questions of weighing the particular against the general, and the individual's work against the undertow of the times and the inherent bias of institutions.

V

If Fitzpatrick's rise and regime in Ireland does seem to have anticipated at many points the 'nineteenth-century revolution in government', we face the problem that several elements of critical importance in the developments of the period 1825-75 were missing in his time. How could a substantially similar process unfold without them? I shall attempt to provide an answer by examining at some length the largest and most obvious lack of all.

The greatest difficulty in predicating the development of the regulatory state in the eighteenth century is probably the absence of central government in the relevant area of activity. Rudimentary departments exercised some control over the raising and spending of revenue, foreign relations and national defence. Public order, religion and law were indirectly subject to some degree of crown surveillance. But otherwise government was a matter for the localities and ultimately managed not by paid, professional, permanent officials but by amateurs who generally owed their power to their formal rank rather than their individual capacities. How then could the state possibly make its way into spheres totally lacking a bureaucratic overlordship or agency in the metropolis?

In the case of Ireland, at least, it may be feasible to supply a solution to this apparently irresolvable problem. Centralised authoritarianism and national uniformity were inherent tendencies in Irish government at all levels, including the local, even in the eighteenth century. Why? One reason was that the Irish ruling class was much too few in number and too scattered in residence to govern individually or in small groups in the English fashion. Another was that Ireland was, in general, much too poor for so small a unit as the parish to be administratively self-sufficient.[23] A third was that the Irish ruling caste, alien in religion, language, interest and habit to the mass of their fellow countrymen, bound themselves together on national rather than parish, county or even regional lines. Their primary identification was with their own order spread thinly across the entire country, not with a particular place or neighbourhood. Their common ground was Dublin; the time and occasion for their concerted action, the parliamentary session and its attendant 'season'. All this is not to say that Irish local government was either powerless or insignificant. The general constitutional structure of post-Tudor Ireland so faithfully reproduced the English institutions that this would have been impossible. But it does help to explain why and how Ireland was predisposed to centralisation and uniformity in government. It does not, however, of itself explain how, in the absence of a departmental system, central government could operate at all in the fields of social administration. The 'missing link' is still to be found.

The location of this 'link' would seem to be in certain forms of the parliamentary committee.[24] It seems fair to say that a species of informal central government gradually established itself in Ireland in the second half of the eighteenth century through the use of committees of inquiry and committees on petitions in both Houses, but particularly in the House of Commons. Grand committees, such as those on trade or religion, and standing committees, such as those on supply or privileges and elections, had always been part of the parliamentary process. But committees of inquiry (often deriving from an *ad hoc* petition committee) were rare before 1750. Thereafter they grew in number and variety of business at an extraordinary rate.

In the early 1750s, there were on average six such committees in each parliamentary session; in the later 1750s, twelve and, by 1765, thirty. By the mid-1760s their work ranged from inquiries into roads, canals and drainage to inquiries into the state of various manufacturers, police and prisons. Some had already virtually a permanent existence. For example, military barracks, a major drain on revenue, were considered by committees in every session of Parliament but one between 1750 and 1765. Similarly, a committee to inquire into lapsed or temporary statutes was missing from only one of the sessions (1769) between 1753 and 1771. Some large-scale public works moved from one committee to another as they progressed. Canals provide one example. In 1757 a committee inquired into the expenditure upon the Grand Canal, which was to link Dublin and the Shannon. Four years later another committee inquired into its construction to date and the need for further investment. In the following session, a third committee was appointed to review progress on the appointments of the undertaking; and in the three succeeding sessions the Grand Canal was considered by a more general committee on expenditure which had been set up in 1765 to consolidate 'under one roof' the supervision of all major public works in progress.

Thus by the 1760s investigative committees were numerous and in several fields practically continuous. More and more often they were allowed or enjoined to sit beyond the end of the parliamentary session. Unfortunately we have no evidence on how long these extra-sessional meetings continued. Presumably they did not outlive the Dublin season unless a considerable proportion of the members lived permanently in the capital. None the less, the prolongation of the life of the committees, by whatever period of time, is an interesting indication of the way in which they were beginning to take on a governmental character. So too is the growing practice of regular reportage to committees. For instance, the inspector general of barracks was coming to report almost every session to the barracks committees, and the trust which managed the Grand Canal, the Inland Navigation Corporation, to whatever committee was dealing with the Grand Canal at that particular time.

A further indication of the institutionalisation and bureaucratisation of the committee system would be continuity of membership. Here again, unfortunately, we lack the decisive evidence. Usually the only names recorded were those of the chairman and perhaps one, two or three of the leading members. But it seems inherently probable that the membership would not have been altered greatly where a committee was revived session after session; and in fact there are indications that this was the case, at any rate for members with a particular expertise or hobby horse. In our own particular field, Peter Holmes belonged to every one of the eleven gaol inquiry committees which sat between 1780 and 1794; Griffith was a member of all which sat during his years in Parliament; and five or six others can be identified as serving on two or more.

The classical test for the emergence of the modern civil service in Great Britain is whether or not the administration (or branch of the administration) was permanent, continuous and devoted to state, as against party or a particular ministry's, policy. It would be too much to say that the inquiry or petition committee of the Irish House of Commons in the last thirty or forty years of the eighteenth century satisfied this test completely. Yet in certain fields it went far towards doing so; and prisons were indisputably in this category. During the 1780s gaol committees were appointed, as we have seen, in every parliamentary session, and were sometimes ordered to remain in being after the session's end. They were supra-factional in composition. They were also increasingly constant in both membership and leadership. They tended to gather business other than the conduct and state of prisons proper into their hands; in the end the release of insolvent debtors or the pursuit of prison malefactors were generally added to their agenda. Most important of all, perhaps, they prepared legislation and, in the latter half of the decade, supervised (or rather were led by) a field executive, in the person of Sir Jeremiah. In essentials, this matched point for point the interaction of, say, the Home Office and the mines inspectorate in the field of coal mining in the 1850s.

Of course it is paradoxical to speak of such a 'body' as the succession of gaols committees as permanent and continuous. It fell away in 1791 and although there were decided indications of a revival in 1793 this might well have come to nothing, even if war had not intervened. On average, Parliament was not in session for more than five months of the year and the extra-sessional meetings of the committee may have sometimes extended to no more than a week or fortnight. Similarly, it may well seem extravagant to speak of the committees as devoted to state policy. Formally, they merely represented the House of Commons. The Irish executive, though occasionally involved obliquely, was in general detached from the affair; and the two House of Lords gaols committees of the period were both independent and fruitless undertakings. Thus the parallel between the 1780s and the 1850s may seem strained.

But this is not really so. Politico-governmental Ireland was, as has been said, extremely small and intimate in the eighteenth century. The Commons gaols committees sat long and regularly enough to conduct their central business, and had their policy been in conflict with that of Dublin Castle, the executive would have intervened decisively in Parliament to check or change it. Meanwhile, in its heyday, the Irish system worked in all the major matters in precisely the same fashion as mid-nineteenth-century central government in Great Britain. Of course, elements critical to Victorian administration were quite missing in Grattan's Ireland. The point is that effective surrogates could be, and were, there.

The real question then would seem to be, not whether the Irish system met substantially the classical test of a 'modern' civil service but why it failed to survive, let alone develop. The first, most obvious answer, is that this particular form of centralisation needed virtually annual renewal. The committee had to be reconstituted by a vote of the House each session. Moreover the issue of reconstitution would not be so much as raised without the positive action of some member or members. It was not part of the set parliamentary agenda. The next step of a standing committee on gaols was never taken or even considered before the Irish Parliament's demise in 1800. Secondly and consequentially, the process was fatally dependent upon extraordinary individual exertion, in particular by backbench MPs. There could be no guarantee of a succession of Holmeses, Griffiths and Blaquieres, or even that such men would maintain their interest in the field of reform they had temporarily adopted. Blaquiere, for instance, became absorbed instead in the foundling hospitals question in the later 1790s.[25]

Curiously enough, the individual who stood at the centre of the whole early development, Fitzpatrick, was more dispensable than his sponsors. This was because he had secured a statutory office. Even though it was left unfilled for more than two years after his departure, and even though his successor was appointed for the most sordid political instead of professional reasons, the office lived on. Moreover, inadequate though Archer may have been, the statutory duty to present his annual reports kept the subject in the parliamentary purview; and when at last in 1809 interested members of the House of Commons (now of the United Kingdom) were again to be found,[26] they had something on which to build the next body of legislation.[27] Still further, the continuance of the office eventually produced its own multiplication. In course of time, Archer's reports made it clear that the work was overwhelming, so that when he had to be replaced in 1822, two inspectors general were appointed.[28] In turn, after various customary developments in terms of government growth, these appointments led on to the setting up of a formal 'board of directors of convict prisons' in Ireland in 1854.[29] Thus despite the lacunae and inexpertise — we might even add some unfortunate first-hand experience, for Palmer, one of the Archer's successors as inspector general, was himself imprisoned for debt while in office in the 1830s![30] — the 1786 and 1787 Acts, in establishing the inspector generalship, ensured the survival of a post from which ultimately a full and regular branch of government could be developed.

The inspectorship of madhouses in Ireland followed a similar, though even more wavering, course. We know little of Fitzpatrick's work in this office; and his successor appears to have been ignorant of or indifferent to the additional duty of protecting lunatics. But the plight of these unfortunates attracted the attention of the House of Commons in 1804 and 1811, with the respective select committees of these two years[31] producing recommendations strikingly similar to Fitzpatrick's proposals of 1790 for penitentiaries. The first suggested provincial asylums, and the second the provision of a network of asylums on the districtal plan. As with the St James's Street penitentiary of 1791, one national institution, opened in Dublin in 1815, was the only immediate fruit of these inquiries.[32] But the logic of a situation in which the bulk of lunatics in public custody were lodged in gaols and bridewells reasserted itself in 1826. The two newly appointed inspectors general of prisons were directed to inspect madhouses as well — apparently the requirement of the 1787 Act that they should do so had dropped completely out of mind — and when in 1842 the licensing of private asylums became compulsory, it was they who were empowered to recommend when a licence should be withdrawn.[33] Three years later these tasks were transferred to a new corps under the direct control of the Irish executive.[34] In this final regularisation of the central management of the insane in Ireland, there was one particular irony worthy of Swift himself. Two inspectors of lunatics were appointed, not so much because of the press of business as to enable both a Protestant and a Catholic to serve!

Meanings 321

Thus, nearly seventy years were to pass before such a centralising consummation as the formal junction of inspectors and responsible department was to be reached in the case of Irish gaols; and over half a century passed before this happened in the field of lunacy. The fundamental reason for such long delays was that the parliamentary committee failed to provide, and doubtless could never have provided, a lasting substitute for a bureaucratic structure of authority. It is true that, in one respect, the Act of Union of 1801 helped to mitigate the effects of the parliamentary committee's failure. With the disappearance of the Irish Parliament, and the consequent list towards crown-colonyhood in Ireland, the Irish executive greatly extended its central supervising and controlling roles in the extra-political fields. Especially after 1822, the prisons were increasingly absorbed into a general Irish administrative system. But it was only after 1854 that they were fitted completely into a modern governmental system, with clearly marked channels of command. (The madhouses preceded them by a few years in either case.) By then, of course, two other vital developments had taken place. In Ireland, the chief secretary had emerged as a species of one-man Cabinet. The new prisons board was effectively related to both the executive and legislature in being made directly responsible to him. Secondly, in the United Kingdom, departmental government for the 'social' fields had also emerged, and was well on the way towards becoming standardised, as well as comparatively sophisticated. Thus by 1854 the missing link in Irish prison reform was missing only in the sense of not having yet been intruded into that particular area: it was readily to be found elsewhere. But seventy years earlier it was not to be found at all. Both the provision of a substitute in the 1780s, and the inherent fragility of that substitute are, therefore, of equal as well as first importance in understanding the early formation of the regulatory state.

VI

In certain respects Fitzpatrick was the antithesis of the titans of nineteenth-century reform, the Chadwicks, Trevelyans, Nightingales and Mary Carpenters. Ego-driven, universalist and apocalyptic in their calls to action, they moved to the accompaniment of Wagnerian clashings. But against such a company Fitzpatrick's seems the bureaucracy of Moore's Melodies, striking the ingenuous and pathetic notes. So far from exaggerating his originality, he tended to disguise it. He tried to rest wherever possible on the authority of others, Howard, Lind or Pringle or the great continental chemists and naturalists. He either failed to see or thought it prudent to suppress the innovatory character of his schemes and devices. Nor was he a doctrinaire or an *a priori* planner. On the contrary, he practised self-conscious and deliberate pragmatism, even to the extent of choosing the *pis aller* repeatedly, lest no change whatever be effected. Moreover he often adopted for his own purposes organisational forms which already existed in other branches of government; and he even allowed for the organic and evolutionary nature of administration in his plans. Thus he sometimes presented regulation as a process of habituating people to initially irksome but ultimately prized modes of conduct, with the need for formal rule withering away gradually in time.

He did not look forward to a brave new world. Instead, he assumed that it had arrived already. What needed to be done was not so much to innovate as to bring everyday practice into conformity with the superior principles and values which had been established in the course of his 'glorious' century. Again and again, his argument for change was that current usage belonged to 'the darkened ages' and had no place in the bright noonday which mankind had now attained. Thus, he presented reform as essentially a matter of adjusting what was actually happening to what all men of good will and good sense generously assumed to be happening, or about to happen. Nor was bridging the gap between the good and the actual conceived of as inherently a difficult affair. Whichever of the four great and now well-marked roads one chose – Common Sense, Humanity, Economy or Policy – the same destination would be reached. Homely wisdom, the desire to reduce the sum of human pain, abhorrence of waste, and the politic management of society inevitably converged upon this goal, for they all expressed either sound reason or good feeling; and even these two last were but different manifestations or qualities of the same entity, enlightened man.

Thus Fitzpatrick presents himself to posterity as a stock Enlightenment figure, not only accepting, but even attempting to sanction his actions by, the mere watchwords and slogans of the movement. Yet these simple shibboleths appear to have provided him with an everflowing rationale for his endeavours, sustaining him in the face of continual rebuffs. They may even have been, in one special sense, the source of some of his administrative originality. When materials were lacking to achieve what Humanity or Economy or Policy suggested should already be in being, what was there to do but simply to set about and make them? Hence perhaps the matter-of-fact fashion in which he deployed his names and numbers into columns, composed his statistical 'charts', and devised his model ventilators or arm rests or marine ovens, as the particular need appeared. After all it was but Common Sense.

Nor was there in Fitzpatrick any element of the grand design or strategy of social reform. It is true that he saw a basic similarity, or even identity, in many of the problems which he took up. Gaol fever and camp fever, he believed, were indistinguishable from any other form of fever associated with dense living; negroes and convicts felt pain as acutely as free Britons; transportees' wives were no less wives than gaolers' spouses. But this simply expressed the generalism, or methodological uniformity, inherent in eighteenth-century medicine and benevolence, and like Howard and others Fitzpatrick even carried such generalism so far as to see society in the image of the body and the reformer in the roles of diagnostician and healer. The fact remains that Fitzpatrick's career of reform was quite unplanned. He accumulated his fields of interest by a succession of chance encounters, and almost always by seeing or touching some physical evil for himself. Systematic social investigation or engineering lay altogether outside his imaginative range, as it lay outside Howard's or Perceval's or Fry's.

In short, although Fitzpatrick was divided from the Victorian titans by only two or three generations, he inhabited a world alien to theirs at many points. Can we visualise Shaftesbury challenged to a duel by some official he had denounced, or Southwood Smith carrying pocket pistols in self-defence? Can we envisage a Victorian reforming career reading — as does Sir Jeremiah's — like a picaresque novel, a succession of apparently random governmental and geographical peregrinations? It is true that the nineteenth century still produced bureaucrats-by-accident, and that some of the latter-day titans accumulated fields for reform like colonial empires. But the first age of modern administrative discovery was then over, and even the most pioneering of the Victorians was not a frontiersman in the early fashion. Smollett had given way to Smiles.

Despite this accumulation of differences, most of the basic elements of Victorian administration were, as we have seen, also discernible in this eighteenth-century career. Perhaps the most important element of all, the state inspectorate, was not only embodied in Fitzpatrick but also thoroughly explored by him as both a concept and a machine. Enforcement was of course its initial function. That indeed was its *raison d'être*: for that it would always be indispensable. But Fitzpatrick rose above a mere static view of government. To the primitive coercive role, that of the initial 'disciplinary invigilator' (in Herman Finer's phrase),[35] he added the advisory and the creative. He saw the inspector as supplying both data and new proposals; he saw him as providing, through his systematic reports, the materials by which his political masters could both evaluate the effectiveness of the current regulation, and apprehend the directions in which they ought to move in amending the legislation. Of course he fully realised that, in ordinary circumstances, the inspector's 'advice' would practically determine the issue. It was in this sense that he spoke of the inspector as a creative agent, and that he regarded the process for which the inspector provided the motive power as dynamic.

He did not, as we shall see, comprehend the inspector as an expert in the Victorian sense of the term, although he naturally assumed that medical matters should be left to the doctors, and even hinted broadly that, trained in observation and enumeration as they were, they constituted the best pool of general administrative talent. Similarly, his grasp of organisational forms — in particular, of the delegation of authority and the provision of a network of subordinate officers — was imperfect. In one or two instances he adumbrated hierarchical schemes. But generally he failed to develop such ideas. These were, however, the ultimate refinements, and by and large, they depended on forces of the future which could not have been foreseen in the years from 1783 to 1802. Overall, Fitzpatrick certainly understood the essentials of the modern office. He conceived of the inspector as a professional — paid, permanent, full-time and specialised in his administrative career or careers.

Thus Fitzpatrick came very close to the early and mid-Victorian inspectorate in action and idea alike. In fact, few nineteenth-century practitioners or theorists had a better grasp of its nature or the 'laws' of its development. His comprehension and exploitation of the fundamental similarities of problem and solution in widely varying administrative fields, and of the virtues and values of deliberate pragmatism in administration, were especially remarkable — and rare.

But these points are not made in any spirit of aggrandisement on Sir Jeremiah's behalf, or to claim him as the 'originator' of a tradition. The pursuit of 'origins' is commonly a ploughing of the sands in history; certainly it seems futile in this particular instance. Doubtless the simplest elements of the inspectorial system are implicit in any bureaucracy, in particular when it turns, as bureaucracies must quickly turn, to the raising of public revenue. In the most general sense, the inspector is coeval with 'Western Europe', discernible in rough outline even in the workings of the Carolingian church and state. Overleaping nine hundred years, we find seventeenth-century France crisscrossed by sophisticated inspectorial networks, mainly judicial and revenue-raising, and ultimately connected to a coercive and regulatory central power. Closer still to him in time and place, Fitzpatrick must have been thoroughly familiar with established patterns of both national and local inspection before he so much as entered the Irish service. The Irish barracks and linen boards, with their inspectors general and peripatetic subordinate officers, and even the Gaols Acts with their assignment of duties of surveillance, enforcement and report to the clergy of the relevant parishes, furnished ready-made if imperfect models of centralised administration. Sir Jeremiah had only to transfer to other fields and improve upon what was already part of the Irish governmental structure. Similarly, Keate was already an inspector general (of military hospitals) in both name and full modern function before Fitzpatrick ever inserted himself into army health.

All this is by no means to deny that Fitzpatrick made a significant original contribution to both the operation and the theory of the inspectorate. To extend it to new fields, to discern the identity of function beneath circumstantial variety upon the surface, to project and elaborate fresh powers and procedures, and above all to think about the institution as such and its general relationship to government, constitutes a remarkable innovatory achievement. None the less it is innovation from within − or rather drawing from − long evolving systems. Of course, Sir Jeremiah's own gifts and urges were crucial to the particular developments which this book has described. It is quite conceivable that no general prisons or lunacy inspectorate would have emerged in pre-union Ireland without his intervention. It is morally certain that without him the inspectorship of army health would not have been conceived during the Revolutionary wars. His existence then mattered, and matters, for people live only once, and briefly. The fact remains, however, that he worked altogether with the grain of an historical process, and fell in faithfully with the logic of contemporary institutional development.

However we judge an individual's part in governmental growth − and his own qualities of head, hand, heart and indispensability at specific junctures, would seem to be among the best criteria − we must also set him in the stream deriving force and direction from both past patterns and the current exigencies of enforcement. Perhaps the essential point about such a phenomenon as the inspectorate is that it is an enduring general tendency in government, varying in its shape and stresses according to the possibilities of the time. Thus, for example, Fitzpatrick did not consider the inspector as an expert torn by conflicting professional and bureaucratic loyalties, as in the case, say, of an analytical chemist in government with duties to his professional organisation and his academic discipline as well as to his department and 'the public'. An inspector of this kind was not born until the mid-nineteenth century; he was dependent for his existence upon certain scientific developments, and upon the rise of professional associations. Conversely, Fitzpatrick could and did conceive of the inspector as an expert in a sense unimaginable a century before. In the interval, the medical profession had developed both a grammar of public health and a statistical methodology which he transferred — and indeed regarded as indispensable — to the business of governmental regulation. Sir Jeremiah took it for granted that social administration required minds trained in a particular way, or at least certain mental habits, quite foreign to pre-Georgian man.

The inspectorate is to be considered therefore in terms of the potentialities of the day. Retrospectively speaking it seems to have been possible, surprisingly often and to a surprising degree, to find rough substitutes for elements crucial to a later form but not as yet developed. The Irish parliamentary committee system and the concentrated metropolitan opinion of the 1780s are cases in point. But Whig interpretations (I use the phrase in Butterfield's sense, of course) must be avoided. The late-eighteenth-century inspectorate as conceived and performed by Fitzpatrick is not to be evaluated according to its degree of conformity or otherwise to its later, 'successful' counterpart. True, in the search for explanations and causes of the early and mid-Victorian offices, it is important to gauge the measure of their anticipation by half a century or more. But it is also vital to place Sir Jeremiah's achievements — or those of any other period — into their contemporary setting, political, social, governmental, economic and sentimental. Once this is done, both the contemporary expression of the eternal inspectorial impulse and the contribution of discoverable individuals to releasing, advancing and moulding it, can be fairly estimated.[36]

Meanings 327

VII

It would be cold, I think, to end a book devoted to one man upon the note of abstract reasoning. Not that it is mandatory to throw philosophy from the window to enable a person to come in at the door. Duns Scotus, for one, achieves the reconciliation between the singular and the genus in terms to which historians should instinctively respond. Of course, generality is valid, not to say necessary, to organise experience in the mind or on the page. But every phenomenon, every stretch of past reality, has its own inimitable form and markings, and every human actor his own 'particular glimpse', and every life its own 'most special image'. Haecceity holds the delicate balance. The great press of events and 'inexorable' social movement are, paradoxically, unique in each of their innumerable historical expressions.

This element of quiddity is, needless to say, all the more powerful where a single individual sustains so much of a protracted endeavour by himself as did Fitzpatrick. But it would be altogether wrong to leave him struck forever in the attitude of an Atlas, or a Hercules, or any antique deity: Don Quixote is a more fitting prototype. Once when Shaw lay close to death (though typically he was to live for half a century more) he wrote an article declaring that his hearse should be drawn by all the animals which he had not eaten.[37] Humans are not particularly grateful; but — in the same strain — if no more than one in ten of all the murderers, Rightboys, prostitutes, inebriates, assaulters, insolvents, charity children, madmen, transportees, settlers, soldiers' wives, soldiers' families, widows, naval ratings, East Indian fusiliers, French priests and Hanoverian mercenaries, whose sufferings Fitzpatrick tried to lessen, had drawn his funeral carriage, even London itself might have been astonished by the train.

Notes

1. O. MacDonagh, 'The Nineteenth-Century Revolution in Government: a Reappraisal', *Historical Journal*, vol. i (1958), pp. 52-67. The leading books and articles bearing on the issue include A.V. Dicey, *Lectures on the Relation between Law and Public Opinion in England during the Nineteenth Century* (London, 1905); J.B. Brebner, '*Laissez-faire* and State Intervention in Nineteenth-Century Britain', *Journal of Economic History*, vol. viii (1948), supplement, pp. 59-73; S.E. Finer, *The Life and Times of Sir Edwin Chadwick* (London, 1952); H.J. Parris, 'The Nineteenth-Century Revolution in Government: a Reappraisal Reappraised', *Historical Journal*, vol. iii (1960), pp. 17-37; MacDonagh, *Pattern of Government Growth*; Lambert, 'A Victorian National Health Service'; R.J. Lambert, *Sir John Simon, 1816-1904, and English Social Administration*

328 *Meanings*

(London, 1963); J. Hart, 'Nineteenth-Century Social Reform: a Tory Interpretation of History', *Past and Present*, no. 31 (1965), pp. 39-61; H.J. Parris, *Constitutional Bureaucracy: the Development of British Central Administration since the Eighteenth Century* (New York, 1969); H.S. Gordon, 'The Ideology of Laissez-Faire' in A.W. Coats (ed.), *The Classical Economists and Economic Policy* (London, 1971); W.C. Lubenow, *The Politics of Government Growth: Early Victorian Attitudes toward State Intervention* (Hawden, Conn., 1971); G. Sutherland (ed.), *Studies in the Growth of Nineteenth Century Government* (London, 1972); J.R. Hay, *The Origins of the Liberal Welfare Reforms 1906-1914* (London, 1975); MacDonagh, *Early Victorian Government*. Two particularly good commentaries on the 'debate' at different junctures are V. Cromwell, 'Interpretations of Nineteenth-Century Administration: an Analysis', *Victorian Studies*, vol. ix (1966), pp. 245-55, and R.M. MacLeod, 'Statesmen Undisguised', *American Historical Review*, vol. lxxviii (1973), pp. 1386-1405.

    2. Cromwell, 'Interpretations', pp. 247-50.

    3. MacDonagh, *Government Growth*, pp. 320-50.

    4. For an excellent discussion of the use of 'models' in history-writing, see P.D. McClelland, *Causal Explanation and Model-Building in History, Economics and Economic History* (Ithaca, N.Y., 1975), especially ch. 2.

    5. MacDonagh, 'Nineteenth-Century Revolution', p. 58.

    6. Ibid., pp. 59-60.

    7. Ibid., p. 60.

    8. *Report of the Select Committee on the Factory Regulation Act*, H.C., 1841, session 1 (56), ix.

    9. *Report of the Select Committee on Coal Mines*, H.C., 1852 (509), v.

    10. 7 & 8 Vic., c.15 and 18 & 19 Vic., c.108, respectively.

    11. See generally, Finer, *Chadwick*; Lambert, *Simon*; R.L. Lewis, *Edwin Chadwick and the Public Health Movement* (London, 1952).

    12. Despite the hiatus between Fitzpatrick's departure and the appointment of a successor, and Archer's weakness as an inspector general, some momentum in government growth was maintained. For example, central control was increased by an Amendment Act of 1810, 50 Geo. III, c.103, which empowered King's Bench to dismiss summarily any prison official it considered guilty of misconduct. In 1822 a further Amendment Act, 3 Geo. IV, c.64, strengthened considerably the hand of the inspector general (or inspectors general). He could now, in effect, dismiss errant prisons officers because it was he who was charged with reporting their misconduct to King's Bench; he could compel counties to furnish bedding and other prison supplies; and it was he who would compose the mandatory 'dietary table' for each prison in future. These changes followed the appointment of new inspectors general, and are typical examples of the manner in which further regulation and bureaucratic discretions are generated from within the administration itself, as answers to some of the practical difficulties of enforcement which have been experienced. Again characteristically, the resumed process of administrative growth was soon to express itself in a consolidating measure, 7 Geo. IV, c.74, enacted in 1826. *Inter alia*, this brought the sanctioning of prison building, and to a large extent its financing, into the sphere of central government.

    13. Pellew, 'Explosives Act of 1875', pp. 177-8, 180-94.

    14. D.M. Vess, *Medical Revolution in France, 1789-1796* (Gainesville, Florida, 1975), pp. 185-93.

    15. C. Maxwell, *Dublin under the Georges 1714-1830* (London, 1946), p. 58.

    16. Irish Catholics were not enfranchised until 1793, and had of course another thirty-six years to wait before they were permitted to sit in Parliament.

    17. B. Inglis, *The Freedom of the Press in Ireland 1784-1841* (London, 1954), appendix C, pp. 232-4.

Meanings 329

18. Ibid., pp. 52-105.
19. Lambert, *Simon*, chs. 13-20.
20. E.M. Johnston, *Great Britain and Ireland 1760-1800: a Study in Political Administration* (London, 1963), pp. 214-56.
21. Maxwell, *Dublin under the Georges*, p. 20.
22. Ibid., pp. 102-3. The concert was held for the benefit of the Charitable Musical Society, whose main object of charity was the debtors imprisoned in Dublin; ibid., p. 100. £400 was collected at the concert, the attendance being enlarged by the request that ladies come without hoops, and gentlemen without swords!
23. O. MacDonagh, *Ireland: the Union and its Aftermath* (London, 1977).
24. The particulars of the Irish parliamentary committees of 1750-94 are drawn from the Irish *House of Commons Journals*, vols. v-xvi, supplemented by the Irish *Parliamentary Register* for the years from 1781 onward.
25. Maxwell, *Dublin under the Georges*, pp. 132-5. Blaquiere took up the scandal of the foundling hospitals in 1796-7, collected statistics, procured a parliamentary committee of inquiry and secured a 'reform'. It was disclosed that between 1784 and 1796, 17,000 of the 25,000 children admitted to the Dublin Foundling Hospital had died there or while being nursed out. But the mortality rate was even higher after 1796, for in the next thirty years 41,000 died out of the 52,000 admitted.
26. *Cobbett's Parliamentary Debates*, vol. xi, 1131, 2 July 1808; vol. xv, 468, 19 February 1810. Sheridan was the prime mover of the new inquiry into the state of Irish gaols. Foster took part in the debate of 1810.
27. 50 Geo. III, c.103.
28. R.B. McDowell, *The Irish Administration 1801-1914* (London, 1964), p. 151.
29. 17 & 18 Vic., c.76 provided for the appointment of such a board by the lord lieutenant. The first board, consisting of Sir Walter Crofton, Captain Knight (former governor of Portsmouth prison) and Dr Lentaigne, was particularly strong, and under the chief secretary constituted a virtually autonomous force controlling the inspectorial system.
30. McDowell, *Irish Administration*, p. 151.
31. *Report from the Committee Respecting the Poor of Ireland*, H.C., 1803-4, v (109); *Report from the Select Committee on the Lunatic Poor in Ireland*, H.C., 1817, viii (430).
32. This was the Richmond asylum, authorised by 55 Geo. III, c.107. See also McDowell, *Irish Administration*, pp. 172-3; A.P. Williamson, 'The Origins of the Irish Mental Hospital Service, 1800-1843' (MLitt dissertation, Dublin University), pp. 101-18.
33. 5 & 6 Vic., c.123.
34. 8 & 9 Vic., c.107.
35. H. Finer, in J.S. Harris, *British Government Inspection as a Dynamic Process: the Local Services and the Central Department* (New York, 1955), pp. viii-ix.
36. I am particularly indebted to Professor R.M. MacLeod for his part in discussions on this section, although of course he bears no responsibility for the views expressed therein.
37. G.K. Chesterton, *George Bernard Shaw* (Guild edition, London, 1949), p. 34.

APPENDIX I: CHARTER SCHOOLS VISITED BY FITZPATRICK

School	County	School	County
Arklow	Wicklow	Longford	Longford
*Athlone	Westmeath	Loughrea	Galway
Ballinrobe	Mayo	Maynooth	Kildare
Ballycastle	Antrim	Newmarket	Clare
Ballykelly	Derry	Newport	Tipperary
Castlebar	Mayo	†Ranelagh	Dublin
Castle Carbery	Kildare	Ray	Donegal
Castleisland	Kerry	*Roscommon	Roscommon
Charleville	Cork	Santry	Dublin
Clonmel	Tipperary	Sligo	Sligo
Creggane	Armagh	Stradbally	Queen's
Dundalk	Louth	Strand	Dublin
Farra	Westmeath	Strangford	Down
Frankfurt	King's	Trim	Meath
Galway	Galway	Waterford	Waterford
Kilkenny	Kilkenny		

*Athlone and Roscommon were not, strictly speaking, Charter Schools proper, being instead on the Ranelagh Foundation.
†Ranelagh Road House was a 'nursery' Charter School.

APPENDIX II: LORDS LIEUTENANT AND CHIEF SECRETARIES OF IRELAND, 1772-1806

30.11.1772	Earl of Harcourt	Sir John Blaquiere
7.12.1776	Earl of Buckinghamshire	Sir Richard Heron
29.11.1780	Earl of Carlisle	William Eden
8. 4.1782	Duke of Portland	Richard Fitzpatrick
15. 8.1782	Earl Temple	W.W. Grenville
3. 5.1783	Earl of Northington	William Windham, Thomas Pelham
12. 2.1784	Duke of Rutland	Thomas Orde
27.10.1787	Lords justices	
6.11.1787	Marquess of Buckingham	A. Fitzherbert
24.10.1789	Earl of Westmorland	Robert Hobart
13.12.1794	Earl Fitzwilliam	Lord Milton
13. 3.1795	Earl Camden	Thomas Pelham
14. 6.1798	Marquis Cornwallis	Viscount Castlereagh
24. 4.1801	Earl of Hardwicke	Charles Abbot

Source: *Handbook of British Chronology* (London, 1961), pp. 166-7, 170.

SELECT BIBLIOGRAPHY

I Primary Sources

1. MANUSCRIPT
Public Record Office, United Kingdom
Admiralty Papers, files 108/20, 36, 38, 46, 48, 49, 51, 53, 57, 66, 68, 69, 70
Colonial Office Papers, files 194/38; 201/15, 20, 23; 324/112; 384/80
Home Office Papers, files 1/2, 51/147
War Office Papers, files 1/896; 1/897; 2/1; 7/101, 102; 71/170; 72/17
Public Record Office, Northern Ireland
Foster/Massereene MS., cited as Foster Papers
Anglesea Papers
National Library of Ireland
Bolton Papers
O'Connell Papers
National Library of Scotland
Melville Papers
Scottish Record Office
Melville Papers
British Library
Hardwicke Papers
Huskisson Papers
Liverpool Papers
Pelham Papers
University College Library, London
Bentham Papers
Trinity College, Dublin
Conolly Papers
Incorporated Society Board book
Registry of Deeds, Dublin
Royal College of Physicians Library, Dublin
Kirkpatrick bequest: a collection of biographical notes, newscuttings etc. relating to Irish doctors compiled by Dr T.P.C. Kirkpatrick

2. PARLIAMENTARY PAPERS
Report of the Committee Appointed to Enquire into the State of the Gaols and Prisons in this Kingdom, 15 June 1782, *Journals of the*

Select Bibliography

House of Commons (Ire.), vol. x

Report from the Committee Appointed to Enquire into the Present State, Situation, and Management of the Public Prisons, Jails and Bridewells, of this Kingdom, 17 December 1783, *Journals of the House of Commons* (Ire.), vol. xi

Report of the Committee to Enquire into the Present State, Situation and Management of the Public Prisons, Jails, and Bridewells of this Kingdom, 4 May 1785, *Journals of the House of Commons* (Ire.), vol. xi

Report from the Committee Appointed to Enquire into the Present State, Situation and Management of the Public Prisons, Gaols and Bridewells of this Kingdom, 12 March 1787, *Journals of the House of Commons* (Ire.), vol. xii

Report on State of Gaols and Prisons, 3 March 1788, *Journals of the House of Commons* (Ire.), vol. xii

Report on the State of the Protestant Charter Schools, 14 April 1788, *Journals of the House of Commons* (Ire.), vol. xii

Report from the Commissioners of Police, of the Present State of the Several Gaols and Prisons within the District of the Metropolis, wherein Persons charged with or Guilty of Treason, Felony, Misdemeanour or Breach of the Peace, are Confined, 23 January 1792, *Journals of the House of Commons* (Ire.), vol. xv

Report of the Committee appointed to Inquire into the Present State and Situation of the Public Gaols and Prisons throughout this Kingdom, 11 July 1793, *Journals of the House of Commons* (Ire.), vol. xv

House of Commons Sessional Papers of the Eighteenth Century, 100, reports and papers 1795-6

A Report on the Prisons of Ireland for the Year 1797 by the Inspector General, 21 March 1798, *Journals of the House of Commons* (Ire.), vol. xvii

A Report on the Prisons of Ireland for the Year 1798 by the Inspector General, 20 March 1799, *Journals of the House of Commons* (Ire.), vol. xviii

A Report on the Prisons of Ireland for the Year 1799 by the Inspector General, 24 March 1800, *Journals of the House of Commons* (Ire.), vol. xix

Report from the Committee Respecting the Poor of Ireland, H.C., 1803-4, v (109)

Fifth Report of the Commissioners of Military Enquiry, Army, Medical Department, H.C., 1808, v (6)

Report of Inspector General of Prisons, H.C., 1808, ix (239)

334 *Select Bibliography*

Third Report of the Commissioners of the Board of Education in Ireland on the Protestant Charter Schools, H.C., 1809, vii (142)
Report from the Select Committee on the Lunatic Poor in Ireland, H.C., 1817, viii (430)
Report of the Select Committee on the Factory Regulation Act, H.C., 1841, session I, ix (56)
Report of the Select Committee on Coal Mines, H.C., 1852, v (509)

3. STATUTES
The Statutes at Large, passed in the Parliament held in Ireland . . ., 20 vols. (Dublin, 1786-1801)
The Statutes at Large from Magna Charta to 1800, 18 vols. (London, 1763-1800)
The Statutes of the United Kingdom of Great Britain and Ireland . . ., 27 vols. (London, 1804-66)

4. PARLIAMENTARY DEBATES
Cobbett's Parliamentary Debates
The Parliamentary History of England from the Earliest Period to the year 1803
Journals of the House of Commons (Ire.)
Journals of the House of Lords (Ire.)
Parliamentary Register (Ire.)

5. PUBLISHED SELECT DOCUMENTS AND LETTERS
Aspinall, A. (ed.) *The Later Correspondence of George III*, 5 vols. (Cambridge, 1962-70)
Copeland, T.W. (ed.) *The Correspondence of Edmund Burke*, 9 vols. (Cambridge, 1958-70)
Dropmore Papers, 7 vols. (Historical Manuscripts Commission), thirteenth report: the manuscripts of J.B. Fortescue Esq. preserved at Dropmore
Harcourt, E.W. (ed.) *The Harcourt Papers*, 14 vols. (Oxford, n.d.)
Historical Records of Australia, series I, 26 vols. (Canberra, 1914-25)
Historical Records of New South Wales, 7 vols. (Sydney, 1892-1901)

6. NEWSPAPERS AND PERIODICALS
Dublin Evening Post
Flying Post (Exeter)
Freeman's Journal (Dublin)
Gentleman's Magazine
Hampshire Chronicle

Monthly Review
The Times

7. CONTEMPORARY PRINTED SOURCES
Dublin Gazette
Fitzpatrick, J. *An Essay on Gaol Abuses, and on the Means of Redressing Them: together with the General Method of Treating Disorders to which Prisoners are Most Incident* (Dublin, 1784)
Fitzpatrick, J. *Suggestions on the Slave Trade, for the Consideration of the Legislature of Great Britain* (London, 1797)
Fitzpatrick, J. *Thoughts on Penitentiaries* (Dublin, 1790)
Howard, J. *An Account of the Principal Lazarettos in Europe; with Various Papers relative to the Plague: together with Further Observations on some Foreign Prisons and Hospitals; and Additional Remarks on the Present State of those in Great Britain and Ireland* (Warrington, 1789)
Howard, J. *The State of the Prisons in England and Wales with Preliminary Observations and an Account of Some Foreign Prisons and Hospitals* (1st edn, Warrington, 1777)
Wesley, J. *Journal*, 8 vols. (London, 1938)
Wilson's Dublin Directory

II Secondary Sources

1. BOOKS AND ARTICLES
Bartlett, T. 'The Townshend Viceroyalty 1767-72' in T. Bartlett and D.W. Hayton (eds.), *Penal Era and Golden Age: Essays in Irish History, 1690-1800* (Belfast, 1979)
Bateson, C. *The Convict Ships 1787-1868* (Glasgow, 1959)
Blanco, R.L. 'The Soldier's Friend – Sir Jeremiah Fitzpatrick, Inspector of Health for Land Forces', *Medical History*, vol. xx (1976)
Blanco, R.L. *Wellington's Surgeon General: Sir James McGrigor* (Durham, N.C., 1974)
Bodkin, M. 'Notes on the Irish Parliament in 1773', *Proceedings of the Royal Irish Academy*, vol. xlviii, section C, no. 4
Bowen, D. *The Protestant Crusade in Ireland, 1800-70* (Dublin, 1978)
Brebner, J.B. '*Laissez-faire* and State Intervention in Nineteenth-Century Britain', *Journal of Economic History*, vol. viii (1948), supplement
Burgess, R. *Catalogue of Portraits of Doctors and Scientists in the Well-*

336 *Select Bibliography*

come Institute of the History of Medicine (London, 1973)
Cantlie, N. *A History of the Army Medical Department*, 2 vols. (Edinburgh, 1974)
Cook, E. *The Life of Florence Nightingale*, 2 vols. (London, 1913)
Cooper, R.A. 'Ideas and their Execution: English Prison Reform', *Eighteenth Century Studies*, vol. x (1976)
Cromwell, V. 'Interpretations of Nineteenth-Century Administration: An Analysis', *Victorian Studies*, vol. ix (1966)
Crowe, K.E. 'The Walcheren Expedition and the New Army Medical Board: a Reconsideration', *English Historical Review*, vol. lxxxviii, no. cccxlix (1973)
Cullen, L.M. *Life in Ireland* (London, 1968)
Dicey, A.V. *Lectures on the Relation between Law and Public Opinion in England during the Nineteenth Century* (London, 1905)
Drew, R. *Commissioned Officers in the Medical Services of the British Army 1660-1960*, 2 vols. (London, 1968)
Finer, S.E. *The Life and Times of Sir Edwin Chadwick* (London, 1952)
Fortescue, J.W. *A History of the British Army*, 13 vols. (London, 1910-30)
Foucault, M. *The Birth of the Clinic* (New York, 1975)
Foucault, M. *Discipline and Punish: the Birth of the Prison* (London, 1977)
Furber, H. *Henry Dundas, First Viscount Melville 1742-1811* (London, 1931)
Glover, R. *Peninsular Preparation: the Reform of the British Army 1795-1809* (Cambridge, 1964)
Gordon, H.S. 'The Ideology of *Laissez-faire*' in A.W. Coats (ed.), *The Classical Economists and Economic Policy* (London, 1971)
Gwynn, D. *Daniel O'Connell* (Oxford, 1947)
Harris, J.S. *British Government Inspection as a Dynamic Process: the Local Services and the Central Departments* (New York, 1955)
Hart, J. 'Nineteenth-Century Social Reform: a Tory Interpretation of History', *Past and Present*, no. 31 (1965)
Hay, J.R. *The Origins of the Liberal Welfare Reforms 1906-1914* (London, 1975)
Inglis, B. *The Freedom of the Press in Ireland 1784-1841* (London, 1954)
Johnston, E.M. *Great Britain and Ireland 1760-1800: a Study in Political Administration* (London, 1963)

Johnston, E.M. *Ireland in the Eighteenth Century* (Dublin, 1974)
Johnston, E.M. 'Members of the Irish Parliament, 1784-7', *Proceedings of the Royal Irish Academy*, vol. lxxi, section C, no. 5
Johnston, E.M. 'The State of the Irish House of Commons in 1791', *Proceedings of the Royal Irish Academy*, vol. lix, section C, no. 1
Jones, M.G. *The Charity School Movement: a Study of Eighteenth Century Puritanism in Action* (Cambridge, 1938)
Kiernan, T.J. *The Irish Exiles in Australia* (Dublin, 1954)
Kramnick, I. *The Rage of Edmund Burke: Portrait of an Ambivalent Conservative* (New York, 1977)
Lambert, R. *Sir John Simon, 1816-1904, and English Social Administration* (London, 1963)
Lambert, R. 'A Victorian National Health Service: State Vaccination 1855-71', *Historical Journal*, vol. iv (1962)
Lecky, W.E.H. *A History of Ireland in the Eighteenth Century*, 5 vols. (London, 1952)
Lewis, R.L. *Edwin Chadwick and the Public Health Movement (London, 1952)*
Locker Lampson, G. *A Consideration of the State of Ireland in the Nineteenth Century* (London, 1907)
Lubenow, W.C. *The Politics of Government Growth: Early Victorian Attitudes toward State Intervention* (Hawden, Conn., 1971)
McClelland, P.D. *Causal Explanation and Model-Building in History, Economics and Economic History* (Ithaca, NY, 1975)
MacDermot, F. *Theobald Wolfe Tone: a Biographical Study* (London, 1939)
MacDonagh, O. *Early Victorian Government 1830-1870* (London, 1977)
MacDonagh, O. *Ireland: the Union and its Aftermath* (London, 1977)
MacDonagh, O. 'The Nineteenth-Century Revolution in Government: a Reappraisal', *Historical Journal*, vol. i (1958)
MacDonagh, O. *A Pattern of Government Growth 1800-60; the Passenger Acts and their Enforcement* (London, 1961)
MacDonagh, O. 'The Politicization of the Irish Catholic Bishops, 1800-50', *Historical Journal*, vol. xviii (1975)
McDowell, R.B. *The Irish Administration 1801-1914* (London, 1964)
McDowell, R.B. *Irish Public Opinion, 1750-1800* (London, 1944)
McDowell, R.B. *Public Opinion and Government Policy in Ireland, 1801-1846* (London, 1952)
McDowell, R.B. (ed.) *Social Life in Ireland 1800-45* (Dublin, 1957)
McGrigor, J. *The Autobiography and Services of Sir James McGrigor*

Bart., late Director General of the Army Medical Department (London, 1861)

MacLeod, R.M. 'The Alkali Acts Administration, 1863-84: the Emergence of the Civil Scientist', *Victorian Studies*, vol. ix (1965)

MacLeod, R.M. 'Government and Resource Conservation: the Salmon Acts Administration, 1860-86', *Journal of British Studies*, vol. vii (1968)

MacLeod, R.M. 'Social Administration and the "Floating Population": the Canal Boat Acts, 1877-1899', *Past and Present*, no. 35 (1966)

MacLeod, R.M. 'Statesmen Undisguised', *American Historical Review*, vol. lxxviii (1973)

Mahoney, T.H.D. *Edmund Burke and Ireland* (Cambridge, Mass., 1960)

Malcolmson, A.P.W. *John Foster: the Politics of the Anglo-Irish Ascendancy* (Oxford, 1978)

Martin, J. [recte G.] 'Convict Transportation to Newfoundland in 1789', *Acadiensis*, vol. v (1975)

Maxwell, C. *Dublin under the Georges 1714-1830* (London, 1946)

Moir, E. 'Sir George Onesiphorous Paul' in H.P.R. Finberg (ed.), *Gloucestershire Studies* (Leicester, 1957)

Morgan, R. 'Divine Philanthropy: John Howard Reconsidered', *History* vol. lxii, no. 206 (1977)

Nelson, R.R. *The Home Office 1782-1801* (Durham, N.C., 1969)

O'Donovan, D. 'The Money Bill Dispute' in T. Bartlett and D.W. Hayton (eds.), *Penal Era and Golden Age: Essays in Irish History, 1690-1800* (Belfast, 1979)

Officer of the Guards, *An Accurate and Impartial Narrative of the War*, 2 vols. (London, 1785)

O'Malley, I.B. *Florence Nightingale, 1820-1856: a Study of her Life down to the End of the Crimean War* (London, 1931)

Pakenham, T. *The Year of Liberty: the Story of the Great Irish Rebellion of 1798* (London, 1969)

Parris, H.J. *Constitutional Bureaucracy: the Development of British Central Administration since the Eighteenth Century* (New York, 1969)

Parris, H.J. 'The Nineteenth-Century Revolution in Government: a Reappraisal Reappraised', *Historical Journal*, vol. iii (1960)

Pellew, J.H. 'The Home Office and the Explosives Act of 1875', *Victorian Studies*, vol. xviii (1974)

Radzinowicz, L. *A History of English Criminal Law and its Administration from 1750*, 4 vols. (London, 1948)

Sainty, J.C. *Colonial Office Officials 1794-1870* (London, 1975)

Sainty, J.C. *Home Office Officials 1782-1870* (London, 1975)

Sayles, G.O. 'Contemporary Sketches of the Members of the Irish Parliament in 1782', *Proceedings of the Royal Irish Academy*, vol. lvi, section C, no. 3

Sutherland, G. (ed.) *Studies in the Growth of Nineteenth Century Government* (London, 1972)

Vess, D.M. *Medical Revolution in France, 1789-1796* (Gainsville, 1975)

Wall, M. *The Penal Laws, 1691-1760* (Dublin Historical Association pamphlet, 1961)

Ward, B. *The Eve of Catholic Emancipation* (London, 1911)

Ward, S.G.P. *Wellington's Headquarters: a Study of the Administrative Problems in the Peninsula 1809-1814* (Oxford, 1957)

Watson, S. *The Reign of George III* (Oxford, 1960)

Youngson, A.J. *The Scientific Revolution in Victorian Medicine* (Canberra, 1979)

Ziegler, P. *Addington: a Life of Henry Addington, First Viscount Sidmouth* (London, 1965)

2. UNPUBLISHED THESES

Berryman, K.M. 'Great Britain and the French Refugees, 1789-1802: the Administrative Response' (PhD dissertation, Australian National University)

Condon, M.E. 'The Administration of the Transport Service during the War against Revolutionary France' (PhD dissertation, London University)

Heaney, H.J. 'Richmond General Penitentiary, Dublin: the Failure of an Experiment' (MA thesis, Queen's University, Belfast)

King, A. 'The Relations of the British Government with the Emigrés and Royalists of Western France, 1793-5' (PhD dissertation, London University)

Williamson, A.P. 'The Origins of the Irish Mental Hospital Service, 1800-1843' (MLitt dissertation, Dublin University)

INDEX

Addington, Henry 253-4
administrative revolution 295; bureaucratic conflict in 305; dynamic reform 301-2; House committees as part of 318-19, 321; Inspectorates in 317, 320, 323-5; Ireland 18th Century 318-19; progress in 315; theoretical stages of 296-8
Alien Office 228-9
Archer, Rev. Foster 143-4, 319-20
Army, British: bureaucratic structure 308-9
Army, British: Medical Board 156; advice on military diets 166; operation of 228-9; prevents provisioning of hospital ships 214; reform of 215, 225; relations with Fitzpatrick, Sir J. 153, 161, 164, 199, 207-10, 304, conflict with 175, 191, 195, 206-7, reports to Windham on 202, 220, restricts his entry to military hospitals 215; staff recruitment by 205, 208, 209

Barrack Board 198
Bentham, Jeremy 140
Blaquiere, Sir John 50, 51, 319; campaign on Dublin gaols 118; inquiry into Dublin Bridewell 118-19; proposal for Dublin inspectorate 120; report on prison inspectorate 112
Boone, John 194-5, 196, 198-9, 202; Fitzpatrick to 205, 215; condemnation of his actions 225-6
bridewells 142-3
Burgh, Hussey 42

Carlow gaol 57
Charter schools: Fitzpatrick's evidence against 91-2; House of Commons Committee on 90-3; House of Lords proposed Committee on 93; Howard, John and 89, 93-4; Orde's plans for 90-1; role of 86-7; Wesley's evidence against 94
City Marshalsea 47; appointment of Keeper 80; condition of 121; outbreak of fever 76, 120
civil service 318; England 318; Ireland 318-19
Cloyne, Bishop of 93
Commissary of Health for the Army: Fitzpatrick's proposals for 159-61
Commission of Military Inquiry, fifth 225-7
convicts: condition on transports 268-9; Fitzpatrick, Sir J.: approaches to King 270, 278-9, conflict with Graham on 280-1, power to land diseased 276-7, programme of reform 270-4, 281, proposed inspectorate 271, 280, role 267, 280, 282-4, seeks Pelham's support 279, system for implemented 277-8, Transport Office supports requests 273; *see also* Fitzpatrick, Sir J.; health 268, 269, 279-80; inspector of appointed 280; on the *Hillsborough* 275-6

defaulting debtors 44
dependants of Irish soldiers *see* Irish soldiers
Dublin 310; Bridwell 58, 72-3, 118-19; gaols, effect of 1787 Amendment Act on 115, 122, Fitzpatrick's report on 105, provisions for under 1786 Act 81-2; report of House of Commons Committee 1788 on 127; *see also* City Marshalsea and New Prison; press 310-11
Dundas, Henry (Lord Melville) 167; appointed Secretary of War 158, 159; returns to office 254; sets troop transport standards 242-3; *see also* Fitzpatrick, Sir J.
Durrow Abbey 19

East India Troops 240-3
Eden, William 49, 50, 54; influence

340

Index 341

on Fitzpatrick's writing 135
Elliot, William 202; court martial 210-11; verdict 214
English Hard Labour Act 1779 50
Essay on gaol abuses 63-9 *passim*

Fitzpatrick, Elizabeth 19, 21, 25, 26; death 254
Fitzpatrick, Hugh 22
Fitzpatrick, Sir Jeremiah: army medicine: at Cork 1793 149-50, at Holland 157, 167, at Netherlands 171-2, entry to 149-55 *passim*, establishment of hospital ship 149, gaol fever experience 159, letter to Moira 155, 156, programme for health of soldiers 153, 165-6, proposal for commissary of health 159, 160-1, support for army work 158, 235, work on troop transports 151, 162, 217; birthplace 19; career structure 25, 27, 36; charter schools: first inspection 87-8, further inspections 89, method of inspection 102, reason for inspection 88-9, 91, relations with Incorporated Society for 90, 91-2, 93, 95, 100, results of work for 95, 98-9; children 23, 25; collector of statistics 79, 96-8, 108; convicts: achievements for 282, 283, approaches to King 270, 278-9, claims recompense for work 282, embarkation powers 277, 280, health scheme implemented 277-8, passed-over for inspector 280, per capita payment for good health 274, proposes family reunion for 281, proposes inspectorate for 270, 271-2, seeks transfer to Ireland 279-80, self appointed role 267, work for 269, 271-2; death 25; dependants of Irish soldiers 257-9, 307: approach to Dundas 258-61, approach to Portland 261, scheme for 262, 264-6, East India Transports 240-3; education 19-20; *Essay on Gaol Abuses* 63-9 *passim*; income 26-7; inspection of prisons 56; Inspector General of Prisons, Ireland 79, 106-9, 113, 319: abandons position 156, 161, action on gaol fever 119, appointment 83, Burgh, Hussey influence of 42, criminal chart 79, expenses incurred as 129, first task as 105, on transportation 134, 135, report on Dublin Prisons 105, role in prison reform 300-3, routine of 144, salary 129-30, 144-5, 168; Inspector of Health for the Land Forces: appointment 161, at Deal 179-80, 81, 191, at Netherlands 171-5, 176, 177-9, at Plymouth 191-2, 193-4, 197, 216, changed role 233, charges against army surgeons 195, 196, court martial of Elliot 202-3, 211, 214, exclusion from Army hospitals 232, expenses, payment of 238-9, inspectorate wound-up 252, loss of authority 221, patient record sheets 204-5, relations with Army Medical Board 161-6 *passim*, 175, 191, 195-6, 199, 200, 205, 206-10, 215, 304, 307, reform for army hospitals 163-4, 199, 201, 203, 222, 233-6, 247, 248, 304; Inspector of the Insane 114, 122-3; intellectual inspiration 33, 64-5, 135, 322; inventions 64, 157, 197, 216, 235; knighthood 24; marriage 19, 21; medical training 20-1; metropolitan police scheme 70; motivation 35, 37; parents 19; personality 321-3; political role 28, 29, 31-3, 312-13; practice as physician 21, 25, 49; prison reformer 42, 57-9, 64, 66, 76, 300-3, 315, achievements of reform period 140-2, influence of Wymondham on 134, influence on legislation 1786 73, 82-3, inspectorate proposal 68-9, knowledge of existing inspectorates 68, 82, penitentiary experiment, Dublin 139, penitentiary proposals 136-7, 302, role of religion in 65, 135, witness to House of Commons Committees 56-8, 72-3; public health 33; religion 21-4, 93; retirement 22, 25, 254; social reporter 95-6, 97-8, 99, 100-2; slave trade 284.

285-7, anti-slaver 285, inspectorates 290; *Suggestions on the Slave Trade* 284-9 passim, 290-1; *Thoughts on Penitentiaries* 134-5; wool industry scheme 69-70

gaol fever 44, 48-9, 63, 323; at Cavan 144: City Marshalsea 76, 120, Clonmel 119, *Hillsborough* 276, Langston hulks 275, Newgate, London 275; Fitzpatrick's expertise 159; in the army 156, 158; role in prison reform 299
government: England modern civil service 318; Ireland 18th Century 310, 312-13, 316-17, 319
Graham, A.: appointed inspector of convicts 280; character 280-1
grand juries: responsibilities 81
Griffith, Richard 50, 51, 59, 62, 112; association with Fitzpatrick 313; draft legislation 76; loss of seat 132; Prison Amendment Bill 1788 129; Prison Amendment Bill 1789 131; Prison reform proposals 74-5

Handel, G.F.: Messiah, first performance 314
Hard Labour Act 1779, England 50
Hard Labour Act 1778, Ireland 47-8
Hillsborough 275-7
Hobart, Lord Roberts 251, 252-3
Holmes, Peter 50-63 passim, 71, 73-4; Amendment Act 1787 111; association with Fitzpatrick 313; draft legislation 76; Insolvent Debtors Bill 1788 126; Membership of Committees 318; Prison Amendment Bill 1788 129; revives Prisons Reform Bills 77; role in prison reform 300
Hospitals: Charitable infirmary 21; Military hospitals: charges against 175, Deal 179, general hospitals 173-4, Gosport 248-9, refitting of 180-1, reform proposals by Fitzpatrick 203, 205, Plymouth 225; prison 279; ships: baking equipment 221, reforms for 181; temporary 191; Simpson's 21
Howard, John 33, 42-3, 44, 49-50, 54, 64-5; as influence on Fitzpatrick's writings 135; charter schools: evidence against 93, 94, visits to 89; influence on legislation 49-50, 82
hulks 47
Huskisson, William 167; promotion to war department 196; see Fitzpatrick, Sir J.
Hutchison, Sir Francis 129-30

Incorporated Society for Promoting English Protestant Schools in Ireland 86-7, 90, 130; defence against criticism 93-4 inquiry into, 1809, 94; relations with Fitzpatrick 90, 91
Inspector general of prisons 81; appointment of Archer, Rev. Foster as 143-4, 319; appointment of Fitzpatrick, Sir J. as 83; as collector of statistics 79; establishment of 78; expenses of 129; growth of 320; permanency of 115-16; position of: abandoned by Fitzpatrick 156, 161; expanded 113-14; strengthened 114; routine of 144; salary of 81, 128-30, 144-5; see also Fitzpatrick, Sir J. as
Inspector of Health for the Land Forces: appointment 161; changed role 233; commission revised 199; differences from Inspectorship of Prisons 167-8; exclusion from army hospitals 232; factors effecting success 305, 307; inspectorate wound-up 252; lateral extension of office 305-6; loss of authority 221; power to deputise 176; planning of military buildings 250, 305; remuneration 168; scope of role 192, 199; tasks 163-4, 199, 304; Transport Commissioners support for work 234; see also Fitzpatrick, Sir J. as
Inspectorates: administrative repercussions 297, 319-20, 323-5; Fitzpatrick's view of 324-6; of convicts 280 see also convicts; of Health for the Land Forces see Inspector of Health for the Land

Index

Forces; of madhouses 320
see also Fitzpatrick, Sir J.; of
prisons *see* prison inspectorates,
see also Inspector General, for
prisons
insane 114, 320
insolvent debtors: role in prison
reform 299, 314
Irish Hard Labour Act 1778 47-8
Irish soldiers: dependants of
257-60; Fitzpatrick's scheme
for 264-6; gratuities for
263-4

Keate, Thomas 164, 206, 235,
325; criticises Fitzpatrick
220-1; condemned by
military inquiry 225-8
King, John 270, 278-9
Kilkenny Charter School 87-8

Lennox, Lord George 150-4 *passim*;
relations with Fitzpatrick
202-3, 214, 215; support for
Fitzpatrick 158, 192, 194,
195; to Dundas 197-8
Lucas, Dr Charles 45, 46, 47

Moira, Earl of (Hastings, Francis)
154; enlists Fitzpatrick's aid
157; letter from Fitzpatrick
155-6; support for Fitzpatrick
158
Moucher, General 149-50

Naas Gaol 57-8
Nepean, Evan 158, 159, 164, 167,
188, 196; assistance sought
by Fitzpatrick 223-4
nepotism 24, 228
Newgate (New Prison Dublin) 47,
48, 54, 63; condition of 121;
Fitzpatrick's report on 108-9;
sale of liquor 127; women's
chambers 72
Nightingale, Florence: reasons
for her success 187-8;
similarity of position with
Fitzpatrick 185-7

O'Connell, Daniel 22, 30, 211
Orange Societies 29
Orde, Thomas 62, 65, 89-90, 119

parliamentary process: England
19th Century 311-12, 314; Ireland
18th Century 311-12, 314
Parnell, Sir John 112, 140
Parnell, Sir John (younger) 49, 51
penitentiaries: act to commute
transportation to 138; fate of
system 140-1; first Dublin
experiment 138-9
Philadelphia fever 149
Portland, Duke of 24; convict
health 274; criticism of
administration 93; effect of new
administration 167; Irish soldiers'
dependants 274
prison inspectorates: bill to establish
76-80; centralized inspectorate
301; Dublin inspectorate 75, 80,
113, 120, 122; Griffith's proposal
for 74-5; Inspector general *see*
Inspector general of Prisons; local
inspectorate 49, expanded role
114, 142, part-time 81; precursor
of 49; role in reform 301
prison reform: England 42-3, 49
prison reform: Ireland 42, 44, 53;
appointment of prison medical
staff 49, 80; Acts: Acquitted
Prisoners 1763 42-4, Acquitted
Prisoners Fees 1784 62, Gaols
1784 300, Gaols 1786 301, Gaol
Regulation 1763 55, Gaol Regulation 1778 55, Hard Labour 1778
47-8, Penitentiary 1792 138,
Prisoners Health 1778 48-9,
Prisons 1729 43, Prisons 1763
42-4, 53, 55, Prisons 1782 55,
Prisons 1784 59, 62, 64, Prisons
1786 69, Prisons 1788 300-1,
Prisons Amendment 1786 132,
301, Prisons Amendment 1787
111-13, 114, 115-17, 118, 122,
127-8, 301, 320, Prisons
Inspection 1786 79-83; Bills:
Acquitted Prisoners 1763 42,
Acquitted Prisoners 1782 53,
Acquitted Prisoners 1784 76,
Acquitted Prisoners Fees Amendment 1786 77, Bridewells 1786
77, Gaols 1788 131, Gaols 1789 93-
4, 131, Insolvent Debtors 1763 42-
3, Insolvent Debtors 1784 62-3,
Insolvent Debtors 1787 119,

Prison Amendment 1788 93-4, 129, 130-1, Prison Inspection 1786 77-9; detonators of 299-30; House of Commons Committee on 109, 318, 1777 48, 1780 52, 1781 52, 1782 52-5, 1783 56, 300, 1785 71, 73-4, 300, 1786 77, 1787 107-8, 109, 110, 127, 1788 126-7, 128, 129, 1789 131, 1793 141, 145, 302; Inquiry into Dublin Bridewell 118; movement 49; newspaper support for 45-6; results of period 141-2; role of Eden, William in 50; role of Fitzpatrick in 42, 300-3, 315; role of gaol fever in 48, 299; role of insolvent debtors in 314
prisoners: food for 114; Health Act 1778 48, 49, 53; health of 48, 54, 56-7

Slave trade: involvement of Fitzpatrick 284-8
Suggestions on the Slave Trade 284-9 *passim*, 290-1

Thoughts on Penitentiaries 134-5
Tone, Theobald Wolfe 29, 30
Transport Board 160, 162, 163, 165; acceptance of Fitzpatrick's role 234; instructions for health of convicts 277; operation of 228-9; responsibility for convict transports 267, 271, 273, 274
Trench, Frederick: member for Maryborough 112-13
typhoid fever 33, 151, 154, 299
typhus 173, 183

volunteerism 52

Warren, Nathaniel 78, 120
Wesley, John: evidence on Charter Schools 94
Wexford Rising 30, 144
Whiteway, John 122
Windham, William: secretary at war 163-6; relations with Fitzpatrick 202, 215, 260
Woodward, Richard: Cloyne, Bishop of 93
Wymondham House of Correction 133-4

York, Duke of: army in Netherlands 158, 171, 177; army reforms 253; departure for England 177; dependants' gratuities 263

For Product Safety Concerns and Information please contact our EU representative GPSR@taylorandfrancis.com
Taylor & Francis Verlag GmbH, Kaufingerstraße 24, 80331 München, Germany

www.ingramcontent.com/pod-product-compliance
Lightning Source LLC
Chambersburg PA
CBHW061426300426
44114CB00014B/1556